Contents

GW00420072

First published in 1997 by George Philip Ltd
a division of Octopus Publishing Group Ltd
2–4 Heron Quays, London E14 4JP

www.philips-maps.co.uk

Fifth edition 2001
First impression 2001

Cartography by Philip's
Copyright © 2001 George Philip Ltd

This product includes mapping data licenced from Ordnance Survey®, with the permission of the Controller of Her Majesty's Stationery Office. © Crown copyright 2001. All rights reserved. Licence number 100011710

To the best of the Publisher's knowledge, the information in this atlas was correct at the time of going to press. No responsibility can be accepted for any errors or their consequences.

The representation in this atlas of any road, drive or track is no evidence of the existence of a right of way

The town plans of Cork and Dublin are based on Ordnance Survey Ireland by permission of the Government. Permit number 7315 © Government of Ireland.

The town plans of Belfast and Londonderry are based upon the Ordnance Survey map by permission of the Controller of Her Majesty's Stationery Office © Crown Copyright. Permit number 1728.

Information for Tourist Attractions in England supplied by the British Tourist Authority / English Tourist Board.

Information for National Parks, Areas of Outstanding Natural Beauty, National Trails and Country Parks in Wales supplied by the Countryside Council for Wales.

Information for National Parks, Areas of Outstanding Natural Beauty, National Trails and Country Parks in England supplied by the Countryside Commission.

Data for Regional Parks, Long Distance Footpaths and Country Parks in Scotland provided by Scottish Natural Heritage.

Gaelic name forms used in the Western Isles provided by Comhairle nan Eilean.

Printed and bound in Great Britain by Scotprint

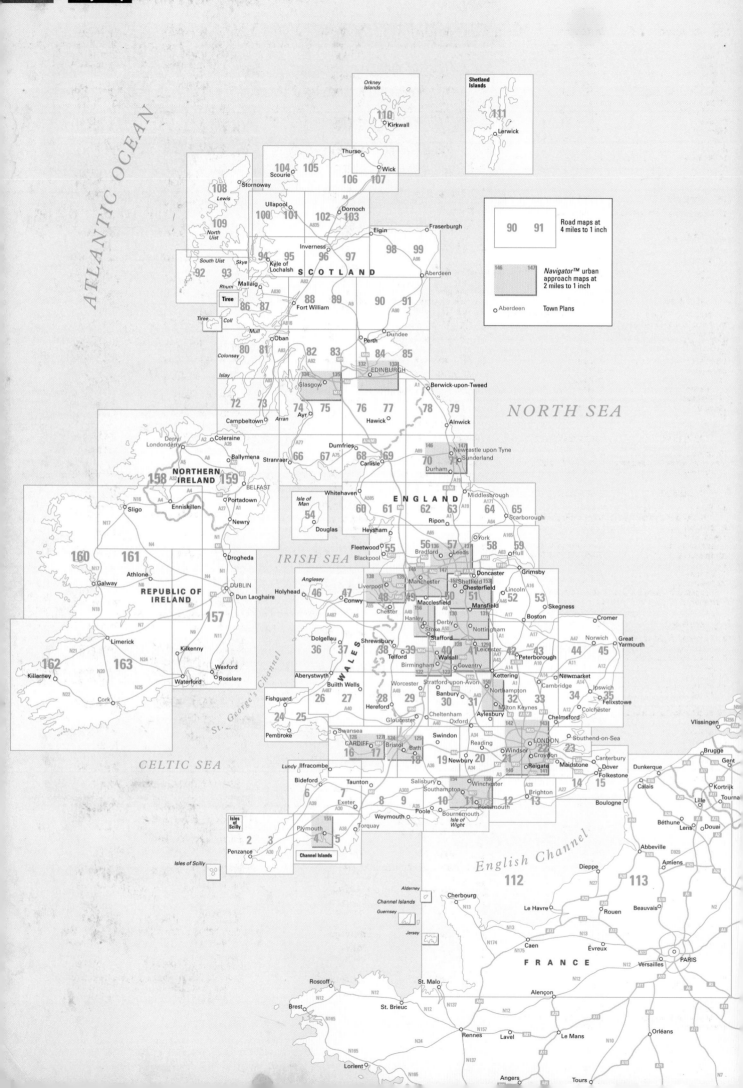

M1

	Northbound	Southbound
2	No exit	No access
4	No exit	No access
6a	No exit	No access
	Access from M25 only	Exit to M25 only
7	No exit	No access
	Access from M10 only	Exit to M10 only
17	No access	No exit
	Exit to M45 only	Access from M45 only
19	No access to A14	No access from A14
21a	No access	No exit
23a		Exit to A42 only
24a	No exit	No access
35a	No access	No exit
43		No exit to M621 northbound
48	No exit to A1 southbound	

M2

	Eastbound	Westbound
1	Access from A2 eastbound only	Exit to A2 westbound only

M3

	Eastbound	Westbound
8	No exit	No access
10	No access	No exit
13		No access to M27 eastbound
14	No exit	No access

M4

	Eastbound	Westbound
1	Exit to A4 eastbound only	Access from A4 westbound only
2	Access to A4 eastbound only	Access to A4 westbound only
21	No exit	No access
23	No access	No exit
25	No exit	No access
25a	No exit	No access
29	No exit	No access
38		No access
39	No exit or access	No exit
41	No access	No exit
41a	No exit	No access
42		Exit to A483 only

M5

	Northbound	Southbound
10	No exit	No access
11a	No access from A417 eastbound	No exit to A417 westbound
12	No access	No exit

M6

	Northbound	Southbound
4a	No exit	No access
	Access from M42 southbnd only	Exit to M42 only
5	No access	No exit
10a	No access	Access from M54 only
	Exit to M54 only	
20	No exit to M56 eastbound	No access from M56 westbound
24	No exit	No access
25	No access	No exit
30	No exit	No access
	Access from M61 nthbnd only	Exit to M61 southbound
31a	No access	No exit

M8

	Eastbound	Westbound
3	Exit to A899 southbound only	Exit to A899 southbound only
	Access from A899 nthbnd only	Access from A899 northbnd only
8	No exit to M73 northbound	No access from M73 southbound
9	No access	No exit
14	No access	No exit
16	No exit	No access
17	No exit	No access
18		No exit
19	No exit to A814 eastbound	No access from A814 westbound
20	No exit	No access
21	No access	No exit
22	No exit	No access
	Access from M77 only	Exit to M77 only
23	No exit	No access
25	Exit to A739 northbound only	Exit to A739 northbound only
	Access from A739 southbnd only	Access from A739 southbnd only
25a	No exit	No access
28	No exit	No access
28a	No exit	No access

M9

	Eastbound	Westbound
1a	No exit	No access
2	No access	No exit
3	No exit	No access
6	No access	No exit
8	No exit	No access

M11

	Northbound	Southbound
4	No exit	No access
5	No access	No exit
9	No access	No exit
13	No access	No exit
14	No exit to A428 westbound	No exit
		Access from A14 westbound only

M20

	Eastbound	Westbound
2	No access	No exit
3	No exit	No access
	Access from M26 eastbound only	Exit to M26 westbound only
11a	No exit	No access

M23

	Northbound	Southbound
7	No exit to A23 southbound	No access from A23 northbound
10a	No exit	No access

M25

	Clockwise	Anticlockwise
5	No exit to M26 eastbound	No access from M26 westbound
19	No access	No exit
21	No exit to M1 southbound	No access to M1 southbound
	Access from M1 southbound only	Access from M1 southbound only
31	No exit	No access

M27

	Eastbound	Westbound
10	No exit	No access
12	No access	No exit

M40

	Eastbound	Westbound
3	No exit	No access
7	No exit	No access
13	No exit	No access
14	No access	No exit
16	No access	No exit

M42

	Northbound	Southbound
1	No exit	No access
7	No access	No exit
	Exit to M6 northbound only	Access from M6 northbound only
7a	No access	No exit
	Exit to M6 only	Access from M6 northbound only
8	No exit	Exit to M6 northbound
	Access from M6 southbnd only	Access from M6 southbound only

M45

	Eastbound	Westbound
Junction with M1		
	Access to M1 southbound only	No access from M1 southbound
Junction with A45 (Dunchurch)		
	No access	No exit

M49

	Southbound	
18a	No exit to M5 northbound	

M53

	Northbound	Southbound
11	Exit to M56 eastbound only	Exit to M56 eastbound only
	Access from M56 westbnd only	Access from M56 westbound only

M56

	Eastbound	Westbound
2	No exit	No access
4	No exit	No access
7		No access
8	No exit or access	No exit
9	No access from M6 northbound	No access to M6 southbound
15	No exit to M53	No access from M53 northbound

M57

	Northbound	Southbound
3	No exit	No access
5	No exit	No access

M58

	Eastbound	Westbound
1	No exit	No access

M60

	Clockwise	Anticlockwise
2	No exit	No access
3	No exit to A34 northbound	No exit to A34 northbound
4	No access to M56	No exit to M56
5	No exit to A5103 southbound	No access to A5103 northbound
7	No access	No exit (Exit from J8 only)
14	No exit to A580	No access from A580
16	No exit	No access
25	No access	
26		No exit or access
27	No exit	No access

M61

	Northbound	Southbound
2	No access from A580 eastbound	No exit from A580 westbound
3	No access from A580 eastbound	No exit from A580 westbound
Junction with M6 junction 30		
	No exit to M6 southbound	No access from M6 northbound

M62

	Eastbound	Westbound
23	No access	No exit

M65

	Eastbound	Westbound
9	No access	No exit
11	No exit	No access

M67

	Eastbound	Westbound
1a	No access	No exit
2	No exit	No access

M69

	Northbound	Southbound
2	No exit	No access

M73

	Northbound	Southbound
2	No access from M8 or A89 estbnd	No exit to M8 or A89 westbound
	No exit to A89	No access from A89
3	Exit to A80 northbound only	Access from A80 southbound only

M74

	Northbound	Southbound
2	No access	No exit
3	No exit	No access
7	No exit	No access
9	No exit or access	No access
10		No exit
11	No exit	No access
12	No exit	No access

M77

	Northbound	Southbound
4	No exit	No access
Junction with M8 junction 22		
	Exit to M8 eastbound only	Access from M8 westbound only

M80

	Northbound	Southbound
3	No access	No exit
5	No access from M876	No exit to M876

M90

	Northbound	Southbound
2a	No access	No exit
7	No access	No exit
8	No access	No exit
10	No access from A912	No exit to A912

M180

	Northbound	Southbound
1	No access	No exit

M621

	Eastbound	Westbound
4	No exit or access	
5	No exit	No access
6	No access	No exit

M876

	Northbound	Southbound
2	No access	No exit

A1(M)

	Northbound	Southbound
2		No access
3		No access
5	No exit	No access
44	No exit, access from M1 only	Exit to M1 only
57	No access	No exit
65	No access	No exit

A3(M)

	Northbound	Southbound
1		No access
4	No access	No exit

A38(M)

	Northbound	Southbound
Junction with Victoria Road (Park Circus)		
	No exit	No access

A48(M)

	Northbound	Southbound
Junction with M4 Junction 29		
	Exit to M4 eastbound only	Access from M4 westbound only
29a	Access from A48 eastbound only	Exit to A48 westbound only

A57(M)

	Eastbound	Westbound
Junction with A5103		
	No access	No exit
Junction with A34		
	No access	No exit

A58(M)

		Southbound
Junction with Park Lane/Westgate		No access

A64(M)

	Eastbound	Westbound
Junction with A58 (Clay Pit Lane)		
	No access	No exit
Junction with Regent Street		
	No access	No exit

A74(M)

	Northbound	Southbound
18	No access	No exit
19		No access

A167(M)

	Northbound	Southbound
Newcastle Central Motorway Junction with Camden Street		
	No exit	No exit or access

A194(M)

	Northbound	Southbound
Junction with A1 and A1(M) Gateshead Western By-pass		
	Access from A1(M) northbound only	Exit to A1(M) southbound only

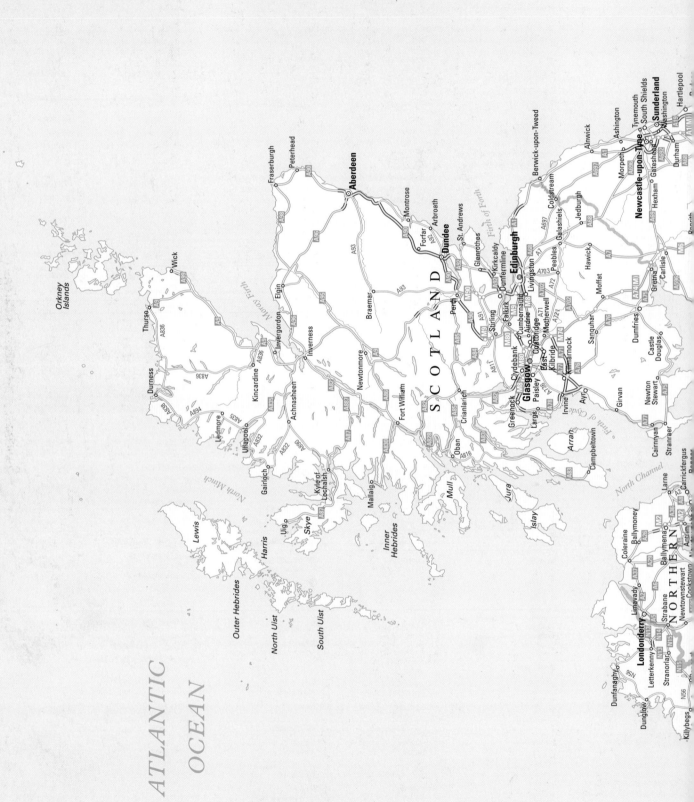

Road map symbols

M6	Motorway
4 5	Motorway junction full, restricted access
S S	Motorway service area full, restricted access
= = = =	Motorway under construction
A453	Primary route – dual, single carriageway
S O	Service area, multi-level junction
= = = = =	Primary route under construction
	Narrow primary route
Derby	Primary destination
A34	
	A road – dual, single carriageway
■ ■ ■ ■ ■	A road under construction
	Narrow A road
B2135	B road – dual, single carriageway
= = = =	B road under construction
	Narrow B road
	Other road
	Other road under construction
2	Distance in miles
= = = = (	Tunnel
TOLL	Toll, steep gradient – arrow points downhill
⚲	National trail – England and Wales
⚜	Long distance footpath – Scotland
•	Railway with station
✕ ✕ (	Level crossing, tunnel
•	Preserved railway with station
■ ■ ■ ■	National boundary
	County / unitary authority boundary
⛴ ⛴	Car ferry, catamaran
⛴ ⛴	Passenger ferry, catamaran
- - - -	Hovercraft
CALAIS 1:15 Ferry	Ferry destination, journey time – hrs : mins
	Car ferry – river crossing
✈ ✈	Principal airport, other airport
	National park, area of outstanding natural beauty, forest park
	Woodland
	Beach
■ ■ ■	Linear antiquity
☀ ▲795	Viewpoint, spot height – in metres
⚑ △	Golf course, youth hostel
29	Adjoining page number – road maps

Zeichenerklärung

Autobahn	M6
Autobahnanschlußstelle – Voller/begrenzter Zugang	4 5
Raststätte – Voller/begrenzter Zugang	S S
Autobahn im Bau	= = = =
Schnellstraße – zweispurig/einspurig	A453
Raststätte, Kreuz	S O
Schnellstraße im Bau	= = = = =
Enge Schnellstraße	
Zielort	**Derby**
	A34
Hauptverkehrsstraße – zweispurig/einspurig	
Hauptverkehrsstraße im Bau	■ ■ ■ ■ ■
Enge Hauptverkehrsstraße	
Nebenstraße – zweispurig/einspurig	B2135
Nebenstraße im Bau	= = = =
Enge Nebenstraße	
Nebenstrecke	
Nebenstrecke im Bau	
Entfernung in Meilen	2
Tunnel	= = = = (
Zahlstelle – Gebührenpflichtige Straße	TOLL
Steigung/Gefälle – in Pfeilrichtung	
Nationaler Wanderweg – England und Wales	⚲
Nationaler Wanderweg – Schottland	⚜
Eisenbahn mit Bahnhof	•
Bahnübergang, Eisenbahntunnel	✕ ✕ (
Museumsbahn mit Bahnhof	•
Staatsgrenze	■ ■ ■ ■
Kreis oder Gemeinde	
Autofähre, Katamaran	⛴ ⛴
Personenfähre, Katamaran	⛴ ⛴
Luftkissenfahrzeug	
Ziel, Fahrtzeit – Stunden : minuten	CALAIS 1:15 Ferry
Autofähre – Fluß	
Hauptflughafen, Sonstige Flughäfen	✈ ✈
Nationalpark, landschaftlich besonders schön, Forst	
Wald	
Strand	
Lineare Altertümer	■ ■ ■
Aussichtspunkt, Höhenangabe in Meter	☀ ▲795
Golfplatz, Jugendherberge	⚑ △
Weiterführende Seitenzahl	29

Légende

M6	Autoroute
4 5	Autoroute avec échangeur – accès libre / accès réglementé
S S	Autoroute avec aire de service – accès libre / accès réglementé
= = = =	Autoroute en construction
A453	Voie principale – chaussées séparées / chaussée sans séparation
S O	Aire de service, échangeur
= = = = =	Voie principale en construction
	Voie principale étroite
Derby	Destination d'itinéraire principal
A34	Route principale – chaussées séparées / chaussée sans séparation
■ ■ ■ ■ ■	Route principale en construction
	Route principale étroite
B2135	Route secondaire – chaussées séparées / chaussée sans séparation
= = = =	Route secondaire en construction
	Route secondaire étroite
	Autre route
	Autre route en construction
2	Distance en miles
= = = = (	Tunnel routier
TOLL	Péage,
	Pente – flèche dans le sens de la descente
⚲	Chemin de grande randonnée – Angleterre et Pays de Galles
⚜	Chemin de grande randonnée – Écosse
•	Chemin de fer, gare
✕ ✕ (	Passage à niveau, Tunnel Ferroviaire
•	Chemin de fer touristique avec gare
■ ■ ■ ■	Frontière d'Etat
	Limite de département
⛴ ⛴	Bac passant les autos, Catamaran
⛴ ⛴	Bac pour piétons, Catamaran
	Aéroglisseur
CALAIS 1:15 Ferry	Destination, durée du voyage en heures:mns
	Traversée de rivière en bac – autos
✈ ✈	Aéroport principal, Autre aéroport
	Parc National, Région d'extrême beauté, Parc Forestier
	Bois
	Plage
■ ■ ■	Antiquité linéaire
☀ ▲795	Point de vue, Altitude en mètres
⚑ △	Terrain de golf, Auberge de jeunesse
29	Référence à la page adjacente

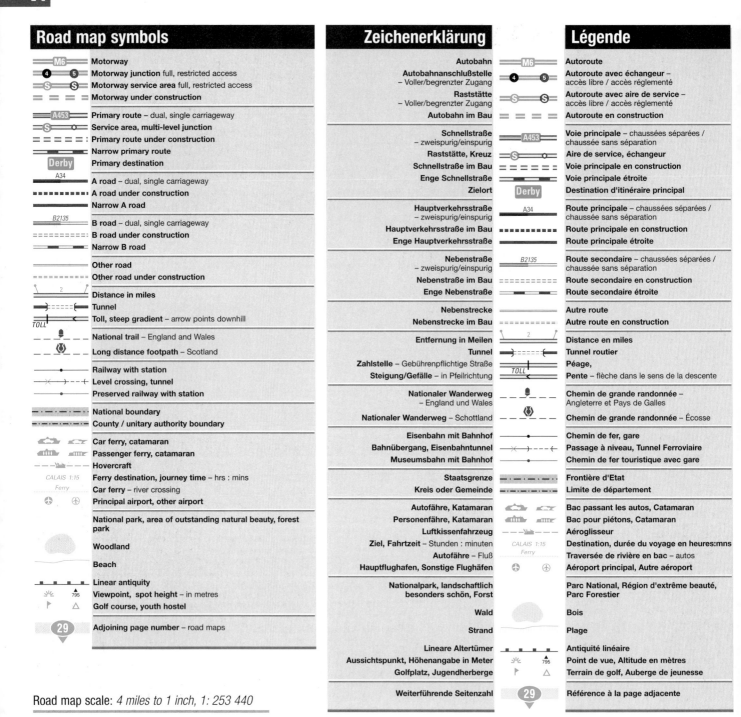

Road map scale: *4 miles to 1 inch, 1: 253 440*

```
0      2      4      6      8 miles
0    2    4    6    8    10   12 kilometres
```

Route-finding system

Town names printed in yellow on a green background are those used on Britain's signposts to indicate primary destinations.

To find your route quickly and easily, simply follow the signs to the primary destination immediately beyond the place you require.

Right Driving from Wakefield to Featherstone, follow the signposts to Pontefract, the first primary destination beyond Featherstone. These will indicate the most direct main route to the side turning for Featherstone.

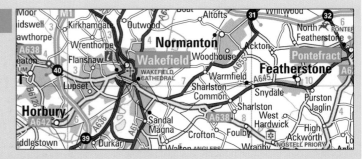

Tourist information

† **Abbey/Cathedral/Priory** — Abbaye, Cathédrale, Prieuré — Abtei, Kathedrale, Priorei	◖▮ **Preserved Railway** — Chemin de fer touristique — Museumsbahn
🏛 **Ancient Monument** — Monument historique — Kulturdenkmal	🏇 **Race Course** — Hippodrome — Pferderennbahn
🐟 **Aquarium** — Aquarium — Aquarium	⚱ **Roman Antiquity** — Antiquité romaine — Römischer Altertümer
🖼 **Art Gallery** — Gallerie d'Art — Kunstgalerie	⋎ **Safari Park** — Parc animalier — Wildpark
🐦 **Bird Collection/Aviary** — Volière — Vogelsammlung/Aviarium	🎡 **Theme Park** — Parc à Thème — Freizeitpark
🏰 **Castle** — Château — Schloß, Burg	ℤ **Tourist Information Centre open all year** — Office de tourisme: ouvert toute l'année — Informationsbüro (Ganzjährij Geöffnet)
⛪ **Church** — Église — Kirche	ℤ **Tourist Information Centre open seasonally** — Office de tourisme: ouvert en saison — Informationsbüro (saisonal geöffnet)
🏞 **Country Park (England & Wales)** — Parc de Loisirs (Angleterrre et Pays de Galles) — Landschaftspark (England und Wales)	🐘 **Zoo** — Zoo — Tiergarten
🏞 **Country Park (Scotland)** — Parc de Loisirs (Écosse) — Landschaftspark (Schottland)	◆ **Other Place of Interest** — Autre curiosité — Sonstige Sehenswürdigkeit
🐄 **Farm Park** — Parc d'Animaux Fermiers — Landwirtschaftspark	
❀ **Garden** — Jardin — Garten	
🏠 **House** — Manoir, Palais — Historisches Haus	
🏠 **House & Garden** — Manoir, Palais avec jardin — Historisches Haus mit Garten	
⚓ **Historic Ship** — Bateau historique — Historisches Schiff	
🏁 **Motor Racing Circuit** — Circuit de Courses automobiles — Autorennbahn	
🏛 **Museum** — Musée — Museum	
🧺 **Picnic Area** — Emplacement de pique-nique — Picknickplatz	

Distance table

How to use this table

	km	miles
Cambridge	*272*	169
Cardiff	*813 253*	505 157
Carlisle	*465 425 446*	289 264 277
Dover	*626 383 201 325*	389 238 125 202
Dundee	*842 245 710 654 692*	523 152 441 406 430

Distances are shown in *kilometres* and miles

Example: the distance between Cambridge and Dundee is *654 km* or 406 miles

Distance matrix (each cell shows *km* in italics above, miles below; reading across to previously listed cities):

London —

Aberdeen — *832* / 517

Aberystwyth — *716 340* / 445 211

Birmingham — *183 676 188* / 114 420 117

Bournemouth — *237 333 908 172* / 147 207 564 107

Brighton — *148 262 407 922 84* / 92 163 253 573 52

Bristol — *237 132 130 201 793 196* / 147 82 81 125 493 122

Cambridge — *272 187 248 161 344 758 87* / 169 116 154 100 214 471 54

Cardiff — *306 72 293 188 166 169 813 253* / 190 45 182 117 103 105 505 157

Carlisle — *465 425 446 596 552 315 360 356 484* / 289 264 277 370 343 196 224 221 301

Dover — *626 383 201 325 132 280 312 478 947 114* / 389 238 125 202 82 174 194 292 588 71

Dundee — *842 245 710 654 692 832 797 562 605 108 721* / 523 152 441 406 430 517 495 349 376 67 448

Edinburgh — *90 744 154 620 555 600 734 707 470 515 201 628* / 56 462 96 385 345 373 456 439 292 320 125 390

Fishguard — *642 740 533 478 180 435 248 468 357 274 90 811 418* / 399 460 331 297 112 270 154 291 222 170 56 504 260

Fort William — *782 232 204 959 332 781 771 782 926 867 631 692 240 821* / 486 144 127 596 206 485 479 486 575 539 392 430 149 510

Glasgow — *163 605 71 134 786 154 620 599 600 753 707 470 515 233 639* / 101 376 44 83 488 96 385 372 373 468 439 292 320 145 397

Gloucester — *557 731 246 562 660 307 398 90 198 56 256 159 90 164 753 175* / 346 454 153 349 410 191 247 56 123 35 159 99 56 102 468 109

Harwich — *316 695 874 542 665 755 201 541 396 108 349 206 301 269 452 861 122* / 196 432 543 337 413 469 125 336 246 67 217 128 187 167 281 535 76

Holyhead — *562 307 531 705 269 536 634 580 237 348 435 332 538 463 238 179 707 433* / 349 191 330 438 167 333 394 360 231 216 270 206 334 288 148 111 439 269

Inverness — *763 916 811 267 106 872 254 212 1001 422 884 813 867 993 961 737 782 169 885* / 474 569 504 166 66 542 158 132 622 262 549 505 539 617 597 458 486 105 550

John o' Groats — *208 970 1116 1011 475 314 1080 459 417 1201 629 1094 1014 1075 1193 1165 924 967 373 1067* / 129 603 693 628 295 195 671 285 259 747 391 680 668 741 724 574 601 232 663

Kingston upon Hull — *834 634 372 316 272 409 594 451 377 475 412 254 393 224 395 216 359 586 296* / 518 394 231 196 198 254 369 280 234 295 256 158 244 139 233 245 264 134 223 364 184

Land's End — *678 1397 1193 652 628 378 922 1104 568 924 1033 613 768 394 602 322 496 330 452 504 1114 478* / 421 868 741 405 390 235 573 686 353 574 642 381 477 245 374 200 308 205 281 313 692 297

Leeds — *652 89 784 579 283 359 280 346 530 381 325 414 410 182 272 526 304* / 405 55 487 360 176 223 174 215 329 237 202 258 260 119 232 145 194 260 255 113 169 327 189

Lincoln — *109 597 71 892 687 348 249 256 468 642 438 415 505 325 307 335 137 295 317 336 145 320 616 211* / 68 371 44 554 427 216 155 159 291 399 272 258 314 202 191 208 85 183 197 209 90 199 383 131

Liverpool — *208 121 581 209 822 615 164 427 225 348 530 257 348 460 481 193 272 312 259 438 377 150 167 549 325* / 129 75 361 130 511 382 102 265 140 216 329 160 216 286 299 120 169 194 161 272 234 93 104 341 202

Manchester — *56 135 64 581 153 805 600 200 367 203 346 530 317 346 459 444 192 295 266 259 414 365 129 208 547 298* / 35 84 40 361 95 500 373 124 228 126 215 329 197 215 285 276 119 183 165 161 257 227 80 129 340 185

Newcastle upon Tyne — *212 270 256 148 802 212 636 431 438 496 428 238 407 529 177 267 576 92 523 388 481 567 558 333 414 378 460* / 132 168 159 92 498 132 395 268 272 308 266 148 253 329 110 166 358 57 325 241 299 352 347 207 257 235 286

Norwich — *425 298 354 169 283 678 240 1053 852 501 117 328 620 811 532 589 697 456 422 100 406 282 344 267 444 798 183* / 264 185 220 105 176 421 149 654 529 311 73 204 385 504 343 366 422 174 289 262 62 252 175 214 166 276 496 114

Oban — *792 375 494 496 623 494 1070 557 393 188 687 843 710 148 79 774 108 188 942 303 768 753 748 910 853 618 663 286 803* / 492 233 307 308 387 307 665 346 244 117 427 524 441 92 49 481 123 117 585 188 477 468 465 565 530 384 412 178 499

Oxford — *744 233 418 232 277 221 270 441 309 1056 856 383 233 84 573 760 330 599 697 227 418 174 134 119 174 145 103 248 777 92* / 462 145 260 144 172 137 168 274 192 656 532 238 145 52 356 472 205 372 433 141 260 108 83 74 108 90 64 154 483 57

Plymouth — *320 945 552 660 455 455 472 509 143 571 1271 1069 528 497 253 797 958 425 798 888 483 642 269 472 196 361 206 327 382 990 351* / 199 587 343 410 283 283 293 316 89 355 790 664 328 309 157 495 595 264 496 552 300 399 167 293 122 224 128 203 237 615 218

Sheffield — *455 217 546 235 201 61 116 74 53 581 105 837 632 270 301 203 399 560 346 378 468 394 245 312 193 259 364 348 122 256 579 256* / 283 135 339 146 125 38 72 46 33 361 65 520 393 168 187 126 248 348 215 235 291 245 152 194 120 161 226 216 76 159 360 159

Shrewsbury — *132 362 171 586 330 323 111 93 214 175 448 705 182 386 124 438 615 233 441 531 404 283 179 258 542 124 642 258* / 82 225 106 364 205 201 69 58 133 109 303 169 567 438 113 240 77 272 382 145 274 330 251 176 111 159 103 226 185 45 77 399 160

Southampton — *298 320 243 103 853 332 521 356 385 328 373 367 412 1164 963 472 264 169 697 871 375 705 805 230 521 195 238 122 98 50 206 323 880 124* / 185 199 151 64 530 206 324 221 239 204 232 228 256 723 598 293 164 105 433 541 233 438 500 143 324 121 148 76 61 31 128 201 547 77

Stranraer — *716 446 423 805 610 238 649 254 354 356 480 354 942 417 610 422 544 660 552 135 514 631 200 269 798 163 628 610 608 765 715 478 523 367 647* / 445 277 263 500 379 148 403 158 220 221 298 220 585 259 379 262 338 435 343 84 195 392 124 167 496 101 390 379 378 475 444 297 325 228 402

Swansea — *671 259 190 349 332 227 815 485 559 301 314 375 399 459 425 1120 921 296 430 143 658 798 108 663 761 441 497 66 365 137 326 192 117 816 312* / 417 161 118 217 206 141 506 301 347 187 195 233 248 285 264 696 572 184 267 89 409 496 67 412 473 274 309 41 227 85 222 167 119 73 507 194

York — *438 357 415 214 84 536 291 497 291 135 103 159 121 39 661 60 771 566 328 367 304 349 531 420 312 402 454 195 393 266 357 443 433 209 314 513 333* / 272 222 258 133 52 333 181 309 181 84 64 99 75 24 411 37 479 352 204 228 189 217 330 261 194 250 282 121 244 165 222 275 269 130 195 319 207

Isles of Scilly

White Island
St. Helens
St. Martin's
Bryher
CROMWELL'S CASTLE
New Grimsby
Higher Town
Bryher
Tresco
TRESCO ABBEY GARDENS
Eastern Isles
Samson
North West Passage
The Road
Crow Sound
Newford
Maypole
LONGSTONE HERITAGE CEN
St. Mary's
A3110
Hugh Town
ST.MARY'S
Crim Rocks
Old Town
Broad Sound
St. Mary's Sound
Annet
Smith Sound
Gugh
PENZANCE 2:40
(Apr-Nov)
St. Agnes
St. Agnes
Bishop Rock

St. Agnes He
St.

Porthtowan
Portreath
B3301
Godrevy Island
Navax Pt.
Illogan
TEHIDY
CORNISH ENGINES
MINERS MUSEUM
Roscroggan
Godrevy Pt.
Clodgy Pt.
The Island
St. Ives Bay
Gwithian
Kehelland
Pool
225
The Carracks
TATE GALLERY
BARBARA HEPWORTH MUSEUM
St. Ives
Roseworthy
TREVITHICK COTTAGE
SHIRE HORSE FARM
Tuckingmill
Carnkie
CAMBORNE
SOUTH WEST COAST PATH
Carbis Bay
Phillack
Barripper
Troon
Penha
CORNWALL
Gurnard's Head
Halsetown
Connor Downs
Copperhouse
Carnhell Green
Praze-an-Beeble
Penma
The Carracks
Zennor
Towednack
247
Cripplesease
Leelant
PARADISE PARK
Hayle
Praze
Fraddam
Crowan
Burras
Porthmeor
WAYSIDE FOLK MUSEUM
Nancledra
Townshend
Leedstown
Drym
Releath
SOUTH WEST COAST PATH
B3306
Canonstown
St. Erth
Hayle
B3302
Nancegollan
Morvah
252
CHYSAUSTER ANCIENT VILLAGE
Newmill
B3311
Relubbus
Praze
GODOLPHIN HOUSE
Godolphin Cross
Wendron
Bojewyan
Higher Boscaswell
Ludgvan
St. Hilary
Trescowe
Crowntown
A39
GEEVOR TIN MINE MUSEUM
Pendeen
Madron
PENZANCE HELIPORT
Gulval
Crowlas
A30
Goldsithney
Trewellard
A3071
TRENGWAINTON
A30
Carnyorth
B3318
Botallack
St. Just
Newbridge
Heamoor
PENZANCE
Chyandour
Marazion
ST. MICHAEL'S MOUNT
Germoe
Ashton
Sithney
Trewer
Cape Cornwall
Bosavern
Relubbus
Penzance
Helston
The Bisons
BALLOWALL BARROW
LAND'S END (ST. JUST)
Kelynack
224
Sancreed
CARN EUNY VILLAGE
Tredavoe
Res.
TRINITY HOUSE NATIONAL LIGHTHOUSE CENTRE
Perranuthnoe
Praa Sands
Rinsey
VILLAGE THEME PARK
Newlyn
Branne
Lower Drift
Catchall
NEWLYN ART GALLERY
SOUTH WEST COAST PATH
Cudden Pt.
Trewavas Hd.
Porthleven
Crows-an-wra
B3283
Kerris
Paul
Mousehole
A394
Sennen Cove
A30
Longships
St. Buryan
Trewoofe
St. Clement's Island
Porthleven Sands
Sennen
B3315
LAND'S END
LAND'S END
Polgigga
B3315
Lamorna
SOUTH WEST COAST PATH
Gunwalloe
Porthcurno
MUSEUM OF SUBMARINE TELEGRAPHY
Treen
Boskenna
TREGIFFIAN BURIAL CHAMBER
Lamorna Cove
Cury
St. Levan
St. Levan
MOUNTS BAY
Gwennap Hd.
Runnel Stone
Mullion
B3296
ISLES OF SCILLY 2:40
(Apr-Nov)
Mullion Cove
Mullion Cove
Mullion Island
Predannack Wollas
Vellan Hd.
Kynance Cove
Liz
LIZARD POINT

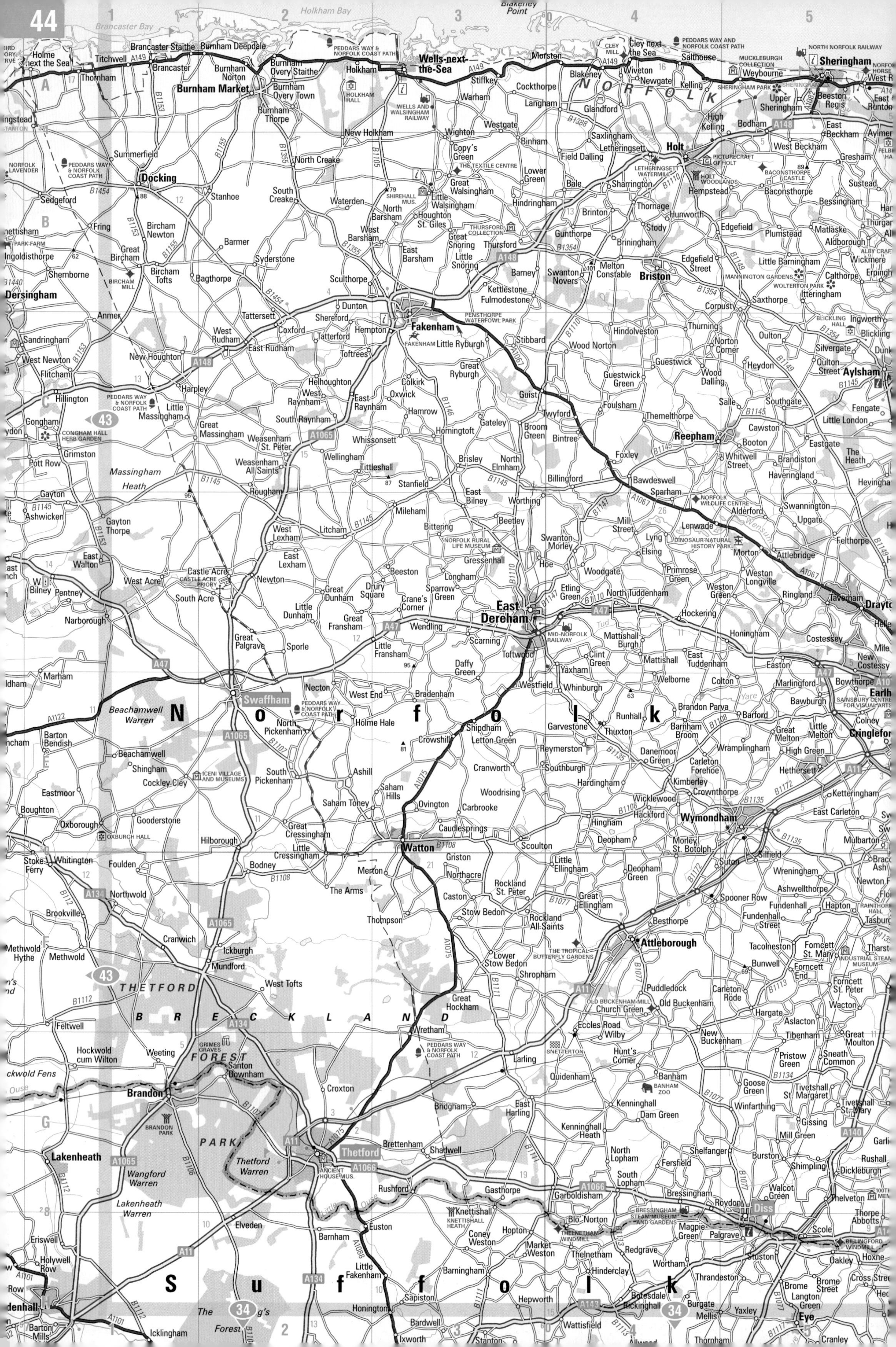

Holkham Bay

Brancaster Bay

Blakeney Point

NORTH NORFOLK RAILWAY

Holme next the Sea
Brancaster Staithe
Burnham Deepdale
Titchwell
Brancaster
Thornham
Burnham Norton
Burnham Overy Staithe
Burnham Overy Town
Holkham
Wells-next-the-Sea
Stiffkey
Warham
Morston
Blakeney
Wiveton
Cley next the Sea
Salthouse
Weybourne
Sheringham
West Runton
Beeston Regis
East Runton

PEDDARS WAY & NORFOLK COAST PATH

Burnham Market
Burnham Thorpe
HOLKHAM HALL
New Holkham
WELLS AND WALSINGHAM RAILWAY
Wighton
Westgate
Binham
Cockthorpe
Langham
Glandford
Newgate
Kelling
High Kelling
Upper Sheringham
Bodham
East Beckham

NORFOLK

Docking
Summerfield
North Creake
South Creake
Waterden
Copy's Green
THE TEXTILE CENTRE
Great Walsingham
Little Walsingham
Houghton St. Giles
Field Dalling
Lower Green
Bale
Sharrington
Hindringham
Thornage
Hunworth
Stody
Edgefield
Plumstead
Matlaske
Aldborough
Gresham
Sustead

NORFOLK LAVENDER
Sedgeford
Fring
Stanhoe
Bagthorpe
Barmer
Bircham Newton
Great Bircham
Syderstone
North Barsham
West Barsham
East Barsham
Little Snoring
Thursford
THURSFORD COLLECTION
Barney
Swanton Novers
Melton Constable
Brinton
Briningham
Briston
Edgefield Street
Little Barningham
Wickmere
Erpingham

Dersingham
Shernborne
Bircham Tofts
BIRCHAM MILL
Anmer
New Houghton
Tattersett
Sculthorpe
Dunton
Fulmodestone
Barney
Thurning
Norton Corner
Corpusty
Saxthorpe
Itteringham
WOLTERTON PARK
MANNINGTON GARDENS
Calthorpe
Aylsham

West Newton
SANDRINGHAM
Flitcham
Hillington
Harpley
West Rudham
East Rudham
Coxford
Shereford
Hempton
Fakenham
FAKENHAM
Little Ryburgh
Stibbard
Wood Norton
Guestwick Green
Guestwick
Wood Dalling
Salle
Heydon
Oulton Street
Silvergate
Ingworth
Blickling
BLICKLING HALL

PENSTHORPE WATERFOWL PARK
Great Ryburgh
Foulsham
Themelthorpe
Southgate
Little London
Fengate

Congham
CONGHAM HALL HERB GARDEN
43
Little Massingham
Helhoughton
West Raynham
East Raynham
Colkirk
Oxwick
Gateley
Broom Green
Bintree
Twyford
Guist
Foxley
Whitwell Street
Brandiston
Reepham
Booton
Eastgate
The Heath
Hevingha

Grimston
Pott Row
Gayton
Great Massingham
Weasenham St. Peter
Weasenham All Saints
Wellingham
South Raynham
Whissonsett
Tittleshall
Brisley
North Elmham
Billingford
Bawdeswell
Sparham
Lenwade
NORFOLK WILDLIFE CENTRE
Alderford
Swannington
Upgate
Haveringland
Cawston

Massingham Heath
Ashwicken
Gayton Thorpe
Roughton
Stanfield
Mileham
Litcham
East Bilney
Beetley
Worthing
Mill Street
Lyng
Elsing
Primrose Green
Weston Green
Morton
Attlebridge
Weston Longville
Ringland
Taverham
Drayton

East Walton
Bilney
Pentney
Narborough
West Acre
Castle Acre
CASTLE ACRE PRIORY
South Acre
Newton
Little Dunham
Great Dunham
Beeston
Gressenhall
NORFOLK RURAL LIFE MUSEUM
Hoe
Swanton Morley
Woodgate
Etling Green
North Tuddenham
Hockering
Honingham
Costessey
Mile
New Costessey

Marham
Barton Bendish
Beachamwell Warren
NORFOLK
Swaffham
A47
Sporle
Great Palgrave
Little Fransham
Great Fransham
Wendling
Scarning
Toftwood
MID-NORFOLK RAILWAY
East Dereham
Mattishall Burgh
Clint Green
Mattishall
East Tuddenham
Easton
Marlingford
Bowthorpe
Earlh

Beachamwell
Shingham
Cockley Cley
ICENI VILLAGE AND MUSEUMS
South Pickenham
North Pickenham
Necton
Holme Hale
West End
Bradenham
Shipdham
Westfield
Whinburgh
Yaxham
Welborne
Colton
Runhall
Barnham Broom
Great Melton
Little Melton
Colney
Cringlefor

Eastmoor
Boughton
Oxborough
OXBURGH HALL
Gooderstone
Hilborough
Ashill
Saham Hills
Ovington
Carbrooke
Woodrising
Southburgh
Hardingham
Hingham
Kimberley
Wicklewood
Hackford
Crownthorpe
Wramplingham
High Green
Hethersett
Ketteringham
East Carleton

Stoke Ferry
Whittington
Foulden
Northwold
Little Cressingham
Great Cressingham
Bodney
Watton
Griston
Merton
Caston
Northacre
Scoulton
Reymerston
Cranworth
Letton Green
Crowshill
Daffy Green
Thuxton
Garveston
Reymerston
Caudlesprings
Deopham
Morley St. Botolph
Wymondham
Silfield
Wreningham
Newton F

Methwold Hythe
Methwold
Cranwich
Ickburgh
Mundford
West Tofts
Thompson
The Arms
Little Ellingham
Great Ellingham
Rockland St. Peter
Rockland All Saints
Stow Bedon
Deopham Green
Besthorpe
Attleborough
Fundenhall
Fundenhall Street
Hapton
Tacolneston
Bunwell
Spooner Row
Ashwellthorpe

43
THETFORD
BRECKLAND
Feltwell
Hockwold cum Wilton
Weeting
GRIMES GRAVES
Santon Downham
Croxton
Bridgham
East Harling
Larling
SNETTERTON
Quidenham
Banham
BANHAM ZOO
Old Buckenham
OLD BUCKENHAM MILL
Church Green
New Buckenham
Carleton Rode
Forncett St. Mary
INDUSTRIAL STEAM MUSEUM
Hargate
Aslacton
Great Moulton
Forncett St. Peter
Wacton
Tibenham

Lakenheath
BRANDON PARK
Brandon
Wangford Warren
Lakenheath Warren
THETFORD FOREST
PARK
Thetford Warren
Thetford
ANCIENT HOUSE MUS.
Brettenham
Shadwell
Kilverstone
Eccles Road
Wilby
Hunt's Corner
Kenninghall
Kenninghall Heath
North Lopham
South Lopham
Garboldisham
Fersfield
Bressingham
BRESSINGHAM STEAM MUSEUM AND GARDENS
Roydon
Diss
Walcot Green
Burston
Shimpling
Dickleburgh
Gissing
Tivetshall St. Margaret
Tivetshall St. Mary

Brandon
Rushford
Gasthorpe
KNETTISHALL HEATH
Coney Weston
Market Weston
Thelnetham
THELNETHAM WINDMILL
Hinderclay
Redgrave
Wortham
Magpie Green
Palgrave
Scole
Billingford WINDMILL
Stuston
Thorpe Abbotts
Oakley
Hoxne

SUFFOLK
Lakenheath
Eriswell
Holywell Row
Barton Mills
Icklingham
Elveden
Barnham
Euston
Little Fakenham
Honington
Sapiston
Ixworth
Bardwell
Stanton
Wattisfield
Botesdale
Rickinghall
Burgate
Mellis
Yaxley
Thrandeston
Brome Street
Cross Street
Eye
Langton Green
Cranley
34

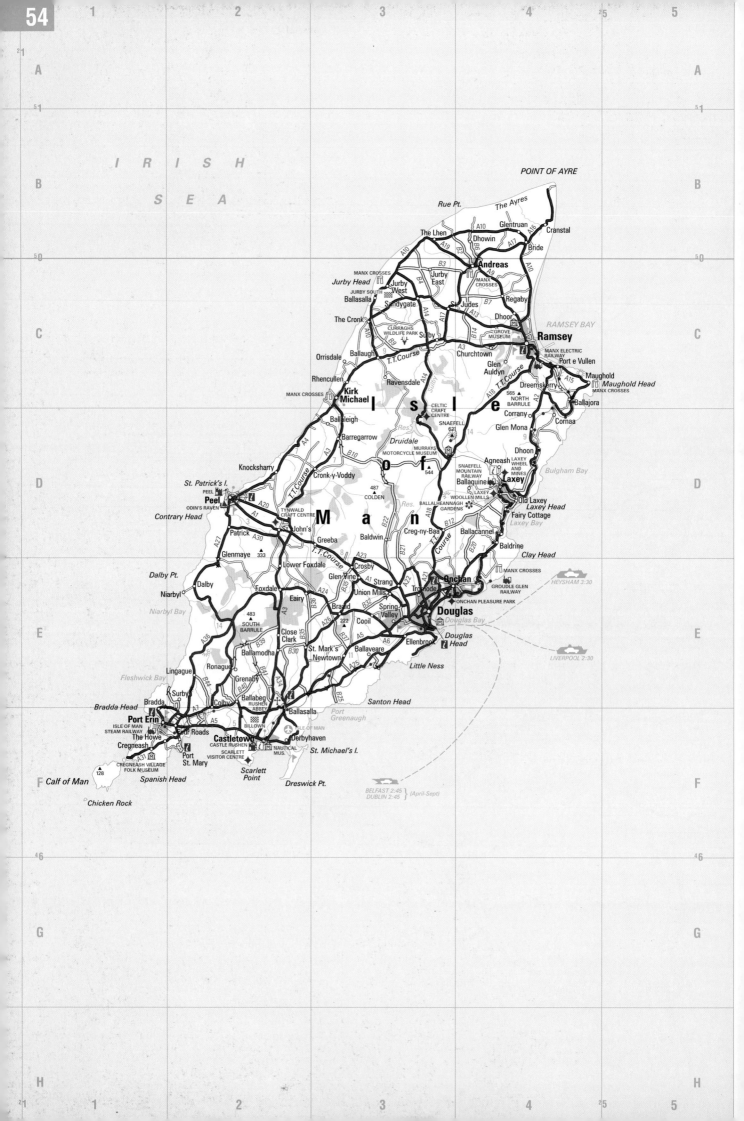

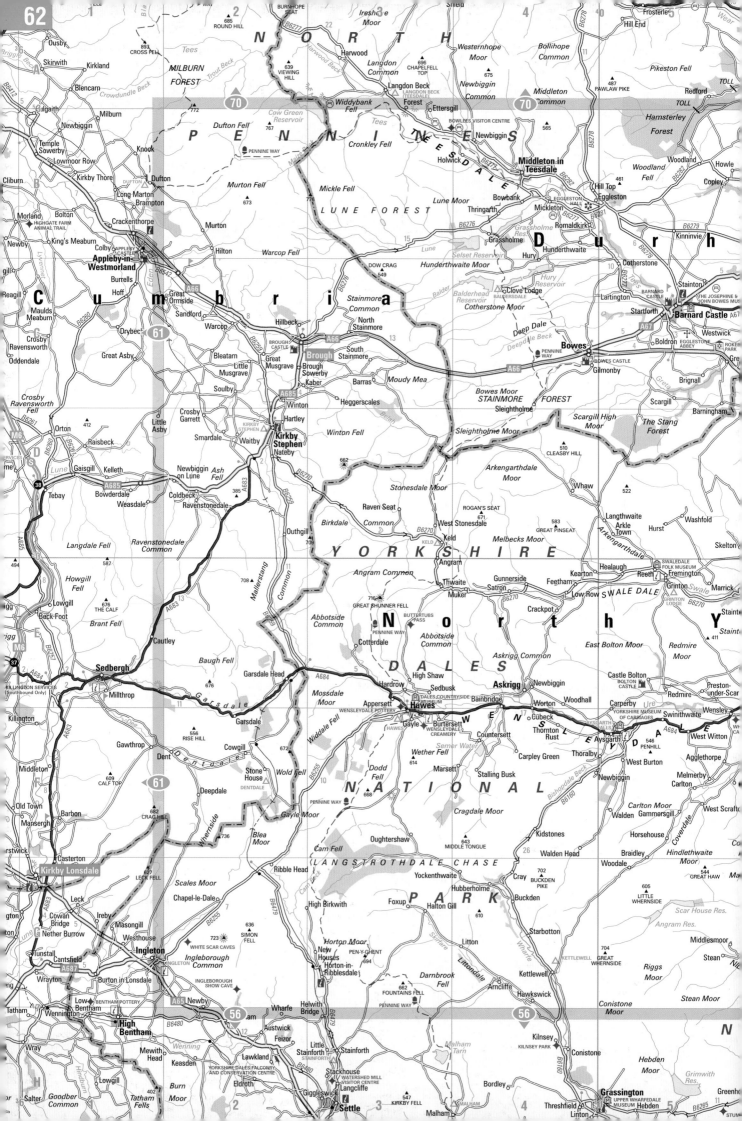

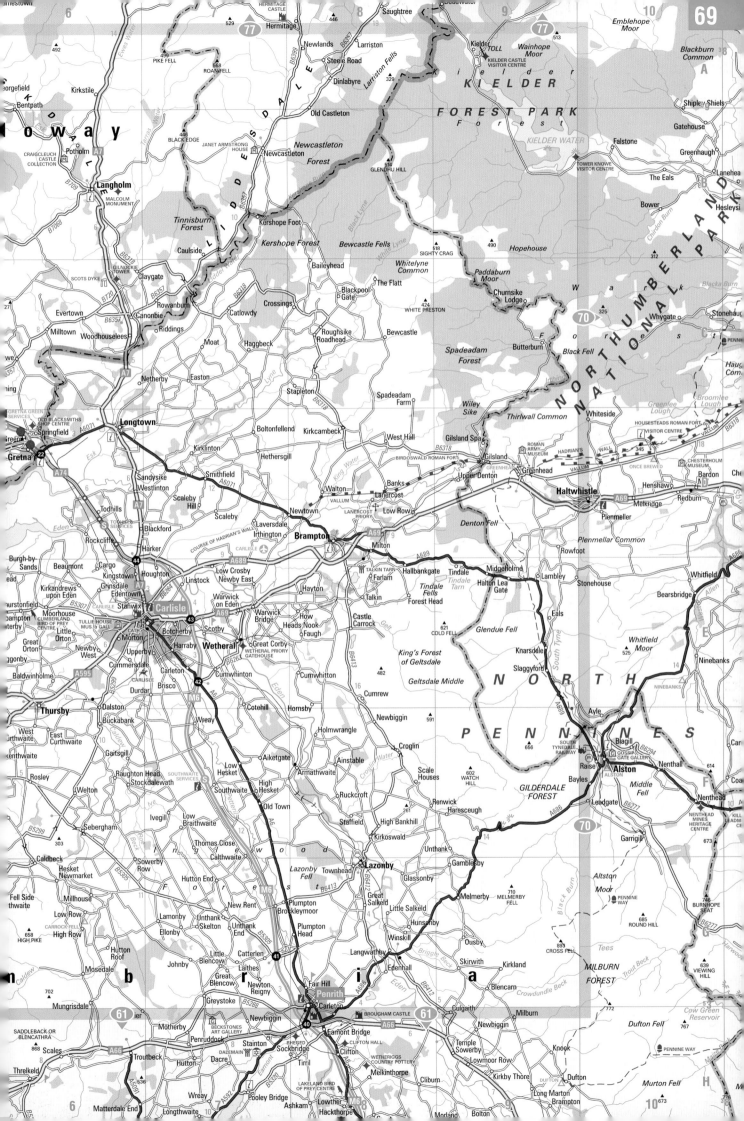

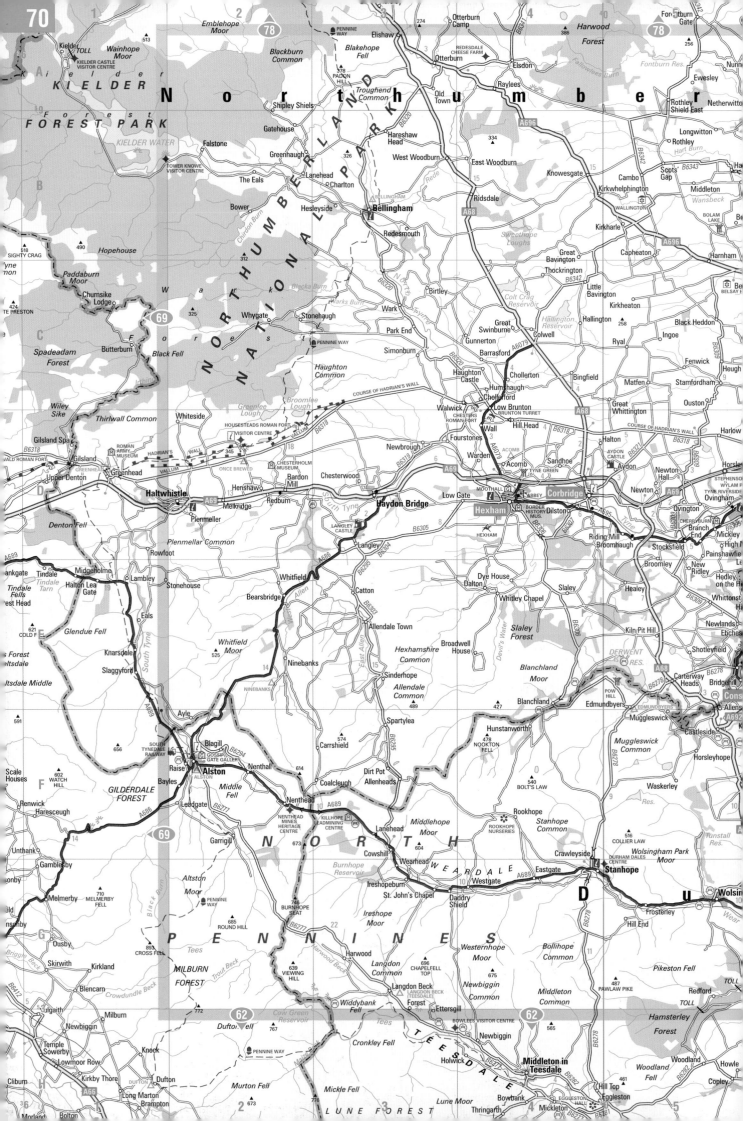

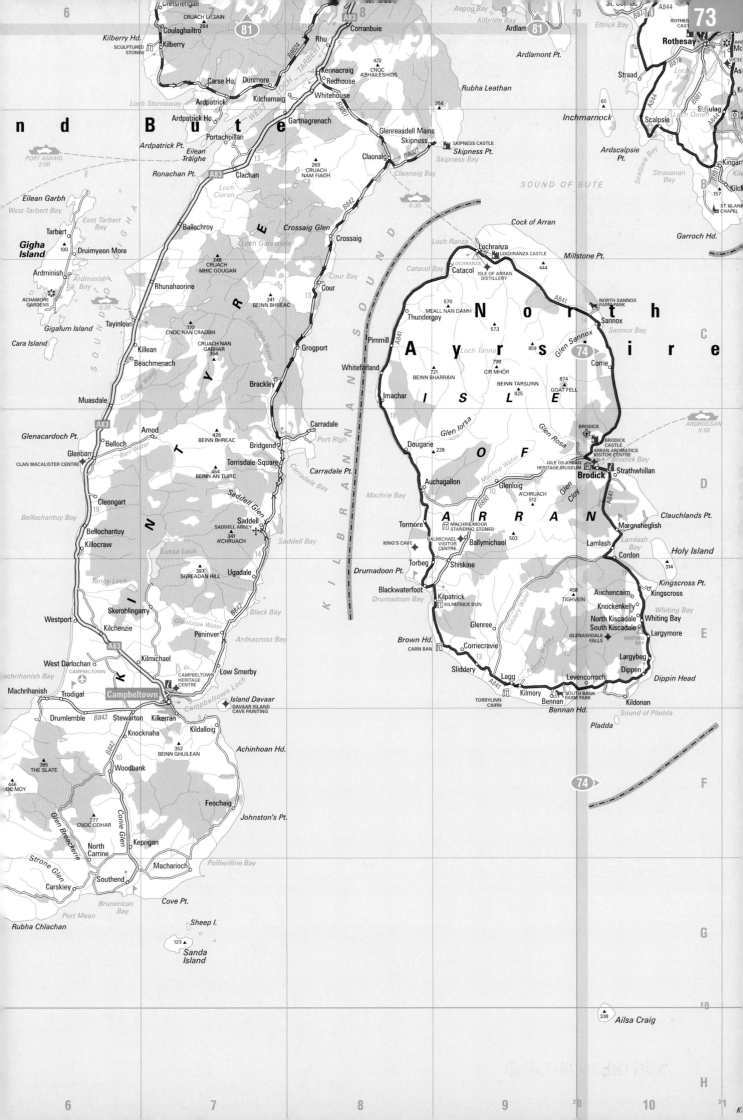

6   7   8   9   10

A

⁶6

B

C

Emmanuel Hd.
**Holy Island
(Lindisfarne)**
LINDISFARNE CASTLE
ay
Holy   Castle Pt.
Island   LINDISFARNE
PRIORY
ds

Guile
Pt.

Farne
Islands

Elwick   Ross   Budle   Staple Sound
Bay
Budle   BAMBURGH   Inner Sound
Budle   CASTLE

Budle
Bamburgh   D

Easington   Waren Mill   B1340
B1342   Burton
Spindlestone   Glororum
lousen   Bradford   B1341
Bellshill   Elford   North   **Seahouses**
Adderstone   Sunderland
Lucker   Newham
Warenford   Hall   Swinhoe   **Beadnell**
LANDS GALLERY   Newham   Fleetham   Benthall
TWO CERAMICS   Newstead   Chathill
Rosebrough   Ellingham   Beadnell
Bay
Brockdam   Preston   High Newton-
PRESTON TOWER   Brunton   by-the-Sea
Brownside   Christon   Low Newton-
North Charlton   Doxford   Bank   by-the-Sea
B6347   Embleton Bay
West   Embleton
Ditchburn   South   Dunstan   Castle Point
ope   Charlton   Steads   DUNSTANBURGH
Rock   CASTLE
Rennington   Dunstan   E
B6347   101   Craster
169   Littlemill   Howick
Shipley   Littlehoughton   Howick Haven
HULNE ABBEY   **Longhoughton**
lington   ALNWICK   Denwick   Boulmer   F
don Hall   ABBEY   Boulmer Haven
250   Hawkhill
Alnwick   Lesbury
Abberwick   HOUSE OF
Broome Park   HARDY MUS.
Lemmington   Bilton
Hall   A1   **Alnmouth**
DLINGHAM   Alnmouth Bay
CASTLE   High
B634   250   Shilbottle   Buston
dlingham   A1068
Low Buston   G
Newton-   179   Birling
on-the-Moor   Eastfield   Warkworth
Hall
A697   **a**   **n**   **d**   Coquet I.
Hazon   Gloster
Swarland   Guyzance   Hill   **Amble**
Estate   North   Hauxley
Brainshaugh   Togston
Swarland   Acklington   Togston   Radcliffe
ngframlington   Broomhill   DRURIDGE BAY
B6345   South
LONGFRAMLINGTON   Felton   Broomhill   Red Row
GARDENS
B6344   West   East
Weldon   Thirston   Thirston
sleyhurst   A1068   Druridge Bay
Eshott   West
Chevington
Helm   Widdrington   H
ingates   71   Causey   Widdrington
Longhorsley   Park Bridge   Stobswood   Station   The Scars
A1   Cresswell

6   7   8   9   10

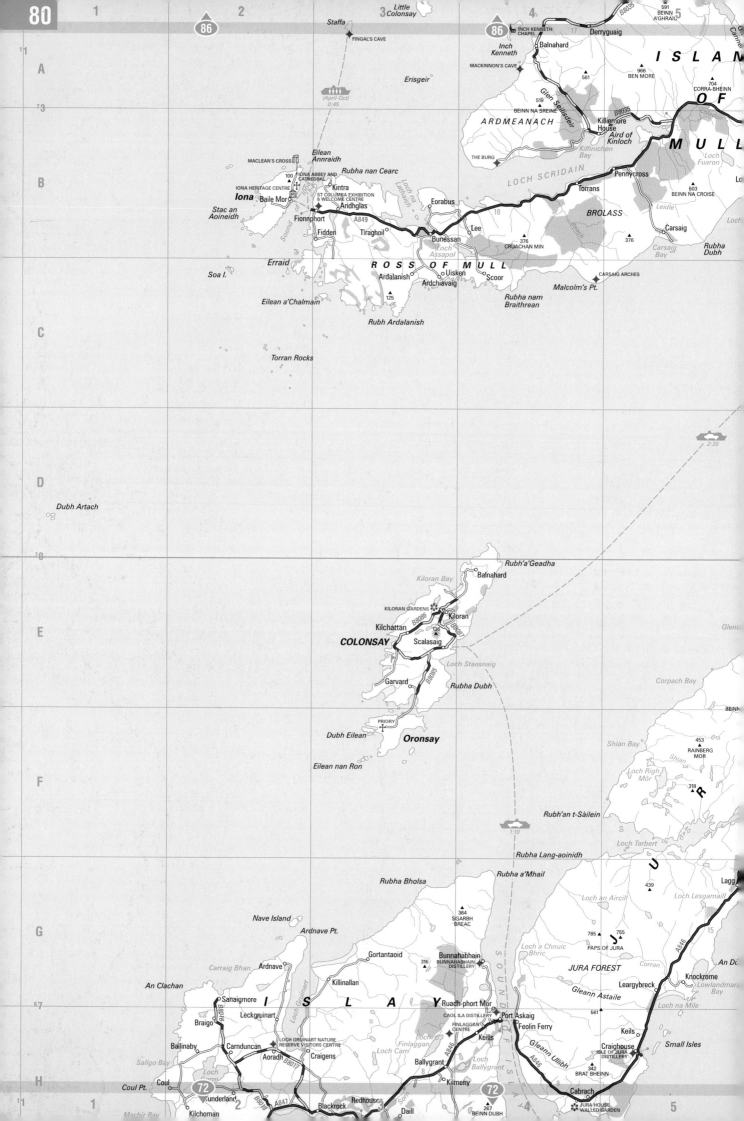

ISLAN

OF

MULL

Staffa

Little Colonsay

FINGAL'S CAVE

Erisgeir

(April-Oct) 0:45

Inch Kenneth Chapel

Inch Kenneth

Derryguaig

B8035

591 BEINN A'GHRAIG

MACKINNON'S CAVE

Balnahard

561

966 BEN MORE

704 CORRA-BHEINN

519

BEINN NA SREINE

Glen Seilisdeir

ARDMEANACH

Killiemore House

B8035

503

MACLEAN'S CROSS

Eilean Annraidh

Rubha nan Cearc

Aird of Kinloch

THE BURG

Kilfinichen Bay

Loch Fuaron

IONA ABBEY AND CATHEDRAL

100

Kintra

ST COLUMBA EXHIBITION & WELCOME CENTRE

Pennycross

Lo

IONA HERITAGE CENTRE

Iona

Baile Mor

Eorabus

Torrans

BEINN NA CROISE

Stac an Aoineidh

Aridhglas

Loch na Lathaich

LOCH SCRIDAIN

BROLASS

Carsaig

Fionnphort

A849

Lee

Leidle

Fidden

Tiraghoil

Bunessan

18

Carsaig Bay

Rubha Dubh

Erraid

Loch Assapol

ROSS OF MULL

376

CRUACHAN MIN

376

Soa I.

Ardalanish

Uisken

Scoor

CARSAIG ARCHES

Eilean a'Chalmain

125

Ardchiavaig

Rubha nam Braithrean

Malcolm's Pt.

Rubh Ardalanish

Torran Rocks

2:20

Dubh Artach

Rubh'a'Geadha

Kiloran Bay

Balnahard

KILORAN GARDENS

Kiloran

B8086

Kilchattan

B8087

136

COLONSAY

Scalasaig

B8085

Garvard

Loch Staosnaig

Rubha Dubh

Corpach Bay

BEINN

Dubh Eilean

PRIORY

Oronsay

453 RAINBERG MOR

Eilean nan Ron

Shian Bay

Loch Righ Mor

Shian

318 R

Rubh'an t-Sàilein

1:10

Loch Tarbert

Rubha Lang-aoinidh

U

Rubha a'Mhail

439

Lagg

Rubha Bholsa

Loch an Aircill

Loch Lesgamaill

Nave Island

364 SGARBH BREAC

SOUND OF ISLAY

An Du

Ardnave Pt.

Gortantaoid

316

JURA FOREST

785 J

755 J

PAPS OF JURA

Loch a Chnuic Bhric

Corran

An Clachan

Ardnave

Killinallan

Bunnahabhain

BUNNAHABHAIN DISTILLERY

Gleann Astaile

Knockrome

Carraig Bhan

561

Leargybreck

Loch na Mile

Sanaigmore

I S L A Y

Ruadh-phort Mor

Keils

Braigo

B8018

Leckgruinart

CAOL ILA DISTILLERY

Port Askaig

Small Isles

Ballinaby

Carnduncan

LOCH GRUINART NATURE RESERVE VISITORS CENTRE

FINLAGGAN CENTRE

Feolin Ferry

Keills

Craighouse

ISLE OF JURA DISTILLERY

Gleann Ullibh

Aoradh

Craigens

A846

Ballygrant

342 BRAT BHEINN

Saligo Bay

B8017

Ballygrant

Loch Ballygrant

A846

Coul Pt.

72

Loch Gorm

Blackrock

Redhouse

Daill

Kilmeny

72

Cabrach

Machir Bay

Kilchoman

underland

A847

B8018

267 BEINN DUBH

JURA HOUSE WALLED GARDEN

15

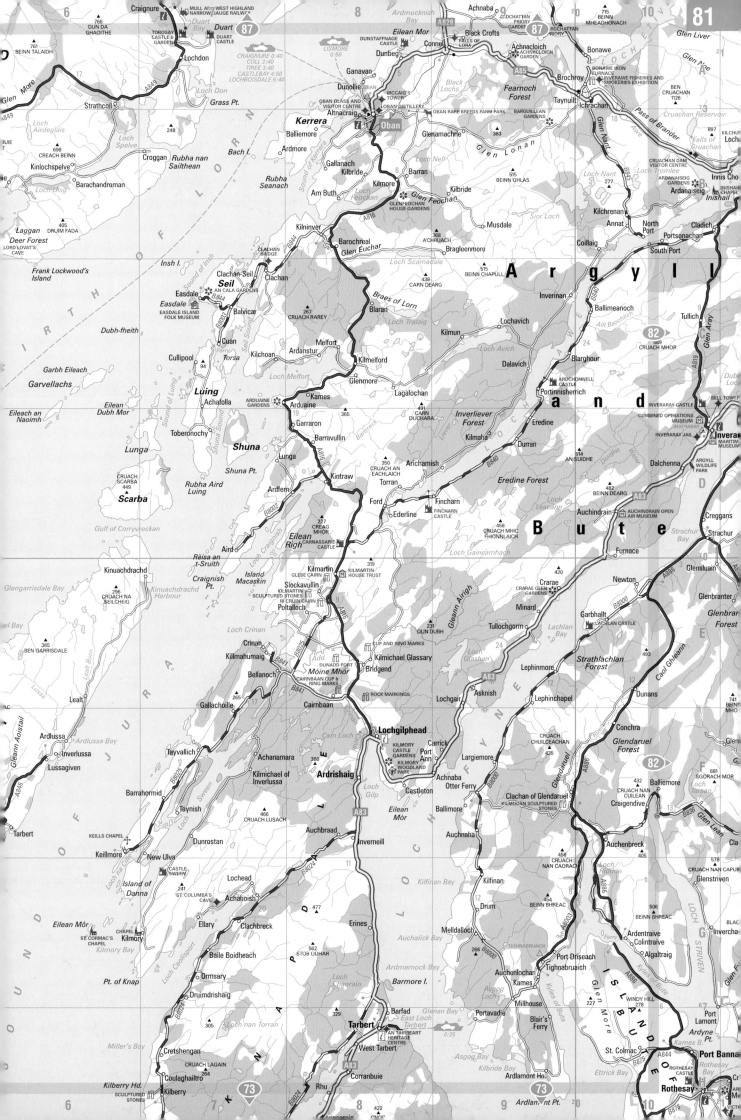

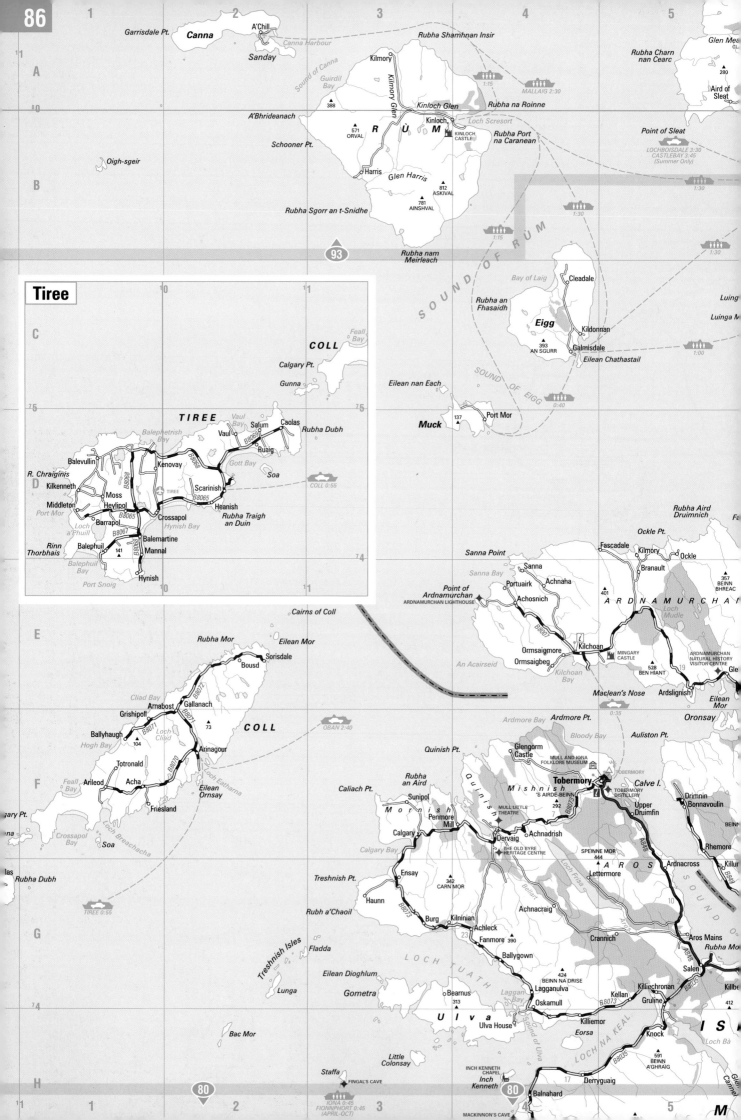

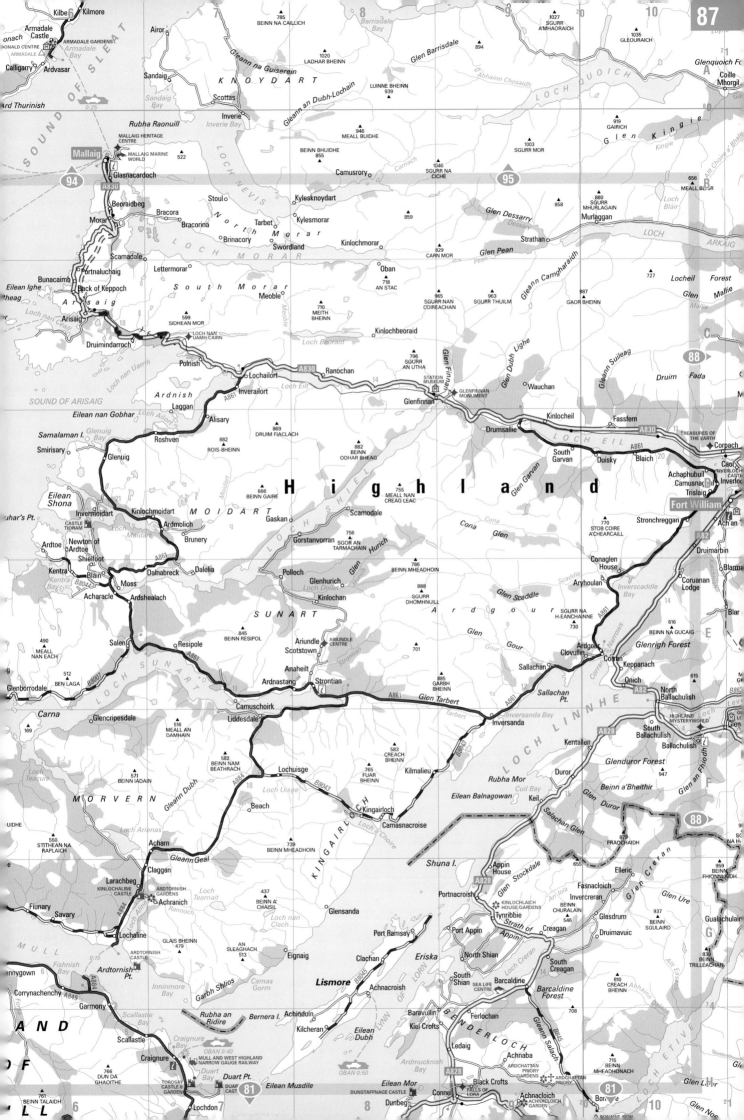

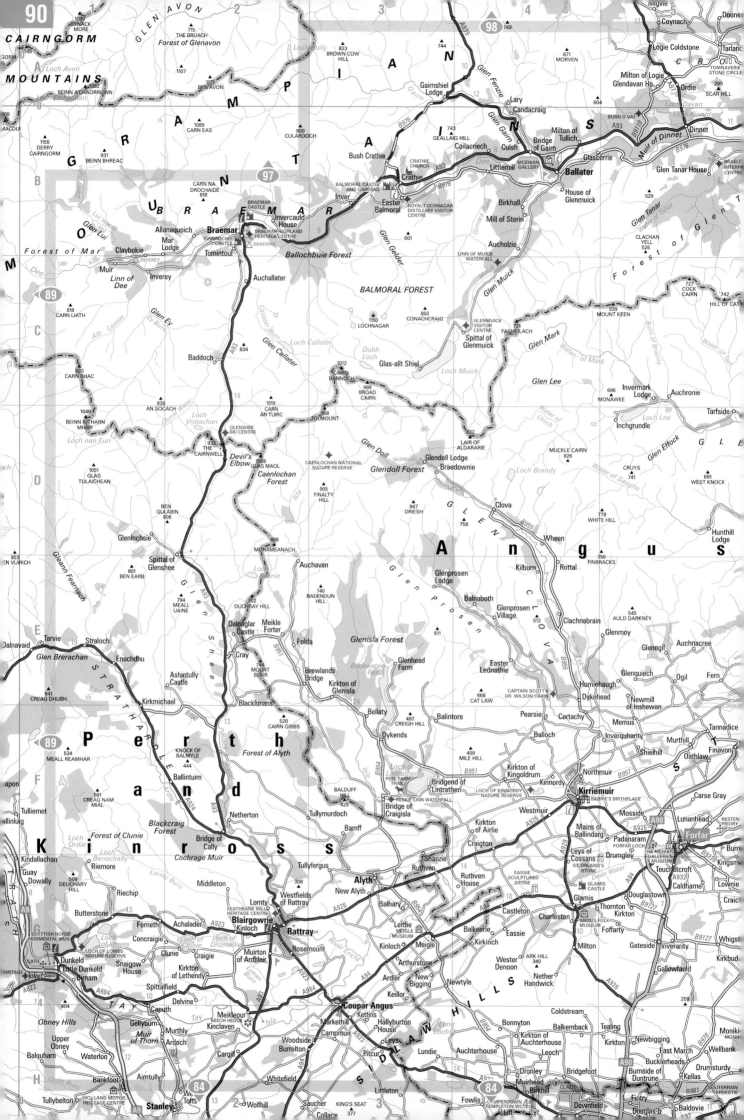

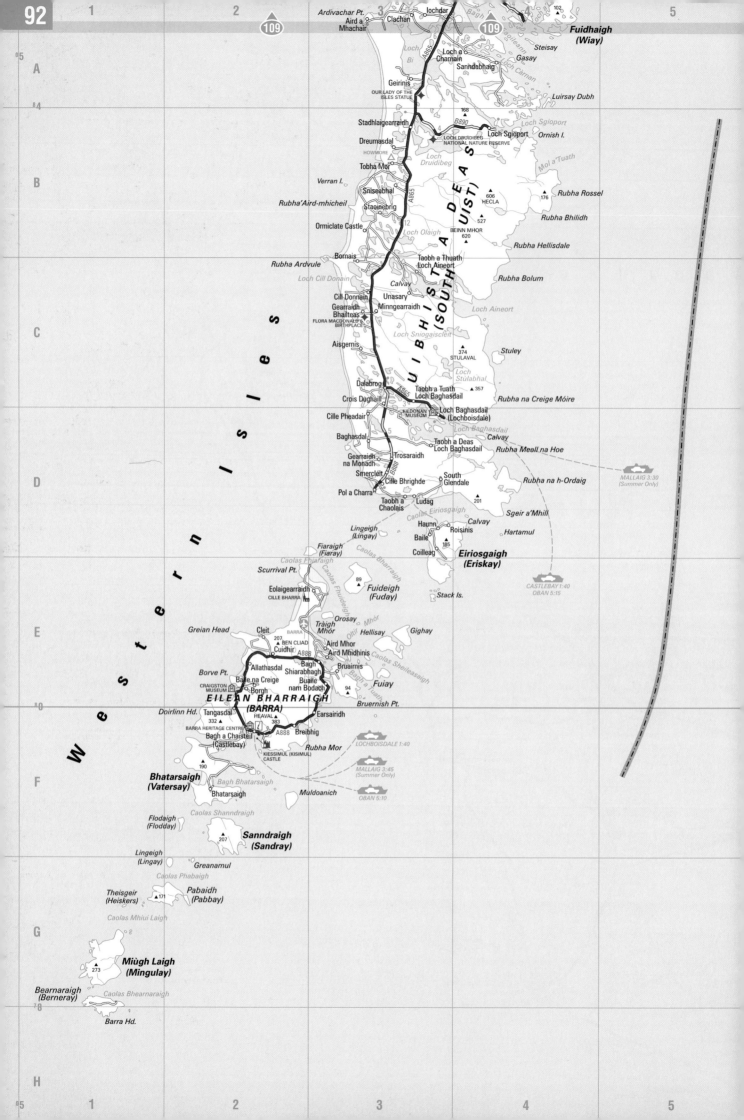

Ardivachar Pt.
Aird a
Mhachair
Clachan
Iochdar
109
109

Fuidhaigh
(Wiay)

Steisay

Gasay

A865
Loch a
Charnain
Sanndabhaig
Loch
Bì
Geirinis
Luirsay Dubh
OUR LADY OF THE
ISLES STATUE

Loch
Càrnan

168
B890
Stadhlaigearraidh
Loch Sgioport
Ornish I.
Dreumasdal
LOCH DRUIDIBEG
NATIONAL NATURE RESERVE
Loch Sgioport
Loch Druidibeg

Mol a'Tuath

HOWMORE

Tobha Mor

Verran I.
Sniseabhal
Staoinebrig

A865

606
HECLA
176
Rubha Rossel

527
Rubha'Aird-mhicheil

BEINN MHOR
620
Rubha Bhilidh

Ormiclate Castle
Loch Olàigh

Rubha Hellisdale

Bornais

12

Taobh a Thuath
Loch Aineort

Rubha Ardvule

Loch Cill Donain

Calvay

Rubha Bolum

Cill Donnain
Unasary
Gearraidh
Bhailteas
Minngearraidh
FLORA MACDONALD'S
BIRTHPLACE

Loch Aineort

Aisgernis

Loch Sniogaiscleit

374
STULAVAL
Stuley

Loch
Stùlabhal

Dalabrog
Taobh a Tuath
Loch Baghasdail

A865

357
Rubha na Creige Móire

Crois Dùghaill

KILDONAN
MUSEUM
Loch Baghasdail
(Lochboisdale)

Cille Pheadair

Loch Baghasdail
Calvay

Baghasdal
Taobh a Deas
Loch Baghasdail
Rubha Meall na Hoe

Gearraidh
na Monadh
Trosaraidh

Smercleit
Cille Bhrighde
South
Glendale
Rubha na h-Ordaig
MALLAIG 3:30
(Summer Only)

Pol a Charra
Taobh a
Chaolais
Ludag
201
Sgeir a'Mhill

Caolas Eiriosgaigh

Haunn
Calvay
Hartamul

Lingeigh
(Lingay)
Baile
Roisinis

Fiaraigh
(Fiaray)
Coilleag
185

Eiriosgaigh
(Eriskay)

Caolas Phlàraigh

Scurrival Pt.
Caolas Bharraigh

CASTLEBAY 1:40
OBAN 5:15

Eolaigearraidh
89
CILLE BHARRA
Fuideigh
(Fuday)
Stack Is.

Greian Head
Cleit
Orosay
Hellisay
Gighay

BARRA
207 BEN CLIAD
Cuidhir
Traigh
Mhór

Oitir Mhór
Aird Mhor
A888
Aird Mhidhinis

Borve Pt.
Allathasdal
Bagh
Shiarabhagh
Bruairnis
Fuiay

CRAIGSTON
MUSEUM
Baile na Creige
Buaile
nam Bodach
94

Borgh

Caolas Sheileasaigh

Bagh a'Tuath

EILEAN BHARRAIGH
(BARRA)

Bruernish Pt.

Doirlinn Hd.
Tangasdal
Earsairidh
332
HEAVAL
383
A888
Breibhig
BARRA HERITAGE CENTRE
Rubha Mor
LOCHBOISDALE 1:40

Bagh a Chaisteil
(Castlebay)
KIESSIMUL (KISIMUL)
CASTLE
MALLAIG 3:45
(Summer Only)

190

Bhatarsaigh
(Vatersay)
Muldoanich
OBAN 5:10

Bhatarsaigh
Bagh Bhatarsaigh

Flodaigh
(Flodday)
Caolas Shanndraigh

207
Sanndraigh
(Sandray)

Lingeigh
(Lingay)
Greanamul

Caolas Phabaigh

Theisgeir
(Heiskers)
171
Pabaidh
(Pabbay)

Caolas Mhiui Laigh

273
Miùgh Laigh
(Mingulay)

Bearnaraigh
(Berneray)
Caolas Bhearnaraigh

Barra Hd.

Western Isles

UIBHIST A DEAS (SOUTH UIST)

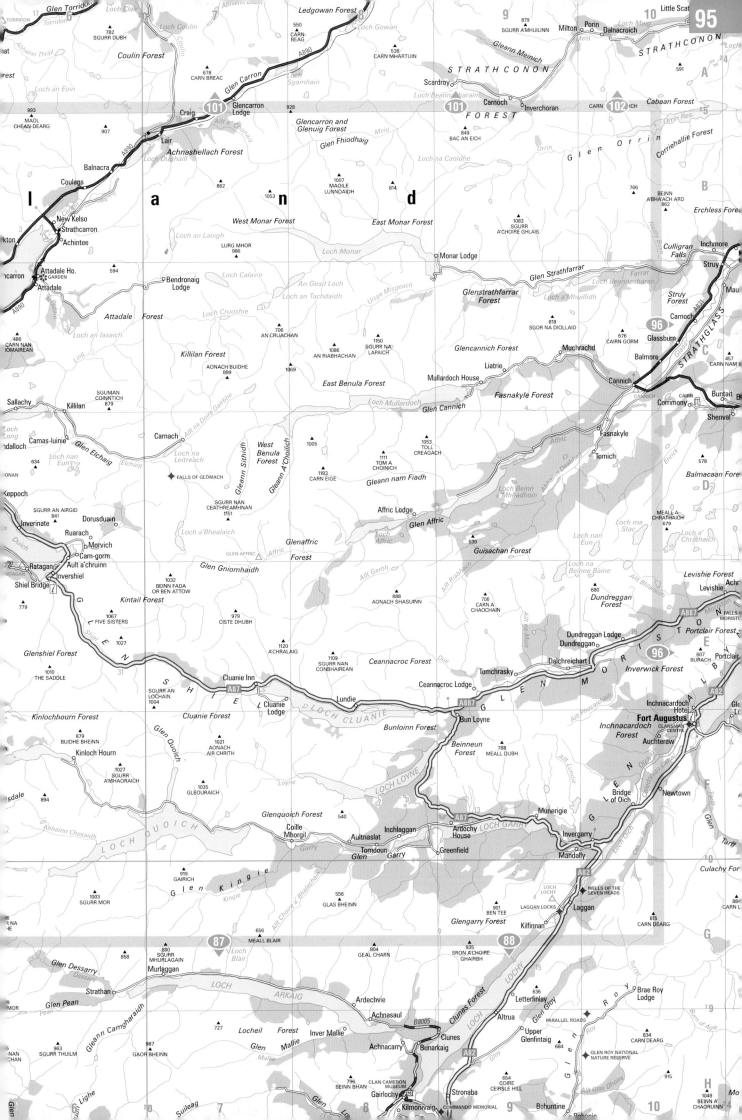

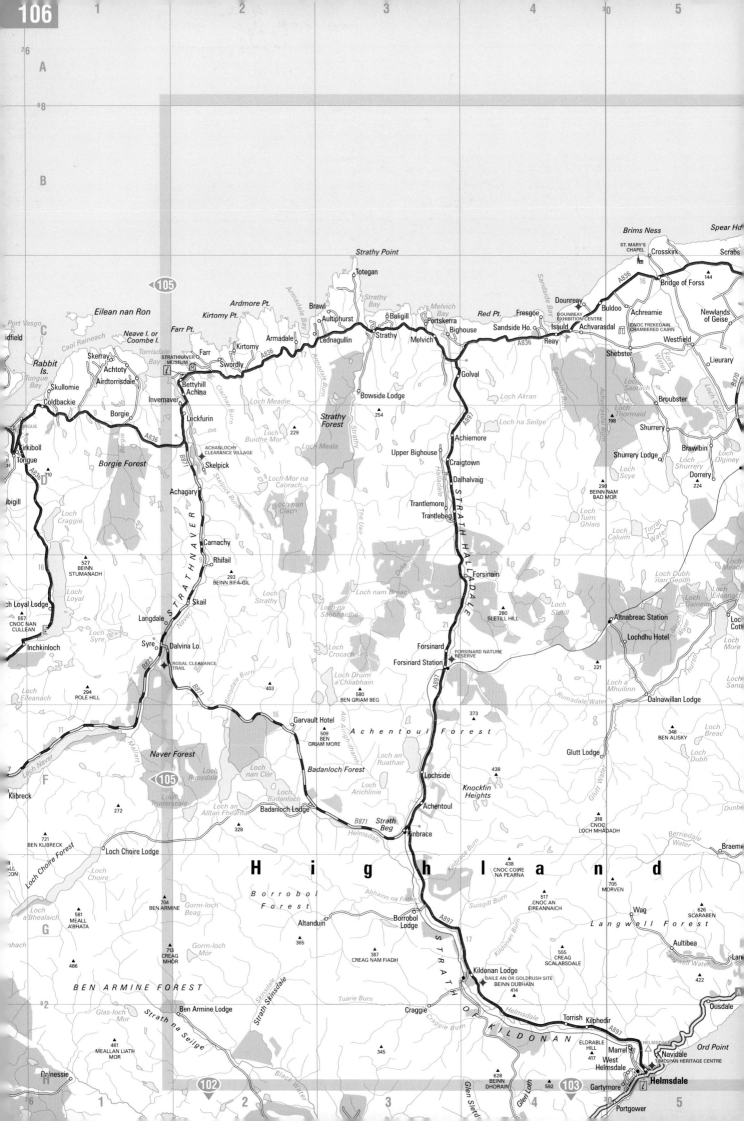

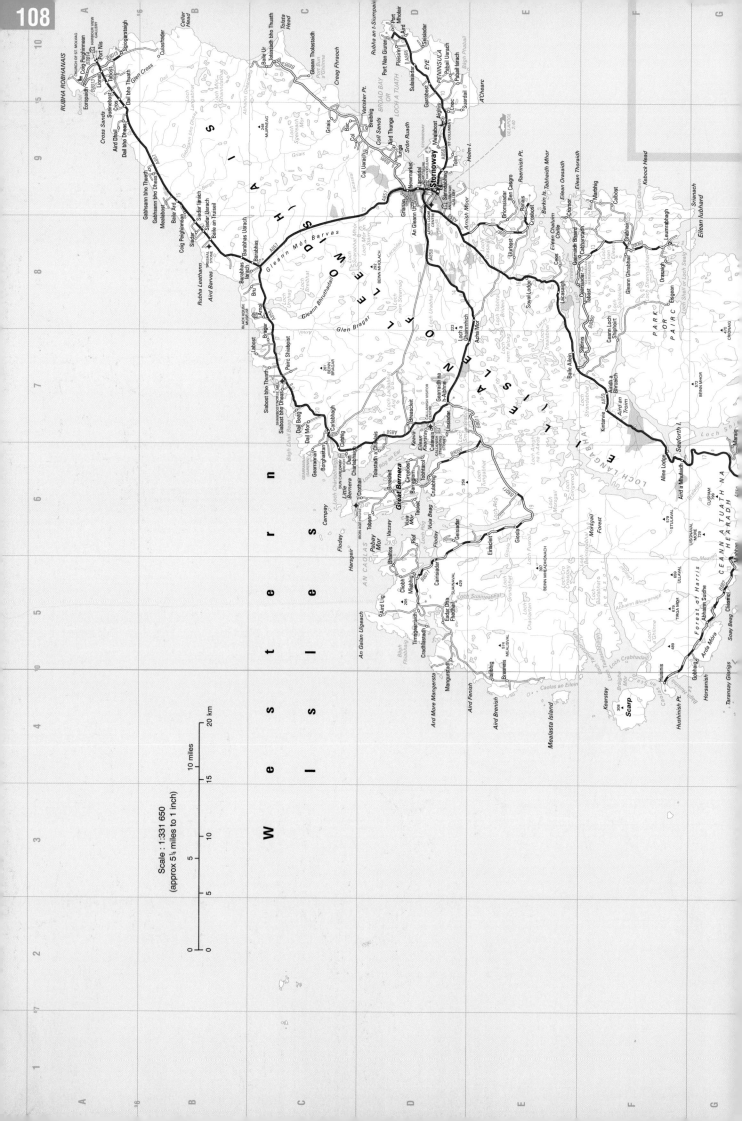

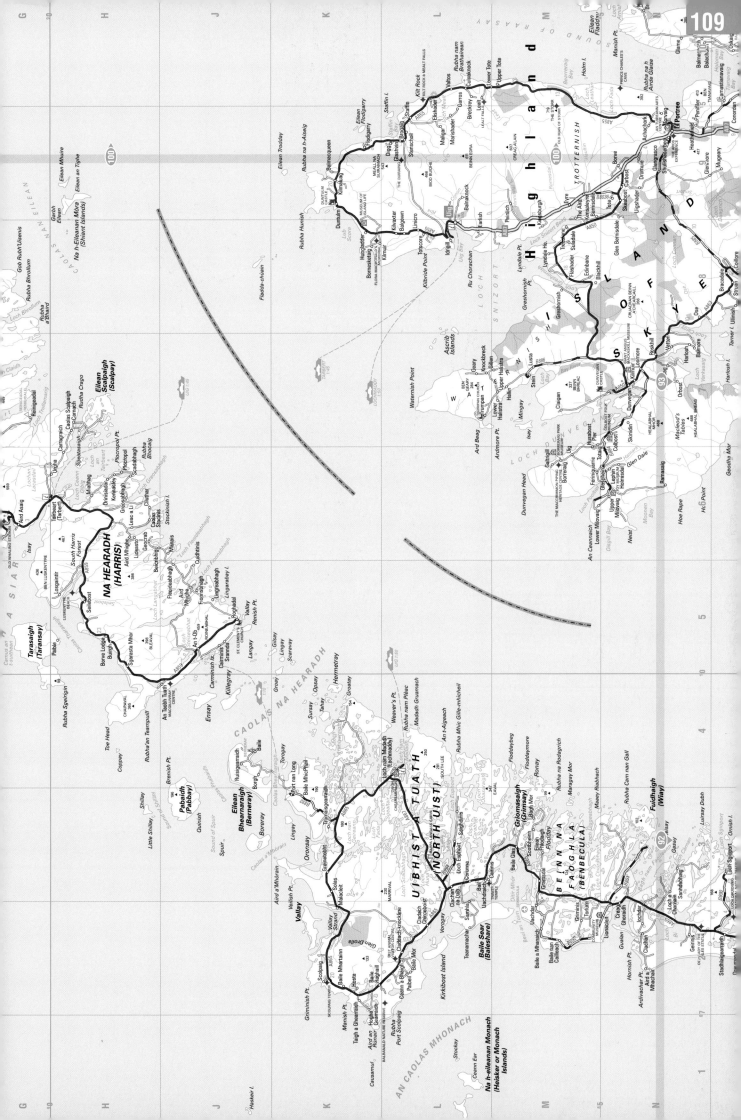

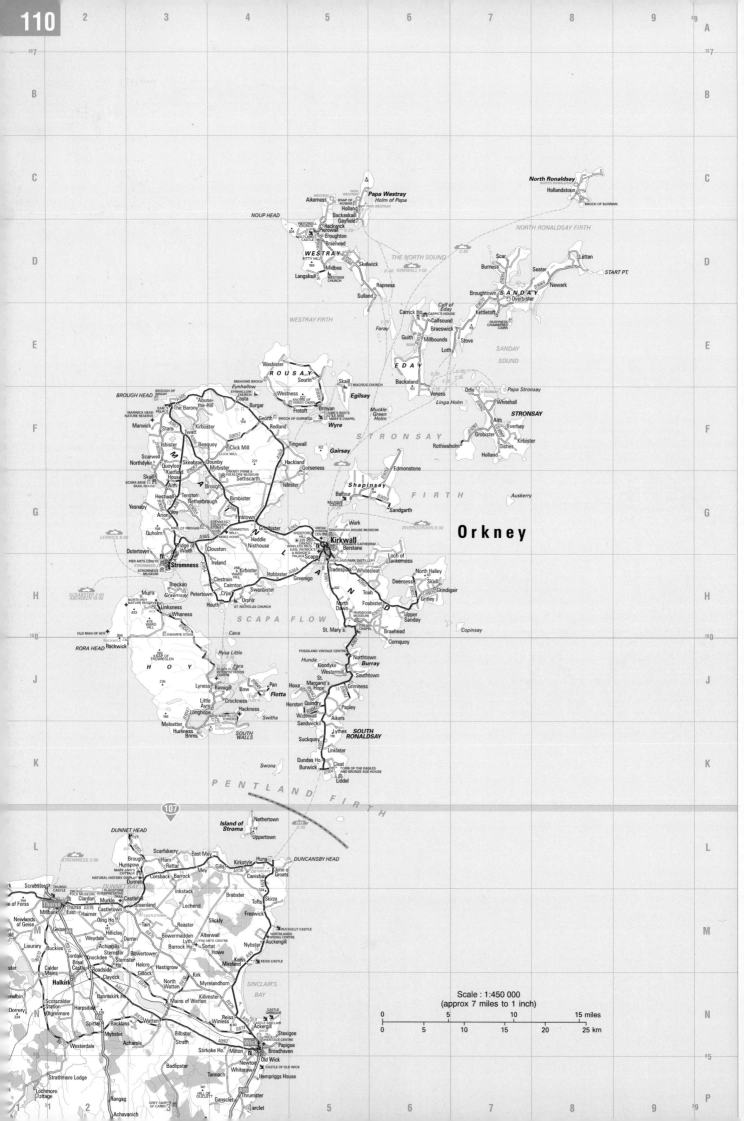

Orkney

North Ronaldsay
Hollandstoun
BROCH OF BURRIAN

NORTH RONALDSAY FIRTH

Papa Westray
Holm of Papa
Aikerness
KNAP OF HOWAR
Holland
Backaskaill
Gayfield
Rackwick
Pierowall
Broughton
Braehead

NOUP HEAD

THE NORTH SOUND

KIRKWALL 1:50

WESTRAY

Midbea
Skelwick
Scar
Burness
Seater
Lettan
START PT.
Langskaill
WESTSIDE CHURCH
Rapness
Broughtown
SANDAY
Sulland
Overbister
Newark

Carrick Ho.
Calf of Eday
Kettletoft
Faray
CARRICK HOUSE
Calfsound
QUOYNESS CHAMBERED CAIRN
Guith
Braeswick

WESTRAY FIRTH
Millbounds
Stove
Loth
SANDAY SOUND

Wasbister
ROUSAY
Sourin
Skaill
ST MAGNUS CHURCH
MIDHOWE BROCH
Eynhallow
Westness
KNOWE OF YARSO CAIRN
Veness
Papa Stronsay
Odie
Whitehall
Linga Holm
BROUGH HEAD
BROUGH OF BIRSAY
Costa
Burgar
Frotoft
Brinyan
CUBBIE ROO'S CASTLE AND ST. MARY'S CHAPEL
Muckle Green Holm
STRONSAY
Aith
Everbay
Abune-the-Hill
Georth
BROCH OF GURNESS
Wyre
Kirbister
Grobister
MARWICK HEAD NATURE RESERVE
EARL'S PALACE
The Barony
Kirbuster
Redland
Rothiesholm
Dishes
Holland
Marwick
Stara
Twatt
Tingwall
GAIRSAY
Dishes
Isbister
Beaquoy
B9057
Gairsay
Scarwell
CLICK MILL
Dounby
Hackland
Edmonstone
Northdyke
Quoyloo
Skaill
Kierfiold House
Mirbister
ORKNEY FARM & FOLKLORE MUSEUM
Settiscarth
Gorseness
Shapinsay
Auskerry
SCARA BRAE SKAIL HOUSE
Aith
Brough
Isbister
Balfour
Hestwall
Tenston
Netherbrough
Bimbister
BALFOUR CASTLE
Yesnaby
Voy
Arion
Finstown
Grimbister
Work
Sandgarth
Quholm
RING OF BROGAR
STENNESS STANDING STONES
Heddle
WIDEFORD HILL
TANKERNESS HOUSE MUSEUM
FIRTH
Outertown
LERWICK 8:00
Bridge of Waith
MAES HOWE
Clouston
Nisthouse
ORTAK VISITOR CENTRE
ORKNEY WIRELESS MUSEUM
Berstane
INVERGORDON 8:30
PIER ARTS CENTRE
Ireland
EARL PATRICK'S & BISHOPS PALACE
Kirkwall
Scapa
HIGHLAND PARK DISTILLERY
Loch of Tankerness
STROMNESS MUSEUM
Stromness
Kirbister
Hobbister
Greenigo
Tradespark
Whitecleat
North Halley
Breckan
Clestrain
Cairnton
Swanbister
Toab
Deerness
Skaill
Grindigair
Murra
Graemsay
Petertown
Crya
Orphir
North Dawn
Foubister
Gritley
NORTH HOY NATURE RESERVE
Linksness
Houton
ST. NICHOLAS CHURCH
NORWOOD MUSEUM
Upper Sanday
Whaness
OLD MAN OF HOY
WARD HILL
DWARFIE STANE
Cava
ITALIAN CHAPEL
St. Mary's
Braehead
Copinsay
RORA HEAD
Rackwick
SCAPA FLOW
Cornquoy
HOY
Rysa Little
FOSSILAND VINTAGE CENTRE
Hunda
Northtown
KNAP OF TROWIEGLEN
Rysa
SCAPA FLOW INTERPRETATION CENTRE
Klondyke
Burray
Lyness
Rinnigill
Pan
Westermill
Southtown
Little Ayre
Bow
Flotta
Hoxa
St. Margaret's Hope
Grimness
Longhope
Crockness
Hackness
Herston
Quindry
Papley
Melsetter
MARTELLO TOWERS
Swartha
Widewall
Aikers
Hurliness
Brims
LONGHOPE
Sandwick
SOUTH RONALDSAY
SOUTH WALLS
Suckquoy
Lythes
Linklater
Swona
Dundas Ho.
Cleat
Burwick
TOMB OF THE EAGLES AND BRONZE AGE HOUSE
Liddel

PENTLAND FIRTH

Netherton
Island of Stroma
Uppertown

107

DUNCANSBY HEAD

STROMNESS 2:00
DUNNET HEAD
Scarfskerry
East Mey
Huna
John o' Groats
Brough
Ham
Gills
Kirkstyle
Hunspow
Rattar
Mey
Canisbay
MARY-ANN'S COTTAGE
Corsback
Barrock
NATURAL HISTORY DISPLAY
Dunnet
NORTHLANDS VIKING CENTRE
BUCHOLLY CASTLE
Scrabster
THURSO CASTLE
Clardon
Castlehill
Inkstack
Brabster
THURSO FOLK MUSEUM
FLAGSTONE INTERPRETATIVE
Murkle
Greenland
Skirza
of Forss
Thurso
Castletown
Lochend
Freswick
Newlands of Geise
East
Hairmer
Olrig Ho.
Tain
Slickly
Millbank
Reaster
Geise
Weydale
Durran
Bowermadden
Alterwall
Nybster
Lieurary
Hilliclay
LYTH ARTS CENTRE
Auckengill
Buckies
Achingills
Stemster
Lyth
Howe
Keiss
KEISS CASTLE
Sordale
Bowertower
Sortat
Mireland
Calder Mains
Braal Castle
Knockdee
Barrock Ho.
Kirk
Myrelandhorn
Roadside
Stemster
Halcro
North Watten
Gillock
Killimster
Reiss
CASTLE GIRNIGOE
Halkirk
Claysock
Hastigrow
Winless
CASTLE SINCLAIR
Bannskirk Ro.
Mains of Watten
SINCLAIR'S BAY
Scotscalder Station
Harpsdale
Watten
Bilbster
Ackergill
Olgrinmore
Spittal
Backlass
Staxigoe
Dorrery
Mybster
Strath
Milton
Papigoe
Westerdale
Acharole
Stirkoke Ho.
Wick
Broadhaven
Newton
Old Wick
Badlipster
Tannach
Whitrow
CASTLE OF OLD WICK
Strathmore Lodge
Rangag
Hempriggs House
Lochmore Cottage
Hill of Olrig
GREY CAIRN OF CAMSTER
Ganslet
Thrumster
Achavanich
Arclet

Scale : 1:450 000
(approx 7 miles to 1 inch)

0   5   10   15 miles
0   5   10   15   20   25 km

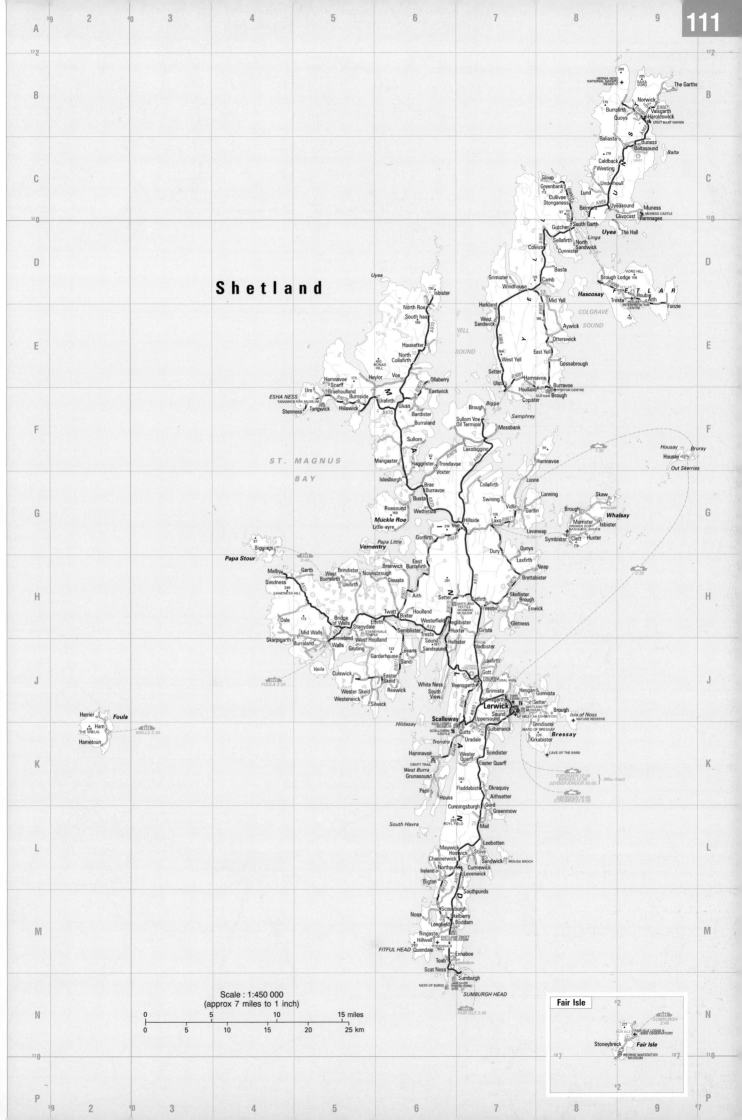

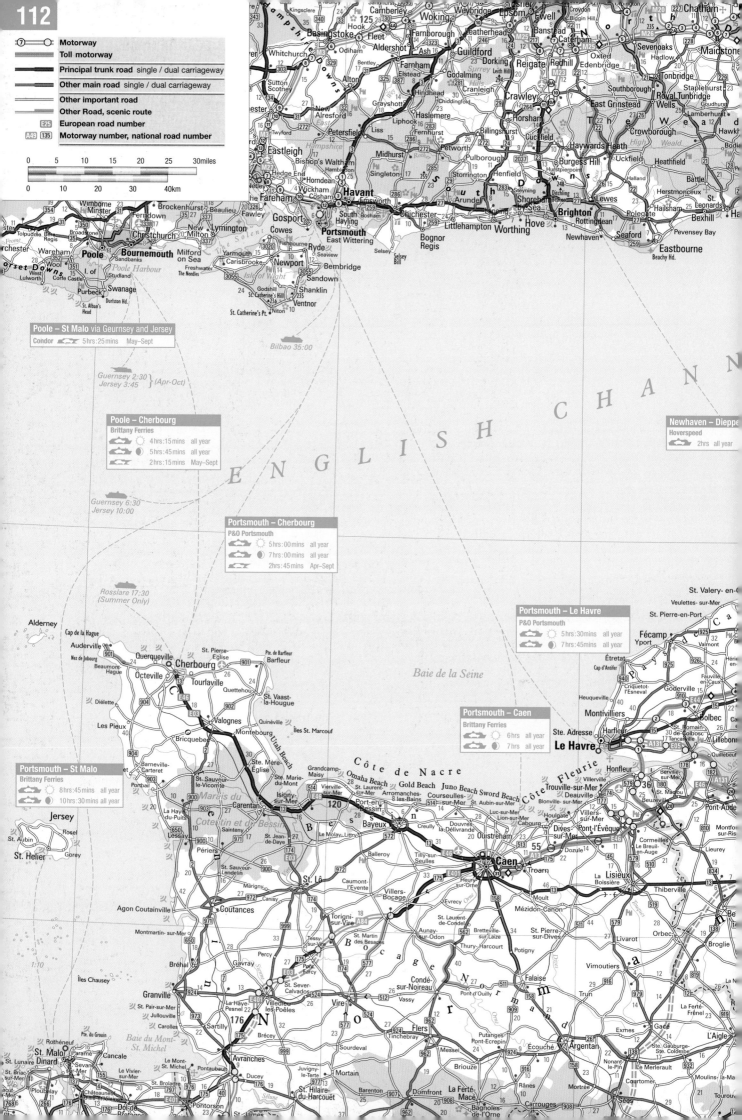

Key to Town Plan Symbols

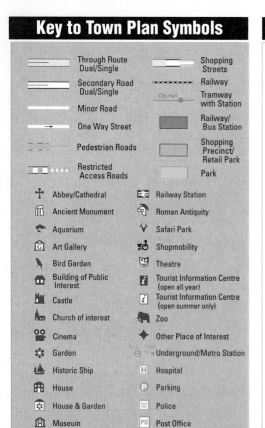

	Through Route Dual/Single		Shopping Streets
	Secondary Road Dual/Single		Railway
	Minor Road	City Hall	Tramway with Station
	One Way Street		Railway/ Bus Station
	Pedestrian Roads		Shopping Precinct/ Retail Park
	Restricted Access Roads		Park

✠ Abbey/Cathedral		Railway Station
Ancient Monument		Roman Antiquity
Aquarium		Safari Park
Art Gallery		Shopmobility
Bird Garden		Theatre
Building of Public Interest		Tourist Information Centre (open all year)
Castle		Tourist Information Centre (open summer only)
Church of interest		Zoo
Cinema		Other Place of Interest
Garden		Underground/Metro Station
Historic Ship		Hospital
House		Parking
House & Garden		Police
Museum		Post Office
Preserved Railway		Youth Hostel

Key to Approach Mapping Symbols

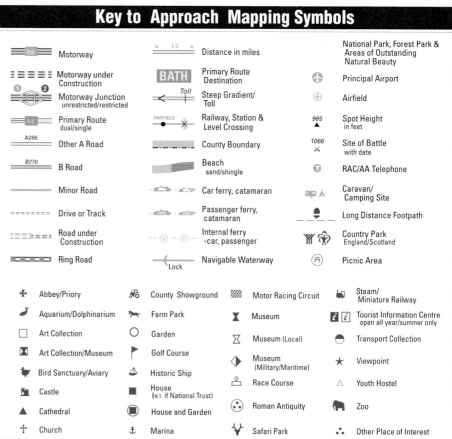

M6 Motorway	Distance in miles	National Park, Forest Park & Areas of Outstanding Natural Beauty
Motorway under Construction	BATH Primary Route Destination	Principal Airport
Motorway Junction unrestricted/restricted	Steep Gradient/ Toll	Airfield
A6 Primary Route dual/single	FAIRFIELD Railway, Station & Level Crossing	965 Spot Height in feet
A286 Other A Road	County Boundary	1066 Site of Battle with date
B270 B Road	Beach sand/shingle	RAC/AA Telephone
Minor Road	Car ferry, catamaran	Caravan/ Camping Site
Drive or Track	Passenger ferry, catamaran	Long Distance Footpath
Road under Construction	Internal ferry -car, passenger	Country Park England/Scotland
Ring Road	Navigable Waterway Lock	Picnic Area

✠ Abbey/Priory	County Showground	Motor Racing Circuit	Steam/ Miniature Railway
Aquarium/Dolphinarium	Farm Park	Museum	Tourist Information Centre open all year/summer only
Art Collection	Garden	Museum (Local)	Transport Collection
Art Collection/Museum	Golf Course	Museum (Military/Maritime)	Viewpoint
Bird Sanctuary/Aviary	Historic Ship	Race Course	Youth Hostel
Castle	House (N.T. if National Trust)	Roman Antiquity	Zoo
Cathedral	House and Garden	Safari Park	Other Place of Interest
✝ Church	Marina		

Aberdeen

0 Miles ¼

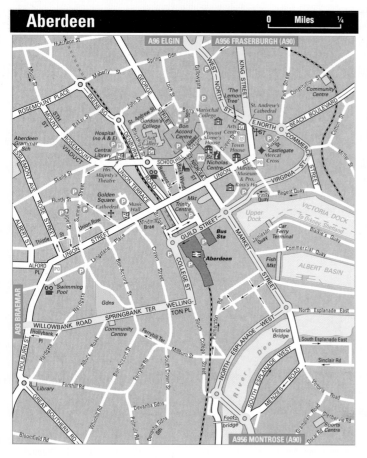

Blackpool

0 Miles ¼

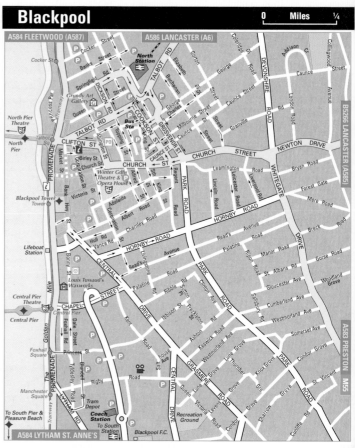

Bournemouth

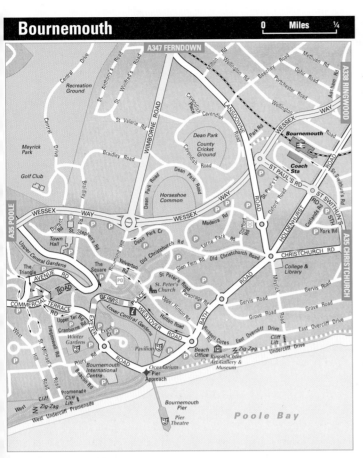

Brighton

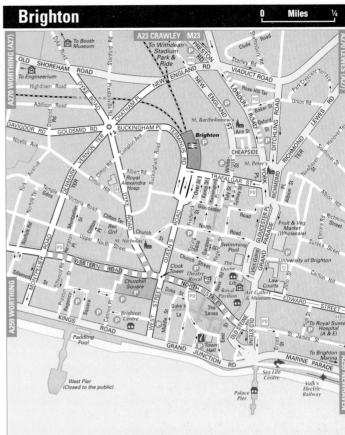

Cambridge

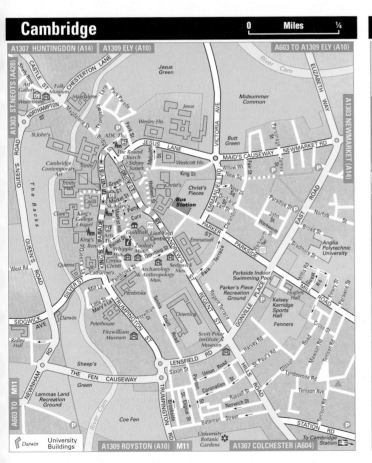

Canterbury

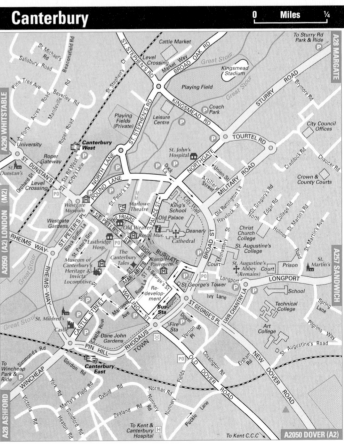

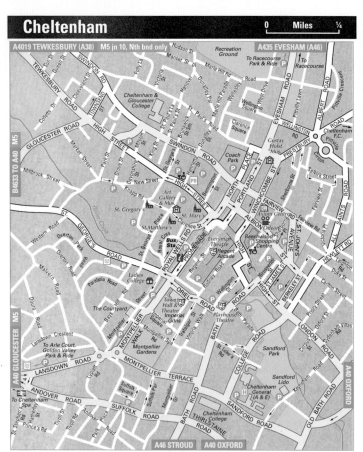

Cheltenham

0 Miles ¼

Chester

0 Miles ¼

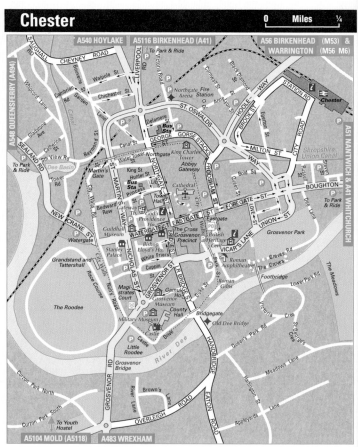

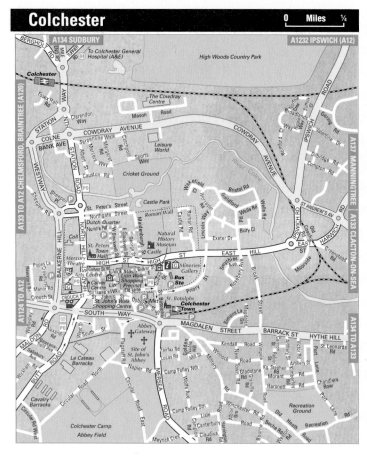

Colchester

0 Miles ¼

Croydon

0 Miles ¼

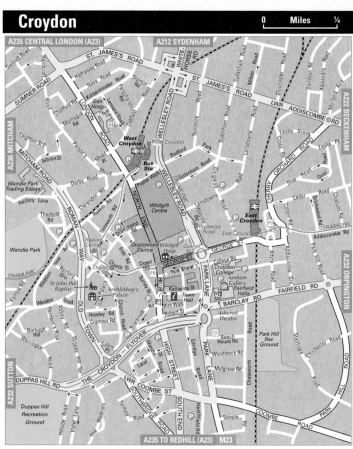

Dundee

0 Miles ¼

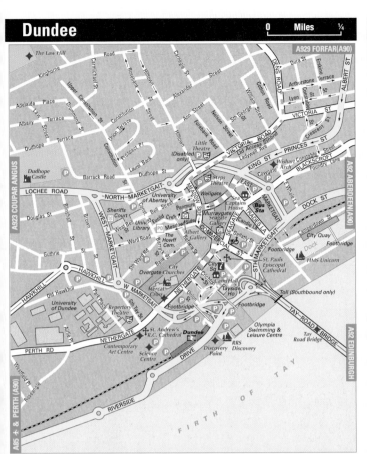

Durham

0 Miles ¼

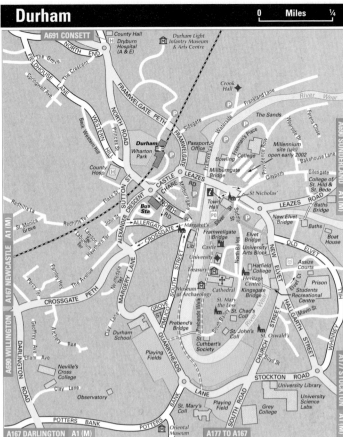

Exeter

0 Miles ¼

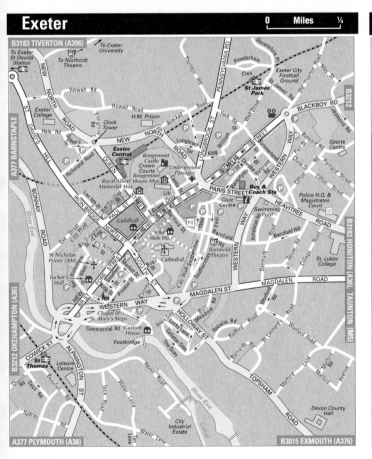

Gloucester

0 Miles ¼

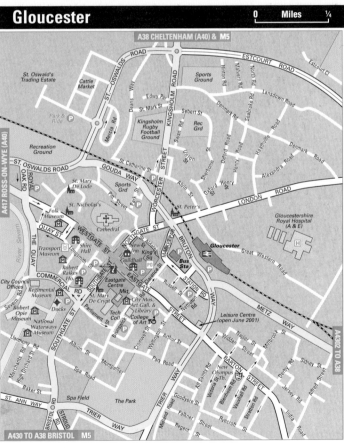

118 **Hull Ipswich Lincoln Middlesbrough**

Hanley page 156 • Leeds page 137 • Leicester page 129 • Liverpool page 138 • London page 140 – 145 • Manchester page 147 • Milton Keynes page 150

Hull

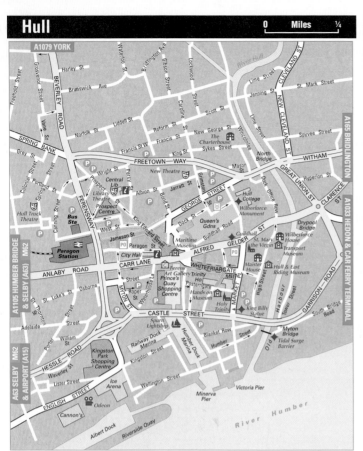

Ipswich

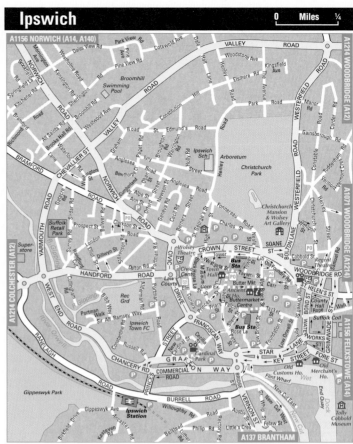

Lincoln

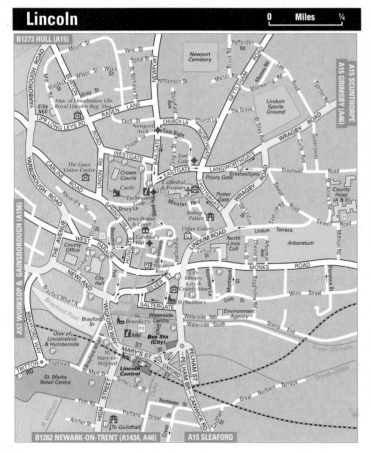

Middlesbrough

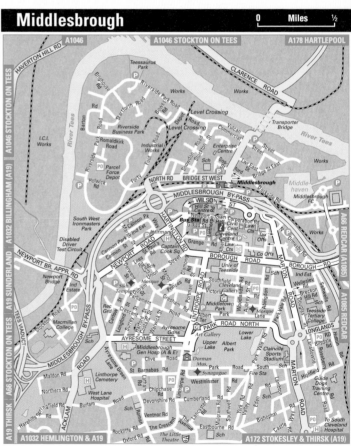

Norwich

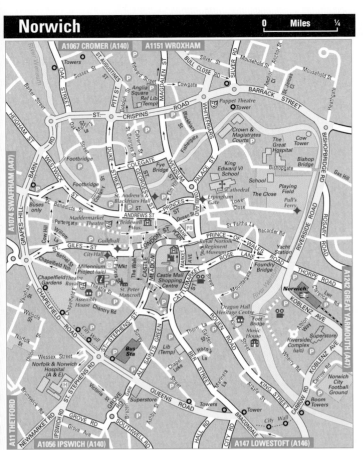

Oxford

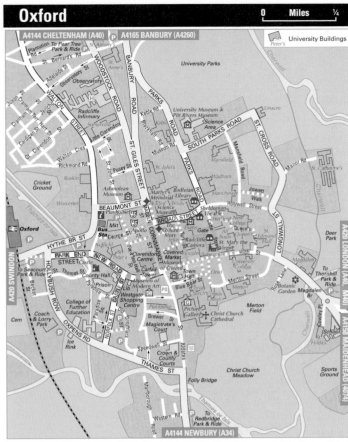

Reading

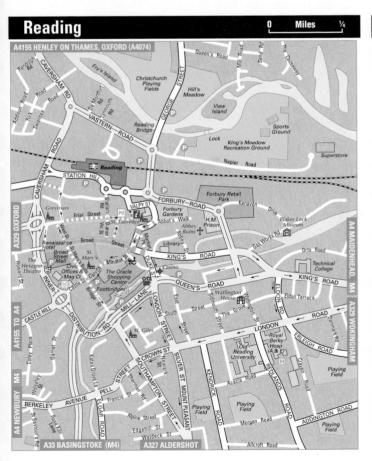

Salisbury

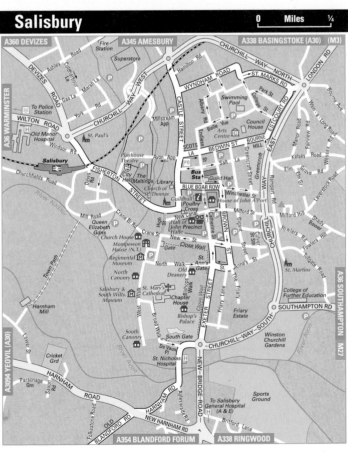

Scarborough

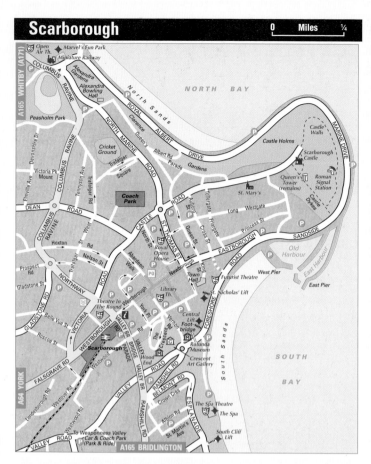

Southend

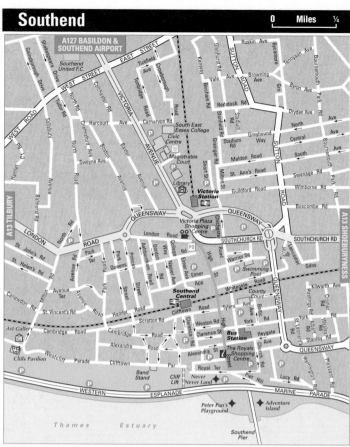

Stratford-upon-Avon

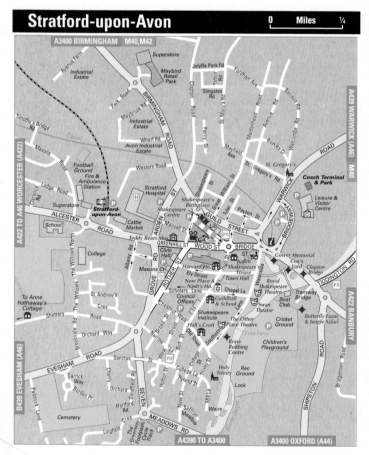

Swansea

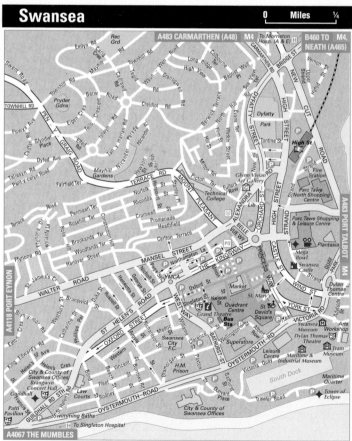

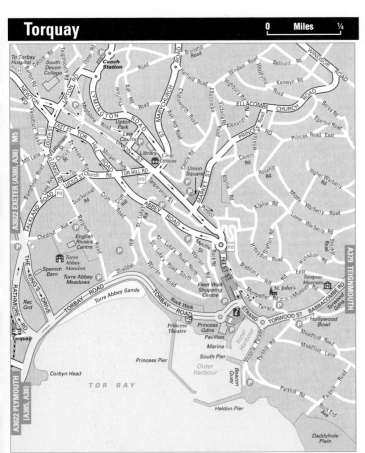

Torquay

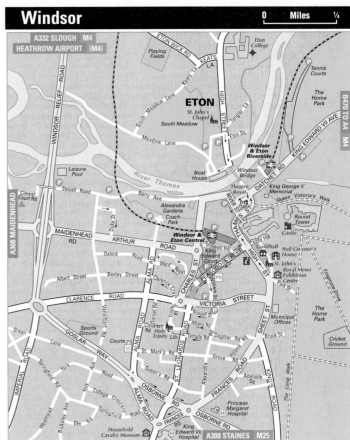

Windsor

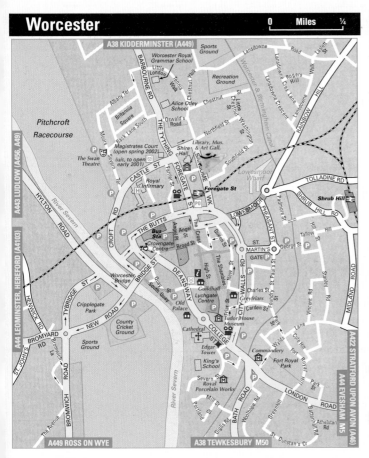

Worcester

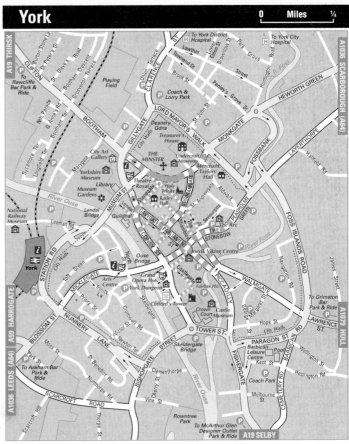

York

Bristol

SEVERN ESTUARY

MIDDLE GROUNDS

NORTH SOMERSET

CHEPSTOW

AVONMOUTH

PORTISHEAD

CLEVEDON

Nailsea

Backwell

Yatton

Congresbury

Wrington

Churchill

Sandford

Banwell

Weston super Mare

Weston Bay

Sand Bay

Uphill

Locking

Hutton

Oldmixon

0   Miles   ¼

A37 SHEPTON MALLET   A4 BATH

A38 TAUNTON

Coventry

B4098 TAMWORTH (A51) · B4113 NUNEATON (A444) · M6

0 — Miles — ¼

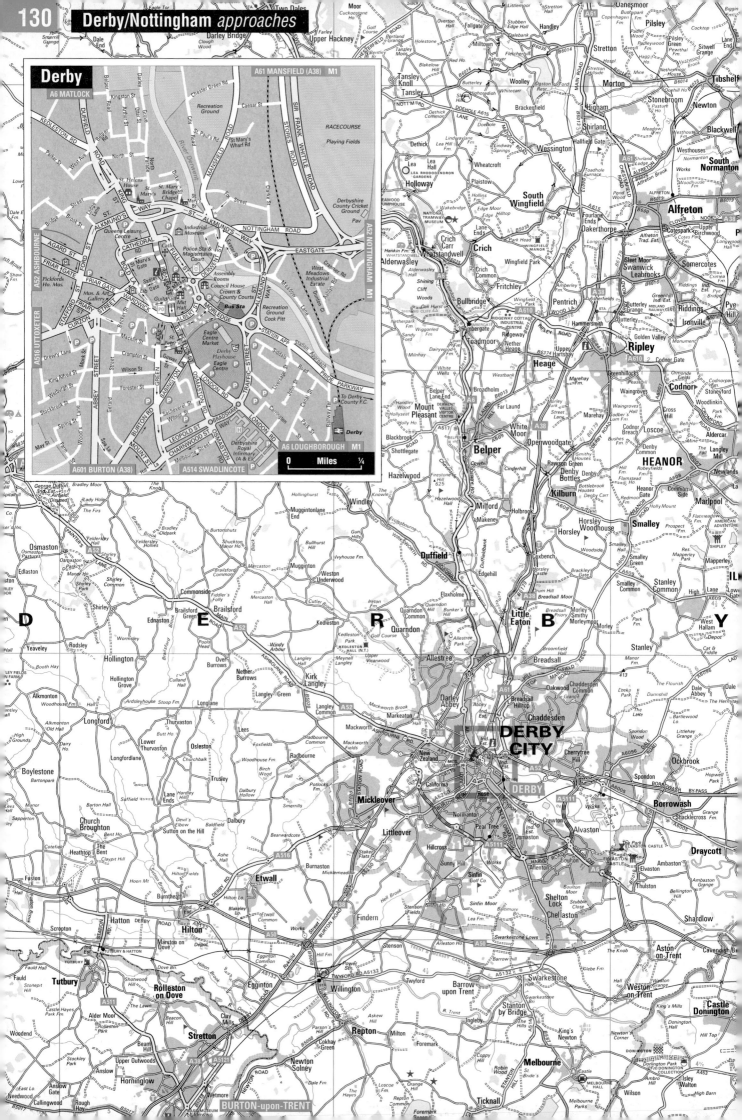

Edinburgh

FORTH

Miles 0 ¼

A702 CARLISLE & M74 TO A7   A7 GALASHIELS & JEDBURGH (A68)

A90 FORTH ROAD BRIDGE & PERTH (M90)

A8 GLASGOW & STIRLING (M8) (M9)

A900 LEITH

A1 BERWICK UPON TWEED

EAST LOTHIAN

LOTHIAN

LAMMERMUIR HILLS

Hope Hills

Portobello
Joppa
Musselburgh
Prestonpans
Cockenzie and Port Seton
Longniddry
Haddington
Gifford
Tranent
Macmerry
Ormiston
Pencaitland
Gladsmuir
Athelstaneford
Dalkeith
Eskbank
Newtongrange
Mayfield
Gorebridge
Pathhead
Humbie
Fala
Wallyford
Elphinstone
Cousland
New Winton
New Town
Nisbet
Bolton
Saltoun Forest
Glenkinchie Distillery
North Middleton
Crichton Castle
Soutra Hill

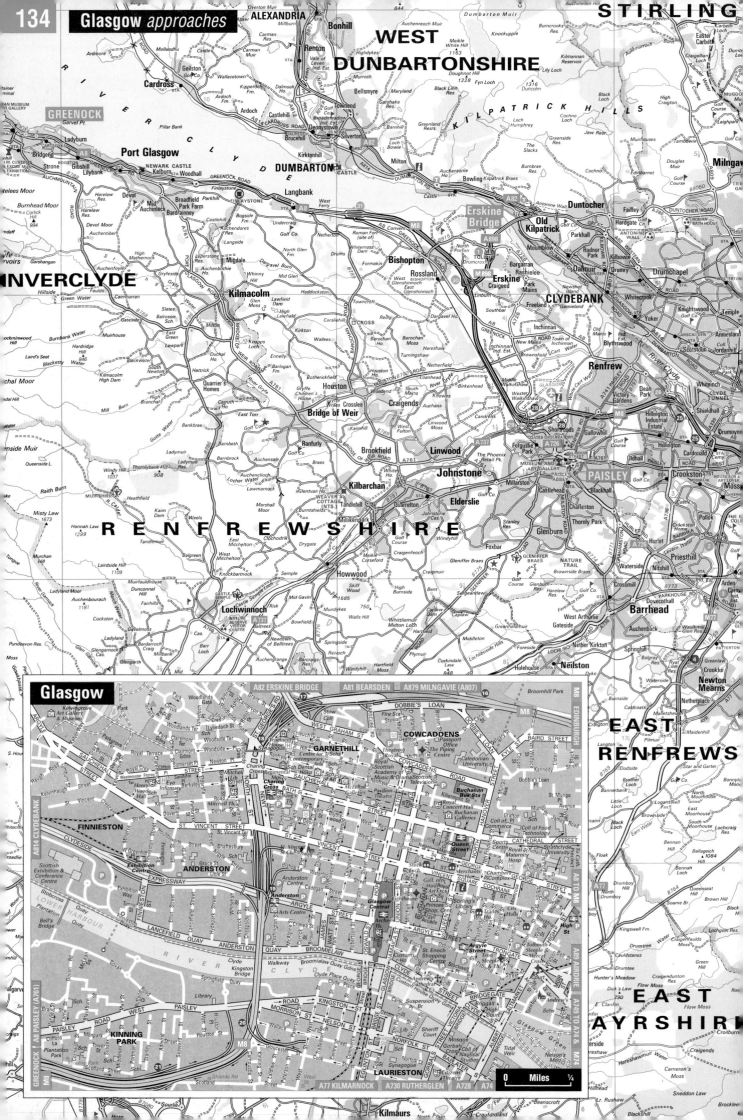

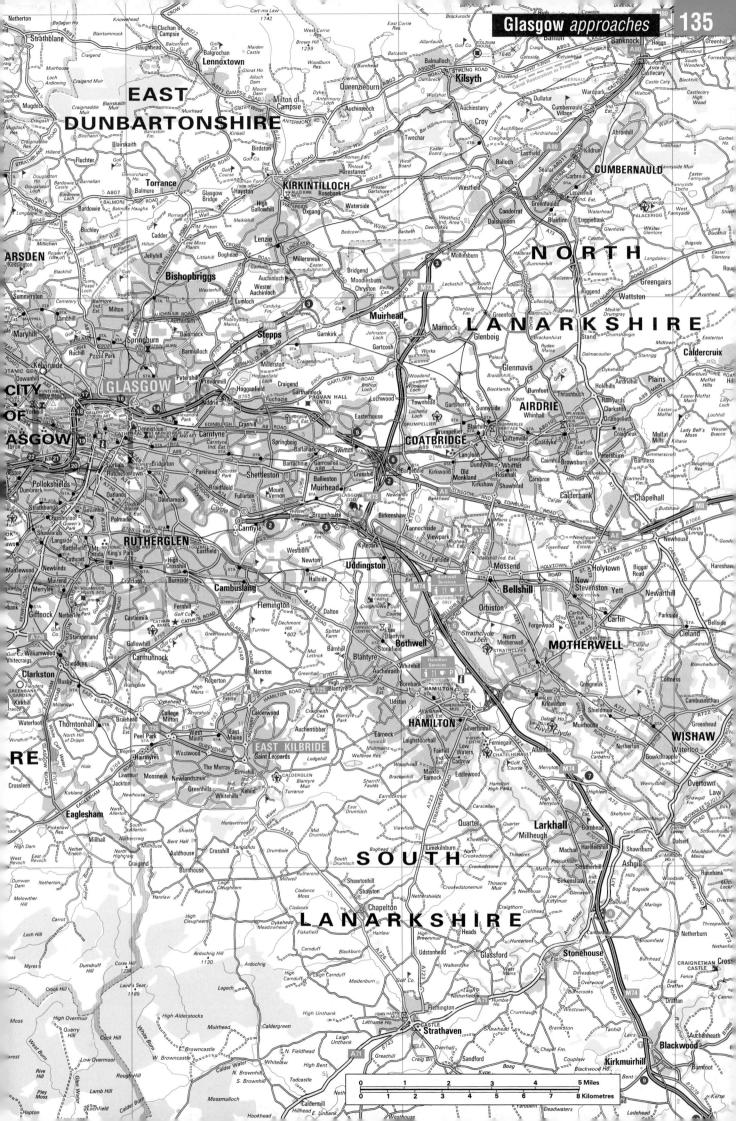

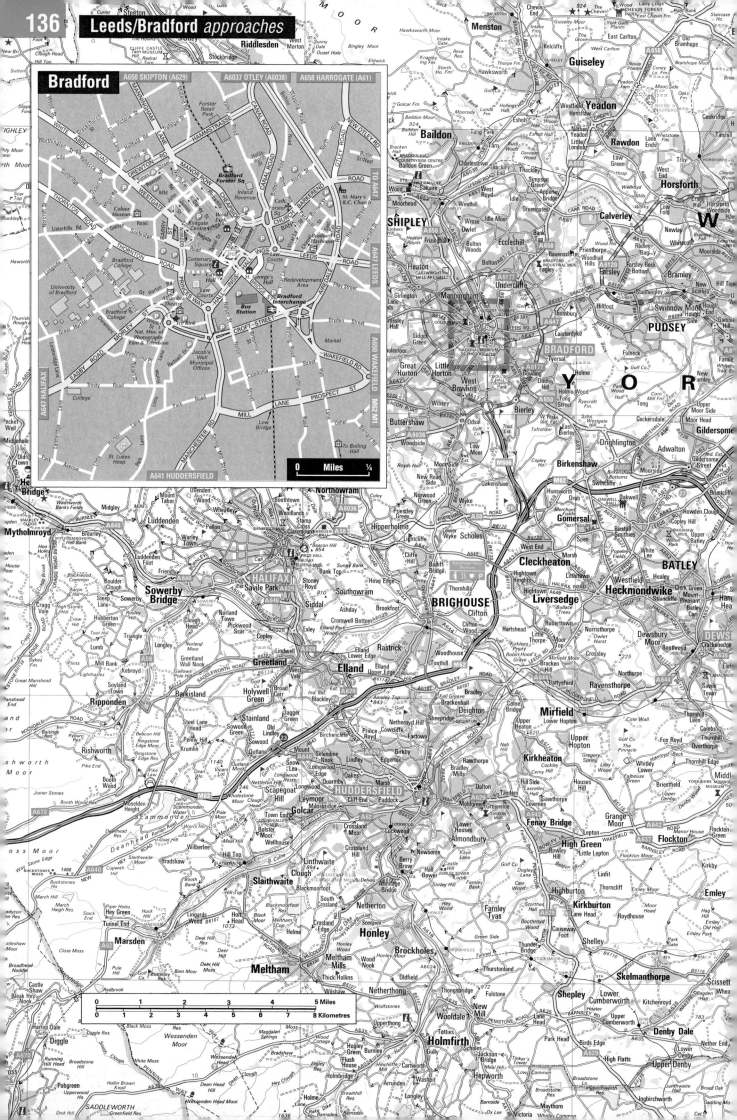

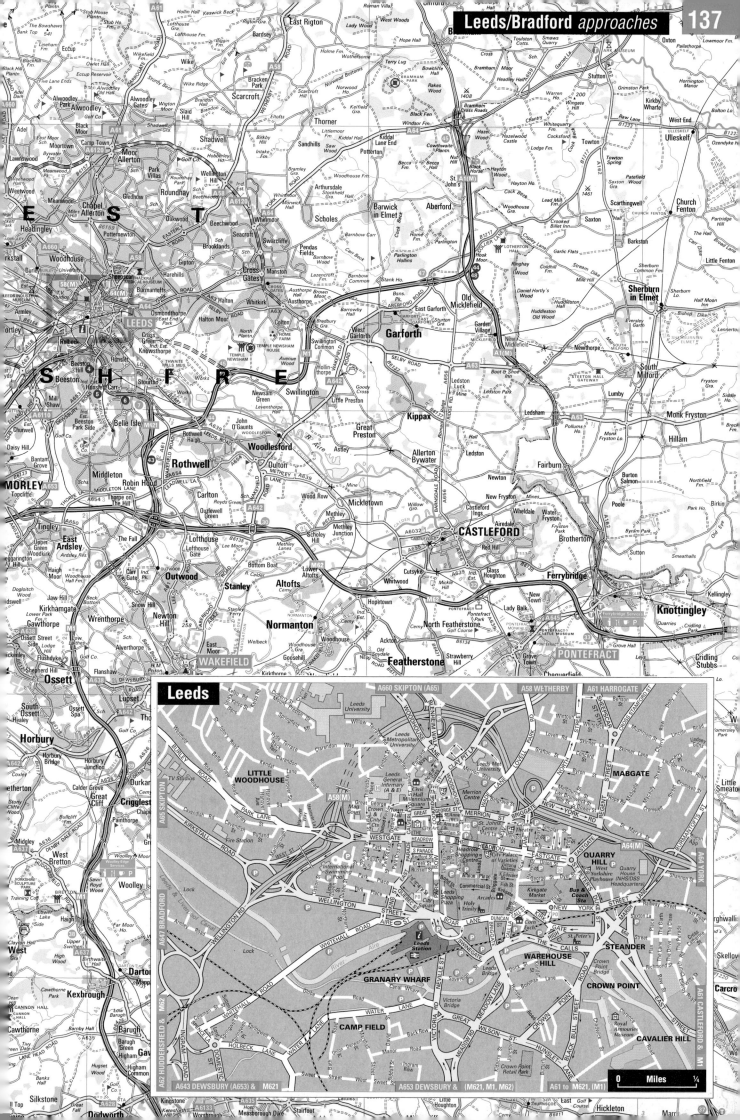

Leeds

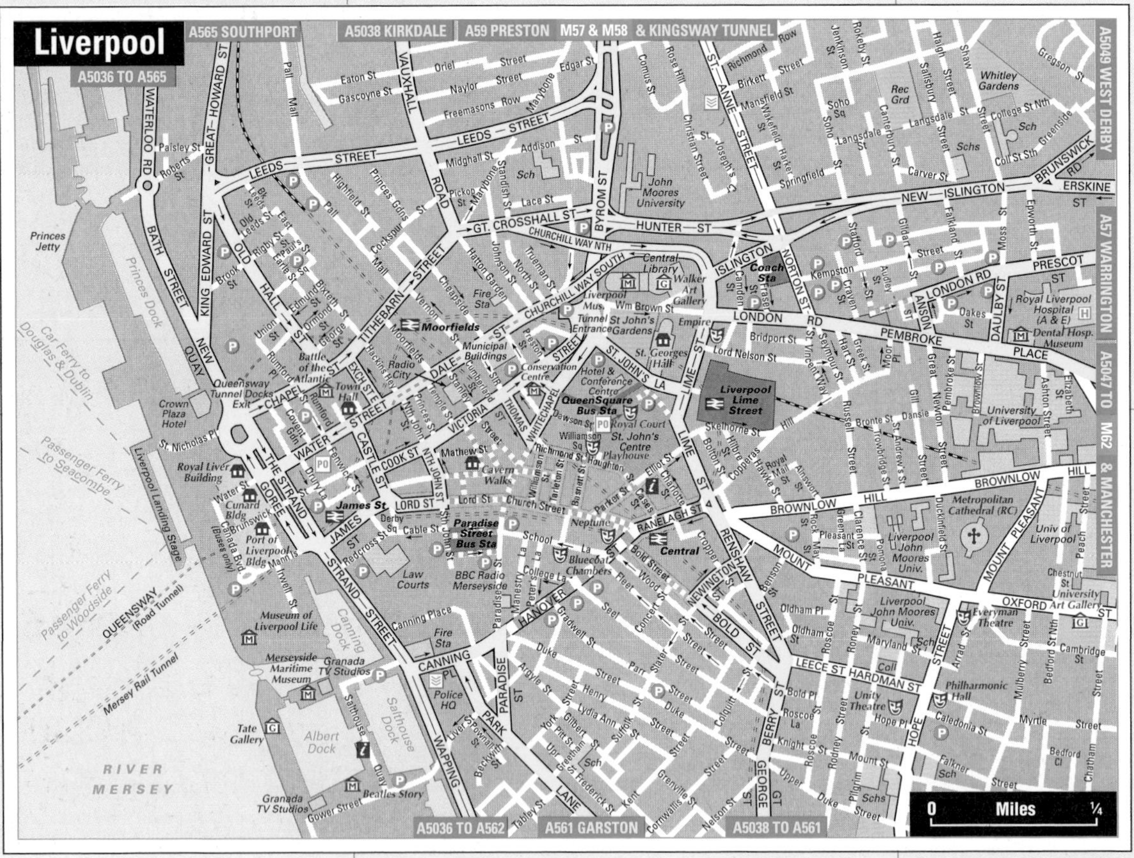

Liverpool
A5036 TO A565

A565 SOUTHPORT | A5038 KIRKDALE | A59 PRESTON | M57 & M58 & KINGSWAY TUNNEL

A5036 TO A562 | A561 GARSTON | A5038 TO A561

0 Miles ¼

RIVER MERSEY

Princes Jetty
Car Ferry to Douglas & Dublin
Crown Plaza Hotel
Passenger Ferry to Seacombe
Queensway Tunnel Docks Exit
St Nicholas Pl
Royal Liver Building
Cunard Bldg
Port of Liverpool Bldg
QUEENSWAY (Road Tunnel)
Mersey Rail Tunnel
Museum of Liverpool Life
Merseyside Maritime Museum
Tate Gallery
Albert Dock
Granada TV Studios
Beatles Story
Canning Dock
Salthouse Dock
Wapping
Queensway to Woodside
Passenger Ferry to Woodside

Moorfields
Municipal Buildings
Conservation Centre
Central Library
Walker Art Gallery
Liverpool Mus.
Wm Brown St
World Entrance Gardens
Empire
St Georges Hall
Coach Sta
Royal Court
St John's Centre
St John's La
Hotel & Conference Centre
QueenSquare Bus Sta
Williamson Sq
Playhouse
Cavern Walk
James St
Paradise Street Bus Sta
Bluecoat Chambers
College La
Central
Neptune
BBC Radio Merseyside
Law Courts
Fire Sta
Police HQ
Liverpool Lime Street
Metropolitan Cathedral (RC)
Univ of Liverpool
University of Liverpool
Liverpool John Moores Univ.
Everyman Theatre
Oxford Art Gallery
Philharmonic Hall
Unity Theatre
Royal Liverpool Hospital (A&E)
Dental Hosp. Museum

WALLASEY
HOYLAKE
West Kirby
Meols
Moreton
Leasowe
Bidston
Upton
Greasby
Woodchurch
Grange
Newton
Frankby
Irby Hill
Arrowe Hill
Arrowe Park
Landican
Caldy
Thurstaston
Irby
Thingwall
Pensby
Barnston
Oldfield
Poll Hill
HESWALL
Gayton
Parkgate
Neston
Little Neston

North Wirral Coastal Park
East Hoyle Bank
Dove Point
Red Rocks
Hilbre Island
Little Hilbre Island
Lime Wharf
Tanskey Rocks
Marine Lake
Caldy Blacks
Thurstaston Caravan Park
The Dungeon
THE WIRRAL
Gayton Sands
Backwood Hall

CROSBY CHANNEL
Taylor's Bank
Crosby East Training Bank
Crosby West Training Bank
Great Burbo Bank
BELFAST 8:30
DOUGLAS 2:30
DUBLIN 6:30
DUBLIN 3:45 (Mar.-Nov)
Blundellsands
Brighton

Formby
Formby Pt.
Ravenmeols Hills
Holiday Caravan Park
Formby Bank
Ranges Danger Area
Freshfield

West Hoyle Bank
Welsh Channel
POINT OF AYR
Wild Road
Salisbury Bank
Salisbury Middle
Dawpool Bank
Holywell Bank
Bagillt Bank
The Marsh
Flint Sands

The Warren
Talacre
Tyn-y-Morfa
Warren Ho
Llwynd
Abbey
Gwespyr
Tanlan Banks
Tan-lan
Llanasa
Gronant
PRESTATYN
Y Frith
Meliden
Gwaenysgor
Gwaenysgor
Brynllystyn
Ffynnongroyw
Picton
Pen-y-ffordd
Mostyn Bank
Mostyn Quay
Mostyn
Rhewl-Mostyn
Glan-y-don
Llannerch-y-môr
Golden Gro
Gyrn Castle
Gop Hill
Trelogan-uchaf
Trelogan
Wern Fm
Bychton
Maes Pennant
Bryniau
Axton
Marian
Berthengam
Plasychau
Pantasaph
Dyserth
Trelawnyd
Sarn
Walwen
Downing
Glol
Gelli
Mertyn
Mertyn Hall
Greenfield
The Moor
BASINGWERK ABBEY
Greenfield Valley Heritage Park
Whitford
Pentre-mawr
Carmel
Holway
Bryn-celyn
Pen-y-maes
Walwen
Whelston
Bagillt
HOLYWELL
Pen-y-cefn
Calcoed
Smithy Gate
Milwr
Dolphin
Brynford
Oaklands
Tynypistyll
Holywell Common
Graig
Babell
Lixwm
Mount Pleasant

DENBIGHSHIRE
Rhuddlan
Rhyddlan
Bodrhyddan Hall
Diserth
Marian Mill
Criccin
Ddwylig Isaf
Penpalmant
Waen Gate
Pont Dafydd
St Asaph
CATHEDRAL
Eryl Hall
Llanerch-y-mor

FLINTSHIRE
Caerwys
Ysceifiog
Afon-wen
Bodfari
Tremeirchion
Waen
Rhual
Moel Maenefa
Nannerch
Rhes-y-cae
Halkyn
Pentre Halkyn
Flint
Flint Mountain
FLINT CASTLE
Mount Pleasant
Pentre Fwrndan
Oakenholt
Leadbrook Hall
Kelsterton
Rockcliffe

London Docklands

Manchester

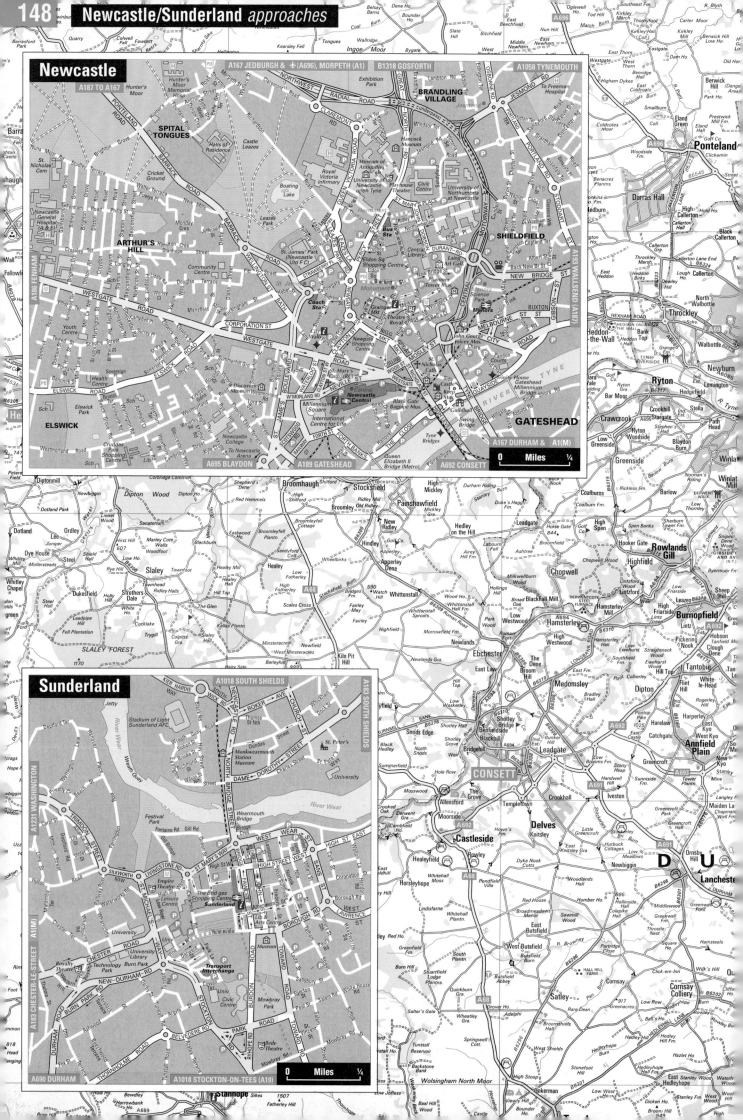

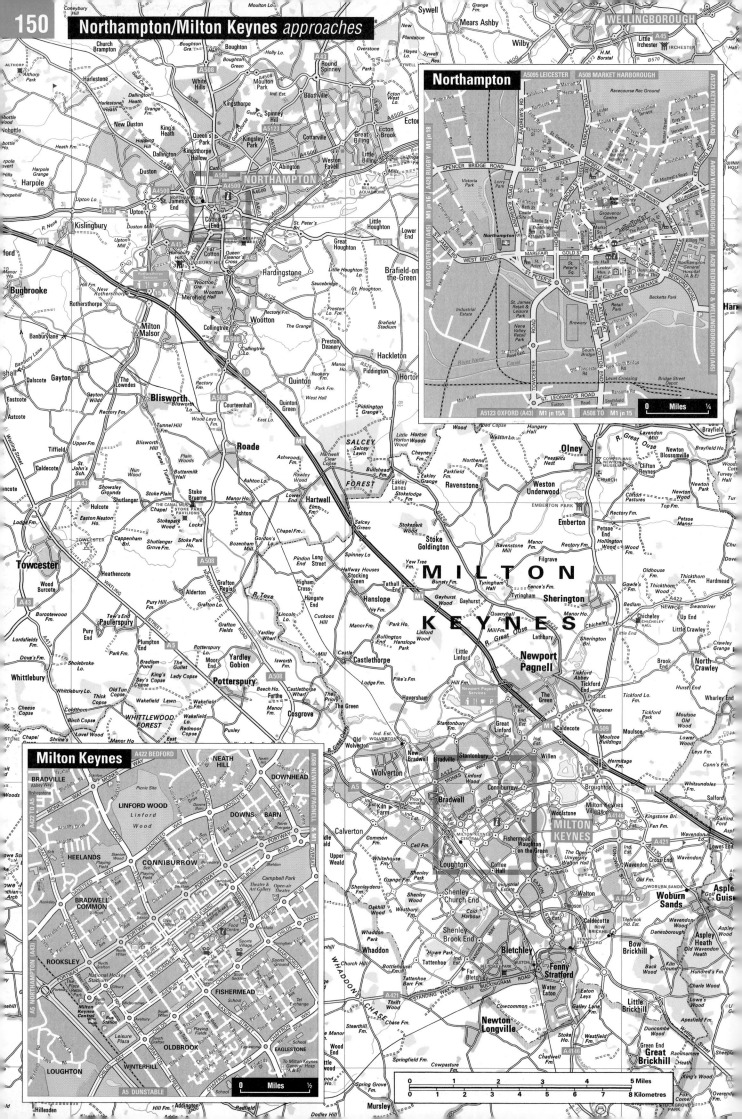

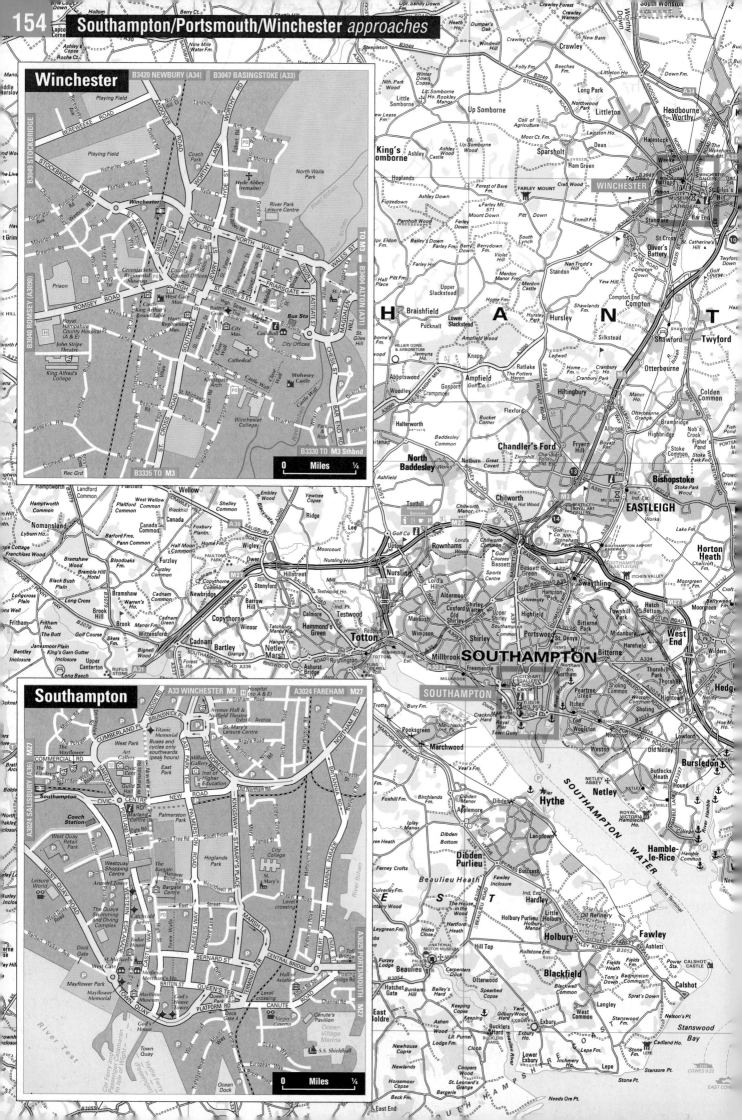

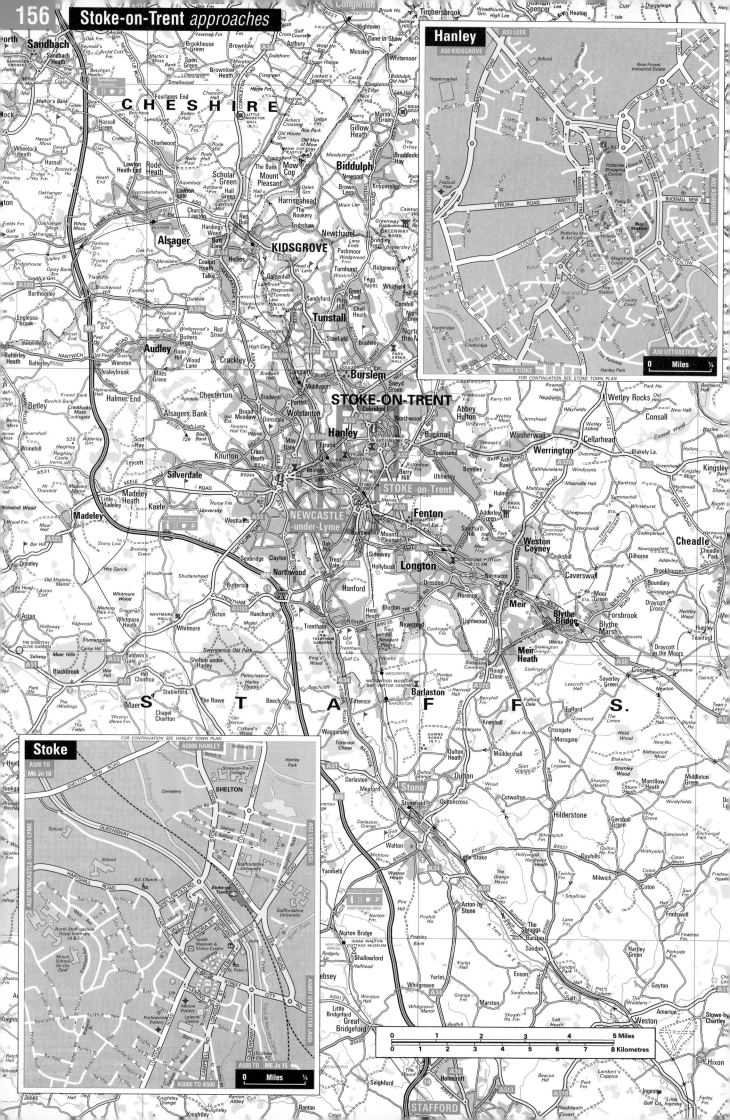

Broad Haven

Benwee Hd.

Portacloy

Downpatrick Hd.

Lenadoon Pt.

Erris Hd.

Belderg

Rathlacken

Ballycastle

Killala Bay

Corlogh

Graghil

Knockalina

MAUMAKEOGH
▲ 380

Creeragh

Inishcrone

Kilc

Annagh Hd.

Belmullet

Glenamoy

R314

R314

Killala

Corba

An Geata Mór

Bunahowen

R315

Beville

Carrowmore L.

R313

Owenmore

Muilet

Srahmore

Bangor

Largan

Crossmolina

Ballina

Crockets Town

Inishkea North

Gwessalia

Bellacorick

N59

Ardnaree

R26

Inishkea South

Blacksod Bay

N59

N59

Deel

L. Conn

Fallmore

Ballycroy

▲ 722

▲ 627

Lahardaun
806
NEPHIN

R10

Blacksod Pt.

Castlehill

Pontoon

Strade
Friary

Foxford

Callo

Saddle Hd.

SLIEVEMORE

NEPHIN BEG RANGE

714

R317

L. Cullin

N58

R319

Achill Hd.

▲ 672

Doogort

L. Feeagh

Beltra

Bellavary

Bohola

Dooagh

Keel

R319

Rosturk

N59

Beltra L.

Castlebar

R312

N5

Kiltama

Chasel

ACHILL I.

Mallaranny

Newport

R311

Derrycoosh

N60

Manulla

Dooega Hd.

Corraun Pen.

Achill Sd.

Newport B.

Balla

R324

Achillbeg I.

Westport B.

Westport

N5

Ballyhean

Mayo

Ballyglass

O

CLARE I.

Clew Bay

R330

Lugatemp

Caher I.

Louisburgh

R335

Killadangan

765
CROAGH PATRICK

Killavally

Aghagower

Ballintober

Cornanagh

Inishturk

Killadoon

M

Sheeffry Hills

Carrowkennedy

▲ 392

Partry

L. Carra

Hollymount

Inishbofin

Cregganbaun

763

A

PARTRY MTS.

Toomakeady

Ballinrobe

Inishshark

▲ 819
MWEELREA

R335

▲ 683

Y

Lough Mask

R331

Kilmaine

Killary Harbour

Srahnalong

N59

Tully Cross

Gowlaun

Leenaun

Joyce Country

Clonbur

Cong

Neale

N84

Cleggan

Letterfrack

N59

MAUMTURK MTS.

Maum

Cornamona

R346

Shrule

Moyard
Streamstown

BENBAUN
730 ▲ CONNEMARA
NAT. PARK

R344

R336

Maam Cross

R345

Headford

R334

Clifden

N59

Recess

660

N59

Ballyhale

Clifden B.

CONNEMARA

R336

Oughterard

Kilgarrif

Ballyconneely

Toombeola

R342

R340

Derryrush

Rosscahill

Slyne Hd.

Roundstone

R341

Glinsk

Kylesa

Kilbrickan

Screeb

Moycullen

N59

G

A

L

Callow

Ballyconneely Bay

Kilkieran

Bertraghboy Bay

Carna

Ardmore

Lettermore I.

Lettermore

Costelloe

Ballagh

Menlough

Galway

Carraroe

Gorumna

Rossaveel

Caher

R336

Barna

Salthill

Lettermullan

Inveran

Spiddle

Cashla Bay

Galway Bay

North Sound

Black Hd.

Burren

Kilmurvy

Kilronan

Murroogh

R477

Ballyvaghan

INISHMORE

Inishmaan

R480

South Sd.

345
SL. ELVA

Carra

ARAN IS.

R479

N67

Inisheer

R478

Lisdoonvarna

Doolin

Kilfenora

Killinabo

Kilshanny

R476

R481

R476

Cliffs of Moher

Hags Hd.

R478

Ennistimon

Corrofin

Liscannor

N85

Liscannor Bay

Lehinch

N67

R460

C L A

Fountain Cross

Spanish Pt.

Milltown
Malbay

Inagh

Mal Bay

SLIEVECALLEN
391

R474

Kilmaley

N85

Mutton I.

Shanovogh

Darragh

Quilty

Kilmurry

A

B

C

D

54°N

53°N

Belfast

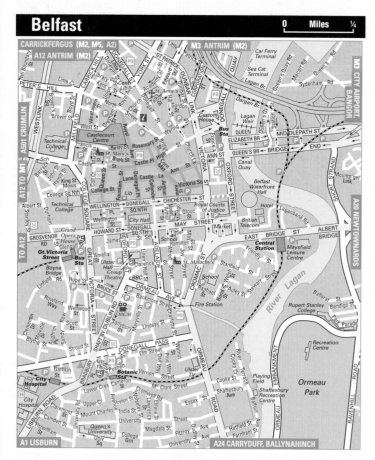

Cork

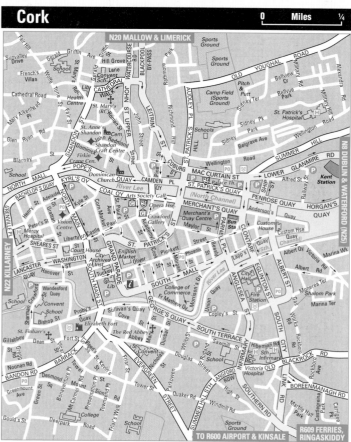

Derry / Londonderry

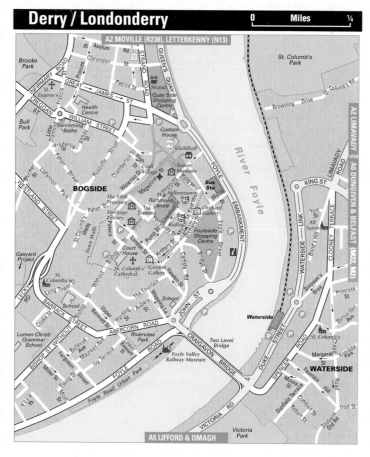

Dublin

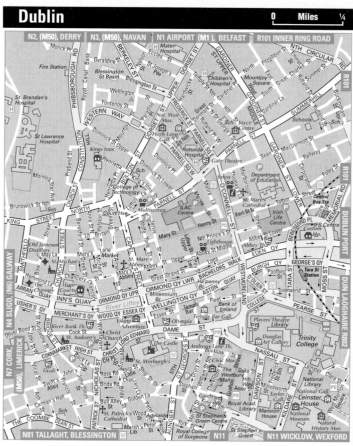

A

Abbey Galway 161 C6
Abbeydorney Kerry 162 B3
Abbeyfeale Limerick 162 B4
Abbeyleix Laois 157 C2
Abington Limerick 163 A6
Achill Mayo 160 B3
Aclare Sligo 161 A5
Acton Armagh 159 C6
Adamstown Waterford 157 D2
Adare Limerick 163 A5
Adcarn Roscommon 161 B6
Adrigole Cork 162 C3
Aghagower Mayo 160 B4
Aghalee Antrim 159 B6
Aghavannagh Wicklow 157 C4
Aghaville Cork 162 C4
Aghern Cork 163 B6
Aghnacliff Longford 161 B7
Aglish Waterford 163 B7
Ahascragh Galway 161 C6
Ahoghill Antrim 159 B6
Allen Kildare 157 B3
Allenwood Kildare 157 B3
Allihies Cork 162 C2
An Geata Mor Mayo 160 A2
Anacotty Limerick 163 A5
Anascaul Kerry 162 B2
Annacarty Tipperary 163 A6
Annacloy Down 159 C7
Annagassan Louth 159 D6
Annahilt Down 159 C7
Annalong Down 159 C7
Annestown Waterford 157 D2
Antrim Antrim 159 B6
Araglin Tipperary 163 B6
Arboe Tyrone 159 B5
Ardagh Limerick 162 B4
Ardagh Longford 161 B7
Ardahy Monaghan 159 C5
Ardara Donegal 158 B2
Ardcath Meath 157 A4
Ardcrony Tipperary 161 D6
Ardee Louth 159 D5
Ardfert Kerry 162 B3
Ardfinnane Tipperary 163 B7
Ardglass Down 159 C7
Ardgroom Cork 162 C3
Ardkearagh Kerry 162 C2
Ardkeen Down 159 C7
Ardmore Galway 160 C3
Ardmore Waterford 163 C7
Ardnacrusha Clare 163 A5
Ardnamona Donegal 158 B2
Ardnaree Mayo 160 A4
Ardnasodan Galway 161 C5
Ardpatrick Limerick 163 B5
Ardrahan Galway 161 C5
Ardreagh Londonderry 159 A5
Ardscull Kildare 157 B3
Ardstraw Tyrone 158 B4
Arklow Wicklow 157 C4
Arless Laois 157 C2
Armagh Armagh 159 C5
Armoy Antrim 159 A6
Arney Fermanagh 158 C3
Arthurstown Wexford 157 D3
Articlave Londonderry 159 A5
Artigarvan Tyrone 158 B4
Arvagh Cavan 161 B7
Ashbourne Meath 157 A4
Ashford Wicklow 157 B4
Ashville Louth 159 D5
Askeaton Limerick 163 A5
Astee Kerry 162 A3
Athboy Meath 157 A3
Athea Limerick 162 B4
Athenry Galway 161 C5
Athlacca Limerick 163 B5
Athleague Roscommon 161 B6
Athlone Westmeath 161 C7
Athy Kildare 157 C3
Attical Down 159 C6
Attymon Galway 161 C5
Aucloggeen Galway 161 C5
Augher Tyrone 158 C4
Aughnacloy Tyrone 159 C5
Aughrim Clare 161 C5
Aughrim Galway 161 C6
Aughrim Wicklow 157 C4
Avoca Wicklow 157 C4

B

Bailieborough Cavan 159 D5
Balbriggan Dublin 157 A4
Baldoyle Dublin 157 B4
Balla Mayo 160 B4
Ballagh Galway 160 C4
Ballagh Limerick 162 B4
Ballagh Tipperary 163 A7
Ballaghaderreen Roscommon 161 B5
Ballickmoyler Laois 157 C2
Ballin Cloher Kerry 162 B3
Ballina Mayo 160 A4
Ballina Tipperary 163 A6
Ballinadee Cork 163 C5
Ballinafad Sligo 158 C2
Ballinagar Offaly 157 B2
Ballinakill Laois 157 C2
Ballinalack Westmeath 157 A2
Ballinalea Wicklow 157 B4
Ballinalee Longford 161 B7
Ballinamallard Fermanagh 158 C3
Ballinameen Roscommon 161 B6
Ballinamore Bridge Galway 161 C6
Ballinamore Leitrim 158 C3
Ballinascarty Cork 163 C5
Ballinasloe Galway 161 C6
Ballincollig Cork 163 C5
Ballincurrig Cork 163 C6
Ballindaggan Wexford 157 C3
Ballinderreen Galway 161 C5
Ballinderry Upr. Antrim 159 B6
Ballinderry Tipperary 161 C6
Ballindine Mayo 161 B5
Ballindooly Galway 160 C4
Ballineen Cork 163 C5
Ballingarry Limerick 163 B5
Ballingarry Tipperary 163 A7
Ballingarry Tipperary 161 C6
Ballingeary Cork 162 C4
Ballinhassig Cork 163 C5
Ballinlea Antrim 159 A6
Ballinlough Roscommon 161 B5
Ballinrobe Mayo 160 B4
Ballinskelligs Kerry 162 C2
Ballinspittle Cork 163 C5
Ballintober Mayo 160 B4
Ballintober Roscommon 161 B6
Ballintoy Antrim 159 A6
Ballintra Donegal 158 B2
Ballintroohan Donegal 158 A4
Ballinunty Tipperary 163 A7
Ballinure Tipperary 163 A7
Ballitore Kildare 157 B3
Ballivor Meath 157 A3
Ballon Carlow 157 C3
Ballure Donegal 158 B2
Ballyagran Limerick 163 B5
Ballybay Monaghan 159 C5
Ballybofey Donegal 158 B3
Ballyboghil Dublin 157 A4
Ballybogy Antrim 159 A5
Ballybritt Offaly 161 C7
Ballybrittas Laois 157 B2
Ballybrophy Laois 161 D7
Ballybunion Kerry 162 A3
Ballycahill Tipperary 163 A7
Ballycanew Wexford 157 C4
Ballycarney Wexford 157 C3
Ballycarry Antrim 159 B7
Ballycastle Mayo 160 A4
Ballycastle Antrim 159 A6
Ballyclare Antrim 159 B7
Ballyclerahan Tipperary 163 B7
Ballyclogh Cork 163 B5
Ballycolla Laois 157 C2
Ballyconneely Galway 160 C2
Ballyconnell Cavan 158 C3
Ballyconnell Sligo 158 C1
Ballycotton Cork 163 C6
Ballycrossaun Galway 161 C6
Ballycroy Mayo 160 A3
Ballycumber Offaly 161 C7
Ballydangan Roscommon 161 C6
Ballydavid Galway 161 C6
Ballydavid Kerry 162 B2
Ballydavis Laois 157 B2
Ballydehob Cork 162 C4
Ballydonegan Cork 162 C2
Ballyduff Kerry 162 B3
Ballyduff Waterford 163 B6
Ballydugan Down 159 C7
Ballyfarnan Roscommon 158 C2
Ballyferriter Kerry 162 B2
Ballyfin Laois 157 B2
Ballyforan Roscommon 161 C6
Ballygar Galway 161 B6
Ballygarrett Wexford 157 C4
Ballygawley Sligo 158 C2
Ballygawley Tyrone 158 C4
Ballyglass Mayo 160 B4
Ballygorman Donegal 158 A4
Ballygowan Down 159 B7
Ballyhaght Limerick 163 B5
Ballyhahill Limerick 162 A4
Ballyhaise Cavan 158 C4
Ballyhalbert Down 159 C8
Ballyhale Galway 160 C4
Ballyhaunis Mayo 161 B5
Ballyhean Mayo 160 B4
Ballyheige Kerry 162 B3
Ballyhooly Cork 163 B6
Ballyhornan Down 159 C7
Ballyjamesduff Cavan 158 D4
Ballykelly Londonderry 158 A4
Ballykillin Donegal 158 A4
Ballylanders Limerick 163 B6
Ballylaneen Waterford 157 D2
Ballyliffin Donegal 158 A4
Ballylongford Kerry 162 A4
Ballylooby Tipperary 163 B7
Ballylynan Laois 157 C2
Ballymacarbry Waterford 163 B7
Ballymacoda Cork 163 C7
Ballymagorry Tyrone 158 B4
Ballymahon Longford 161 B7
Ballymakenny Louth 159 D6
Ballymartin Down 159 C7
Ballymena Antrim 159 B6
Ballymoe Galway 161 B6
Ballymoney Antrim 159 A5
Ballymore Eustace Kildare 157 B3
Ballymore Westmeath 161 C7
Ballymote Sligo 158 C1
Ballymullakill Roscommon 161 C6
Ballymurphy Carlow 157 C3
Ballymurray Roscommon 161 B6
Ballynabola Wexford 157 D3
Ballynacally Clare 162 A4
Ballynacarrigy Westmeath 161 B7
Ballynacorra Cork 163 C6
Ballynagore Westmeath 157 B2
Ballynahinch Down 159 C7
Ballynahown Westmeath 161 C7
Ballynamona Cork 163 B5
Ballynamult Waterford 163 B7
Ballyneety Limerick 163 A5
Ballynure Antrim 159 B7
Ballyporeen Tipperary 163 B6
Ballyragget Kilkenny 157 C2
Ballyroan Laois 157 C2
Ballyroe Cork 163 B6
Ballyronan Londonderry 159 B5
Ballyroney Down 159 C6
Ballysadare Sligo 158 C1
Ballyshannon Donegal 158 C2
Ballyshannon Kildare 157 B3
Ballyshrule Galway 161 C6
Ballysloe Tipperary 163 A7
Ballysteen Limerick 163 A5
Ballyvaghan Clare 160 C4
Ballyvourney Cork 162 C4
Ballyvoy Antrim 159 A6
Ballywalter Down 159 B8
Ballyward Down 159 C6
Ballywilliam Wexford 157 D3
Balrath Meath 157 A4
Balrothery Dublin 157 A4
Baltimore Cork 162 D4
Baltinglass Wicklow 157 C3
Baltracey Kildare 157 B3
Baltray Louth 159 D6
Banagher Offaly 161 C7
Banbridge Down 159 C6
Bandon Cork 163 C5
Bangor Mayo 160 A3
Bangor Down 159 B7
Bannow Wexford 157 D3
Banteer Cork 163 B5
Bantry Cork 162 C4
Baranailt Londonderry 158 B4
Barefield Clare 161 D5
Barna Galway 160 C4
Barnaderg Galway 161 C5
Barnesmore Donegal 158 B2
Barraduff Kerry 162 B4
Barran Cavan 158 C3
Batterstown Meath 157 B3
Bawnboy Cavan 158 C3
Bealin Westmeath 161 C7
Bealnablath Cork 163 C5
Beaufort Kerry 162 B3
Beech Hill Down 159 C6
Beelaha Clare 162 A3
Belclare Galway 161 C5
Belcoo Fermanagh 158 C3
Belderg Mayo 160 A3
Belfast Antrim 159 B7
Belgooly Cork 163 C6
Bellacorick Mayo 160 A3
Bellaghy Londonderry 159 B5
Bellahy Sligo 161 B5
Bellanagare Roscommon 161 B6
Bellanaleck Fermanagh 158 C3
Bellanamore Donegal 158 B2
Bellananagh Cavan 158 D4
Bellavary Mayo 160 B4
Belleek Donegal 158 C2
Belleek Armagh 159 C6
Belleville Galway 161 C5
Bellinamuck Longford 161 B7
Belmullet Mayo 160 A3
Beltra Mayo 160 B4
Beltra Sligo 158 C1
Belturbet Cavan 158 C4
Benburb Tyrone 159 C5
Bennettsbridge Kilkenny 157 C2
Beragh Tyrone 158 B4
Bessbrook Armagh 159 C6
Bettystown Meath 157 A4
Beville Mayo 160 A4
Birdhill Tipperary 163 A6
Birr Offaly 161 C7
Black Rock Louth 159 D6
Blackrock Dublin 157 B4
Blackwater Wexford 157 D4
Blanchardstown Dublin 157 B4
Blaney Fermanagh 158 C3
Blarney Cork 163 C5
Blessington Wicklow 157 B3
Bodyke Clare 161 D5
Boggaun Leitrim 158 C2
Boherahuca Offaly 161 C7
Boherboy Cork 162 B4
Boherlahan Tipperary 163 A7
Boho Fermanagh 158 C3
Bohola Mayo 160 B4
Bolea Londonderry 159 A5
Boley Kildare 157 B3
Borris in Ossory Laois 161 D7
Borris Carlow 157 C3
Borrisokane Tipperary 161 D6
Borrisoleigh Tipperary 163 A7
Bouladuff Tipperary 163 A7
Boyle Roscommon 161 B6
Bracklin Cavan 159 D5
Bracknagh Offaly 157 B2
Branden Kerry 162 B2
Bray Wicklow 157 B4
Breaghva Clare 162 A3
Breedoge Roscommon 161 B6
Breenagh Donegal 158 B3
Brideswell Roscommon 161 C6
Bridge End Donegal 158 A4
Bridgetown Wexford 157 D3
Brittas Dublin 157 B4
Broadford Clare 163 A5
Broadford Limerick 163 B5
Broadway Wexford 157 D4
Brookeborough Fermanagh 158 C4
Broomfield Monaghan 159 C5
Broughderg Tyrone 159 B5
Broughshane Antrim 159 B6
Bruff Limerick 163 B5
Bruree Limerick 163 B5
Buggan Fermanagh 158 C3
Bullaun Galway 161 C5
Bunahowen Mayo 160 A3
Bunalunn Cork 162 C4
Bunaw Kerry 162 C3
Bunbeg Donegal 158 A2
Bunbrosna Westmeath 157 A2
Bunclody Wexford 157 C3
Buncrana Donegal 158 A4
Bundoran Donegal 158 C2
Bunmahon Waterford 157 D2
Bunnaglass Galway 161 C5
Bunnanaddan Sligo 158 C1
Bunnyconnellan Mayo 160 A4
Bunratty Clare 163 A5
Burnfoot Cork 163 B5
Burnfoot Donegal 158 A4
Burren Clare 160 C4
Burren Down 159 C6
Burtonport Donegal 158 B2
Bushmills Antrim 159 A5
Butler's Bridge Cavan 158 C4
Butlerstown Cork 163 C5
Buttevant Cork 163 B5
Bweeng Cork 163 B5

C

Cabinteely Dublin 157 B4
Cabragh Tyrone 159 C5
Cadamstown Offaly 161 C7
Caher Clare 161 D5
Caher Galway 160 C4
Caher Tipperary 163 B7
Caherciveen Kerry 162 C2
Caherconlish Limerick 163 A6
Caherdaniel Kerry 162 C2
Cahermore Cork 162 C2
Cahermurphy Clare 162 A4
Caledon Tyrone 159 C5
Callan Kilkenny 157 C2
Callow Galway 160 C2
Callow Mayo 160 B4
Calta Galway 161 C6
Camlough Armagh 159 C6
Camolin Wexford 157 C4
Camp Kerry 162 B3
Campile Wexford 157 D3
Camross Wexford 157 D3
Canningstown Cavan 158 D4
Cappagh White Tipperary 163 A6
Cappagh Cork 163 B6
Cappagh Galway 161 C6
Cappamore Limerick 163 A6
Cappeen Cork 163 C5
Cappoquin Waterford 163 B7
Carbury Kildare 157 B3
Carlanstown Meath 159 D5
Carlingford Louth 159 C6
Carlow Carlow 157 C3
Carna Galway 160 C3
Carnaross Meath 157 A3
Carncastle Antrim 159 B7
Carndonagh Donegal 158 A4
Carnew Wicklow 157 C4
Carney Sligo 158 C1
Carnlough Antrim 159 B7
Carracastle Mayo 161 B5
Carragh Kildare 157 B3
Carran Clare 160 C4
Carraroe Galway 160 C3
Carrick on Shannon Roscommon 161 B6
Carrick on Suir Tipperary 157 D2
Carrick Donegal 158 B1
Carrickart Donegal 158 A3
Carrickbeg Waterford 157 D2
Carrickboy Longford 161 B7
Carrickfergus Antrim 159 B7
Carrickmacross Monaghan 159 D5
Carrickmore Tyrone 158 B4
Carrigaholt Clare 162 A3
Carrigahorig Tipperary 161 C6
Carrigaline Cork 163 C6
Carrigallen Leitrim 161 B7
Carriganimmy Cork 162 C4
Carrigfadda Cork 162 C4
Carrigkerry Limerick 162 B4
Carrignavar Cork 163 C6
Carrigtohill Cork 163 C6
Carrowbehy Roscommon 161 B5
Carrowkeel Donegal 158 A3
Carrowkeel Donegal 158 A4
Carrowkeel Galway 161 C6
Carrowkennedy Mayo 160 B3
Carrowreagh Antrim 159 A6
Carrowreilly Sligo 158 C1
Carrowroe Longford 161 B7
Carryduff Down 159 B7
Cashel Galway 161 B5
Cashel Tipperary 163 A7
Castlebar Mayo 160 B4
Castlebellingham Louth 159 D6
Castleblakeney Galway 161 C6
Castleblaney Monaghan 159 C5
Castlebridge Wexford 157 D4
Castlecomer Kilkenny 157 C2
Castleconnell Limerick 163 A6
Castlecor Cork 163 B5
Castledawson Londonderry 159 B5
Castlederg Tyrone 158 B3
Castledermot Kildare 157 C3
Castlefinn Donegal 158 B3
Castlegregory Kerry 162 B2
Castlehill Mayo 160 A3
Castleisland Kerry 162 B4
Castlelyons Cork 163 B6
Castlemaine Kerry 162 B3
Castlemartyr Cork 163 C6
Castleplunket Roscommon 161 B6
Castlepollard Westmeath 157 A2
Castlerea Roscommon 161 B6
Castlerock Londonderry 159 A5
Castletown Bearhaven Cork 162 C3
Castletown Geoghegan Westmeath 157 B2
Castletown Laois 157 C2
Castletown Meath 159 D5
Castletownroche Cork 163 B6
Castletownshend Cork 162 C4
Castlewellan Down 159 C7
Causeway Kerry 162 B3
Cavan Cavan 158 C4
Cavangarden Donegal 158 B2
Celbridge Kildare 157 B3
Chanonrock Louth 159 D5
Charlemont Armagh 159 C5
Charlestown Mayo 161 B5
Charleville Cork 163 B5
Chasel Mayo 160 B3
Church Hill Donegal 158 B3
Church Hill Fermanagh 158 C3
Churchtown Cork 163 C6
Churchtown Wexford 157 D4
Clabby Fermanagh 158 C4
Clady Milltown Armagh 159 C5
Clady Tyrone 158 B3
Clanabogan Tyrone 158 B4
Clane Kildare 157 B3
Clara Offaly 161 C7
Clarahill Laois 157 B2
Clarecastle Clare 163 A5
Clareen Offaly 161 C7
Claregalway Galway 161 C5
Claremorris Mayo 161 B5
Claretuam Galway 161 C5
Clarina Limerick 163 A5
Clarinbridge Galway 161 C5
Clash Cork 163 C6
Clashmore Waterford 163 B7
Claudy Londonderry 158 B4
Cleady Kerry 162 C3
Cleggan Galway 160 B2
Clifden Galway 160 C2
Cliffony Sligo 158 C2
Clogh Kilkenny 157 C2
Clogh Antrim 159 B6
Cloghan Donegal 158 B3
Cloghan Offaly 161 C7
Cloghan Westmeath 157 A2
Cloghane Kerry 162 B2
Cloghaneely Donegal 158 A2
Cloghboy Donegal 158 B1
Clogheen Tipperary 163 B7
Clogher Head Louth 159 D6
Clogher Roscommon 161 B6
Clogher Tyrone 158 C4
Cloghjordan Tipperary 161 D6
Cloghran Dublin 157 B4
Cloghy Down 159 C8
Clomantagh Kilkenny 157 C2
Clonakilty Cork 163 C5
Clonaslee Laois 161 C7
Clonbulloge Offaly 157 B2
Clonbur Galway 160 B4
Cloncurry Kildare 157 B3
Clondalkin Dublin 157 B4
Clonea Waterford 157 D2
Clonee Meath 157 B4
Cloneen Tipperary 163 B7
Clonelly Fermanagh 158 B3
Clones Monaghan 158 C4
Cloney Kildare 157 B2
Clonfert Galway 161 C6
Clonlee Mayo 161 B5
Clonmacnoise Offaly 161 C7
Clonmany Donegal 158 A4
Clonmel Tipperary 163 B7
Clonmellon Westmeath 157 A2
Clonmore Carlow 157 C3
Clonmore Offaly 157 B2
Clonmore Tipperary 163 A7
Clonord Meath 157 B2
Clonroche Wexford 157 D3
Clontarf Dublin 157 B4
Cloodara Longford 161 B7
Cloonacool Sligo 161 A5
Cloonart Longford 161 B7
Cloonbannin Cork 162 B4
Cloonboo Galway 160 C4
Cloone Leitrim 161 B7
Cloonfad Roscommon 161 B5
Cloonkeen Kerry 162 C4
Cloonlara Clare 163 A5
Cloonlough Sligo 161 B6
Cloonmore Mayo 161 B5
Clorbern Galway 161 B5
Clough Down 159 C7
Cloyne Cork 163 C6
Coachford Cork 163 C5
Coagh Tyrone 159 B5
Coalisland Tyrone 159 B5
Cobh Cork 163 C6
Colehill Longford 161 B7
Coleraine Londonderry 159 A5
Collinstown Westmeath 157 A2
Collon Louth 159 D6
Collooney Sligo 158 C2
Comber Down 159 B7
Commeen Donegal 158 B3
Cong Mayo 160 B4
Conlig Down 159 B7
Conna Cork 163 B6
Connagh Galway 161 D6
Connonagh Cork 162 C4
Connor Antrim 159 B6
Convoy Donegal 158 B3
Cookstown Tyrone 159 B5
Coola Sligo 158 C2
Coolaney Sligo 158 C1
Coolbaun Tipperary 161 D6
Coolderg Galway 161 B5
Coole Westmeath 157 A2
Coolgreany Wexford 157 C4
Coolmore Donegal 158 B2
Coolrain Laois 161 D7
Cooneen Fermanagh 158 C4
Cooraclare Clare 162 A4
Cootehill Cavan 158 C4
Corbally Laois 157 C2
Corbally Sligo 160 A4
Cordal Kerry 162 B4
Corgary Tyrone 158 B3
Cork Cork 163 C6
Corlea Longford 161 B7
Corlogh Mayo 160 A2
Cornafulla Roscommon 161 C7
Cornamona Galway 160 B4
Cornanagh Mayo 160 B4
Cornhaw Cavan 158 C3
Corranny Fermanagh 158 C4
Corrawalleen Leitrim 158 C3
Corrigeenroe Roscommon 158 C2
Corrofin Clare 160 D4
Corvally Monaghan 159 D5
Corvoy Monaghan 159 C5
Costelloe Galway 160 C3
Courtmacsherry Cork 163 C5
Courtown Wexford 157 C4
Craanford Wexford 157 C4
Craigavon Armagh 159 C6
Cranagh Tyrone 158 B4
Crataloe Limerick 162 B4
Craughwell Galway 161 C5
Creaghanroe Monaghan 159 C5
Creegh Clare 162 A4
Creeragh Mayo 160 A4
Creeslough Donegal 158 A3
Creeve Tyrone 159 B5
Creeves Limerick 162 A4
Creggan Tyrone 158 B4
Cregganbaun Mayo 160 B3
Creggs Galway 161 B6
Crindle Londonderry 159 A5
Crinkill Offaly 161 C7
Croagh Limerick 163 A5
Crockets Town Mayo 160 A4
Croghan Offaly 157 B2
Croghan Roscommon 161 B6
Crolly Donegal 158 A2
Crookedwood Westmeath 157 A2
Crookhaven Cork 162 D3
Crookstown Cork 163 C5
Croom Limerick 163 A5
Cross Barry Cork 163 C5
Cross Keys Meath 157 A3
Crossakiel Meath 157 A2
Crossdoney Cavan 158 D4
Crossgar Down 159 C7
Crosshaven Cork 163 C6
Crossmaglen Armagh 159 C5
Crossmolina Mayo 160 A4
Crumlin Dublin 157 B4
Crumlin Antrim 159 B6
Crusheen Clare 161 D5
Culdaff Donegal 158 A4
Cullaville Armagh 159 C5
Cullen Tipperary 163 A6
Cullion Tyrone 158 B4
Cullyhanna Armagh 159 C5
Curraglass Cork 163 B6
Curry Sligo 161 B5
Curryglass Cork 162 C3
Cushendall Antrim 159 A6
Cushendun Antrim 159 A6
Cushina Offaly 157 B2

D

Dacklin Roscommon 161 B6
Daingean Offaly 157 B2
Dalkey Dublin 157 B4
Dalystown Galway 161 C6
Damerstown Kilkenny 157 C2
Darkley Armagh 159 C5
Darragh Clare 162 A4
Deelish Cork 162 C4
Delvin Westmeath 157 A2
Derry Sligo 158 C2
Derry/Londonderry Londonderry 158 B4
Derrybeg Donegal 158 A2
Derryboy Down 159 C7
Derrybrien Galway 161 C5
Derrycoosh Mayo 160 B4
Derrygonnelly Fermanagh 158 C3
Derrygorry Monaghan 158 C4
Derrygrogan Offaly 157 B2
Derrykeighan Antrim 159 A5
Derrylin Fermanagh 158 C3
Derrymore Kerry 162 B3
Derrynacreeve Cavan 158 C3
Derrynane Kerry 162 C2
Derryrush Galway 160 C3
Derrytrasna Armagh 159 B5
Dervock Antrim 159 A6
Desertmartin Londonderry 159 B5
Diamond Down 159 C6
Dingle Kerry 162 B2
Dirtagh Londonderry 159 A5
Doagh Antrim 159 B6
Dolla Tipperary 163 A6
Donabate Dublin 157 B4
Donadea Kildare 157 B3
Donagh Fermanagh 158 C4
Donaghadee Down 159 B7
Donaghmore Laois 161 D7
Donaghmore Tyrone 159 B5
Donard Wicklow 157 B3
Donegal Donegal 158 B2
Doneraile Cork 163 B5
Donohill Tipperary 163 A6
Donore Meath 157 A4
Donoughmore Cork 163 C5
Dooagh Mayo 160 B2
Doocharry Donegal 158 B2
Doogary Cavan 158 C3
Doogort Mayo 160 A2
Dooish Tyrone 158 B4
Doolin Clare 160 C4
Doon Limerick 163 A6
Doonaha Clare 162 A3
Doonbeg Clare 162 A3
Douglas Cork 163 C6
Downhill Londonderry 159 A5
Downies Donegal 158 A3
Downpatrick Down 159 C7
Dowra Cavan 158 C2
Drangan Tipperary 163 A7
Draperstown Londonderry 159 B5
Dreenagh Kerry 162 B3
Drimoleague Cork 162 C4
Drinagh Cork 162 C4
Dripsey Cork 163 C5
Drogheda Louth 157 A4
Dromahair Leitrim 158 C2
Dromara Down 159 C6
Dromard Sligo 158 C1
Dromcolliher Limerick 163 B5
Dromin Louth 159 D6
Dromina Cork 163 B5
Dromineer Tipperary 161 D6
Dromiskin Louth 159 D6
Dromkeen Limerick 163 A6
Dromod Leitrim 161 B7
Dromore West Sligo 161 A5
Dromore Down 159 C6
Dromore Tyrone 158 B4
Drum Monaghan 158 C4
Drumaduff Londonderry 159 B5
Drumahoe Londonderry 158 B4
Drumakilly Tyrone 158 B4
Drumbad Longford 161 B7
Drumbadmeen Fermanagh 158 C3
Drumbear Monaghan 159 C5
Drumbeg Donegal 158 B3
Drumbeg Down 159 B7
Drumbilla Louth 159 C6
Drumbo Monaghan 159 D5
Drumcard Fermanagh 158 C3
Drumcliff Sligo 158 C1
Drumcondra Dublin 157 B4
Drumcondra Meath 159 D5
Drumcoo Monaghan 158 C4
Drumcree Westmeath 157 A2
Drumdallagh Antrim 159 A6
Drumfin Sligo 158 C2
Drumfree Donegal 158 A4
Drumkeeran Leitrim 158 C2
Drumlegagh Tyrone 158 B4
Drumlish Longford 161 B7
Drumnacross Donegal 158 B3
Drumquin Tyrone 158 B4
Drumramer Londonderry 159 A5
Drumsallan Armagh 159 C5
Drumsaragh Londonderry 159 B5
Drumshanbo Leitrim 158 C2
Drumskinny Fermanagh 158 B3
Drumsna Leitrim 161 B6
Drumsurn Londonderry 159 A5
Dublin Dublin 157 B4
Duleek Meath 157 A4
Dun Laoghaire Dublin 157 B4
Dunaff Donegal 158 A4
Dunboyne Meath 157 B4
Duncormick Wexford 157 D3
Dundalk Louth 159 C6
Dunderrow Cork 163 C5
Dunderry Meath 157 A3
Dundonald Down 159 B7
Dundrod Antrim 159 B6
Dundrum Dublin 157 B4
Dundrum Tipperary 163 A6
Dundrum Down 159 C7
Dunfanaghy Donegal 158 A3
Dungannon Tyrone 159 B5
Dungarvan Waterford 163 B7
Dungiven Londonderry 159 B5
Dunglow Donegal 158 B2
Dungourney Cork 163 C6
Dunheeda Meath 159 D5
Dunkerrin Offaly 161 D7
Dunkineely Donegal 158 B2
Dunlavin Wicklow 157 B3
Dunleer Louth 159 D6
Dunloy Antrim 159 A6
Dunmanway Cork 162 C4
Dunmore East Waterford 157 D3
Dunmore Galway 161 B5
Dunmurry Antrim 159 B6
Dunnamanagh Tyrone 158 B4
Dunsany Meath 157 A3
Dunshaughlin Meath 157 A3
Durrow Abbey Offaly 161 C7
Durrow Laois 157 C2
Durrus Cork 162 C3
Dyan Tyrone 159 C5
Dysart Westmeath 157 B2

E

Eargantea Londonderry 159 A5
Earlstown Galway 161 C6
Easky Sligo 161 A5
Eden Antrim 159 B7
Edenaveagh Fermanagh 158 B3
Edenderry Offaly 157 B2
Ederny Fermanagh 158 B3
Edgeworthstown Longford 161 B7
Edmondstown Louth 159 D5
Eglinton Londonderry 158 A4
Eglish Tyrone 159 C5
Eighter Cavan 158 D4
Ellistrin Donegal 158 B3
Elphin Roscommon 161 B6
Emly Tipperary 163 B6
Emmoo Roscommon 161 B6
Emyvale Monaghan 159 C5
Ennis Clare 163 A5
Enniscorthy Wexford 157 C3
Enniskean Cork 163 C5
Enniskerry Wicklow 157 B4
Enniskillen Fermanagh 158 C3
Ennistimon Clare 160 D4
Errill Laois 163 A7
Essexford Monaghan 159 D5
Eyrecourt Galway 161 C6

F

Falcarragh Donegal 158 A2
Fallmore Mayo 160 A2
Fardrum Westmeath 161 C7
Farranfore Kerry 162 B3
Feakle Clare 161 D5
Fedamore Limerick 163 A5
Feeard Clare 162 A3
Feenhanagh Limerick 163 B5
Feeny Londonderry 158 B4
Fenagh Leitrim 158 C3
Fenit Kerry 162 B3
Fennagh Carlow 157 C3
Ferbane Offaly 161 C7
Fermoy Cork 163 B6
Ferns Wexford 157 C4
Fethard Tipperary 163 B7
Fethard Wexford 157 D3
Fiddown Kilkenny 157 D2
Fincarn Londonderry 159 B5
Finglas Dublin 157 B4
Finnea Westmeath 158 D4
Finnis Down 159 C6
Fintona Tyrone 158 C4
Fintown Donegal 158 B2
Finvoy Antrim 159 A6
Five Alley Offaly 161 C7
Fivemiletown Tyrone 158 C4
Flagmount Clare 161 C5
Fontstown Kildare 157 B3
Ford Wexford 157 C4
Fordstown Meath 157 A3
Fore Westmeath 157 A2
Forgney Longford 161 B7
Forkill Armagh 159 C6
Foulkesmill Wexford 157 D3
Fountain Cross Clare 162 A4
Four Mile House Roscommon 161 B6
Foxford Mayo 160 B4
Foygh Longford 161 B7
Foynes Limerick 162 A4
Frankville Down 159 C7
Freemount Cork 163 B5
Frenchpark Roscommon 161 B6
Freshford Kilkenny 157 C2
Fuerty Roscommon 161 B6
Fybagh Kerry 162 B3

G

Galbally Limerick 163 B6
Galmoy Kilkenny 163 A7
Galway Galway 160 C4
Garbally Galway 161 C6
Garrane Cork 162 C4
Garrison Fermanagh 158 C2
Garristown Dublin 157 A4
Garryvoe Cork 163 C6
Garvagh Londonderry 159 B5
Garvaghy Down 159 C6
Garvaghy Tyrone 158 C4
Garvary Fermanagh 158 C3
Gattabaun Kilkenny 157 C2
Gay Brook Westmeath 157 B2
Geashill Offaly 157 B2
Gilford Down 159 C6
Glandore Cork 162 C4
Glanworth Cork 163 B6
Glasdrumman Down 159 C7
Glaslough Monaghan 159 C5
Glasnevin Dublin 157 B4
Glassan Westmeath 161 C7
Glastry Down 159 C8
Glen Donegal 158 A3
Glen Fermanagh 158 C2
Glenade Leitrim 158 C2
Glenamoy Mayo 160 A3
Glenariff Antrim 159 A6
Glenarm Antrim 159 B7
Glenavy Antrim 159 B6
Glenbeigh Kerry 162 B3
Glencar Kerry 162 B3
Glencolumbkille Donegal 158 B1
Glendalough Wicklow 157 B4
Glendree Clare 161 D5
Gleneely Wicklow 157 C4
Gleneely Donegal 158 A4
Glenfarn Leitrim 158 C3
Glenfesk Kerry 162 B4
Glengarriff Cork 162 C3
Glengavlen Cavan 158 C3
Glengormly Antrim 159 B7
Glennamaddy Galway 161 B5
Glenoe Antrim 159 B7

How to use the index

Example: **Westcott** *Devon* **8 D2**
- grid square
- page number
- county or unitary authority

Places of special interest are highlighted in red

Abbreviations

Aberd C	Aberdeen City	Brighton/Hove	Brighton and Hove	Clack	Clackmannanshire
Aberds	Aberdeenshire	Bristol	City and County of Bristol	Corn'w'l	Cornwall
Angl	Isle of Anglesey	Bucks	Buckinghamshire	Cumb	Cumbria
Arg/Bute	Argyll & Bute	C/Edinb	City of Edinburgh	D'lington	Darlington
Bath/NE Som'set	Bath & North East Somerset	C/Glasg	Glasgow City	Denbs	Denbighshire
Beds	Bedfordshire	C/York	City of York	Derby	Derbyshire
Bl Gwent	Blaenau Gwent	Caerph	Caerphilly	Derby C	Derby City
Blackb'n	Blackburn with Darwen	Cambs	Cambridgeshire	Dumf/Gal	Dumfries & Galloway
Blackp'l	Blackpool	Card	Cardiff	Dundee C	Dundee City
Bournem'th	Bournemouth	Carms	Carmarthenshire	E Ayrs	East Ayrshire
Brack'nl	Bracknell Forest	Ceredig'n	Ceredigion	E Dunb	East Dunbartonshire
Bridg	Bridgend	Ches	Cheshire	E Loth	East Lothian

E Renf	East Renfrewshire	Herts	Hertfordshire	Newp	Newport
ER Yorks	East Riding of Yorkshire	I/Man	Isle of Man	Northants	Northamptonshire
E Sussex	East Sussex	I/Scilly	Isles of Scilly	Northum	Northumberland
Falk	Falkirk	I/Wight	Isle of Wight	Nott'ham	City of Nottingham
		Invercl	Inverclyde	Notts	Nottinghamshire
		Kingston/Hull	Kingston upon Hull	Oxon	Oxfordshire
		Lancs	Lancashire	Pembs	Pembrokeshire
		Leics	Leicestershire	Perth/Kinr	Perth and Kinross
		Leics C	Leicester City	Peterbro	Peterborough
		Lincs	Lincolnshire	Plym'th	Plymouth
		London	Greater London	Portsm'th	Portsmouth
		M/Keynes	Milton Keynes	Redcar/Clevel'd	Redcar and Cleveland
		Mersey	Merseyside	Renf	Renfrewshire
		Merth Tyd	Merthyr Tydfil	Rh Cyn Taff	Rhondda Cynon Taff
		Middlesbro	Middlesbrough	Rutl'd	Rutland
		Midloth	Midlothian	S Ayrs	South Ayrshire
		Monmouths	Monmouthshire	S Glocs	South Gloucestershire
		N Ayrs	North Ayrshire	S Lanarks	South Lanarkshire
		N Lanarks	North Lanarkshire	S Yorks	South Yorkshire
		N Lincs	North Lincolnshire	Scot Borders	Scottish Borders
		N Som'set	North Somerset	Shetl'd	Shetland
		N Yorks	North Yorkshire	Shrops	Shropshire
		NE Lincs	North East Lincolnshire	Som'set	Somerset
		Neath P Talb	Neath Port Talbot		

Southend	Southend-on-Sea
Staffs	Staffordshire
Stirl	Stirling
Stockton	Stockton on Tees
Stoke	Stoke-on-Trent
Swan	Swansea
Telford	Telford and Wrekin
Thurr'k	Thurrock
Torf	Torfaen
Tyne/Wear	Tyne and Wear
V/Glam	Vale of Glamorgan
W Berks	West Berkshire
W Dunb	West Dunbartonshire
W Isles	Western Isles
W Loth	West Lothian
W Midlands	West Midlands
W Sussex	West Sussex
W Yorks	West Yorkshire
Warwick	Warwickshire
Wilts	Wiltshire
Windsor	Windsor and Maidenhead
Worcs	Worcestershire
Wrex	Wrexham

A

Budock Water Cornw'l 3 F6
Buerton Ches 39 A7
Buffler's Holt Bucks 31 E8
Bugbrooke Northants 31 C8
Buglawton Ches 49 F9
Bugle Cornw'l 3 D9
Bugley Wilts 18 G5
Bugthorpe ER Yorks 58 C3
Buildwas Shrops 39 E7
Builth Road Powys 27 C10
Builth Wells Powys 27 C10
Buirgh W Isles 109 H5
Bulby Lincs 42 C3
Bulcote Notts 41 A8
Buldoo H'land 106 C4
Bulford Wilts 19 G8
Bulford Camp Wilts 19 G8
Bulkeley Ches 49 G6
Bulkington Warwick 40 G5
Bulkington Wilts 19 F6
Bulkworthy Devon 6 E4
Bull Hill Hants 11 E6
Bullamoor N Yorks 63 E8
Bullbridge Derby 50 G5
Bullbrook Brackn'l 21 E6
Bulley Glos 29 G8
Bullgill Cumb 68 G3
Bullington Hants 20 G2
Bullington Lincs 52 E3
Bull's Green Herts 32 G5
Bullwood Arg/Bute 82 G2
Bulmer Essex 34 D2
Bulmer N Yorks 58 B2
Bulmer Tye Essex 34 E2
Bulphan Thurr'k 23 C6
Bulverhythe E Sussex 14 H2
Bulwark Aberds 99 D9
Bulwell Nott'ham 51 H7
Bulwick Northants 42 F2
Bumble's Green Essex 33 H7
Bun Abhainn Eadarra W Isles 109 G6
Bun Loyne H'land 95 F9
Bunacaimb H'land 87 C6
Bunarkaig H'land 88 C2
Bunbury Ches 49 G6
Bunbury Heath Ches 49 G6
Bunchrew H'land 96 B4
Bundalloch H'land 94 D5
Buness Shetl'd 111 C9
Bunessan Arg/Bute 80 B3
Bungay Suffolk 45 G7
Bunker's Hill Lincs 52 E2
Bunker's Hill Lincs 52 G5
Bunkers Hill Oxon 31 G6
Bunloit H'land 96 D3
Bunnahabhain Arg/Bute 80 G4
Bunny Notts 41 C7
Buntait H'land 96 C1
Buntingford Herts 33 F6
Bunwell Norfolk 44 F5
Burbage Derby 50 E2
Burbage Leics 41 F6
Burbage Wilts 19 E9
Burchett's Green Windsor 21 C6
Burcombe Wilts 10 A3
Burcot Oxon 20 B3
Burcott Bucks 32 F1
Burdon Tyne/Wear 71 E8
Bures Suffolk 34 E3
Bures Green Suffolk 34 E3
Burford Ches 49 G7
Burford Oxon 30 G4
Burford Shrops 29 B6
Burg Arg/Bute 86 G3
Burgar Orkney 110 F4
Burgate Hants 10 C4
Burgate Suffolk 44 H4
Burgess Hill W Sussex 13 D7
Burgh Suffolk 35 C6
Burgh by Sands Cumb 69 E6
Burgh Castle Norfolk 45 E8
Burgh Heath Surrey 22 F2
Burgh le Marsh Lincs 53 F8
Burgh Muir Aberds 99 F7
Burgh next Aylsham Norfolk 45 C6
Burgh on Bain Lincs 52 D5
Burgh St. Margaret Norfolk 45 D8
Burgh St. Peter Norfolk 45 F8
Burghclere Hants 20 E2
Burghead Moray 103 F10
Burghfield W Berks 20 E4
Burghfield Common W Berks 20 E4
Burghfield Hill W Berks 20 E4
Burghill Heref'd 28 D5
Burghwallis S Yorks 57 G10
Burham Kent 14 B2
Buriton Hants 11 B10
Burland Ches 49 G7
Burlawn Cornw'l 3 B8
Burleigh Brackn'l 21 E6
Burlescombe Devon 8 C2
Burleston Dorset 9 E9
Burley Hants 10 D5
Burley Rutl'd 42 D1
Burley W Yorks 57 E7
Burley Gate Heref'd 29 D6
Burley in Wharfedale W Yorks 57 D6
Burley Lodge Hants 10 D5
Burley Street Hants 10 D5
Burleydam Ches 39 A7
Burlingjobb Powys 28 C3
Burlow E Sussex 13 D9
Burlton Shrops 38 C5
Burmarsh Kent 14 E5
Burmington Warwick 30 E4
Burn N Yorks 58 F1
Burn of Cambus Stirl 83 D8
Burnaston Derby 40 B4
Burnbank S Lanarks 75 B9
Burnby ER Yorks 58 D4
Burncross S Yorks 50 C5
Burneside Cumb 61 E8
Burness Orkney 110 D7
Burneston N Yorks 63 F8
Burnett Bath/NE Som'set 18 E3
Burnfoot Scot Borders 77 F7
Burnfoot Scot Borders 77 F8
Burnfoot E Ayrs 75 G6
Burnfoot Perth/Kinr 84 D1
Burnham Bucks 21 C7
Burnham N Lincs 59 G6
Burnham Deepdale Norfolk 44 A2
Burnham Green Herts 32 G5
Burnham Market Norfolk 44 A2
Burnham Norton Norfolk 44 A2
Burnham on Crouch Essex 23 B9
Burnham on Sea Som'set 17 G8
Burnham Overy Staithe Norfolk 44 A2
Burnham Overy Town Norfolk 44 A2
Burnham Thorpe Norfolk 44 A2
Burnhaven Aberds 99 D11
Burnhead Dumf/Gal 76 H1
Burnhead S Ayrs 74 G4
Burnhervie Aberds 99 G7
Burnhill Green Staffs 39 E8
Burnhope Durham 71 F6
Burnhouse N Ayrs 74 B5
Burniston N Yorks 65 E8
Burnlee W Yorks 50 B3
Burnley Lancs 56 E3
Burnley Lane Lancs 56 E3
Burnmouth Scot Borders 78 A4
Burnopfield Durham 71 E6
Burnsall N Yorks 56 B5
Burnside Angus 91 F6
Burnside E Ayrs 75 F7
Burnside Fife 84 D3
Burnside Shetl'd 111 F5
Burnside S Lanarks 75 A8
Burnside W Loth 84 G2
Burnside of Duntrune Angus 84 A6
Burnswark Dumf/Gal 68 C4
Burnt Heath Derby 50 E4
Burnt Houses Durham 63 B6
Burnt Yates N Yorks 57 B7
Burntcommon Surrey 21 F8
Burnthouse Cornw'l 3 F6
Burntisland Fife 84 F4
Burnton E Ayrs 75 G6
Burntwood Staffs 40 E2
Burnwynd C/Edinb 84 H3
Burpham Surrey 21 F8
Burpham W Sussex 12 E4
Burradon Northum 78 G4
Burradon Tyne/Wear 71 C7
Burrafirth Shetl'd 111 B9
Burraland Shetl'd 111 F6
Burraland Shetl'd 111 J5
Burras Cornw'l 2 F5
Burravoe Shetl'd 111 G6
Burravoe Shetl'd 111 F8
Burrells Cumb 61 C9
Burrelton Perth/Kinr 90 H3
Burridge Devon 7 C6
Burridge Hants 11 C8
Burrill N Yorks 63 F7
Burringham N Lincs 51 B10
Burrington Devon 7 E7
Burrington Heref'd 28 A5
Burrington N Som'set 17 F9
Burrough Green Cambs 33 C9
Burrough on the Hill Leics 41 D9
Burrowbridge Som'set 8 B5
Burrowhill Surrey 21 E7
Burry Swan 25 G9
Burry Green Swan 25 G9
Burry Port Carms 25 F9
Burscough Lancs 55 G4
Burscough Bridge Lancs 55 G4
Bursea ER Yorks 58 E4
Burshill ER Yorks 59 D6
Bursledon Hants 11 D7
Burslem Stoke 49 H9
Burstall Suffolk 34 D4
Burstock Dorset 9 D6
Burston Norfolk 44 G5
Burston Staffs 39 B10
Burstow Surrey 22 G3
Burstwick ER Yorks 59 F8
Burtersett N Yorks 62 F3
Burtle Som'set 17 G8
Burton Ches 48 E4
Burton Ches 49 F6
Burton Dorset 10 E4
Burton Lincs 52 E2
Burton Northum 79 D6
Burton Pembs 24 F4
Burton Som'set 17 G6
Burton Wilts 18 D5
Burton Agnes ER Yorks 59 B7
Burton Bradstock Dorset 9 F6
Burton Dassett Warwick 30 C5
Burton Fleming ER Yorks 65 G8
Burton Green W Midlands 40 H4
Burton Green Wrex 48 G4
Burton Hastings Warwick 41 F6
Burton in Kendal Cumb 61 G8
Burton in Lonsdale N Yorks 61 G9
Burton Joyce Notts 41 A8
Burton Latimer Northants 32 A2
Burton Lazars Leics 41 D9
Burton le Coggles Lincs 42 C2
Burton Leonard N Yorks 57 B8
Burton on the Wolds Leics 41 C7
Burton Overy Leics 41 F8
Burton Pedwardine Lincs 42 A4
Burton Pidsea ER Yorks 59 E8
Burton Salmon N Yorks 57 F9
Burton Stather N Lincs 58 G4
Burton upon Stather N Lincs 58 G4
Burton upon Trent Staffs 40 C4
Burtonwood Warrington 49 C6
Burwardsley Ches 49 G6
Burwarton Shrops 39 G7
Burwash E Sussex 14 F1
Burwash Common E Sussex 13 C10
Burwash Weald E Sussex 13 C10
Burwell Cambs 33 B8
Burwell Lincs 53 E6
Burwen Angl 46 C4
Burwick Orkney 110 K5
Bury Cambs 42 G5
Bury Gtr Man 56 G3
Bury Som'set 7 D10
Bury W Sussex 12 D4
Bury Green Herts 33 F7
Bury St. Edmunds Suffolk 34 B2
Burythorpe N Yorks 58 B3
Busby E Renf 75 B7
Buscot Oxon 19 B9
Bush Bank Heref'd 28 C5
Bush Crathie Aberds 90 B3
Bush Green Norfolk 45 G6
Bushbury W Midlands 39 E10
Bushby Leics 41 E8
Bushey Herts 21 B9
Bushey Heath Herts 21 B9
Bushley Worcs 29 E9
Bushton Wilts 19 D7
Buslingthorpe Lincs 52 D3
Busta Shetl'd 111 G6
Butcher's Cross E Sussex 13 C9
Butcher's Pasture Essex 33 F9
Butcombe N Som'set 18 E2
Butetown Card 17 D6
Butleigh Som'set 9 A7
Butleigh Wootton Som'set 18 H2
Butler's Cross Bucks 31 H10
Butler's End Warwick 40 G4
Butler's Marston Warwick 30 D5
Butley Suffolk 35 C7
Butley High Corner Suffolk 35 D7
Butt Green Ches 49 G7
Butterburn Cumb 69 C9
Buttercrambe N Yorks 58 C3
Butterknowle Durham 63 B6
Butterleigh Devon 8 D1
Buttermere Cumb 60 C4
Buttermere Wilts 19 E10
Buttershaw W Yorks 57 F6
Butterstone Perth/Kinr 90 G1
Butterton Staffs 50 G2
Butterwick Durham 63 B8
Butterwick Lincs 53 H6
Butterwick N Yorks 64 G5
Butterwick N Yorks 65 G7
Buttington Powys 38 E3
Buttonoak Shrops 39 H8
Butt's Green Hants 11 B6
Buttsash Hants 11 D7
Buxhall Suffolk 34 C4
Buxhall Fen Street Suffolk 34 C4
Buxley Scot Borders 78 B3
Buxted E Sussex 13 C8
Buxton Derby 50 E2
Buxton Norfolk 45 C6
Buxworth Derby 50 D2
Bwlch Powys 28 F2
Bwlch Llan Ceredig'n 26 C5
Bwlch y cibau Powys 38 D2
Bwlch y fadfa Ceredig'n 25 B9
Bwlch y ffridd Powys 38 F1
Bwlch y sarnau Powys 27 A10
Bwlchgwyn Wrex 48 G3
Bwlchnewydd Carms 25 D8
Bwlchtocyn Gwyn 36 C3
Bwlchyddar Powys 38 C2
Bwlchygroes Pembs 25 C7
Byermoor Tyne/Wear 71 E6
Byers Green Durham 71 G7
Byfield Northants 31 C7
Byfleet Surrey 21 E8
Byford Heref'd 28 D4
Bygrave Herts 32 E5
Byker Tyne/Wear 71 D7
Bylchau Conwy 47 F9
Byley Ches 49 F8
Bynea Carms 25 G10
Byrness Northum 78 G2
Bythorn Cambs 42 H3
Byton Heref'd 28 B4
Byworth W Sussex 12 C3

C

Cabharstadh W Isles 108 E8
Cablea Perth/Kinr 89 H10
Cabourne Lincs 52 B4
Cabrach Arg/Bute 72 A4
Cabrach Moray 98 F3
Cabus Lancs 55 D4
Cackle Street E Sussex 13 C8
Cadbury Devon 7 F10
Cadbury Barton Devon 7 E7
Cadbury World, Bourneville W Midlands 40 G2
Cadder E Dunb 83 G7
Caddington Beds 32 G3
Caddonfoot Scot Borders 77 D7
Cade Street E Sussex 13 C10
Cadeby Leics 41 E6
Cadeby S Yorks 51 B7
Cadeleigh Devon 7 F10
Cadgwith Cornw'l 3 H6
Cadham Fife 84 D4
Cadishead Gtr Man 49 C8
Cadle Swan 16 B1
Cadley Lancs 55 E5
Cadley Wilts 19 F9
Cadley Wilts 19 E9
Cadmore End Bucks 20 B5
Cadnam Hants 10 C5
Cadney N Lincs 52 B3
Cadole Flints 48 F3
Cadoxton V/Glam 17 E6
Cadoxton Juxta Neath Neath P Talb 16 B2
Cadshaw Blackb'n 56 G2
Cadzow S Lanarks 75 B9
Caeathraw Gwyn 46 F4
Caehopkin Powys 27 G8
Caenby Lincs 52 D3
Caenby Corner Lincs 52 D2
Caer bryn Carms 26 G5
Caer Llan Monmouths 28 H5
Caerau Bridg 16 B3
Caerau Card 17 D6
Caerdeon Gwyn 37 D6
Caerfarchell Pembs 24 D2
Caergeiliog Angl 46 E3
Caergwrle Flints 48 G4
Caerleon Newp 17 B8
Caernarfon Gwyn 46 F4
Caernarfon Castle Gwyn 46 F4
Caerphilly Caerph 17 C6
Caersws Powys 37 F10
Caerwedros Ceredig'n 26 C3
Caerwent Monmouths 17 B9
Caerwych Gwyn 37 B6
Caerwys Flints 48 E2
Caethle Gwyn 37 F6
Cairn Angl 47 D6
Caio Carms 27 E6
Cairinis W Isles 109 L3
Cairisiadar W Isles 108 D5
Cairminis W Isles 109 J5
Cairnbaan Arg/Bute 81 E8
Cairnbanno Ho. Aberds 99 D8
Cairnborrow Aberds 98 D4
Cairnbrogie Aberds 99 F8
Cairnbulg Castle Aberds 99 B10
Cairncross Angus 90 D5
Cairncross Scot Borders 78 A3
Cairndow Arg/Bute 82 C2
Cairness Aberds 99 B10
Cairneyhill Fife 84 F2
Cairnfield Ho. Moray 98 B4
Cairngaan Dumf/Gal 66 G3
Cairngarroch Dumf/Gal 66 F2
Cairnhill Aberds 99 E6
Cairnie Aberds 98 D4
Cairnie Aberds 99 H8
Cairnorrie Aberds 99 D8
Cairnpark Aberds 99 G8
Cairnryan Dumf/Gal 66 D2
Cairnton Orkney 110 H4
Caister on Sea Norfolk 45 D9
Caistor Lincs 52 B4
Caistor St. Edmund Norfolk 45 E6
Caistron Northum 78 G4
Caitha Bowland Scot Borders 77 C7
Caithness Glass Perth/Kinr 84 B2
Calais Street Suffolk 34 E3
Calanais W Isles 108 D7
Calbost W Isles 108 F9
Calbourne I/Wight 11 F7
Calceby Lincs 53 E6
Calcot Row W Berks 20 D4
Calcott Kent 15 B6
Caldback Shetl'd 111 C9
Caldbeck Cumb 69 G6
Caldbergh N Yorks 62 F5
Caldecot Rutl'd 42 F1
Caldecote Cambs 33 C6
Caldecote Cambs 42 G4
Caldecote Herts 32 E5
Caldecote Northants 31 C8
Caldecott Northants 32 B2
Caldecott Oxon 20 B2
Calder Bridge Cumb 60 D3
Calder Hall Cumb 60 D3
Calder Mains H'land 106 D5
Calder Vale Lancs 55 D5
Calderbank N Lanarks 75 A9
Calderbrook Gtr Man 56 G4
Caldercruix N Lanarks 83 H9
Caldermill S Lanarks 75 C8
Calderwood S Lanarks 75 B8
Caldhame Angus 90 G5
Caldicot Monmouths 17 C9
Caldwell Derby 40 D4
Caldwell N Yorks 63 C6
Caldy Mersey 48 D3
Caledrhydiau Ceredig'n 26 C4
Calfsound Orkney 110 E6
Calgary Arg/Bute 86 F3
Califer Moray 103 G9
California Falk 83 G10
California Norfolk 45 D9
Calke Derby 40 C5
Callaly Northum 78 G5
Callander Stirl 83 D7
Callaughton Shrops 39 F7
Callestick Cornw'l 3 D6
Callestock Cider Farm, Truro Cornw'l 3 D6
Calligarry H'land 94 F3
Callington Cornw'l 4 D4
Callow Heref'd 28 E5
Callow End Worcs 29 D9
Callow Hill Wilts 19 C7
Callow Hill Worcs 29 A8
Callows Grave Worcs 29 B6
Calmore Hants 11 C6
Calmsden Glos 30 H2
Calne Wilts 19 D7
Calow Derby 51 E6
Calshot Hants 11 D7
Calstock Cornw'l 4 D5
Calstone Wellington Wilts 19 E7
Calthorpe Norfolk 44 B5
Calthwaite Cumb 69 F7
Calton N Yorks 56 C4
Calton Staffs 50 G3
Calveley Ches 49 G6
Calver Derby 50 E4
Calver Hill Heref'd 28 D4
Calverhall Shrops 39 B7
Calverleigh Devon 7 E10
Calverley W Yorks 57 E7
Calvert Bucks 31 F8
Calverton M/Keynes 31 E9
Calverton Notts 51 H8
Calvine Perth/Kinr 89 E9
Calvo Cumb 68 E4
Calzeat Scot Borders 76 D4
Cam Glos 18 B4
Camas luinie H'land 95 D6
Camasnacroise H'land 87 F8
Camastianavaig H'land 94 C2
Camasunary H'land 94 E2
Camault Muir H'land 96 B3
Camb Shetl'd 111 D8
Camber E Sussex 14 G4
Camberley Surrey 21 E6
Camberwell London 22 D3
Camblesforth N Yorks 58 F2
Cambo Northum 70 B5
Cambois Northum 71 B8
Camborne Cornw'l 2 E5
Cambridge Cambs 33 C7
Cambridge Glos 18 A4
Cambridge Town Southend 23 C9
Cambus Clack 83 E9
Cambusavie Farm H'land 103 C6
Cambusbarron Stirl 83 E8
Cambuskenneth Stirl 83 E9
Cambuslang S Lanarks 75 A8
Cambusmore Lodge H'land 103 C6
Camden London 22 C2
Camelford Cornw'l 4 B2
Camelot Theme Park, Chorley Lancs 55 G5
Camelsdale W Sussex 12 B2
Camerory H'land 97 C8
Camer's Green Worcs 29 E8
Camerton Bath/NE Som'set 18 F3
Camerton Cumb 68 G3
Camerton ER Yorks 59 F8
Camghouran Perth/Kinr 88 F6
Cammachmore Aberds 91 B10
Cammeringham Lincs 52 D2
Camp Hill Warwick 40 F5
Campbeltown Arg/Bute 73 E7
Camperdown Tyne/Wear 71 C7
Campmuir Perth/Kinr 90 H3
Campsall S Yorks 57 G10
Campsey Ash Suffolk 35 C7
Campton Beds 32 E4
Camptown Scot Borders 77 F9
Camrose Pembs 24 D4
Camserney Perth/Kinr 89 G9
Camster H'land 107 E7
Camuschoirk H'land 87 E7
Camuscross H'land 94 E3
Camusnagaul H'land 88 D1
Camusnagaul H'land 101 D8
Camusrory H'land 94 G5
Camusteel H'land 94 B4
Camusterrach H'land 94 B4
Camusvrachan Perth/Kinr 89 G7
Canada Hants 10 C5
Canadia E Sussex 14 G2
Canal Side S Yorks 58 G2
Candacraig Aberds 90 B4
Candacraig Ho. Aberds 98 G3
Candlesby Lincs 53 F7
Candy Mill S Lanarks 76 C3
Cane End Oxon 20 D4
Canewdon Essex 23 B8
Canford Bottom Dorset 10 D3
Canford Cliffs Poole 10 F3
Canford Magna Poole 10 E3
Canham's Green Suffolk 34 B4
Canholes Derby 50 E2
Canisbay H'land 107 B8
Cann Dorset 10 B1
Cann Common Dorset 10 B1
Cannard's Grave Som'set 18 G3
Cannich H'land 95 C10
Cannington Som'set 17 H7
Cannock Staffs 40 E1
Cannock Wood Staffs 40 D2
Canon Bridge Heref'd 28 D5
Canon Frome Heref'd 29 D7
Canon Pyon Heref'd 28 D5
Canonbie Dumf/Gal 69 C6
Canons Ashby Northants 31 C7
Canonstown Cornw'l 2 F4
Canterbury Kent 15 C6
Canterbury Cathedral Kent 15 C6
Canterbury Tales Kent 15 C6
Cantley Norfolk 45 E7
Cantley S Yorks 51 B8
Cantlop Shrops 39 E6
Canton Card 17 D6
Cantraybruich H'land 96 B5
Cantraydoune H'land 96 B5
Cantraywood H'land 96 B5
Cantsfield Lancs 61 G9
Canvey Island Essex 23 C7
Canwick Lincs 52 F2
Canworthy Water Cornw'l 6 G3
Caol H'land 88 D2
Caolas Arg/Bute 86 D2
Caolas Scalpaigh W Isles 109 H7
Caolas Stocinis W Isles 109 H6
Capel Surrey 21 G9
Capel Bangor Ceredig'n 37 G6
Capel Betws Lleucu Ceredig'n 27 C6
Capel Carmel Gwyn 36 C1
Capel Coch Angl 46 D4
Capel Curig Conwy 47 G7
Capel Cynon Ceredig'n 25 B8
Capel Dewi Ceredig'n 25 B9
Capel Dewi Ceredig'n 37 G6
Capel Dewi Carms 25 D9
Capel Garmon Conwy 47 G8
Capel gwyn Angl 46 E3
Capel Gwyn Carms 25 D9
Capel Gwynfe Carms 27 F7
Capel Hendre Carms 26 G5
Capel Hermon Gwyn 37 C7
Capel Isaac Carms 26 F5
Capel Iwan Carms 25 C7
Capel le Ferne Kent 15 E7
Capel Llanilltern Card 16 C5
Capel Mawr Angl 46 E4
Capel Seion Ceredig'n 37 H6
Capel St. Andrew Suffolk 35 D7
Capel St. Mary Suffolk 34 E4
Capel Tygwydd Ceredig'n 25 B7
Capel Uchaf Gwyn 46 H4
Capel y graig Gwyn 46 F5
Capelulo Conwy 47 E7
Capenhurst Ches 48 E4
Capernwray Lancs 61 G8
Capheaton Northum 70 B5
Cappercleuch Scot Borders 76 E5
Capplegill Dumf/Gal 76 G4
Capton Devon 5 E9
Caputh Perth/Kinr 90 H1
Car Colston Notts 41 A9
Carbis Bay Cornw'l 2 F4
Carbost H'land 93 B9
Carbost H'land 109 N9
Carbrook S Yorks 50 D5
Carbrooke Norfolk 44 E3
Carburton Notts 51 E8
Carcant Scot Borders 77 B6
Carcary Angus 91 F7
Carclaze Cornw'l 3 D9
Carcroft S Yorks 57 G10
Cardenden Fife 84 E4
Cardeston Shrops 38 D4
Cardiff Card 17 D6
Cardiff Castle Card 17 D6
Cardigan Ceredig'n 25 B6
Cardington Beds 32 D3
Cardington Shrops 39 F6
Cardinham Cornw'l 4 D2
Cardonald Glasg C 75 A7
Cardow Moray 97 B9
Cardrona Scot Borders 77 D6
Cardross Arg/Bute 82 G4
Cardurnock Cumb 68 E4
Careby Lincs 42 D3
Careston Angus 91 F6
Carew Pembs 24 F5
Carew Cheriton Pembs 24 F5
Carew Newton Pembs 24 F5
Carey Heref'd 29 E6
Carfrae E Loth 85 H7
Cargenbridge Dumf/Gal 68 C2
Cargill Perth/Kinr 90 H2
Cargo Cumb 69 E6
Cargreen Cornw'l 4 D5
Carham Northum 78 D3
Carhampton Som'set 16 G5
Carharrack Cornw'l 3 E6
Carie Perth/Kinr 89 H7
Carie Perth/Kinr 89 F7
Carines Cornw'l 3 D6
Carisbrooke I/Wight 11 F7
Carisbrooke Castle I/Wight 11 F7
Cark Cumb 61 G6
Carlabhagh W Isles 108 C7
Carland Cross Cornw'l 3 D7
Carlby Lincs 42 D3
Carlecotes S Yorks 50 B3
Carlesmoor N Yorks 63 G6
Carleton Cumb 61 B8
Carleton Cumb 69 E7
Carleton Lancs 55 E3
Carleton N Yorks 56 D4
Carleton Forehoe Norfolk 44 E4
Carleton Rode Norfolk 44 F5
Carlin How Redcar/Clevel'd 64 C5
Carlingcott Bath/NE Som'set 18 F3
Carlisle Cumb 69 E7
Carlisle Cathedral Cumb 69 E6
Carlisle Racecourse Cumb 69 E6
Carlops Scot Borders 76 B4
Carlton Beds 32 C2
Carlton Cambs 33 C9
Carlton Leics 40 E5
Carlton Notts 41 A8
Carlton N Yorks 64 F4
Carlton N Yorks 58 F2
Carlton N Yorks 62 F5
Carlton N Yorks 63 C6
Carlton Stockton 63 B8
Carlton Suffolk 35 B7
Carlton S Yorks 57 G8
Carlton W Yorks 57 F8
Carlton Colville Suffolk 45 G9
Carlton Curlieu Leics 41 F8
Carlton Husthwaite N Yorks 63 G9
Carlton in Cleveland N Yorks 64 D3
Carlton in Lindrick Notts 51 D7
Carlton le Moorland Lincs 52 G2
Carlton Miniott N Yorks 63 F8
Carlton on Trent Notts 51 F9
Carlton Scroop Lincs 42 A2
Carluke S Lanarks 75 B10
Carmarthen Carms 25 D9
Carmel Angl 46 D3
Carmel Carms 26 G5
Carmel Flints 48 E2
Carmel Guernsey 4
Carmel Gwyn 46 G4
Carmont Aberds 91 C9
Carmunnock Glasg C 75 B8
Carmyle Glasg C 75 A8
Carmyllie Angus 91 G6
Carn gorm H'land 95 D6
Carnaby ER Yorks 59 B7
Carnach H'land 101 C8
Carnach H'land 95 D7
Carnach W Isles 109 H7
Carnachy H'land 106 D2
Carnbee Fife 85 D7
Carnbo Perth/Kinr 84 D2
Carnbrea Cornw'l 2 E5
Carnduff S Lanarks 75 C8
Carnduncan Arg/Bute 80 H2
Carne Cornw'l 3 F8
Carnforth Lancs 61 G7
Carnhedryn Pembs 24 D3
Carnhell Green Cornw'l 2 F5
Carnkie Cornw'l 3 F6
Carnkie Cornw'l 2 F5
Carno Powys 37 F9
Carnoch H'land 96 C1
Carnoch H'land 101 G10
Carnock Fife 84 F2
Carnon Downs Cornw'l 3 E6
Carnousie Aberds 99 C6
Carnoustie Angus 85 A7
Carnwath S Lanarks 76 C2
Carnyorth Cornw'l 2 F2
Carperby N Yorks 62 F5
Carpley Green N Yorks 62 F4
Carr S Yorks 51 C7
Carr Hill Tyne/Wear 71 D7
Carradale Arg/Bute 73 D8
Carragraich W Isles 109 H6
Carrbridge H'land 97 D7
Carrefour Selous Jersey 4
Carreg wen Pembs 25 B7
Carreglefn Angl 46 D3
Carrick Arg/Bute 81 F9
Carrick Fife 84 B6
Carrick Castle Arg/Bute 82 E2
Carrick Ho. Orkney 110 E6
Carriden Falk 84 F2
Carrington Gtr Man 49 C8
Carrington Lincs 53 G6
Carrington Midloth 77 A6
Carrog Conwy 47 H7
Carrog Denbs 38 A2
Carron Falk 83 F9
Carron Moray 98 D2
Carron Bridge N Lanarks 83 F8
Carronbridge Dumf/Gal 76 H1
Carrshield Northum 70 F3
Carrutherstown Dumf/Gal 68 C4
Carrville Durham 71 F8
Carsaig Arg/Bute 80 B5
Carscreugh Dumf/Gal 66 E4
Carse Gray Angus 90 F5
Carse Ho. Arg/Bute 73 A7
Carsegown Dumf/Gal 67 E6
Carseriggan Dumf/Gal 66 D5
Carsethorn Dumf/Gal 68 E2
Carshalton London 22 E2
Carsington Derby 50 G4
Carskiey Arg/Bute 73 G6
Carsluith Dumf/Gal 67 E6
Carsphairn Dumf/Gal 67 A7
Carstairs S Lanarks 76 C2
Carstairs Junction S Lanarks 76 C2
Carswell Marsh Oxon 19 B10
Carter's Clay Hants 11 B6
Carterton Oxon 30 H4
Carterway Heads Northum 70 E5
Carthew Cornw'l 3 D9
Carthorpe N Yorks 63 F8
Cartington Northum 78 G5
Cartland S Lanarks 76 C1
Cartmel Cumb 61 G6
Cartmel Fell Cumb 61 F7
Carway Carms 25 F9
Cary Fitzpaine Som'set 9 B7
Cascob Powys 28 B3
Cashlie Perth/Kinr 88 G5
Cashmere Visitor Centre, Elgin Moray 98 B2
Cashmoor Dorset 10 C2
Cassey Compton Glos 30 G2
Cassington Oxon 31 G6
Cassop Durham 71 G8
Castell Denbs 48 F2
Castell Coch Card 17 C6
Castell Howell Ceredig'n 25 B9
Castell y bwch Torf 17 B7
Castellau Rh Cyn Taff 16 C5
Casterton Cumb 61 G9
Castle Acre Norfolk 44 D2
Castle Ashby Northants 32 C1
Castle Bolton N Yorks 62 E5
Castle Bromwich W Midlands 40 G3
Castle Bytham Lincs 42 D2
Castle Caereinion Powys 38 E2
Castle Camps Cambs 33 D9
Castle Carrock Cumb 69 E8
Castle Cary Som'set 9 A8
Castle Combe Wilts 18 D5
Castle Craig Scot Borders 76 C4
Castle Donington Leics 41 C6
Castle Douglas Dumf/Gal 67 D9
Castle Drogo, Exeter Devon 7 G8
Castle Eaton Swindon 19 B8
Castle Eden Durham 71 G9
Castle Forbes Aberds 98 G6
Castle Frome Heref'd 29 D7
Castle Green Surrey 21 E7
Castle Gresley Derby 40 D4
Castle Heaton Northum 78 C4
Castle Hedingham Essex 34 E1
Castle Hill Kent 14 D1
Castle Howard, Malton N Yorks 64 G5
Castle Huntly Perth/Kinr 84 B5
Castle Kennedy Dumf/Gal 66 E3
Castle Museum C/York 58 C2
Castle O'er Dumf/Gal 68 A5
Castle Pulverbatch Shrops 38 E5
Castle Rising Norfolk 43 C9
Castle Stuart H'land 96 B5
Castlebythe Pembs 24 D5
Castlecary N Lanarks 83 G8
Castlecraig H'land 103 F7
Castlefairn Dumf/Gal 67 B9
Castleford W Yorks 57 F9
Castlehill Scot Borders 76 D5
Castlehill H'land 107 C6
Castlehill W Dunb 82 G4
Castlemaddy Dumf/Gal 67 B7
Castlemartin Pembs 24 G4
Castlemilk Dumf/Gal 68 C4
Castlemilk Glasg C 75 B8
Castlemorris Pembs 24 C4
Castlemorton Worcs 29 E8
Castleside Durham 70 F5
Castlethorpe M/Keynes 31 D10
Castleton Angus 90 G4
Castleton Arg/Bute 81 F8
Castleton Derby 50 D3
Castleton Gtr Man 56 G3
Castleton Newp 17 C7
Castleton N Yorks 64 D4
Castletown Ches 48 G5
Castletown H'land 107 C6
Castletown H'land 96 B5
Castletown I/Man 54 F2
Castletown Tyne/Wear 71 E8
Castleweary Scot Borders 77 G7
Castley N Yorks 57 D7
Caston Norfolk 44 F3
Castor Peterbro 42 F4
Catacol N Ayrs 73 C9
Catbrain S Gloucs 18 C2
Catbrook Monmouths 18 A2
Catchall Cornw'l 2 G3
Catchems Corner W Midlands 40 H4
Catchgate Durham 71 E6
Catcleugh Northum 78 G2
Catcliffe S Yorks 51 D6
Catcott Som'set 17 H8
Caterham Surrey 22 F3
Catfield Norfolk 45 C7
Catfirth Shetl'd 111 H7
Catford London 22 D3
Catforth Lancs 55 E4
Cathays Card 17 D6
Cathcart Glasg C 75 A7
Cathedine Powys 28 F2
Catherington Hants 11 C9
Catherton Shrops 39 H7
Catlodge H'land 89 B7
Catlowdy Cumb 69 C7
Catmore W Berks 20 C2
Caton Lancs 55 B5
Caton Green Lancs 55 B5
Catrine E Ayrs 75 E7
Cat's Ash Newp 17 B8
Catsfield E Sussex 14 G2
Catshill Worcs 30 A1
Cattal N Yorks 57 C9
Cattawade Suffolk 34 E5
Catterall Lancs 55 D4
Catterick N Yorks 63 E7
Catterick Bridge N Yorks 63 E7
Catterick Garrison N Yorks 63 E6
Catterick Racecourse N Yorks 63 E7
Catterlen Cumb 69 G7
Catterline Aberds 91 D9
Catterton N Yorks 57 D10
Catthorpe Leics 41 H7
Cattistock Dorset 9 E7
Catton Northum 70 E3
Catton N Yorks 63 G8
Catwick ER Yorks 59 D7
Catworth Cambs 32 A3
Caudlesprings Norfolk 44 E3
Caudwell's Mill, Matlock Derby 50 F4
Caulcott Oxon 31 F7
Cauldcots Angus 91 G7
Cauldhame Stirl 83 E7
Cauldmill Scot Borders 77 F8
Cauldon Staffs 50 H2
Caulkerbush Dumf/Gal 68 E2
Caulside Dumf/Gal 69 B7
Caunsall Worcs 39 G9
Caunton Notts 51 G9
Causeway End Dumf/Gal 67 D6
Causeway Foot W Yorks 56 E5
Causeway head Stirl 83 E8
Causewayend S Lanarks 76 D3
Causewayhead Cumb 68 E4
Causey Park Bridge Northum 71 A6
Causeyend Aberds 99 G9
Cautley Cumb 61 E9
Cavendish Suffolk 34 D2
Cavendish Bridge Leics 41 C6
Cavenham Suffolk 34 B1
Caversfield Oxon 31 F7
Caversham Reading 20 D5
Caverswall Staffs 40 A1
Cavil ER Yorks 58 E3
Cawdor H'land 103 G7
Cawdor Castle and Gardens H'land 97 B6
Cawkwell Lincs 52 E5
Cawood N Yorks 58 E1
Cawsand Cornw'l 4 E5
Cawston Norfolk 44 C5
Cawthorne S Yorks 50 B4
Cawthorpe Lincs 42 C3
Cawton N Yorks 64 G4
Caxton Cambs 33 C6
Caynham Shrops 29 A6
Caythorpe Lincs 52 H2
Caythorpe Notts 51 H8
Cayton N Yorks 65 F8
Ceann a Bhaigh W Isles 109 L2
Ceann Loch Shiphoirt W Isles 108 F7
Ceannacroc Lodge H'land 95 E9
Cearsiadar W Isles 108 E8
Cefn Berain Conwy 47 F9
Cefn brith Conwy 47 G9
Cefn Canol Powys 38 B3
Cefn coch Conwy 47 F8
Cefn Coch Powys 38 C2
Cefn coed y cymmer Merth Tyd 27 H10
Cefn Cribbwr Bridg 16 C3
Cefn Cross Bridg 16 C3
Cefn ddwysarn Gwyn 37 B9
Cefn Einion Shrops 38 G3
Cefn gorwydd Powys 27 D9
Cefn mawr Wrex 38 A3
Cefn y bedd Flints 48 G4
Cefn y pant Carms 25 D6
Cefneithin Carms 26 G5
Cei bach Ceredig'n 26 C4
Ceint Angl 46 E4
Cellan Ceredig'n 27 D6
Cellarhead Staffs 50 H1
Cemaes Angl 46 C3
Cemmaes Powys 37 E8
Cemmaes Road Powys 37 E8
Cenarth Carms 25 B7
Cenin Gwyn 46 H4
Central Invercl 82 G3
Ceos W Isles 108 E8
Ceres Fife 84 C6
Cerne Abbas Dorset 9 D8
Cerney Wick Glos 19 B7
Cerrigceinwen Angl 46 E4
Cerrigydrudion Conwy 47 H9
Cessford Scot Borders 78 E2
Ceunant Gwyn 46 F5
Chaceley Glos 29 E9
Chacewater Cornw'l 3 E6
Chackmore Bucks 31 E8
Chacombe Northants 31 D6
Chad Valley W Midlands 40 G2
Chadderton Gtr Man 49 B10
Chadderton Fold Gtr Man 49 B9
Chaddesden Derby C 40 B5
Chaddesley Corbett Worcs 29 A9
Chaddleworth W Berks 20 D2
Chadlington Oxon 30 F5
Chadshunt Warwick 30 C5
Chadwell Leics 41 C9
Chadwell St. Mary Thurr'k 23 D6
Chadwick End W Midlands 30 A4
Chadwick Green Mersey 49 C6
Chaffcombe Som'set 8 C5
Chagford Devon 5 B8
Chailey E Sussex 13 D7
Chain Bridge Lincs 43 A6
Chainbridge Cambs 43 E7
Chainhurst Kent 14 D2
Chalbury Dorset 10 D3
Chalbury Common Dorset 10 D3
Chaldon Surrey 22 F3
Chaldon Herring or Dorset 9 F9
Chale I/Wight 11 G7
Chale Green I/Wight 11 G7
Chalfont Common Bucks 21 B8
Chalfont St. Giles Bucks 21 B7
Chalfont St. Peter Bucks 21 B8
Chalford Glos 18 A5
Chalgrove Oxon 20 B4
Chalk Kent 23 D6
Challacombe Devon 7 B7
Challoch Dumf/Gal 66 D5
Challock Lees Kent 14 C5
Chalton Beds 32 F3
Chalton Hants 11 C10
Chalvington E Sussex 13 E9
Champany Falk 84 G2
Chancery Ceredig'n 36 H5
Chandler's Ford Hants 11 B7
Channerwick Shetl'd 111 L7
Chantry Som'set 18 G4
Chantry Suffolk 34 D5
Chapel Fife 84 E4
Chapel Allerton Som'set 17 F9
Chapel Allerton W Yorks 57 E8
Chapel Amble Cornw'l 3 B8
Chapel Brampton Northants 31 B9
Chapel Chorlton Staffs 39 B9
Chapel en le Frith Derby 50 D2
Chapel End Warwick 40 F5
Chapel Green Warwick 40 G4
Chapel Green Warwick 31 B6
Chapel Haddlesey N Yorks 58 F1
Chapel Head Cambs 43 G6
Chapel Hill Aberds 99 E10
Chapel Hill Lincs 52 G5
Chapel Hill Monmouths 18 B2
Chapel Hill N Yorks 57 D8
Chapel Lawn Shrops 38 H4
Chapel le Dale N Yorks 62 G2
Chapel Milton Derby 50 D2
Chapel of Garioch Aberds 99 F7
Chapel Row W Berks 20 E3
Chapel St. Leonards Lincs 53 E8
Chapel Stile Cumb 61 D6
Chapelgate Lincs 43 C7
Chapelhall N Lanarks 75 A9
Chapelhill Dumf/Gal 68 A3
Chapelhill H'land 103 E7
Chapelhill N Ayrs 74 C4
Chapelhill Perth/Kinr 84 B4
Chapelhill Perth/Kinr 84 A2
Chapelknowe Dumf/Gal 69 C6
Chapelton Angus 91 G7
Chapelton Devon 7 D6
Chapelton H'land 97 E7
Chapelton S Lanarks 75 C8
Chapeltown Blackb'n 56 G2
Chapeltown Moray 98 F2
Chapeltown S Yorks 50 C5
Chapmans Well Devon 6 G4
Chapmanslade Wilts 18 G5
Chapmore End Herts 33 G6
Chappel Essex 34 F2
Chard Som'set 8 D5
Chardstock Devon 8 D5
Charfield S Gloucs 18 B4
Charford Worcs 30 B1
Charing Kent 14 D4
Charing Cross Dorset 10 C4
Charing Heath Kent 14 D4
Charingworth Glos 30 E4
Charlbury Oxon 30 G5
Charlcombe Bath/NE Som'set 18 E4
Charlecote Warwick 30 C4
Charlecote Park, Wellesbourne Warwick 30 C4
Charles Devon 7 C7
Charles Manning's Amusement Park, Felixstowe Suffolk 35 E6
Charles Tye Suffolk 34 C4
Charlesfield Dumf/Gal 68 D4
Charleston Angus 90 G4
Charleston Renf 75 A6
Charlestown Aberd C 91 A10
Charlestown Cornw'l 3 D9
Charlestown Derby 50 C2
Charlestown Dorset 9 G8
Charlestown Fife 84 F2
Charlestown Gtr Man 49 B9
Charlestown H'land 96 B4
Charlestown H'land 101 E6
Charlestown W Yorks 56 F4
Charlestown of Aberlour Moray 98 D2
Charlesworth Derby 50 C2
Charleton Devon 5 F8
Charlton London 22 D4
Charlton Hants 20 G1
Charlton Herts 32 F4
Charlton Northants 31 E7
Charlton Northum 70 B3
Charlton Som'set 18 F3
Charlton Telford 39 D6
Charlton Wilts 10 B2
Charlton Wilts 19 F8
Charlton Wilts 19 C6
Charlton Worcs 30 D2
Charlton W Sussex 12 D2
Charlton Abbots Glos 30 F2
Charlton Adam Som'set 9 B7
Charlton All Saints Wilts 10 B4
Charlton Horethorne Som'set 9 B8
Charlton Kings Glos 30 F1
Charlton Mackerell Som'set 9 B7
Charlton Marshall Dorset 10 D1
Charlton Musgrove Som'set 9 B9
Charlton on Otmoor Oxon 31 G7
Charltons Redcar/Clevel'd 64 C4
Charlwood Surrey 22 G2
Charlynch Som'set 17 H7
Charminster Dorset 9 E8
Charmouth Dorset 8 E5
Charndon Bucks 31 F8
Charney Bassett Oxon 20 B1
Charnock Richard Lancs 55 G5
Charsfield Suffolk 35 C6
Chart Corner Kent 14 C2
Chart Sutton Kent 14 D3
Charter Alley Hants 20 F3
Charterhouse Som'set 17 F9
Charterville Allotments Oxon 30 G5
Chartham Kent 15 C6
Chartham Hatch Kent 15 C6
Chartridge Bucks 21 A7
Chartwell, Westerham Kent 22 F4
Charvil Wokingham 20 D5
Charwelton Northants 31 C7
Chasetown Staffs 40 E2
Chastleton Oxon 30 F4
Chasty Devon 6 F4
Chatburn Lancs 56 D2
Chatcull Staffs 39 B8
Chatham Medway 14 B2
Chathill Northum 79 E6
Chatsworth, Bakewell Derby 50 E4
Chattenden Medway 23 D7
Chatteris Cambs 43 G6
Chattisham Suffolk 34 D4
Chatto Scot Borders 78 F2
Chatton Northum 78 E5
Chawleigh Devon 7 E8
Chawley Oxon 20 A2
Chawston Beds 32 C4
Chawton Hants 20 H5
Cheadle Gtr Man 49 D9
Cheadle Staffs 40 A2
Cheadle Heath Gtr Man 49 D9
Cheadle Hulme Gtr Man 49 D9
Cheam London 22 E2
Cheapside Surrey 21 F8
Chearsley Bucks 31 G9
Chebsey Staffs 39 C9
Checkendon Oxon 20 C4
Checkley Ches 49 H8
Checkley Heref'd 29 E6
Checkley Staffs 40 B2
Chedburgh Suffolk 34 C1
Cheddar Som'set 17 F9
Cheddar Showcaves and Gorge Som'set 17 F9
Cheddington Bucks 32 G2
Cheddleton Staffs 50 G1
Cheddon Fitzpaine Som'set 8 B4
Chedglow Wilts 19 B6
Chedgrave Norfolk 45 F7
Chedington Dorset 9 D6
Chediston Suffolk 45 H7
Chedworth Glos 30 G2
Chedworth Roman Villa Glos 30 G2
Chedzoy Som'set 17 H8
Cheeklaw Scot Borders 78 B2
Cheeseman's Green Kent 14 E5
Cheglinch Devon 7 B6
Cheldon Devon 7 E8
Chelford Ches 49 E9
Chell Heath Stoke 49 G9
Chellaston Derby C 40 B5
Chellington Beds 32 C2
Chelmarsh Shrops 39 G8
Chelmer Village Essex 33 H10
Chelmondiston Suffolk 35 E6
Chelmorton Derby 50 F3
Chelmsford Essex 33 H10
Chelsea London 22 D2
Chelsfield London 22 E4
Chelsworth Suffolk 34 D3
Cheltenham Glos 29 F10
Cheltenham Racecourse Glos 30 F1
Chelveston Northants 32 B2
Chelvey N Som'set 17 E9
Chelwood Bath/NE Som'set 18 E3
Chelwood Common E Sussex 13 C8
Chelwood Gate E Sussex 13 C8
Chelworth Wilts 19 B6
Chelworth Green Wilts 19 B7
Chemistry Shrops 39 A6
Chenies Bucks 21 B8
Cheny Longville Shrops 38 G5
Chepstow Monmouths 18 B2
Chepstow Racecourse Monmouths 17 B10
Chequerfield W Yorks 57 F9
Cherhill Wilts 19 D7
Cherington Glos 19 B6
Cherington Warwick 30 E4
Cheriton Devon 7 B8
Cheriton Hants 11 B8
Cheriton Kent 15 E6
Cheriton Swan 25 G9
Cheriton Bishop Devon 7 G8
Cheriton Fitzpaine Devon 7 F9
Cheriton or Stackpole Elidor Pembs 24 G4
Cherrington Telford 39 C7
Cherry Burton ER Yorks 58 D5
Cherry Hinton Cambs 33 C7
Cherry Orchard Worcs 29 C9
Cherry Willingham Lincs 52 E3
Cherrybank Perth/Kinr 84 B3
Chertsey Surrey 21 E8
Cheselbourne Dorset 9 E9
Chesham Bucks 21 A7
Chesham Bois Bucks 21 B7
Cheshire Candle Workshops, Burwardsley Ches 49 G6
Cheshunt Herts 22 A3
Cheslyn Hay Staffs 40 E1
Chessington London 21 E9
Chessington World of Adventures London 21 E9
Chester Ches 48 F5
Chester Cathedral Ches 48 F4
Chester Le Street Durham 71 E7
Chester Moor Durham 71 F7
Chester Racecourse Ches 48 F4
Chester Zoo Ches 48 E5
Chesterblade Som'set 18 G3
Chesterfield Derby 50 E5
Chesters Scot Borders 77 F9
Chesters Scot Borders 77 E9
Chesters Roman Fort Northum 70 C4
Chesterton Cambs 42 F4
Chesterton Cambs 33 B7
Chesterton Glos 19 A7
Chesterton Oxon 31 F7
Chesterton Shrops 39 F8
Chesterton Staffs 49 H9
Chesterton Warwick 30 C5
Chesterwood Northum 70 D3
Chestfield Kent 15 B6
Cheston Devon 5 E7
Cheswardine Shrops 39 C8
Cheswick Northum 78 C5
Chetnole Dorset 9 D8
Chettiscombe Devon 8 C1
Chettisham Cambs 43 G8
Chettle Dorset 10 C2
Chetton Shrops 39 F7
Chetwode Bucks 31 F8
Chetwynd Aston Telford 39 D8
Cheveley Cambs 33 B9
Chevening Kent 22 F4
Chevington Suffolk 34 C1
Chevithorne Devon 8 C1
Chew Magna Bath/NE Som'set 18 E2
Chew Stoke Bath/NE Som'set 18 E2
Chewton Keynsham Bath/NE Som'set 18 E3
Chewton Mendip Som'set 18 F2
Chicheley M/Keynes 32 D2
Chichester W Sussex 12 E2
Chichester Cathedral W Sussex 12 E2
Chickerell Dorset 9 F8
Chicklade Wilts 10 A2
Chicksgrove Wilts 10 A2
Chidden Hants 11 C9
Chiddingfold Surrey 12 B3
Chiddingly E Sussex 13 D9
Chiddingstone Kent 22 G4
Chiddingstone Causeway Kent 22 G5
Chiddingstone Hoath Kent 22 G4
Chideock Dorset 9 E6
Chidham W Sussex 12 E1
Chidswell W Yorks 57 F7
Chieveley W Berks 20 D2
Chignall Smealy Essex 33 G9
Chignall St. James Essex 33 H9
Chigwell Essex 22 B4
Chigwell Row Essex 22 B4
Chilbolton Hants 20 H1
Chilcomb Hants 11 B8
Chilcombe Dorset 9 E7
Chilcompton Som'set 18 F3
Chilcote Leics 40 D4
Child Okeford Dorset 9 C10
Childer Thornton Ches 48 E4
Childrey Oxon 20 C1
Child's Ercall Shrops 39 C7
Childswickham Worcs 30 E2
Childwall Mersey 48 D5
Childwick Green Herts 32 G4
Chilfrome Dorset 9 E7
Chilgrove W Sussex 12 D2
Chilham Kent 14 C5
Chilhampton Wilts 10 A3
Chilla Devon 6 F5
Chillaton Devon 4 B5
Chillenden Kent 15 C7
Chillerton I/Wight 11 F7
Chillesford Suffolk 35 C7
Chillingham Northum 78 E5
Chillington Devon 5 F8
Chillington Som'set 8 C5
Chilmark Wilts 10 A2
Chilson Oxon 30 G5
Chilsworthy Cornw'l 4 C5
Chilsworthy Devon 6 F4
Chilthorne Domer Som'set 9 C7
Chiltington E Sussex 13 D7
Chilton Bucks 31 G8
Chilton Durham 63 B7
Chilton Oxon 20 C2
Chilton Cantelo Som'set 9 B7
Chilton Foliat Wilts 19 D10
Chilton Lane Durham 71 G8
Chilton Polden Som'set 17 H8
Chilton Street Suffolk 34 D1
Chilton Trinity Som'set 17 H7
Chilvers Coton Warwick 40 F5
Chilwell Notts 41 B7
Chilworth Hants 11 C7
Chilworth Surrey 21 G8
Chimney Oxon 20 A1
Chineham Hants 20 F4
Chingford London 22 B3
Chinley Derby 50 D2
Chinley Head Derby 50 D2
Chinnor Oxon 20 A5
Chipnall Shrops 39 B8
Chippenhall Green Suffolk 45 H6
Chippenham Cambs 33 B9
Chippenham Wilts 19 D6
Chipperfield Herts 21 A8
Chipping Herts 33 E6
Chipping Lancs 55 D6
Chipping Campden Glos 30 E3
Chipping Hill Essex 34 G2
Chipping Norton Oxon 30 F5
Chipping Ongar Essex 22 A5
Chipping Sodbury S Gloucs 18 C4
Chipping Warden Northants 31 D6
Chipstable Som'set 8 B2
Chipstead Kent 22 F4
Chipstead Surrey 22 F2
Chirbury Shrops 38 F3
Chirk Wrex 38 B3
Chirk Bank Shrops 38 B3
Chirk Castle Wrex 38 B3
Chirmorie S Ayrs 66 C4
Chirnside Scot Borders 78 B3
Chirnsidebridge Scot Borders 78 B3
Chirton Wilts 19 F7
Chisbury Wilts 19 E9
Chiselborough Som'set 9 C6
Chiseldon Swindon 19 D8
Chiserley W Yorks 56 F5
Chislehampton Oxon 20 B3
Chislehurst London 22 D4
Chislet Kent 15 B7
Chiswell Green Herts 21 A9
Chiswick London 22 D2
Chiswick End Cambs 33 D6
Chisworth Derby 50 C1
Chithurst W Sussex 12 C2
Chittering Cambs 33 A7
Chitterne Wilts 19 G6
Chittlehamholt Devon 7 D7
Chittlehampton Devon 7 D7
Chittoe Wilts 19 E6
Chivenor Devon 7 C6
Chobham Surrey 21 E7
Choicelee Scot Borders 78 B2
Cholderton Wilts 19 G9
Cholesbury Bucks 32 H2
Chollerford Northum 70 C4
Chollerton Northum 70 C4
Cholmondeston Ches 49 F7
Cholsey Oxon 20 C3

Cholstrey Heref'd 28 C5
Chop Gate N Yorks 64 E3
Choppington Northum 71 B7
Chopwell Tyne/Wear 71 E6
Chorley Ches 49 G6
Chorley Lancs 55 G5
Chorley Shrops 39 G7
Chorley Staffs 40 D2
Chorleywood Herts 21 B8
Chorlton cum Hardy Gtr Man 49 C9
Chorlton Lane Ches 48 H5
Choulton Shrops 38 G4
Chowdene Tyne/Wear 71 E7
Chowley Ches 48 G5
Chrishall Essex 33 E7
Christ Church Oxford Oxon 31 H7
Christchurch Cambs 43 F7
Christchurch Dorset 10 E4
Christchurch Glos 29 G6
Christchurch Newp 17 C8
Christchurch Priory Dorset 10 E4
Christian Malford Wilts 19 D6
Christleton Ches 48 F5
Christmas Common Oxon 20 B5
Christon N Som'set 17 F8
Christon Bank Northum 79 E7
Christow Devon 5 B9
Chryston N Lanarks 83 G7
Chudleigh Devon 5 C9
Chudleigh Knighton Devon 5 C9
Chulmleigh Devon 7 E7
Chunal Derby 50 C2
Church Lancs 56 F2
Church Aston Telford 39 D8
Church Brampton Northants 31 B9
Church Broughton Derby 40 B4
Church Crookham Hants 21 F6
Church Eaton Staffs 39 D9
Church End Beds 32 F2
Church End Beds 32 E4
Church End Beds 32 E2
Church End Cambs 42 G5
Church End Cambs 43 E6
Church End ER Yorks 59 C6
Church End Essex 33 D8
Church End Essex 33 F10
Church End Hants 20 F4
Church End Lincs 42 B5
Church End Warwick 40 F4
Church End Warwick 40 F4
Church End Wilts 19 D7
Church Enstone Oxon 30 F5
Church Fenton N Yorks 57 E10
Church Green Devon 8 E3
Church Green Norfolk 44 F4
Church Gresley Derby 40 D4
Church Hanborough Oxon 31 G6
Church Hill Ches 49 F7
Church Houses N Yorks 64 E4
Church Knowle Dorset 10 F2
Church Laneham Notts 51 E10
Church Langton Leics 41 F9
Church Lawford Warwick 41 H6
Church Lawton Ches 49 G9
Church Leigh Staffs 40 B2
Church Lench Worcs 30 C2
Church Mayfield Staffs 40 A3
Church Minshull Ches 49 F7
Church Norton W Sussex 12 F2
Church Preen Shrops 39 F6
Church Pulverbatch Shrops 38 E5
Church Stoke Powys 38 F3
Church Stowe Northants 31 C8
Church Street Kent 23 D7
Church Stretton Shrops 38 F5
Church Town N Lincs 51 B9
Church Town Surrey 22 F3
Church Village Rh Cyn Taff 16 C5
Church Warsop Notts 51 F7
Churcham Glos 29 G8
Churchbank Shrops 38 H3
Churchbridge Staffs 40 E1
Churchdown Glos 29 G9
Churchend Essex 33 F9
Churchend Essex 23 B10
Churchend S Gloucs 18 B4
Churchfield W Midlands 40 F2
Churchgate Street Essex 33 G7
Churchill Devon 7 B6
Churchill Devon 8 D5
Churchill N Som'set 17 F9
Churchill Oxon 30 F4
Churchill Worcs 39 H9
Churchill Worcs 29 C10
Churchinford Som'set 8 C4
Churchover Warwick 41 G7
Churchstanton Som'set 8 C3
Churchstow Devon 5 F8
Churchtown Derby 50 F4
Churchtown I/Man 54 C4
Churchtown Lancs 55 D4
Churchtown Mersey 55 G3
Churnsike Lodge Northum 69 C9
Churston Ferrers Torbay 5 E10
Churt Surrey 12 B2
Churton Ches 48 G5
Churwell W Yorks 57 F7
Chute Standen Wilts 19 F10
Chwilog Gwyn 36 B4
Chyandour Cornw'l 2 F3
Cilan Uchaf Gwyn 36 C2
Cilcain Flints 48 F2
Cilcennin Ceredig'n 26 B5
Cilfor Gwyn 37 B6
Cilfrew Neath P Talb 16 A2
Cilfynydd Rh Cyn Taff 16 B5
Cilgerran Pembs 25 B6
Cilgwyn Carms 27 F7
Cilgwyn Gwyn 46 G4
Cilgwyn Pembs 24 C5
Ciliau Aeron Ceredig'n 26 C4
Cill Donnain W Isles 92 C3
Cille Bhrighde W Isles 92 D3
Cille Pheadair W Isles 92 D3
Cilmery Powys 27 C10
Cilsan Carms 26 F5
Ciltalgarth Gwyn 37 A8
Cilwendeg Pembs 25 C7
Cilybebyll Neath P Talb 16 A2
Cilycwm Carms 27 E7
Cimla Neath P Talb 16 B2
Cinderford Glos 29 G7
Cippyn Pembs 24 B6
Cirbhig W Isles 108 C6
Circebost W Isles 108 D6
Cirencester Glos 19 A7
City Powys 38 G3
City Dulas Angl 46 D4
City of London London 22 C3
Clachaig Arg/Bute 82 F2
Clachan Arg/Bute 73 B7
Clachan Arg/Bute 81 C7
Clachan Arg/Bute 87 G8
Clachan Arg/Bute 82 C2
Clachan H'land 94 C2
Clachan W Isles 109 N2
Clachan na Luib W Isles 109 L3
Clachan of Campsie E Dunb 83 G7
Clachan of Glendaruel Arg/Bute 81 F9
Clachan Seil Arg/Bute 81 C7
Clachaneasy Dumf/Gal 66 C5
Clachanmore Dumf/Gal 66 F2
Clachbreck Arg/Bute 81 G7
Clachnabrain Angus 90 E4
Clachtoll H'land 104 G3
Clackmannan Clack 83 E10
Clacton on Sea Essex 34 G5
Cladach Chireboist W Isles 109 L2
Claddach knockline W Isles 109 L2
Cladich Arg/Bute 82 B1
Claggan H'land 87 G6
Claggan H'land 88 D2
Claigan H'land 109 M7
Claines Worcs 29 C9
Clandown Bath/NE Som'set 18 F3
Clanfield Hants 11 C9
Clanfield Oxon 19 A9
Clanville Hants 19 G10
Claonaig Arg/Bute 73 B8
Claonel H'land 102 B4
Clap Hill Kent 14 E5
Clapgate Dorset 10 D3
Clapgate Herts 33 F7
Clapham Beds 32 C3
Clapham London 22 D2
Clapham N Yorks 56 B2
Clapham W Sussex 12 E4
Clappers Scot Borders 78 B4
Clappersgate Cumb 61 D6
Clapton Som'set 9 D6
Clapton in Gordano N Som'set 17 D9
Clapton on the Hill Glos 30 G3
Clapworthy Devon 7 D7
Clara Vale Tyne/Wear 71 D6
Clarach Ceredig'n 37 G6
Clarbeston Pembs 24 D5
Clarbeston Road Pembs 24 D5
Clarborough Notts 51 D9
Clardon H'land 107 C6
Clare Suffolk 34 D1
Clarebrand Dumf/Gal 67 D9
Claremont Landscape Garden, Esher Surrey 21 E9
Clarencefield Dumf/Gal 68 D3
Clarilaw Scot Borders 77 F8
Clark's Green Surrey 12 B5
Clarkston E Renf 75 B7
Clashandorran H'land 96 B3
Clashcoig H'land 102 C5
Clashindarroch Aberds 98 E4
Clashmore H'land 104 F3
Clashmore H'land 102 D6
Clashnessie H'land 104 F3
Clashnoir Moray 98 F2
Clathy Perth/Kinr 84 C1
Clatt Aberds 98 F5
Clatter Powys 37 F9
Clatterford I/Wight 11 F7
Clatterin Bridge Aberds 91 D7
Clatworthy Som'set 8 A2
Claughton Lancs 55 D5
Claughton Lancs 55 B5
Claughton Mersey 48 D4
Claverdon Warwick 30 B3
Claverham N Som'set 17 E9
Clavering Essex 33 E7
Claverley Shrops 39 F8
Claverton Bath/NE Som'set 18 E4
Clawdd newydd Denbs 48 G1
Clawthorpe Cumb 61 G8
Clawton Devon 6 G4
Claxby Lincs 52 C4
Claxby Lincs 53 E7
Claxton Norfolk 45 E7
Claxton N Yorks 58 B2
Clay Common Suffolk 45 G8
Clay Coton Northants 41 H7
Clay Cross Derby 50 F5
Clay Hill W Berks 20 D3
Clay Lake Lincs 42 C5
Claybokie Aberds 90 B1
Claybrooke Magna Leics 41 G6
Claybrooke Parva Leics 41 G6
Claydon Oxon 31 C6
Claydon Suffolk 34 C5
Claygate Dumf/Gal 69 C6
Claygate Kent 14 D2
Claygate Surrey 21 E9
Claygate Cross Kent 23 F6
Clayhanger Devon 8 B2
Clayhanger W Midlands 40 E2
Clayhidon Devon 8 C3
Clayhill E Sussex 14 F3
Clayhill Hants 11 D6
Clayock H'land 107 D6
Claypole Lincs 52 H1
Clayton Staffs 39 A9
Clayton S Yorks 51 B6
Clayton W Sussex 13 D6
Clayton W Yorks 57 E6
Clayton Green Lancs 55 F5
Clayton le Moors Lancs 56 E2
Clayton le Woods Lancs 55 F5
Clayton West W Yorks 57 G7
Clayworth Notts 51 D9
Cleadale H'land 86 C4
Cleadon Tyne/Wear 71 D8
Clearbrook Devon 5 D6
Clearwell Glos 29 H6
Cleasby N Yorks 63 C7
Cleat Orkney 110 K5
Cleatlam Durham 63 C6
Cleator Cumb 60 C3
Cleator Moor Cumb 60 C3
Cleckheaton W Yorks 57 F6
Clee St. Margaret Shrops 39 G6
Cleedownton Shrops 39 G6
Cleehill Shrops 39 H6
Cleethorpes NE Lincs 53 B6
Cleeton St. Mary Shrops 39 H7
Cleeve N Som'set 17 E9
Cleeve Hill Glos 30 F1
Cleeve Prior Worcs 30 D2
Clegymant Powys 37 E9
Clehonger Heref'd 28 E5
Cleish Perth/Kinr 84 E2
Cleit W Isles 92 E2
Cleland N Lanarks 75 B10
Clench Common Wilts 19 E8
Clenchwarton Norfolk 43 C8
Clent Worcs 39 H10
Cleobury Mortimer Shrops 39 H7
Cleobury North Shrops 39 G7
Cleongart Arg/Bute 73 D6
Clephanton H'land 103 G7
Clerklands Scot Borders 77 E8
Clestrain Orkney 110 H4
Clett Shetl'd 111 G8
Cleuch Head Scot Borders 77 F8
Cleughbrae Dumf/Gal 68 C3
Clevancy Wilts 19 D7
Clevedon N Som'set 17 D9
Cleveley Oxon 30 F5
Cleveleys Lancs 55 D3
Cleverton Wilts 19 C6
Clevis Bridg 16 D3
Clewer Som'set 17 F9
Cley next the Sea Norfolk 44 A4
Cliasmol W Isles 108 G5
Cliburn Cumb 61 B8
Click Mill Orkney 110 F4
Cliddesden Hants 20 G4
Cliff End E Sussex 14 G3
Cliffburn Angus 91 G7
Cliffe Medway 23 D7
Cliffe N Yorks 58 E2
Cliffe Woods Medway 23 D7
Clifford Heref'd 28 D3
Clifford W Yorks 57 D9
Clifford Chambers Warwick 30 C3
Clifford's Mesne Glos 29 F8
Cliffsend Kent 15 B8
Clifton Beds 32 E4
Clifton Bristol 18 D2
Clifton Cumb 61 B8
Clifton Derby 40 A3
Clifton Lancs 55 E4
Clifton Nott'ham 41 B7
Clifton Northum 71 B7
Clifton N Yorks 57 D6
Clifton Oxon 31 E6
Clifton Stirl 82 A4
Clifton S Yorks 51 C7
Clifton Worcs 29 D9
Clifton C/York 58 C1
Clifton Campville Staffs 40 D4
Clifton Green Gtr Man 49 B8
Clifton Hampden Oxon 20 B3
Clifton Reynes M/Keynes 32 C2
Clifton upon Dunsmore Warwick 41 H7
Clifton upon Teme Worcs 29 B8
Cliftoncote Scot Borders 78 E3
Cliftonville Kent 15 A8
Climaen gwyn Neath P Talb 27 H7
Climping W Sussex 12 E4
Climpy S Lanarks 76 B2
Clink Som'set 18 G4
Clint N Yorks 57 C7
Clint Green Norfolk 44 D4
Clintmains Scot Borders 77 D9
Cliobh W Isles 108 D5
Clippesby Norfolk 45 D8
Clipsham Rutl'd 42 D2
Clipston Northants 41 G9
Clipstone Notts 51 F7
Clitheroe Lancs 56 D2
Cliuthar W Isles 109 H6
Clive Shrops 39 C6
Clivocast Shetl'd 111 C9
Clixby Lincs 52 B4
Clocaenog Denbs 48 G1
Clochan Moray 98 B4
Clock Face Mersey 49 C6
Clockmill Scot Borders 78 B2
Cloddiau Powys 38 E3
Clodock Heref'd 28 F4
Clola Aberds 99 D10
Clophill Beds 32 E3
Clopton Northants 42 G3
Clopton Suffolk 35 C6
Clopton Corner Suffolk 35 C6
Clopton Green Suffolk 34 C1
Close Clark I/Man 54 E2
Closeburn Dumf/Gal 68 A1
Closworth Som'set 9 C7
Clothall Herts 32 E5
Clotton Ches 49 F6
Clough Foot W Yorks 56 F4
Cloughton N Yorks 65 E8
Cloughton Newlands N Yorks 65 E8
Clousta Shetl'd 111 H6
Clouston Orkney 110 G3
Clova Aberds 98 F4
Clova Angus 90 D4
Clove Lodge Durham 62 C4
Clovelly Devon 6 D4
Clovelly Village Devon 6 D4
Clovenfords Scot Borders 77 D7
Clovenstone Aberds 99 G7
Clovullin H'land 87 E10
Clow Bridge Lancs 56 F3
Clowne Derby 51 E6
Clows Top Worcs 29 A8
Cloy Wrex 38 A4
Cluanie Inn H'land 95 E7
Cluanie Lodge H'land 95 E7
Clun Shrops 38 G4
Clunbury Shrops 38 G4
Clunderwen Carms 24 E6
Clunes H'land 88 C3
Clungunford Shrops 38 H4
Clunie Aberds 98 C6
Clunie Perth/Kinr 90 G2
Clunton Shrops 38 G4
Cluny Fife 84 E4
Cluny Castle H'land 89 B7
Clutton Bath/NE Som'set 18 F3
Clutton Ches 48 G5
Clwt grugoer Conwy 47 F9
Clwt y bont Gwyn 46 F5
Clydach Monmouths 28 G3
Clydach Swan 16 A1
Clydach Vale Rh Cyn Taff 16 B4
Clydebank W Dunb 82 G5
Clydey Pembs 25 C7
Clyffe Pypard Wilts 19 D7
Clynder Arg/Bute 82 F3
Clyne Neath P Talb 16 A3
Clynelish H'land 103 B7
Clynnog fawr Gwyn 46 G4
Clyro Powys 28 D3
Clyst Honiton Devon 8 E1
Clyst Hydon Devon 8 D2
Clyst St. George Devon 8 F1
Clyst St. Lawrence Devon 8 D2
Clyst St. Mary Devon 8 E1
Cnoc W Isles 108 D9
Cnwch coch Ceredig'n 37 H6
Coachford Aberds 98 D4
Coad's Green Cornw'l 4 C3
Coal Aston Derby 50 E5
Coalbrookdale Telford 39 E7
Coalbrookvale Bl Gwent 28 H2
Coalburn S Lanarks 75 D10
Coalburns Tyne/Wear 71 D6
Coalcleugh Northum 70 F3
Coaley Glos 18 A4
Coalhall E Ayrs 75 F6
Coalhill Essex 23 B7
Coalpit Heath S Gloucs 18 C3
Coalport Telford 39 E7
Coalsnaughton Clack 83 E10
Coaltown of Balgonie Fife 84 E4
Coaltown of Wemyss Fife 84 E5
Coalville Leics 41 D6
Coalway Glos 29 G6
Coat Som'set 9 B6
Coatbridge N Lanarks 83 H8
Coatdyke N Lanarks 75 A9
Coate Swindon 19 C8
Coate Wilts 19 E7
Coates Cambs 43 F6
Coates Glos 19 A6
Coates Lancs 56 D3
Coates Notts 51 D10
Coates W Sussex 12 D3
Coatham Redcar/Clevel'd 64 B3
Coatham Mundeville D'lington 63 B7
Coatsgate Dumf/Gal 76 G3
Cobbaton Devon 7 D7
Cobbler's Green Norfolk 45 F6
Coberley Glos 30 G1
Cobham Kent 14 B1
Cobham Surrey 21 E9
Cobholm Island Norfolk 45 E9
Cobleland Stirl 83 E6
Cobnash Heref'd 28 B5
Coburty Aberds 99 B9
Cock Bank Wrex 48 H4
Cock Clarks Essex 23 A8
Cockayne N Yorks 64 E4
Cockayne Hatley Cambs 32 D5
Cockburnspath Scot Borders 85 G9
Cockenzie and Port Seton E Loth 84 G6
Cockerham Lancs 55 C4
Cockermouth Cumb 68 G4
Cockernhoe Green Herts 32 F4
Cockfield Durham 63 B6
Cockfield Suffolk 34 C3
Cockfosters London 22 B2
Cocking W Sussex 12 D2
Cockington Torbay 5 D9
Cocklake Som'set 17 G9
Cockley Beck Cumb 60 D5
Cockley Cley Norfolk 44 E1
Cockshutt Shrops 38 C5
Cockthorpe Norfolk 44 A3
Cockwood Devon 8 F1
Cockyard Heref'd 28 E5
Codda Cornw'l 4 C2
Coddenham Suffolk 34 C5
Coddington Ches 48 G5
Coddington Heref'd 29 D8
Coddington Notts 51 G10
Codford St. Mary Wilts 19 H6
Codford St. Peter Wilts 19 H6
Codicote Herts 32 G5
Codmore Hill W Sussex 12 C4
Codnor Derby 51 H6
Codrington S Gloucs 18 D4
Codsall Staffs 39 E9
Codsall Wood Staffs 39 E9
Coed Mawr Gwyn 46 E5
Coed Morgan Monmouths 28 G4
Coed Talon Flints 48 G3
Coed y bryn Ceredig'n 25 B8
Coed y paen Monmouths 17 B8
Coed yr ynys Powys 28 F2
Coed Ystumgwern Gwyn 36 C5
Coedely Rh Cyn Taff 16 C5
Coedkernew Newp 17 C7
Coedpoeth Wrex 48 G3
Coedway Powys 38 D4
Coelbren Powys 27 G8
Coffinswell Devon 5 D9
Cofton Hackett Worcs 40 H2
Cogan V/Glam 17 D6
Cogenhoe Northants 31 B10
Cogges Oxon 30 H5
Coggeshall Essex 34 F2
Coggeshall Hamlet Essex 34 F2
Coggins Mill E Sussex 13 C9
Coig Peighinnean W Isles 108 B9
Coig Peighinnean W Isles 108 A10
Coignafearn Lodge H'land 96 E4
Coilacriech Aberds 90 B4
Coilantogle Stirl 83 D6
Coillaig Arg/Bute 81 B10
Coille Mhorgil H'land 95 F8
Coilleag W Isles 92 D3
Coillore H'land 93 B9
Coire Bhachdaidh Lodge Perth/Kinr 88 D6
Coity Bridg 16 C4
Col W Isles 108 C9
Col Uarach W Isles 108 D9
Colaboll H'land 102 A4
Colan Cornw'l 3 C7
Colaton Raleigh Devon 8 F2
Colbost H'land 109 N7
Colburn N Yorks 63 E6
Colby Cumb 61 B9
Colby I/Man 54 E2
Colby Norfolk 45 B6
Colchester Essex 34 F4
Colchester Zoo Essex 34 F3
Colcot V/Glam 17 E6
Cold Ash W Berks 20 E3
Cold Ashby Northants 41 H8
Cold Ashton S Gloucs 18 D4
Cold Aston Glos 30 G3
Cold Blow Pembs 24 E6
Cold Brayfield M/Keynes 32 C2
Cold Hanworth Lincs 52 D3
Cold Harbour Lincs 42 B2
Cold Hatton Telford 39 C7
Cold Hesledon Durham 71 F9
Cold Higham Northants 31 C8
Cold Kirby N Yorks 64 F3
Cold Newton Leics 41 E9
Cold Northcott Cornw'l 4 B3
Cold Norton Essex 23 A8
Cold Overton Leics 41 D10
Coldbackie H'land 105 D9
Coldbeck Cumb 62 D2
Coldblow London 22 D5
Coldean Brighton/Hove 13 E7
Coldeast Devon 5 C9
Colden W Yorks 56 F4
Colden Common Hants 11 B7
Coldfair Green Suffolk 35 B8
Coldham Cambs 43 E7
Coldharbour Glos 18 A2
Coldharbour Kent 22 F5
Coldharbour Surrey 21 G9
Coldingham Scot Borders 85 H11
Coldrain Perth/Kinr 84 D2
Coldred Kent 15 D7
Coldridge Devon 7 F7
Coldstream Angus 90 H4
Coldstream Scot Borders 78 D3
Coldwaltham W Sussex 12 D4
Coldwells Aberds 99 E11
Coldwells Croft Aberds 98 F5
Coldyeld Shrops 38 F4
Cole Som'set 9 A8
Cole Green Herts 32 G5
Cole Henley Hants 20 F2
Colebatch Shrops 38 G4
Colebrook Devon 8 D2
Colebrooke Devon 7 G8
Coleby Lincs 52 F2
Coleby N Lincs 58 G4
Coleford Devon 7 F8
Coleford Glos 29 G6
Coleford Som'set 18 G3
Colehill Dorset 10 D3
Coleman's Hatch E Sussex 13 B8
Colemere Shrops 38 B5
Colemore Hants 11 A10
Colenden Perth/Kinr 84 B3
Coleorton Leics 41 D6
Colerne Wilts 18 D5
Cole's Green Suffolk 35 B6
Coles Green Suffolk 34 D4
Colesbourne Glos 30 G1
Colesden Beds 32 C4
Coleshill Bucks 21 B7
Coleshill Oxon 19 B9
Coleshill Warwick 40 G4
Colestocks Devon 8 D2
Colgate W Sussex 13 B6
Colgrain Arg/Bute 82 F4
Colinsburgh Fife 85 D6
Colinton C/Edinb 84 H4
Colintraive Arg/Bute 81 G10
Colkirk Norfolk 44 C3
Collace Perth/Kinr 84 A4
Collafirth Shetl'd 111 G7
Collaton St. Mary Torbay 5 E9
College Milton S Lanarks 75 B8
Collessie Fife 84 C4
Collier Row London 22 B5
Collier Street Kent 14 D2
Collier's End Herts 33 F6
Collier's Green Kent 14 E2
Colliery Row Tyne/Wear 71 F8
Collieston Aberds 99 F10
Collin Dumf/Gal 68 C3
Collingbourne Ducis Wilts 19 F9
Collingbourne Kingston Wilts 19 F9
Collingham Notts 51 F10
Collingham W Yorks 57 D8
Collington Heref'd 29 B7
Collingtree Northants 31 C9
Collins Green Warrington 49 C6
Colliston Angus 91 G7
Collmuir Aberds 98 H5
Collycroft Warwick 40 G5
Collynie Aberds 99 E8
Collyweston Northants 42 E2
Colmonell S Ayrs 66 B3
Colmworth Beds 32 C4
Coln Rogers Glos 30 H2
Coln St. Aldwyn's Glos 30 H3
Coln St. Dennis Glos 30 G2
Colnabaichin Aberds 98 H2
Colnbrook Slough 21 D8
Colne Cambs 43 H6
Colne Lancs 56 D3
Colne Edge Lancs 56 D3
Colne Engaine Essex 34 E2
Colney Norfolk 44 E5
Colney Heath Herts 32 H5
Colney Street Herts 21 A9
Colpy Aberds 98 E6
Colquhar Scot Borders 77 C6
Colsterdale N Yorks 63 F6
Colsterworth Lincs 42 C2
Colston Bassett Notts 41 B8
Coltfield Moray 103 F10
Colthouse Cumb 61 E6
Coltishall Norfolk 45 D6
Coltness N Lanarks 75 B10
Colton Cumb 61 F6
Colton Norfolk 44 E5
Colton N Yorks 57 D10
Colton Staffs 40 C2
Colton W Yorks 57 E8
Colva Powys 28 C3
Colvend Dumf/Gal 68 E1
Colvister Shetl'd 111 D8
Colwall Green Heref'd 29 D8
Colwall Stone Heref'd 29 D8
Colwell Northum 70 C4
Colwich Staffs 40 C2
Colwick Notts 41 A8
Colwinston V/Glam 16 D4
Colworth W Sussex 12 E3
Colwyn Bay Conwy 47 E8
Colyford Devon 8 E4
Colyton Devon 8 E4
Combe Heref'd 28 B4
Combe Oxon 31 G6
Combe W Berks 20 E1
Combe Common Surrey 12 B3
Combe Down Bath/NE Som'set 18 E4
Combe Florey Som'set 8 A3
Combe Hay Bath/NE Som'set 18 F4
Combe Martin Devon 7 B6
Combe Moor Heref'd 28 B4
Combe Raleigh Devon 8 D3
Combe St. Nicholas Som'set 8 C5
Combeinteignhead Devon 5 C10
Comberbach Ches 49 E7
Comberton Cambs 33 C6
Comberton Heref'd 28 B5
Combpyne Devon 8 E4
Combridge Staffs 40 B2
Combrook Warwick 30 C5
Combs Derby 50 E2
Combs Suffolk 34 C4
Combs Ford Suffolk 34 C4
Combwich Som'set 17 G7
Comers Aberds 99 H6
Comins Coch Ceredig'n 37 G6
Commercial End Cambs 33 B8
Commins Capel Betws Ceredig'n 27 C6
Commins Coch Powys 37 E8
Common Edge Blackp'l 55 E3
Common Side Derby 50 E5
Commondale N Yorks 64 C4
Commonmoor Cornw'l 4 D3
Commonside Ches 49 E6
Compstall Gtr Man 50 C1
Compton Devon 5 D9
Compton Hants 11 B7
Compton Surrey 21 G6
Compton Surrey 21 G7
Compton W Berks 20 D3
Compton Wilts 19 F8
Compton W Sussex 12 D1
Compton Abbas Dorset 10 C1
Compton Abdale Glos 30 G2
Compton Acres Poole 10 F3
Compton Bassett Wilts 19 D7
Compton Beauchamp Oxon 19 C9
Compton Bishop Som'set 17 F8
Compton Chamberlayne Wilts 10 B3
Compton Dando Bath/NE Som'set 18 E3
Compton Dundon Som'set 9 A6
Compton Martin Bath/NE Som'set 18 F2
Compton Pauncefoot Som'set 9 B8
Compton Valence Dorset 9 E7
Comrie Fife 84 F2
Comrie Perth/Kinr 83 B8
Conaglen House H'land 87 E10
Conchra Arg/Bute 81 F10
Concraigie Perth/Kinr 90 G2
Conder Green Lancs 55 C4
Conderton Worcs 30 E1
Condicote Glos 30 F3
Condorrat N Lanarks 83 G8
Condover Shrops 38 E5
Coney Weston Suffolk 44 H3
Coneyhurst W Sussex 12 C5
Coneysthorpe N Yorks 64 G5
Coneythorpe N Yorks 57 C8
Conford Hants 12 B2
Congash H'land 97 D8
Congdon's Shop Cornw'l 4 C3
Congerstone Leics 40 E5
Congham Norfolk 43 C10
Congl y wal Gwyn 37 A7
Congleton Ches 49 F9
Congresbury N Som'set 17 E9
Congreve Staffs 39 D10
Conicavel Moray 103 G8
Coningsby Lincs 52 G5
Conington Cambs 42 G4
Conington Cambs 33 B6
Conisbrough S Yorks 51 C7
Conisby Arg/Bute 72 A2
Conisholme Lincs 53 C7
Coniston Cumb 61 E6
Coniston ER Yorks 59 E7
Coniston Cold N Yorks 56 C4
Conistone N Yorks 56 B4
Connah's Quay Flints 48 F3
Connel Arg/Bute 81 A9
Connel Park E Ayrs 75 F8
Connor Downs Cornw'l 2 F4
Conon Bridge H'land 102 G4
Conon House H'land 102 G4
Cononley N Yorks 56 D4
Conordan H'land 94 C2
Consall Staffs 50 H1
Consett Durham 71 E6
Constable Burton N Yorks 63 E6
Constantine Cornw'l 3 G6
Constantine Bay Cornw'l 3 B7
Contin H'land 102 G3
Contlaw Aberd C 91 A9
Conwy Conwy 47 E7
Conwy Castle Conwy 47 E7
Conyer Kent 14 B4
Conyers Green Suffolk 34 B2
Cooden E Sussex 14 H2
Cooil I/Man 54 E3
Cookbury Devon 6 F5
Cookham Windsor 21 C6
Cookham Dean Windsor 21 C6
Cookham Rise Windsor 21 C6
Cookhill Worcs 30 C2
Cookley Suffolk 45 H7
Cookley Worcs 39 G9
Cookley Green Oxon 20 B4
Cookney Aberds 91 B9
Cookridge W Yorks 57 D7
Cooksbridge E Sussex 13 D8
Cooksmill Green Essex 33 H9
Coolham W Sussex 12 C5
Cooling Medway 23 D7
Coombe Cornw'l 6 E3
Coombe Cornw'l 3 D8
Coombe Hants 11 B9
Coombe Wilts 19 F8
Coombe Bissett Wilts 10 B4
Coombe Hill Glos 29 F9
Coombe Keynes Dorset 9 F10
Coombes W Sussex 12 E5
Coopersale Common Essex 22 A4
Cootham W Sussex 12 D4
Copdock Suffolk 34 D5
Copford Green Essex 34 F3
Copgrove N Yorks 57 B8
Copister Shetl'd 111 F7
Cople Beds 32 D4
Copley Durham 62 B5
Coplow Dale Derby 50 E3
Copmanthorpe C/York 58 D1
Coppathorne Cornw'l 6 F3
Coppenhall Staffs 39 D10
Coppenhall Moss Ches 49 G8
Copperhouse Cornw'l 2 F4
Coppingford Cambs 42 G4
Coppleridge Dorset 9 B10
Copplestone Devon 7 F8
Coppull Lancs 55 G5
Coppull Moor Lancs 55 G5
Copsale W Sussex 12 C5
Copster Green Lancs 56 E1
Copston Magna Warwick 41 G6
Copt Heath W Midlands 40 H3
Copt Hewick N Yorks 63 G8
Copt Oak Leics 41 D6
Copthorne Shrops 38 D5
Copthorne W Sussex 13 B7
Copy's Green Norfolk 44 B3
Copythorne Hants 11 C6
Corbets Tey London 22 C5
Corbridge Northum 70 D4
Corby Northants 42 G1
Corby Glen Lincs 42 C2
Cordon N Ayrs 74 D2
Coreley Shrops 29 A7
Cores End Bucks 21 C7
Corfe Som'set 8 C4
Corfe Castle Dorset 10 F2
Corfe Castle Dorset 10 F2
Corfe Mullen Dorset 10 E2
Corfton Shrops 38 G5
Corgarff Aberds 98 H2
Corhampton Hants 11 B9
Corlae Dumf/Gal 75 H8
Corley Warwick 40 G5
Corley Ash Warwick 40 G4
Corley Moor Warwick 40 G4
Cornaa I/Man 54 D4
Cornabus Arg/Bute 72 C3
Cornel Conwy 47 F7
Corner Row Lancs 55 E4
Corney Cumb 60 E4
Cornforth Durham 71 G8
Cornhill Aberds 98 C5
Cornhill on Tweed Northum 78 D3
Cornholme W Yorks 56 F4
Cornish Hall End Essex 33 E9
Cornquoy Orkney 110 J6
Cornsay Durham 71 F6
Cornsay Colliery Durham 71 F6
Corntown H'land 102 G4
Corntown V/Glam 16 D4
Cornwell Oxon 30 F4
Cornwood Devon 5 E7
Cornworthy Devon 5 E9
Corpach H'land 88 D1
Corpusty Norfolk 44 B5
Corran H'land 87 E10
Corran H'land 94 F5
Corranbuie Arg/Bute 81 H8
Corrany I/Man 54 D4
Corrie N Ayrs 74 C2
Corrie Common Dumf/Gal 68 B5
Corriecravie N Ayrs 73 E9
Corriekinloch H'land 105 G6
Corriemoillie H'land 102 F2
Corrievorrie H'land 96 D5
Corrimony H'land 96 C1
Corringham Lincs 52 C1
Corringham Thurr'k 23 C7
Corris Gwyn 37 E7
Corris Uchaf Gwyn 37 E7
Corrour Shooting Lodge H'land 88 E5
Corrow Arg/Bute 82 D2
Corry H'land 94 D3
Corry of Ardnagrask H'land 96 B3
Corrymuckloch Perth/Kinr 83 A9
Corrynachenchy Arg/Bute 87 G6
Cors y Gedol Gwyn 36 C5
Corsback H'land 107 B7
Corscombe Dorset 9 D7
Corse Aberds 98 D6
Corse Lawn Worcs 29 E9
Corse of Kinnoir Aberds 98 D5
Corsewall Dumf/Gal 66 D2
Corsham Wilts 18 D5
Corsindae Aberds 99 H6
Corsley Wilts 18 G5
Corsley Heath Wilts 18 G5
Corsock Dumf/Gal 67 C9
Corston Bath/NE Som'set 18 E3
Corston Wilts 19 C6
Corstorphine C/Edinb 84 G3
Cortachy Angus 90 F4
Corton Suffolk 45 F9
Corton Wilts 19 G6
Corton Denham Som'set 9 B8
Coruanan Lodge H'land 87 E10
Corunna W Isles 109 L3
Corwen Denbs 38 A1
Coryton Devon 4 B5
Coryton Thurr'k 23 C7
Cosby Leics 41 F7
Coseley W Midlands 39 F10
Cosgrove Northants 31 D9
Cosham Portsm'th 11 D9
Cosheston Pembs 24 F5
Cossall Notts 41 A6
Cossington Leics 41 D8
Cossington Som'set 17 G8
Costa Orkney 110 F4
Costessey Norfolk 44 D5
Costock Notts 41 C7
Coston Leics 41 C10
Cote Oxon 19 A10
Cotebrook Ches 49 F6
Cotehele House Cornw'l 4 D5
Cotehill Cumb 69 E7
Cotes Cumb 61 F7
Cotes Leics 41 C7
Cotes Staffs 39 B9
Cotesbach Leics 41 G7
Cotgrave Notts 41 B8
Cothall Aberds 99 G8
Cotham Notts 51 H9
Cothelstone Som'set 8 A3
Cotherstone Durham 62 C5
Cothill Oxon 20 B2
Cotleigh Devon 8 D4
Cotmanhay Derby 41 A6
Cotmaton Devon 8 F3
Coton Cambs 33 C7
Coton Northants 31 A8
Coton Staffs 39 C9
Coton Staffs 40 B1
Coton Clanford Staffs 39 C9
Coton Hill Shrops 38 D5
Coton Hill Staffs 40 B1
Coton in the Elms Derby 40 D4
Cotswold Wild Life Park, Burford Oxon 30 H4
Cott Devon 5 D8
Cottam ER Yorks 58 B5
Cottam Lancs 55 E5
Cottam Notts 51 E10
Cottartown H'land 97 C8
Cottenham Cambs 33 B7
Cotterdale N Yorks 62 E3
Cottered Herts 33 F6
Cotteridge W Midlands 40 H2
Cotterstock Northants 42 F3
Cottesbrooke Northants 31 A9
Cottesmore Rutl'd 42 D2
Cotteylands Devon 7 E10
Cottingham ER Yorks 59 E6
Cottingham Northants 41 F10
Cottingley W Yorks 57 E6
Cottisford Oxon 31 E7
Cotton Staffs 50 H2
Cotton Suffolk 34 B4
Cotton End Beds 32 D3
Cottown Aberds 98 F5
Cottown Aberds 99 G7
Cottown Aberds 99 D8
Cotwalton Staffs 39 B10
Couch's Mill Cornw'l 4 E2
Coughton Heref'd 29 F6
Coughton Warwick 30 B2
Coul Arg/Bute 72 A2
Coulaghailtro Arg/Bute 81 H7
Coulags H'land 95 B6
Coulderton Cumb 60 D2
Coull Aberds 91 A6
Coulport Arg/Bute 82 F3
Coulsdon London 22 F2
Coulston Wilts 19 F6
Coulter S Lanarks 76 D3
Coulton N Yorks 64 G4
Cound Shrops 39 E6
Coundon Durham 63 B7
Coundon W Midlands 40 G5
Coundon Grange Durham 63 B7
Countersett N Yorks 62 F4
Countess Wilts 19 G8
Countess Wear Devon 5 B10
Countesthorpe Leics 41 F7
Countisbury Devon 7 B8
County Oak W Sussex 13 B6
Coup Green Lancs 55 F5
Coupar Angus Perth/Kinr 90 G3
Coupland Northum 78 D4
Cour Arg/Bute 73 C8
Courance Dumf/Gal 68 A3
Court at Street Kent 14 E5
Court Henry Carms 26 F5
Courteenhall Northants 31 C9
Courtsend Essex 23 B10
Courtway Som'set 8 A4
Cousland Midloth 84 H5
Cousley Wood E Sussex 14 E1
Cove Arg/Bute 82 F3
Cove Scot Borders 85 G9
Cove Devon 8 C1
Cove Hants 21 F6
Cove H'land 101 C6
Cove Bay Aberd C 91 A10
Cove Bottom Suffolk 45 H8
Covehithe Suffolk 45 G9
Coven Staffs 39 E10
Coveney Cambs 43 G7
Covenham St. Bartholomew Lincs 53 C6
Covenham St. Mary Lincs 53 C6
Coventry W Midlands 40 H5
Coventry Cathedral W Midlands 40 H5
Coverack Cornw'l 3 H6
Coverham N Yorks 63 F6
Covesea Moray 103 E10
Covington Cambs 32 A3
Covington S Lanarks 76 D2
Cow Ark Lancs 56 D1
Cowan Bridge Lancs 61 G9
Cowbeech E Sussex 13 D10
Cowbit Lincs 42 D5
Cowbridge Lincs 53 H6
Cowbridge Som'set 16 G4
Cowbridge V/Glam 16 D4
Cowdale Derby 50 E2
Cowden Kent 22 G4
Cowdenbeath Fife 84 E3
Cowdenburn Scot Borders 76 B5
Cowers Lane Derby 50 H5
Cowes I/Wight 11 E7
Cowesby N Yorks 63 F9
Cowfold W Sussex 13 C6
Cowgill Cumb 62 F2
Cowie Aberds 91 C9
Cowie Stirl 83 F9
Cowley Devon 7 G10
Cowley Glos 30 G1
Cowley London 21 C8
Cowley Oxon 20 A3
Cowleymoor Devon 8 C1
Cowling Lancs 55 G5
Cowling N Yorks 56 D4
Cowling N Yorks 63 F7
Cowlinge Suffolk 33 C10
Cowpe Lancs 56 F3
Cowpen Northum 71 B7
Cowpen Bewley Stockton 63 B9
Cowplain Hants 11 C9
Cowshill Durham 70 F3
Cowstrandburn Fife 84 E2
Cowthorpe N Yorks 57 C9
Cox Common Suffolk 45 G7
Cox Grn. Windsor 21 D6
Cox Moor Notts 51 G7
Coxbank Ches 39 A7
Coxbench Derby 40 A5
Coxford Norfolk 44 C2
Coxford S'thampton 11 C6
Coxheath Kent 14 C2
Coxhill Kent 15 D7
Coxhoe Durham 71 G8
Coxley Som'set 18 G2
Coxwold N Yorks 64 G3
Coychurch Bridg 16 D4
Coylton S Ayrs 75 E6
Coylumbridge H'land 97 E7
Coynach Aberds 98 H4
Coynachie Aberds 98 E4
Coytrahen Bridg 16 C3
Crabadon Devon 5 E8
Crabbs Cross Worcs 30 B2
Crabtree W Sussex 13 C6
Crackenthorpe Cumb 61 B9
Crackington Haven Cornw'l 6 G2
Crackley Warwick 30 A4
Crackleybank Shrops 39 D8
Crackpot N Yorks 62 E4
Cracoe N Yorks 56 B4
Craddock Devon 8 C2
Cradhlastadh W Isles 108 D5
Cradley Heref'd 29 D8
Cradley Heath W Midlands 39 G10
Crafthole Cornw'l 4 E4
Cragg Vale W Yorks 56 F5
Craggan H'land 97 D8
Craggie H'land 106 H3
Craggie H'land 96 C5
Craghead Durham 71 E7
Crai Powys 27 F8
Craibstone Aberd C 99 G8
Craibstone Moray 98 C4
Craichie Angus 91 G6
Craig Dumf/Gal 67 D8
Craig Dumf/Gal 67 D8
Craig H'land 95 B7
Craig Castle Aberds 98 F4
Craig cefn parc Swan 16 A1
Craig Penllyn V/Glam 16 D4
Craig y don Conwy 47 D7
Craig y nos Powys 27 G8
Craiganor Lodge Perth/Kinr 89 F7
Craigdam Aberds 99 E8
Craigdarroch Dumf/Gal 67 A9
Craigdhu H'land 96 B2
Craigearn Aberds 99 G7
Craigellachie Moray 98 D2
Craigencross Dumf/Gal 66 D2
Craigend Perth/Kinr 84 B3
Craigend Stirl 83 F8
Craigendive Arg/Bute 81 F10
Craigendoran Arg/Bute 82 F4
Craigends Renf 82 H5
Craigens Arg/Bute 80 H2
Craigens E Ayrs 75 F7
Craighat Stirl 82 F5
Craighead Fife 85 D8
Craighlaw Mains Dumf/Gal 66 D5
Craighouse Arg/Bute 80 H5
Craigie Aberds 99 G9
Craigie Dundee C 84 A6
Craigie Perth/Kinr 84 B3
Craigie Perth/Kinr 90 G2
Craigie S Ayrs 75 D6
Craigielaw E Loth 85 G6
Craiglockhart C/Edinb 84 G4
Craigmalloch E Ayrs 67 A6
Craigmaud Aberds 99 C8
Craigmillar C/Edinb 84 G4
Craigmore Arg/Bute 82 H2
Craignant Shrops 38 B3
Craigneuk N Lanarks 75 B9
Craigneuk N Lanarks 75 A9
Craignure Arg/Bute 87 H7
Craigo Angus 91 E7
Craigow Perth/Kinr 84 D2
Craigrothie Fife 84 C5
Craigroy Moray 103 G10
Craigruie Stirl 82 B5
Craigston Castle Aberds 99 C7
Craigton Aberd C 91 A9
Craigton Angus 90 F4
Craigton Angus 91 H6
Craigton H'land 102 C5
Craigtown H'land 106 D3
Craik Scot Borders 77 G6
Crail Fife 85 D8
Crailing Scot Borders 77 E9
Crailinghall Scot Borders 77 E9
Craiselound N Lincs 51 C9
Crakehill N Yorks 63 G9
Crakemarsh Staffs 40 B2
Crambe N Yorks 58 B3
Cramlington Northum 71 C7
Cramond C/Edinb 84 G3
Cramond Bridge C/Edinb 84 G3
Cranage Ches 49 F8
Cranberry Staffs 39 B9
Cranborne Dorset 10 C3
Cranbourne Brackn'l 21 D7
Cranbrook Kent 14 E2
Cranbrook Common Kent 14 E2
Crane Moor S Yorks 50 B5
Crane's Corner Norfolk 44 D3
Cranfield Beds 32 D2
Cranford London 21 D9
Cranford St. Andrew Northants 42 H2
Cranford St. John Northants 42 H2
Cranham Glos 29 G9
Cranham London 22 C5
Crank Mersey 49 C6
Crank Wood Gtr Man 49 B7
Cranleigh Surrey 12 B4
Cranley Suffolk 34 A5
Cranmer Green Suffolk 34 A4
Cranmore I/Wight 11 F6
Cranna Aberds 98 C6
Crannich Arg/Bute 86 G5
Crannoch Moray 98 C4
Cranoe Leics 41 F9
Cransford Suffolk 35 B7
Cranshaws Scot Borders 77 A9
Cranstal I/Man 54 B4
Crantock Cornw'l 3 C6
Cranwell Lincs 52 H3
Cranwich Norfolk 44 F1
Cranworth Norfolk 44 E3
Crapstone Devon 5 D6
Crarae Arg/Bute 81 E9
Crask Inn H'land 105 G8
Crask of Aigas H'land 96 B2
Craskins Aberds 98 H5
Craster Northum 79 F7
Craswall Heref'd 28 E3
Cratfield Suffolk 45 H7
Crathes Aberds 91 B8
Crathes Castle and Gardens Aberds 91 B8
Crathie Aberds 90 B3
Crathie H'land 89 B6
Crathorne N Yorks 63 D9
Craven Arms Shrops 38 G5
Crawcrook Tyne/Wear 71 D6
Crawford Lancs 48 B5
Crawford S Lanarks 76 E2
Crawfordjohn S Lanarks 76 E1
Crawick Dumf/Gal 75 F9
Crawley Hants 11 A7
Crawley Oxon 30 G5
Crawley W Sussex 13 B6
Crawley Down W Sussex 13 B7
Crawleyside Durham 70 F4
Crawshawbooth Lancs 56 F3
Crawton Aberds 91 D9
Cray N Yorks 62 G4
Cray Perth/Kinr 90 E2
Crayford London 22 D5
Crayke N Yorks 64 G3
Crays Hill Essex 23 B7
Cray's Pond Oxon 20 C4
Creacombe Devon 7 E9
Creag Ghoraidh W Isles 109 N2
Creagan Arg/Bute 87 G9
Creaguaineach Lodge H'land 88 E4
Creaton Northants 31 A9
Creca Dumf/Gal 68 C5
Credenhill Heref'd 28 D5
Crediton Devon 7 F9
Creebridge Dumf/Gal 67 D6
Creech Heathfield Som'set 8 B4
Creech St. Michael Som'set 8 B4
Creed Cornw'l 3 E8
Creekmouth London 22 C4
Creeting Bottoms Suffolk 34 C5
Creeting St. Mary Suffolk 34 C4
Creeton Lincs 42 C3
Creetown Dumf/Gal 67 E6
Creg ny Baa I/Man 54 D3
Creggans Arg/Bute 82 D1
Cregneish I/Man 54 F1
Cregrina Powys 28 C2
Creich Fife 84 B5
Creigiau Card 16 C5
Cremyll Cornw'l 4 E5
Cressage Shrops 39 E6
Cressbrook Derby 50 E3
Cresselly Pembs 24 F5
Cressing Essex 34 F1
Cresswell Northum 71 A7
Cresswell Staffs 40 B1
Cresswell Quay Pembs 24 F5
Creswell Derby 51 E7
Cretingham Suffolk 35 B6
Cretshengan Arg/Bute 81 H7
Crew Green Powys 38 D4
Crewe Ches 48 G5
Crewe Ches 49 G8
Crewkerne Som'set 9 D6
Crianlarich Stirl 82 B4
Cribyn Ceredig'n 26 C5
Criccieth Gwyn 36 B4
Crich Derby 50 G5
Crichie Aberds 99 D9
Crichton Midloth 77 A6
Crick Monmouths 17 B9
Crick Northants 31 A7
Crickadarn Powys 28 D1
Cricket Malherbie Som'set 8 C5
Cricket St. Thomas Som'set 8 D5
Crickheath Shrops 38 C3
Crickhowell Powys 28 G3
Cricklade Wilts 19 B8
Cricklewood London 22 C2
Cridling Stubbs N Yorks 57 F10
Crieff Perth/Kinr 83 B9
Crieff Visitors' Centre Perth/Kinr 83 B9
Criggion Powys 38 D3
Crigglestone W Yorks 57 G8
Crimond Aberds 99 C10
Crimonmogate Aberds 99 C10
Crimplesham Norfolk 43 E9
Crinan Arg/Bute 81 E7
Cringleford Norfolk 44 E5
Cringles W Yorks 56 D5
Crinow Pembs 24 E6
Cripplesease Cornw'l 2 F4
Cripplestyle Dorset 10 C3
Cripp's Corner E Sussex 14 F2
Croasdale Cumb 60 C3
Crock Street Som'set 8 C5
Crockenhill Kent 22 E5
Crockernwell Devon 7 G8
Crockerton Wilts 18 G5
Crocketford or Ninemile Bar Dumf/Gal 67 C10
Crockey Hill C/York 58 D2
Crockham Hill Kent 22 F4
Crockleford Heath Essex 34 F4
Crockness Orkney 110 J4
Croes goch Pembs 24 C3
Croes lan Ceredig'n 25 B8
Croes y mwyalch Torf 17 B8
Croeserw Neath P Talb 16 B3
Croesor Gwyn 37 A6
Croesyceiliog Carms 25 E9
Croesyceiliog Torf 17 B8
Croesywaun Gwyn 46 G5
Croft Leics 41 F7
Croft Lincs 53 F8
Croft Pembs 25 B6
Croft Warrington 49 C7
Croft on Tees N Yorks 63 D7
Croftamie Stirl 82 F5
Croftmalloch W Loth 76 A2
Crofton Wilts 19 E9
Crofton W Yorks 57 G8
Crofts of Benachielt H'land 107 F6
Crofts of Haddo Aberds 99 E8
Crofts of Inverthernie Aberds 99 D7
Crofts of Meikle Ardo Aberds 99 D8
Crofty Swan 25 G10
Croggan Arg/Bute 81 B7
Croglin Cumb 69 F8
Croick H'land 102 C3
Crois Dughaill W Isles 92 C3
Cromarty H'land 103 F6
Cromblet Aberds 99 E7
Cromdale H'land 97 D8
Cromer Herts 32 F5
Cromer Norfolk 45 A6
Cromford Derby 50 G4
Cromhall S Gloucs 18 B3
Cromhall Common S Gloucs 18 C3
Cromor W Isles 108 E9
Cromra H'land 88 B6
Cromwell Notts 51 F9
Cronberry E Ayrs 75 E8
Crondall Hants 20 G5
Cronk y Voddy I/Man 54 D3
Cronton Mersey 48 D5
Crook Cumb 61 E7
Crook Durham 71 G6
Crook of Devon Perth/Kinr 84 D2
Crookedholm E Ayrs 75 D6
Crookes S Yorks 50 D5
Crookham Northum 78 D4
Crookham W Berks 20 E3
Crookham Village Hants 20 F5
Crookhaugh Scot Borders 76 E4
Crookhouse Scot Borders 78 E2
Crooklands Cumb 61 F8
Croome Court Worcs 29 D9
Cropredy Oxon 31 D6
Cropston Leics 41 D7
Cropthorne Worcs 30 D1
Cropton N Yorks 64 F5
Cropwell Bishop Notts 41 B8
Cropwell Butler Notts 41 B8
Cros W Isles 108 A10
Crosbost W Isles 108 E8
Crosby Cumb 68 G3
Crosby I/Man 54 E3
Crosby Mersey 48 C4
Crosby N Lincs 58 G4
Crosby Garrett Cumb 62 D2
Crosby Ravensworth Cumb 61 C9
Crosby Villa Cumb 68 G3
Croscombe Som'set 18 G2
Cross Som'set 17 F9
Cross Ash Monmouths 28 G5
Cross at Hand Kent 14 D2
Cross Green Devon 4 B4
Cross Green Suffolk 34 C3
Cross Green Suffolk 34 C2
Cross Green Warwick 30 C5
Cross Hands Carms 26 G5
Cross hands Carms 25 D6
Cross Hands Pembs 24 E5
Cross Hill Derby 51 H6
Cross Houses Shrops 39 E6
Cross in Hand E Sussex 13 C9
Cross in Hand Leics 41 G7
Cross Inn Ceredig'n 26 C3
Cross Inn Ceredig'n 26 B5
Cross Inn Rh Cyn Taff 16 C5
Cross Keys Kent 22 F5
Cross Lane Head Shrops 39 F8
Cross Lanes Cornw'l 2 G5
Cross Lanes N Yorks 57 B10
Cross Lanes Wrex 48 H4
Cross Oak Powys 28 F2
Cross of Jackston Aberds 99 E7
Cross o'th'hands Derby 50 H4
Cross Street Suffolk 44 H5
Crossaig Arg/Bute 73 B8
Crossapol Arg/Bute 86 D1
Crossburn Falk 83 G9
Crossbush W Sussex 12 E4
Crosscanonby Cumb 68 G3
Crossdale Street Norfolk 45 B6
Crossens Mersey 55 G3
Crossflatts W Yorks 57 D6
Crossford Fife 84 F2
Crossford S Lanarks 75 C10
Crossgate Lincs 42 C5
Crossgatehall E Loth 84 H5
Crossgates Fife 84 F3
Crossgates Powys 28 B1
Crossgill Lancs 55 B5
Crosshill E Ayrs 75 E6
Crosshill Fife 84 E3
Crosshill S Ayrs 74 G5
Crosshouse E Ayrs 75 D5
Crossings Cumb 69 C8
Crosskeys Caerph 17 B7
Crosskirk H'land 106 B5
Crosslanes Shrops 38 D4
Crosslee Scot Borders 77 F6
Crosslee Renf 82 H5
Crossmichael Dumf/Gal 67 D9
Crossmoor Lancs 55 E4
Crossroads Aberds 91 B8
Crossroads E Ayrs 75 D6
Crossway Heref'd 29 E7
Crossway Monmouths 28 G5
Crossway Powys 28 C1
Crossway Green Worcs 29 B9

Crossways Dorset 9 F9
Crosswell Pembs 24 C6
Crosswood Ceredig'n 27 A6
Crosthwaite Cumb 61 E7
Croston Lancs 55 G4
Crostwick Norfolk 45 D6
Crostwight Norfolk 45 C7
Crothair W Isles 108 D6
Crouch Kent 23 F6
Crouch Hill Dorset 9 C9
Crouch House Green Kent 22 G4
Croucheston Wilts 10 B3
Croughton Northants 31 E7
Crovie Aberds 99 B8
Crow Edge S Yorks 50 B3
Crow Hill Heref'd 29 F7
Crowan Cornw'l 2 F5
Crowborough E Sussex 13 B9
Crowcombe Som'set 17 H6
Crowdecote Derby 50 F3
Crowden Derby 50 C2
Crowell Oxon 20 B5
Crowfield Northants 31 D8
Crowfield Suffolk 34 C5
Crowhurst E Sussex 14 G2
Crowhurst Surrey 22 G3
Crowhurst Lane End Surrey 22 G3
Crowland Lincs 42 D5
Crowlas Cornw'l 2 F4
Crowle N Lincs 58 G3
Crowle Worcs 29 C10
Crowmarsh Gifford Oxon 20 C4
Crown Corner Suffolk 35 A6
Crownhill Plym'th 4 E5
Crownland Suffolk 34 B4
Crownthorpe Norfolk 44 E4
Crowntown Cornw'l 2 F5
Crows an wra Cornw'l 2 G2
Crowshill Norfolk 44 E3
Crowsnest Shrops 38 E4
Crowthorne Brackn'l 21 E6
Crowton Ches 49 E6
Croxall Staffs 40 D3
Croxby Lincs 52 C4
Croxdale Durham 71 G7
Croxden Staffs 40 B2
Croxley Green Herts 21 B8
Croxton Cambs 32 B5
Croxton N Lincs 59 G6
Croxton Norfolk 44 G2
Croxton Staffs 39 B8
Croxton Kerrial Leics 41 C10
Croxtonbank Staffs 39 B8
Croy H'land 96 B5
Croy N Lanarks 83 G8
Croyde Devon 6 C5
Croydon Cambs 33 D6
Croydon London 22 E3
Crubenmore Lodge H'land 89 B7
Cruckmeole Shrops 38 E5
Cruckton Shrops 38 D5
Cruden Bay Aberds 99 E10
Crudgington Telford 39 D7
Crudwell Wilts 19 B6
Crug Powys 28 A2
Crugmeer Cornw'l 3 B8
Crugybar Carms 27 E6
Crulabhig W Isles 108 D6
Crumlin Caerph 17 B7
Crumpsall Gtr Man 49 B9
Crundale Kent 14 D5
Crundale Pembs 24 E4
Cruwys Morchard Devon 7 E9
Crux Easton Hants 20 F2
Crwbin Carms 25 E9
Crya Orkney 110 H4
Cryers Hill Bucks 21 B6
Crymlyn Gwyn 47 E6
Crymych Pembs 25 C6
Crynant Neath P Talb 16 A2
Crynfryn Ceredig'n 26 B5
Cuaig H'land 100 G5
Cuan Arg/Bute 81 C7
Cubbington Warwick 30 B5
Cubeck N Yorks 62 F4
Cubert Cornw'l 3 D6
Cubley S Yorks 50 B4
Cubley Common Derby 40 B3
Cublington Bucks 31 F10
Cublington Heref'd 28 E5
Cuckfield W Sussex 13 C7
Cucklington Som'set 9 B9
Cuckney Notts 51 E7
Cuckoo Hill Notts 51 C9
Cuddesdon Oxon 20 A4
Cuddington Bucks 31 G9
Cuddington Ches 49 E7
Cuddington Heath Ches 48 H5
Cuddy Hill Lancs 55 E4
Cudham London 22 F4
Cudliptown Devon 5 C6
Cudworth Som'set 8 C5
Cudworth S Yorks 50 B5
Cuffley Herts 22 A3
Cuiashader W Isles 108 B10
Cuidhir W Isles 92 E2
Cuidhtinis W Isles 109 J5
Culbo H'land 102 F5
Culbokie H'land 102 G5
Culburnie H'land 96 B2
Culcabock H'land 96 B4
Culcairn H'land 102 F5
Culcharry H'land 103 G7
Culcheth Warrington 49 C7
Culdrain Aberds 98 E5
Culduie H'land 94 B4
Culford Suffolk 34 A2
Culgaith Cumb 61 B9
Culham Oxon 20 B3
Culkein H'land 104 F3
Culkein Drumbeg H'land 104 F4
Culkerton Glos 19 B6
Cullachie H'land 97 D7
Cullen Moray 98 B5
Cullercoats Tyne/Wear 71 C8
Cullicudden H'land 102 F5
Cullingworth W Yorks 56 E5
Cullipool Arg/Bute 81 C7
Cullivoe Shetl'd 111 C8
Culloch Perth/Kinr 83 C8
Culloden Battlefield, Inverness H'land 96 B5
Cullompton Devon 8 D2
Culmaily H'land 103 C7
Culmazie Dumf/Gal 66 E5
Culmington Shrops 38 G5
Culmstock Devon 8 C3
Culnacraig H'land 101 B8
Culnaknock H'land 100 F3
Culpho Suffolk 35 D6
Culrain H'land 102 C4
Culross Fife 84 F1
Culroy S Ayrs 74 F5
Culsh Aberds 99 D8
Culsh Aberds 90 B4
Culshabbin Dumf/Gal 66 E5
Culswick Shetl'd 111 J5
Cultercullen Aberds 99 F9
Cults Aberd C 91 A9
Cults Aberds 98 E5
Cults Dumf/Gal 67 F6
Culverstone Green Kent 23 E6
Culverthorpe Lincs 42 A3
Culworth Northants 31 D7
Culzean Castle, Maybole S Ayrs 74 G4
Culzie Lodge H'land 102 E4
Cumbernauld N Lanarks 83 G8
Cumbernauld Village N Lanarks 83 G8
Cumberworth Lincs 53 E8
Cuminestown Aberds 99 C8
Cumlewick Shetl'd 111 L7
Cummersdale Cumb 69 E6
Cummertrees Dumf/Gal 68 D4
Cummingstown Moray 103 F10
Cumnock E Ayrs 75 E7
Cumnor Oxon 20 A2
Cumrew Cumb 69 E8
Cumwhinton Cumb 69 E7
Cumwhitton Cumb 69 E8
Cundall N Yorks 63 G9
Cunninghamhead N Ayrs 74 C5
Cunningsburgh Shetl'd 111 L7
Cunnister Shetl'd 111 D8
Cupar Fife 84 C5
Cupar Muir Fife 84 C5
Cupernham Hants 11 B6
Curbar Derby 50 E4
Curbridge Hants 11 C8
Curbridge Oxon 30 H5
Curdridge Hants 11 C8
Curdworth Warwick 40 F3
Curland Som'set 8 C4
Curlew Green Suffolk 35 B7
Currarie S Ayrs 66 A3
Curridge W Berks 20 D2
Currie C/Edinb 84 H3
Curry Mallet Som'set 8 B5
Curry Rivel Som'set 8 B5
Curtisden Green Kent 14 D2
Curtisknowle Devon 5 E8
Cury Cornw'l 2 G5
Cushnie Aberds 99 B7
Cushuish Som'set 8 A3
Cusop Heref'd 28 D3
Cutcloy Dumf/Gal 67 G6
Cutcombe Som'set 7 C10
Cutgate Gtr Man 56 G3
Cutiau Gwyn 37 D6
Cutlers Green Essex 33 E8
Cutnal Green Worcs 29 B9
Cutsdean Glos 30 E2
Cutthorpe Derby 50 E5
Cutts Shetl'd 111 K7
Cutty Sark, Greenwich London 22 D3
Cuxham Oxon 20 B4
Cuxton Medway 14 B2
Cuxwold Lincs 52 B4
Cwm Bl Gwent 28 H2
Cwm Denbs 48 E1
Cwm Swan 16 B1
Cwm byr Carms 27 E6
Cwm Cewydd Gwyn 37 D8
Cwm cou Ceredig'n 25 B7
Cwm Dulais Swan 25 F11
Cwm felin fach Caerph 17 B6
Cwm Ffrwd oer Torf 17 A7
Cwm hesgen Gwyn 37 C7
Cwm hwnt Rh Cyn Taff 27 H9
Cwm Irfon Powys 27 D8
Cwm Llinau Powys 37 E8
Cwm mawr Carms 26 G5
Cwm parc Rh Cyn Taff 16 B4
Cwm Penmachno Conwy 47 H7
Cwm y glo Carms 26 G5
Cwm y glo Gwyn 46 F5
Cwmafan Neath P Talb 16 B2
Cwmaman Rh Cyn Taff 16 B4
Cwmann Carms 26 D5
Cwmavon Torf 28 H3
Cwmbach Carms 25 D7
Cwmbach Carms 25 F9
Cwmbach Powys 27 C10
Cwmbach Powys 28 E2
Cwmbâch Rh Cyn Taff 16 A5
Cwmbelan Powys 37 G9
Cwmbran Torf 17 B7
Cwmbrwyno Ceredig'n 37 G7
Cwmcarn Caerph 17 B7
Cwmcarvan Monmouths 28 H5
Cwmcych Pembs 25 C7
Cwmdare Rh Cyn Taff 16 A4
Cwmderwen Powys 37 E9
Cwmdu Carms 27 E6
Cwmdu Powys 28 F2
Cwmdu Swan 16 B1
Cwmduad Carms 25 C8
Cwmdwr Carms 27 E7
Cwmfelin Bridg 16 C3
Cwmfelin Merth Tyd 16 A5
Cwmfelin Boeth Carms 25 E6
Cwmfelin Mynach Carms 25 D7
Cwmffrwd Carms 25 E9
Cwmgiedd Powys 27 G7
Cwmgors Neath P Talb 27 G7
Cwmgwili Carms 26 G5
Cwmgwrach Neath P Talb 16 A3
Cwmhiraeth Carms 25 C8
Cwmifor Carms 27 F6
Cwmisfael Carms 25 E9
Cwmllynfell Neath P Talb 27 G7
Cwmorgan Carms 25 C7
Cwmpengraig Carms 25 C8
Cwmrhos Powys 28 F2
Cwmsychpant Ceredig'n 25 B9
Cwmtillery Bl Gwent 28 H3
Cwmwysg Powys 27 F8
Cwmyoy Monmouths 28 F3
Cwmystwyth Ceredig'n 27 A7
Cwrt Gwyn 37 E6
Cwrt newydd Ceredig'n 25 B9
Cwrt y cadno Carms 27 D6
Cwrt y gollen Powys 28 G3
Cyffylliog Denbs 48 G1
Cyfronydd Powys 38 E2
Cymer Neath P Talb 16 B3
Cyncoed Card 17 C6
Cynghordy Carms 27 D8
Cynheidre Carms 25 F9
Cynwyd Denbs 38 A1
Cynwyl Elfed Carms 25 D8
Cywarch Gwyn 37 D8

D

Dacre Cumb 61 B7
Dacre N Yorks 57 B6
Dacre Banks N Yorks 57 B6
Daddry Shield Durham 70 G3
Dadford Bucks 31 E8
Dadlington Leics 41 F6
Dafarn Faig Gwyn 46 H4
Dafen Carms 25 F10
Daffy Green Norfolk 44 E3
Dagenham London 22 C4
Daglingworth Glos 30 H1
Dagnall Bucks 32 G2
Dail Beag W Isles 108 C7
Dail bho Dheas W Isles 108 A9
Dail bho Thuath W Isles 108 A9
Dail Mor W Isles 108 C7
Daill Arg/Bute 72 A3
Dailly S Ayrs 74 G4
Dairsie or Osnaburgh Fife 84 C6
Daisy Hill Gtr Man 49 B7
Dalabrog W Isles 92 C3
Dalavich Arg/Bute 81 C9
Dalbeattie Dumf/Gal 67 D10
Dalblair E Ayrs 75 F8
Dalbog Angus 91 D6
Dalbury Derby 40 B4
Dalby I/Man 54 E2
Dalby N Yorks 64 G4
Dalcapon Perth/Kinr 89 F10
Dalchalloch Perth/Kinr 89 E8
Dalchalm H'land 103 B8
Dalchenna Arg/Bute 82 D1
Dalchirach Moray 97 C9
Dalchork H'land 102 A4
Dalchreichart H'land 95 E9
Dalchruin Perth/Kinr 83 C8
Dalderby Lincs 52 F5
Dale Pembs 24 F3
Dale Shetl'd 111 H4
Dale Abbey Derby 41 B6
Dale Head Cumb 61 C7
Dalelia H'land 87 E7
Daless H'land 97 C6
Dalgarven N Ayrs 74 C4
Dalgety Bay Fife 84 F3
Dalginross Perth/Kinr 83 B8
Dalguise Perth/Kinr 89 G10
Dalhalvaig H'land 106 D3
Dalham Suffolk 33 B10
Dalinlongart Arg/Bute 82 F2
Dalkeith Midloth 84 H5
Dallam Warrington 49 C6
Dallas Moray 103 G10
Dalleagles E Ayrs 75 F7
Dallinghoo Suffolk 35 C6
Dallington E Sussex 14 G1
Dallington Northants 31 B9
Dallow N Yorks 63 G6
Dalmadilly Aberds 99 G7
Dalmally Arg/Bute 82 B2
Dalmarnock Glasg C 75 A8
Dalmary Stirl 83 E6
Dalmellington E Ayrs 75 G6
Dalmeny C/Edinb 84 G3
Dalmigavie H'land 96 E5
Dalmigavie Lodge H'land 96 D5
Dalmore H'land 102 F5
Dalmuir W Dunb 82 G5
Dalnabreck H'land 87 E6
Dalnacardoch Lodge Perth/Kinr 89 D8
Dalnacroich H'land 102 G2
Dalnaglar Castle Perth/Kinr 90 E2
Dalnahaitnach H'land 97 D6
Dalnaspidal Lodge Perth/Kinr 89 D7
Dalnavaid Perth/Kinr 89 E11
Dalnavie H'land 102 E5
Dalnawillan Lodge H'land 106 E5
Dalness H'land 88 F2
Dalnessie H'land 105 H9
Dalqueich Perth/Kinr 84 D2
Dalquhairn S Ayrs 74 H5
Dalreavoch H'land 103 B6
Dalry N Ayrs 74 C4
Dalrymple E Ayrs 74 F5
Dalserf S Lanarks 75 B10
Dalston Cumb 69 E6
Dalswinton Dumf/Gal 68 B2
Dalton Dumf/Gal 68 C4
Dalton Lancs 48 B5
Dalton Northum 70 E4
Dalton Northum 71 C6
Dalton N Yorks 63 G9
Dalton N Yorks 63 D6
Dalton S Yorks 51 C6
Dalton in Furness Cumb 60 G5
Dalton le Dale Durham 71 F9
Dalton on Tees N Yorks 63 D7
Dalton Piercy Hartlep'l 71 G9
Dalveich Stirl 83 B7
Dalvina Lo. H'land 105 E9
Dalwhinnie H'land 89 C7
Dalwood Devon 8 D4
Dam Green Norfolk 44 G4
Dam Side Lancs 55 D4
Damerham Hants 10 C4
Damgate Norfolk 45 E8
Damnaglaur Dumf/Gal 66 G3
Damside Scot Borders 76 C4
Danbury Essex 34 H1
Danby N Yorks 64 D5
Danby Wiske N Yorks 63 E8
Dandaleith Moray 98 D2
Danderhall Midloth 84 H5
Dane End Herts 33 F6
Danebridge Ches 50 F1
Danehill E Sussex 13 C8
Danemoor Green Norfolk 44 E4
Danesford Shrops 39 F8
Daneshill Hants 20 F4
Dangerous Corner Lancs 55 G5
Danskine E Loth 85 H7
Darcy Lever Gtr Man 49 B8
Darenth Kent 22 D5
Daresbury Halton 49 D6
Darfield S Yorks 51 B6
Darfoulds Notts 51 E7
Dargate Kent 14 B5
Darite Cornw'l 4 D3
Darlaston W Midlands 40 F1
Darley N Yorks 57 C7
Darley Bridge Derby 50 F4
Darley Head N Yorks 57 C6
Darlingscott Warwick 30 D4
Darlington D'lington 63 C7
Darliston Shrops 39 B6
Darlton Notts 51 E9
Darnall S Yorks 50 D5
Darnick Scot Borders 77 D8
Darowen Powys 37 E8
Darra Aberds 99 D7
Darracott Devon 6 C5
Darras Hall Northum 71 C6
Darrington W Yorks 57 F9
Darsham Suffolk 35 B8
Dartford Kent 22 D5
Dartington Devon 5 D8
Dartington Cider Press Centre Devon 5 D8
Dartington Crystal Devon 6 E5
Dartmeet Devon 5 C7
Dartmouth Devon 5 E9
Darton S Yorks 50 B5
Darvel E Ayrs 75 D7
Darwell Hole E Sussex 14 G1
Darwen Blackb'n 56 F1
Datchet Windsor 21 D7
Datchworth Herts 32 G5
Datchworth Green Herts 32 G5
Daubhill Gtr Man 49 B8
Daugh of Kinermony Moray 98 D2
Dauntsey Wilts 19 C6
Davenham Ches 49 E7
Davenport Green Ches 49 E9
Daventry Northants 31 B7
David's Well Powys 38 H1
Davidson's Mains C/Edinb 84 G4
Davidstow Cornw'l 4 B2
Davington Dumf/Gal 76 G5
Daviot Aberds 99 F7
Daviot H'land 96 C5
Davoch of Grange Moray 98 C4
Davyhulme Gtr Man 49 C8
Dawley Telford 39 E7
Dawlish Devon 8 G1
Dawlish Warren Devon 8 G1
Dawn Conwy 47 E8
Daws Heath Essex 23 C8
Daw's House Cornw'l 4 B4
Dawsmere Lincs 43 B7
Dayhills Staffs 40 B1
Daylesford Glos 30 F4
Ddôl Cownwy Powys 37 D10
Ddrydwy Angl 46 E3
Deadwater Northum 77 H9
Deaf Hill Durham 71 G8
Deal Kent 15 C8
Deal Hall Essex 23 B10
Dean Cumb 60 B3
Dean Devon 5 D8
Dean Devon 7 B6
Dean Dorset 10 C2
Dean Hants 11 C8
Dean Som'set 18 G3
Dean Prior Devon 5 D8
Dean Row Ches 49 D9
Deanburnhaugh Scot Borders 77 F6
Deane Gtr Man 49 B7
Deane Hants 20 F3
Deanich Lodge H'land 102 D2
Deanland Dorset 10 C2
Deans W Loth 84 H2
Deanscales Cumb 60 B3
Deanshanger Northants 31 E9
Deanston Stirl 83 D8
Dearham Cumb 68 G3
Dearne S Yorks 51 B6
Debach Suffolk 35 C6
Debden Essex 33 E8
Debden Essex 22 B4
Debden Cross Essex 33 E8
Debenham Suffolk 34 B5
Dechmont W Loth 84 G2
Deddington Oxon 31 E6
Dedham Essex 34 E4
Dedham Heath Essex 34 E4
Deebank Aberds 91 B7
Deene Northants 42 F2
Deenethorpe Northants 42 F2
Deep Sea World, North Queensferry Fife 84 F3
Deepcar S Yorks 50 C4
Deepcut Surrey 21 F7
Deepdale Cumb 62 F2
Deeping Gate Cambs 42 E4
Deeping St. James Lincs 42 E4
Deeping St. Nicholas Lincs 42 D5
Deerhill Moray 98 C4
Deerhurst Glos 29 F9
Deerness Orkney 110 H6
Defford Worcs 29 D10
Defynnog Powys 27 F9
Deganwy Conwy 47 E7
Deighton N Yorks 63 D8
Deighton W Yorks 57 G6
Deighton C/York 58 D2
Deiniolen Gwyn 46 F5
Delabole Cornw'l 4 B1
Delamere Ches 49 F6
Delfrigs Aberds 99 F9
Dell Lodge H'land 97 E8
Delliefure H'land 97 C8
Delnabo Moray 97 E9
Delnadamph Lodge Aberds 98 H2
Delph Gtr Man 50 B1
Delves Durham 71 F6
Delvine Perth/Kinr 90 G2
Dembleby Lincs 42 B3
Denaby Main S Yorks 51 C6
Denbigh Denbs 48 F1
Denbury Devon 5 D9
Denby Derby 50 H5
Denby Dale W Yorks 50 B4
Denchworth Oxon 20 B1
Dendron Cumb 60 G5
Denel End Beds 32 E3
Denend Aberds 98 E6
Denford Northants 42 H2
Dengie Essex 23 A9
Denham Bucks 21 C8
Denham Suffolk 34 B1
Denham Suffolk 34 A5
Denham Green Bucks 21 C8
Denham Street Suffolk 34 A5
Denhead Aberds 99 C9
Denhead Fife 85 C6
Denhead of Arbilot Angus 91 G6
Denhead of Gray Dundee C 84 A5
Denholm Scot Borders 77 F8
Denholme W Yorks 56 E5
Denholme Clough W Yorks 56 E5
Denio Gwyn 36 B3
Denmead Hants 11 C9
Denmore Aberd C 99 G9
Denmoss Aberds 99 D6
Dennington Suffolk 35 B6
Denny Falk 83 F9
Denny Lodge Hants 11 D6
Dennyloanhead Falk 83 F9
Denshaw Gtr Man 56 G4
Denside Aberds 91 B9
Densole Kent 15 D7
Denston Suffolk 34 C1
Denstone Staffs 40 A3
Dent Cumb 62 F2
Denton Cambs 42 G4
Denton D'lington 63 C7
Denton E Sussex 13 E8
Denton Gtr Man 49 C10
Denton Kent 15 D7
Denton Lincs 42 B1
Denton Norfolk 45 G6
Denton Northants 31 C10
Denton N Yorks 57 D6
Denton Oxon 20 A3
Denton's Green Mersey 48 C5
Denver Norfolk 43 E9
Denwick Northum 79 F7
Deopham Norfolk 44 E4
Deopham Green Norfolk 44 F4
Depden Suffolk 34 C1
Depden Green Suffolk 34 C1
Deptford London 22 D3
Deptford Wilts 19 H7
Derby Derby C 40 B5
Derbyhaven I/Man 54 F2
Deri Caerph 17 A6
Derril Devon 6 F4
Derringstone Kent 15 D7
Derrington Staffs 39 C9
Derriton Devon 6 F4
Derry Hill Wilts 19 D6
Derryguaig Arg/Bute 86 H4
Derrythorpe N Lincs 51 B10
Dersingham Norfolk 43 B9
Dervaig Arg/Bute 86 F4
Derwen Denbs 48 G1
Derwenlas Powys 37 F7
Desborough Northants 41 G10
Desford Leics 41 E6
Detchant Northum 78 D5
Detling Kent 14 C2
Deuddwr Powys 38 D3
Devauden Monmouths 17 B9
Devil's Bridge Ceredig'n 37 H7
Devizes Wilts 19 E7
Devol Invercl 82 G4
Devon & Exeter Racecourse Devon 8 F1
Devonport Plym'th 4 E5
Devonside Clack 83 E10
Devoran Cornw'l 3 F6
Dewar Scot Borders 77 C6
Dewlish Dorset 9 E9
Dewsbury W Yorks 57 F7
Dewsbury Moor W Yorks 57 F7
Dewshall Court Heref'd 28 E5
Dhoon I/Man 54 D4
Dhoor I/Man 54 C4
Dhowin I/Man 54 B4
Dial Post W Sussex 12 D5
Dibden Hants 11 D7
Dibden Purlieu Hants 11 D7
Dickleburgh Norfolk 44 G5
Didbrook Glos 30 E2
Didcot Oxon 20 C3
Diddington Cambs 32 B4
Diddlebury Shrops 39 G6
Didley Heref'd 28 E5
Didling W Sussex 12 D2
Didmarton Glos 18 C5
Didsbury Gtr Man 49 C9
Didworthy Devon 5 D7
Digby Lincs 52 G3
Digg H'land 100 F2
Diggle Gtr Man 50 B2
Digmoor Lancs 48 B5
Digswell Park Herts 32 G5
Dihewid Ceredig'n 26 C4
Dilham Norfolk 45 C7
Dilhorne Staffs 40 A1
Dillarburn S Lanarks 75 C10
Dillington Cambs 32 B4
Dilston Northum 70 D4
Dilton Marsh Wilts 18 G5
Dilwyn Heref'd 28 C5
Dinas Carms 25 C7
Dinas Gwyn 36 B2
Dinas Cross Pembs 24 C5
Dinas Dinlle Gwyn 46 G4
Dinas Mawddwy Gwyn 37 D8
Dinas Powys V/Glam 17 D6
Dinder Som'set 18 G2
Dinedor Heref'd 29 E6
Dingestow Monmouths 28 G5
Dingle Mersey 48 D4
Dingleden Kent 14 E3
Dingley Northants 41 G9
Dingwall H'land 102 G4
Dinlabyre Scot Borders 69 A8
Dinmael Conwy 37 A10
Dinnet Aberds 90 B5
Dinnington Som'set 9 C6
Dinnington S Yorks 51 D7
Dinnington Tyne/Wear 71 C7
Dinorwic Gwyn 46 F5
Dinton Bucks 31 G9
Dinton Wilts 10 A3
Dinwoodie Mains Dumf/Gal 68 A4
Dinworthy Devon 6 E4
Dippen N Ayrs 74 E2
Dippenhall Surrey 21 G6
Dipple Moray 98 C3
Dipple S Ayrs 74 G4
Diptford Devon 5 E8
Dipton Durham 71 E6
Dirdhu H'land 97 D8
Dirleton E Loth 85 F7
Dirt Pot Northum 70 F3
Discoed Powys 28 B3
Discovery Point Dundee C 84 B6
Diseworth Leics 41 C6
Dishes Orkney 110 F7
Dishforth N Yorks 63 G8
Disley Ches 50 D1
Diss Norfolk 44 H5
Disserth Powys 27 C10
Distington Cumb 60 B3
Ditchampton Wilts 10 A3
Ditcheat Som'set 18 H3
Ditchingham Norfolk 45 F7
Ditchling E Sussex 13 D7
Ditherington Shrops 39 D6
Dittisham Devon 5 E9
Ditton Halton 48 D5
Ditton Kent 14 C2
Ditton Green Cambs 33 C9
Ditton Priors Shrops 39 G7
Divlyn Carms 27 E7
Dixton Glos 30 E1
Dixton Monmouths 29 G6
Dobcross Gtr Man 50 B1
Dobwalls Cornw'l 4 D3
Doccombe Devon 5 B8
Dochfour Ho. H'land 96 C4
Dochgarroch H'land 96 B4
Docking Norfolk 44 B1
Docklow Heref'd 29 C6
Dockray Cumb 61 B6
Dockroyd W Yorks 56 E5
Dodburn Scot Borders 77 G7
Doddinghurst Essex 22 B5
Doddington Cambs 43 F6
Doddington Kent 14 C4
Doddington Lincs 52 E2
Doddington Northum 78 D4
Doddington Shrops 39 H7
Doddiscombsleigh Devon 5 B9
Dodford Northants 31 B8
Dodford Worcs 29 A10
Dodington S Gloucs 18 C4
Dodleston Ches 48 F4
Dods Leigh Staffs 40 B2
Dodworth S Yorks 50 B5
Doe Green Warrington 49 D6
Doe Lea Derby 51 F6
Dog Village Devon 8 E1
Dogdyke Lincs 52 G5
Dogmersfield Hants 20 F5
Dogridge Wilts 19 C7
Dogsthorpe Peterbro 42 E4
Dol fôr Powys 37 E8
Dôl y Bont Ceredig'n 37 G6
Dol y cannau Powys 28 D3
Dolanog Powys 38 D1
Dolau Powys 28 B2
Dolau Rh Cyn Taff 16 C4
Dolbenmaen Gwyn 36 A5
Dolfach Powys 37 E9
Dolfor Powys 38 G2
Dolgarrog Conwy 47 F7
Dolgellau Gwyn 37 D7
Dolgran Carms 25 C9
Dolhendre Gwyn 37 B8
Doll H'land 103 B7
Dollar Clack 83 E10
Dolley Green Powys 28 B3
Dollwen Ceredig'n 37 G6
Dolphin Flints 48 E2
Dolphinholme Lancs 55 C5
Dolphinton S Lanarks 76 C4
Dolton Devon 7 E6
Dolwen Conwy 47 E8
Dolwen Powys 37 E9
Dolwyd Conwy 47 E8
Dolwyddelan Conwy 47 G7
Dolyhir Powys 28 C3
Doncaster S Yorks 51 B7
Doncaster Racecourse S Yorks 51 B7
Dones Green Ches 49 E7
Donhead St. Andrew Wilts 10 B2
Donhead St. Mary Wilts 10 B2
Donibristle Fife 84 F3
Donington Lincs 42 B5
Donington on Bain Lincs 52 D5
Donington South Ing Lincs 42 B5
Donisthorpe Leics 40 D5
Donkey Town Surrey 21 E7
Donnington Glos 30 F3
Donnington Heref'd 29 E8
Donnington Shrops 39 E6
Donnington Telford 39 D8
Donnington W Berks 20 E2
Donnington W Sussex 12 E2
Donnington Wood Telford 39 D8
Donyatt Som'set 8 C5
Doonfoot S Ayrs 74 F5
Dorback Lodge H'land 97 E8
Dorchester Dorset 9 E8
Dorchester Oxon 20 B3
Dorchester Abbey, Wallingford Oxon 20 B3
Dordon Warwick 40 E4
Dore S Yorks 50 D5
Dores H'land 96 C3
Dorking Surrey 21 G9
Dormansland Surrey 22 G4
Dormanstown Redcar/Clevel'd 64 B3
Dormington Heref'd 29 D6
Dormston Worcs 30 C1
Dornal S Ayrs 66 C4
Dorney Bucks 21 D7
Dornie H'land 94 D5
Dornoch H'land 103 D6
Dornock Dumf/Gal 68 D5
Dorrery H'land 106 D5
Dorridge W Midlands 40 H3
Dorrington Lincs 52 G3
Dorrington Shrops 38 E5
Dorsington Warwick 30 D3
Dorstone Heref'd 28 D4
Dorton Bucks 31 G8
Dorusduain H'land 95 D6
Dosthill Staffs 40 F4
Dottery Dorset 9 E6
Doublebois Cornw'l 4 D2
Dougarie N Ayrs 73 D8
Doughton Glos 18 B5
Douglas I/Man 54 E3
Douglas S Lanarks 75 D10
Douglas & Angus Dundee C 84 A6
Douglas Water S Lanarks 76 D1
Douglas West S Lanarks 75 D10
Douglastown Angus 90 G5
Doulting Som'set 18 G3
Dounby Orkney 110 F3
Doune H'land 102 B3
Doune Stirl 83 D8
Doune Park Aberds 99 B7
Dounepark S Ayrs 74 H3
Douneside Aberds 98 H4
Dounie H'land 102 C4
Dounreay H'land 106 C4
Dousland Devon 5 D6
Dovaston Shrops 38 C4
Dove Cottage and Wordsworth Museum Cumb 61 D6
Dove Holes Derby 50 E2
Dovenby Cumb 68 G3
Dover Kent 15 D8
Dover Castle Kent 15 D8
Dovercourt Essex 35 E6
Doverdale Worcs 29 B9
Doveridge Derby 40 B3
Doversgreen Surrey 22 G2
Dowally Perth/Kinr 89 G11
Dowbridge Lancs 55 E4
Dowdeswell Glos 30 G1
Dowlais Merth Tyd 28 H1
Dowland Devon 7 E6
Dowlish Wake Som'set 8 C5
Down Ampney Glos 19 B8
Down Hatherley Glos 29 F9
Down St. Mary Devon 7 F8
Down Thomas Devon 5 E6
Downcraig Ferry N Ayrs 74 B3
Downderry Cornw'l 4 E4
Downe London 22 E4
Downend I/Wight 11 F8
Downend S Gloucs 18 D3
Downend W Berks 20 D2
Downfield Dundee C 84 A5
Downgate Cornw'l 4 C4
Downham Essex 23 B7
Downham Lancs 56 D2
Downham Northum 78 D3
Downham Market Norfolk 43 E9
Downhead Som'set 18 G3
Downhill Perth/Kinr 84 A2
Downhill Tyne/Wear 71 E8
Downholland Cross Lancs 48 B4
Downholme N Yorks 63 E6
Downies Aberds 91 B10
Downley Bucks 21 B6
Downside Som'set 18 G3
Downside Surrey 21 F9
Downton Hants 10 E5
Downton Wilts 10 B4
Downton on the Rock Heref'd 28 A5
Dowsby Lincs 42 C4
Dowsdale Lincs 42 D5
Dowthwaitehead Cumb 61 B6
Doxey Staffs 39 C10
Doxford Northum 79 E6
Doxford Park Tyne/Wear 71 E8
Doynton S Gloucs 18 D4
Draffan S Lanarks 75 C9
Dragonby N Lincs 58 G5
Drakeland Corner Devon 5 E6
Drakemyre N Ayrs 74 B4
Drake's Broughton Worcs 29 D10
Drakes Cross Worcs 40 H2
Drakewalls Cornw'l 4 C5
Draughton Northants 41 H9
Draughton N Yorks 56 C5
Drax N Yorks 58 F2
Draycote Warwick 31 A6
Draycott Derby 41 B6
Draycott Glos 30 E3
Draycott Som'set 17 F9
Draycott in the Clay Staffs 40 C3
Draycott in the Moors Staffs 40 A1
Drayford Devon 7 E8
Drayton Leics 41 F10
Drayton Lincs 42 B5
Drayton Norfolk 44 D5
Drayton Oxon 31 D6
Drayton Oxon 20 B2
Drayton Portsm'th 11 D9
Drayton Som'set 9 B6
Drayton Worcs 39 H10
Drayton Bassett Staffs 40 E3
Drayton Beauchamp Bucks 32 G2
Drayton Manor Park, Tamworth Staffs 40 E3
Drayton Parslow Bucks 31 F10
Drayton St. Leonard Oxon 20 B3
Dre fach Ceredig'n 26 D5
Dre fach Carms 27 G6
Dreamland Theme Park, Margate Kent 15 A8
Drebley N Yorks 56 C5
Dreemskerry I/Man 54 C4
Dreenhill Pembs 24 E4
Drefach Carms 25 C8
Drefach Carms 26 G5
Drefelin Carms 25 C8
Dreghorn N Ayrs 74 D5
Drellingore Kent 15 D7
Drem E Loth 85 G7
Dresden Stoke 39 A10
Dreumasdal W Isles 92 B3
Drewsteignton Devon 7 G8
Driby Lincs 53 E6
Driffield ER Yorks 59 C6
Driffield Glos 19 B7
Drigg Cumb 60 E3
Drighlington W Yorks 57 F7
Drimnin H'land 86 F5
Drimpton Dorset 9 D6
Drimsynie Arg/Bute 82 D2
Drinisiadar W Isles 109 H6
Drinkstone Suffolk 34 B3
Drinkstone Green Suffolk 34 B3
Drishaig Arg/Bute 82 C2
Drochil Scot Borders 76 C4
Drointon Staffs 40 C2
Droitwich Worcs 29 B9
Droman H'land 104 D4
Dron Perth/Kinr 84 C3
Dronfield Derby 50 E5
Dronfield Woodhouse Derby 50 E5
Drongan E Ayrs 75 F6
Dronley Angus 90 H4
Droxford Hants 11 C9
Droylsden Gtr Man 49 C10
Druid Denbs 37 A10
Druidston Pembs 24 E3
Druimarbin H'land 88 D1
Druimavuic Arg/Bute 87 G10
Druimdrishaig Arg/Bute 81 G7
Druimindarroch H'land 87 C6
Druimyeon More Arg/Bute 73 B6
Drum Arg/Bute 81 G9
Drum Perth/Kinr 84 D2
Drumbeg H'land 104 F4
Drumblade Aberds 98 D5
Drumblair Ho. Aberds 98 D6
Drumbuie Dumf/Gal 67 B7
Drumbuie H'land 94 C4
Drumburgh Cumb 68 E5
Drumburn Dumf/Gal 68 D2
Drumchapel Glasg C 83 G6
Drumchardine H'land 96 B3
Drumchork H'land 101 D6
Drumclog S Lanarks 75 D8
Drumderfit H'land 102 G5
Drumeldrie Fife 84 D6
Drumelzier Scot Borders 76 D4
Drumfearn H'land 94 E3
Drumgask H'land 89 B7
Drumgley Angus 90 F5
Drumguish H'land 96 G5
Drumin Moray 97 C9
Drumlasie Aberds 98 H6
Drumlemble Arg/Bute 73 F6
Drumligair Aberds 99 G9
Drumlithie Aberds 91 C8
Drummoddie Dumf/Gal 66 F5
Drummond H'land 102 F5
Drummore Dumf/Gal 66 G3
Drummuir Castle Moray 98 D3
Drumnadrochit H'land 96 D3
Drumnagorrach Moray 98 C5
Drumoak Aberds 91 B8
Drumpark Dumf/Gal 68 B1
Drumphail Dumf/Gal 66 D4
Drumrash Dumf/Gal 67 C8
Drumrunie H'land 101 B9
Drums Aberds 99 F9
Drumsallie H'land 87 D9
Drumstinchall Dumf/Gal 68 E1
Drumsturdy Angus 90 H5
Drumtochty Castle Aberds 91 D7
Drumtroddan Dumf/Gal 66 F5
Drumuie H'land 94 B1
Drumuillie H'land 97 D7
Drumvaich Stirl 83 D7
Drumwhindle Aberds 99 E9
Drunkendub Angus 91 G7
Drury Flints 48 F3
Drury Square Norfolk 44 D3
Drusillas Park, Polegate E Sussex 13 E9
Dry Doddington Lincs 51 H10
Dry Drayton Cambs 33 B6
Drybeck Cumb 61 C9
Drybridge Moray 98 B4
Drybridge N Ayrs 74 D5
Drybrook Glos 29 G7
Dryburgh Scot Borders 77 D8
Dryhope Scot Borders 76 E5
Drylaw C/Edinb 84 G4
Drym Cornw'l 2 F5
Drymen Stirl 82 F5
Drymuir Aberds 99 D9
Drynoch H'land 93 B10
Dryslwyn Carms 26 F5
Dryton Shrops 39 E6
Dubford Aberds 99 B8
Dubton Angus 91 F6
Duchally H'land 105 H6
Duchlage Arg/Bute 82 F4
Duck Corner Suffolk 35 D7
Duckington Ches 48 G5
Ducklington Oxon 30 H5
Duckmanton Derby 51 E6
Duck's Cross Beds 32 C4
Duddenhoe End Essex 33 E7
Duddingston C/Edinb 84 G4
Duddington Northants 42 E2
Duddleswell E Sussex 13 C8
Duddo Northum 78 C4
Duddon Ches 49 F6
Duddon Bridge Cumb 60 F5
Dudleston Shrops 38 B4
Dudleston Heath Shrops 38 B4
Dudley Tyne/Wear 71 C7
Dudley W Midlands 39 F10
Dudley Port W Midlands 40 F1
Dudley Zoo and Castle W Midlands 39 F10
Duffield Derby 40 A5
Duffryn Newp 17 C7
Duffryn Neath P Talb 16 B3
Dufftown Moray 98 E3
Duffus Moray 103 F10
Dufton Cumb 61 B9
Duggleby N Yorks 58 B4
Duirinish H'land 94 C4
Duisdalemore H'land 94 E4
Duisky H'land 87 D10
Dukestown Bl Gwent 28 G2
Dukinfield Gtr Man 49 C10
Dulas Angl 46 D4
Dulcote Som'set 18 G2
Dulford Devon 8 D2
Dull Perth/Kinr 89 G9
Dullatur N Lanarks 83 G8
Dullingham Cambs 33 C9
Dulnain Bridge H'land 97 D7
Duloe Beds 32 B4
Duloe Cornw'l 4 E3
Dulsie H'land 97 B7
Dulverton Som'set 7 D10
Dulwich London 22 D3
Dumbarton W Dunb 82 G4
Dumbleton Glos 30 E2
Dumcrieff Dumf/Gal 76 G4
Dumfries Dumf/Gal 68 C2
Dumgoyne Stirl 83 F6
Dummer Hants 20 G3
Dumpford W Sussex 12 C2
Dumpton Kent 15 B8
Dun Angus 91 F7
Dun Charlabhaigh W Isles 108 C6
Dunain Ho. H'land 96 B4
Dunalastair Perth/Kinr 89 F8
Dunan Arg/Bute 82 G2
Dunan H'land 94 D2
Dunans Arg/Bute 81 E10
Dunball Som'set 17 G8
Dunbar E Loth 85 G8
Dunbeath H'land 107 G6
Dunbeg Arg/Bute 81 A8
Dunblane Stirl 83 D8
Dunbog Fife 84 C4
Duncanston Aberds 98 F5
Duncanston H'land 102 G4
Dunchurch Warwick 31 A6
Duncote Northants 31 C8
Duncow Dumf/Gal 68 B2
Duncraggan Stirl 83 D6
Duncrievie Perth/Kinr 84 D3
Duncton W Sussex 12 D3
Dundas Ho. Orkney 110 K5
Dundee Dundee C 84 A6
Dundon Som'set 9 A6
Dundonald S Ayrs 74 D5
Dundonnell H'land 101 D8
Dundonnell Hotel H'land 101 D8
Dundonnell House H'land 101 D9
Dundraw Cumb 68 F5
Dundreggan H'land 95 E10
Dundreggan Lodge H'land 95 E10
Dundrennan Dumf/Gal 67 F9
Dundry N Som'set 18 E2
Dunecht Aberds 99 H7
Dunfermline Fife 84 F2
Dunfield Glos 19 B8
Dunford Bridge S Yorks 50 B3
Dungworth S Yorks 50 D4
Dunham Notts 51 E10
Dunham Massey Gtr Man 49 D8
Dunham on the Hill Ches 48 E5
Dunham Town Gtr Man 49 D8
Dunhampton Worcs 29 B9
Dunholme Lincs 52 E3
Dunino Fife 85 C7
Dunipace Falk 83 F9
Dunira Perth/Kinr 83 B8
Dunkeld Perth/Kinr 90 G1
Dunkerton Bath/NE Som'set 18 F4
Dunkeswell Devon 8 D3
Dunkeswick N Yorks 57 D8
Dunkirk Kent 14 C5
Dunkirk Norfolk 45 C6
Dunk's Green Kent 23 F6
Dunlappie Angus 91 E6
Dunley Hants 20 F2
Dunley Worcs 29 B8
Dunlichity Lodge H'land 96 C4
Dunlop E Ayrs 75 C6
Dunmaglass Lodge H'land 96 D3
Dunmore Arg/Bute 73 A7
Dunmore Falk 83 F9
Dunnet H'land 107 B7
Dunnichen Angus 91 G6
Dunninald Angus 91 F8
Dunning Perth/Kinr 84 C2
Dunnington ER Yorks 59 C7
Dunnington Warwick 30 C2
Dunnington C/York 58 C2
Dunnockshaw Lancs 56 F3
Dunollie Arg/Bute 81 A8
Dunoon Arg/Bute 82 G2
Dunragit Dumf/Gal 66 E3
Dunrobin Castle Museum & Gardens H'land 103 B7
Dunrostan Arg/Bute 81 F7
Duns Scot Borders 78 B2
Duns Tew Oxon 31 F6
Dunsby Lincs 42 C4
Dunscore Dumf/Gal 68 B1
Dunscroft S Yorks 51 B8
Dunsdale Redcar/Clevel'd 64 C4
Dunsden Green Oxon 20 D5
Dunsfold Surrey 12 B4
Dunsford Devon 5 B9
Dunshalt Fife 84 C4
Dunshillock Aberds 99 D9
Dunsley N Yorks 65 C6
Dunsmore Bucks 32 H1
Dunsop Bridge Lancs 56 C1
Dunstable Beds 32 F3
Dunstall Staffs 40 C3
Dunstall Common Worcs 29 D9
Dunstall Green Suffolk 33 B10
Dunstan Northum 79 F7
Dunstan Steads Northum 79 E7
Dunster Som'set 16 G4
Dunster Castle, Minehead Som'set 16 G4
Dunston Lincs 52 F3
Dunston Norfolk 45 E6
Dunston Staffs 39 D10
Dunston Tyne/Wear 71 D7
Dunsville S Yorks 51 B8
Dunswell ER Yorks 59 E6
Dunsyre S Lanarks 76 C3
Dunterton Devon 4 C4
Duntisbourne Abbots Glos 30 H1
Duntisbourne Leer Glos 30 H1
Duntisbourne Rouse Glos 30 H1
Duntish Dorset 9 D8
Duntocher W Dunb 82 G5
Dunton Beds 32 D5
Dunton Bucks 31 F10
Dunton Norfolk 44 B2
Dunton Bassett Leics 41 F7
Dunton Green Kent 22 F5
Dunton Wayletts Essex 23 B6
Duntulm H'land 109 K9
Dunure S Ayrs 74 F4
Dunvant Swan 25 G10
Dunvegan H'land 109 N7
Dunvegan Castle H'land 109 N7
Dunwich Suffolk 35 A8
Dunwood Staffs 49 G10
Dupplin Castle Perth/Kinr 84 C2
Durdar Cumb 69 E7
Durgates E Sussex 13 B10
Durham Durham 71 F7
Durham Cathedral Durham 71 F7
Durisdeer Dumf/Gal 76 G1
Durisdeermill Dumf/Gal 76 G1
Durkar W Yorks 57 G8
Durleigh Som'set 17 H7
Durley Hants 11 C8
Durley Wilts 19 E9
Durnamuck H'land 101 C8
Durness H'land 105 C7
Durno Aberds 99 F7
Duror H'land 87 F9
Durran Arg/Bute 81 D9
Durran H'land 107 C6
Durrington Wilts 19 G8
Durrington W Sussex 12 E5
Dursley Glos 18 B4
Durston Som'set 8 B4
Durweston Dorset 10 D1
Dury Shetl'd 111 G7
Duston Northants 31 B9
Duthil H'land 97 D7
Dutlas Powys 38 H3
Duton Hill Essex 33 F9
Dutson Cornw'l 4 B4
Dutton Ches 49 E6
Duxford Cambs 33 D7
Duxford Oxon 20 B1
Duxford Airfield (Imperial War Museum), Sawston Cambs 33 D7
Dwygyfylchi Conwy 47 E7
Dwyran Angl 46 F4
Dyce Aberd C 99 G8
Dye House Northum 70 E4
Dyffryn Bridg 16 B3
Dyffryn Carms 25 D8
Dyffryn Pembs 24 C4
Dyffryn Ardudwy Gwyn 36 C5
Dyffryn Castell Ceredig'n 37 G7
Dyffryn Ceidrych Carms 27 F7
Dyffryn Cellwen Neath P Talb 27 H8
Dyke Devon 6 D4
Dyke Lincs 42 C4
Dyke Moray 103 G8
Dykehead Angus 90 E4
Dykehead N Lanarks 76 B1
Dykehead Stirl 83 E6
Dykelands Aberds 91 E8
Dykends Angus 90 F3
Dykeside Aberds 99 D7
Dykesmains N Ayrs 74 C4
Dylife Powys 37 F8
Dymchurch Kent 14 F5
Dymock Glos 29 E8
Dyrham S Gloucs 18 D4
Dyrham Park S Gloucs 18 D4
Dysart Fife 84 E5
Dyserth Denbs 48 E1

E

Eachwick Northum 71 C6
Eadar Dha Fhadhail W Isles 108 D5
Eagland Hill Lancs 55 D4
Eagle Lincs 52 F1
Eagle Barnsdale Lincs 52 F1
Eagle Moor Lincs 52 F1
Eaglescliffe Stockton 63 C9
Eaglesfield Cumb 60 B3
Eaglesfield Dumf/Gal 68 C5
Eaglesham E Renf 75 B7
Eaglethorpe Northants 42 F3
Eairy I/Man 54 E2
Eakley Lanes M/Keynes 31 C10
Eakring Notts 51 F8
Ealand N Lincs 58 G3
Ealing London 21 C9
Eals Northum 69 E9
Eamont Bridge Cumb 61 B8
Earby Lancs 56 D4
Earcroft Blackb'n 56 F1
Eardington Shrops 39 F8
Eardisland Heref'd 28 C5
Eardisley Heref'd 28 D4
Eardiston Shrops 38 C4
Eardiston Worcs 29 B7
Earith Cambs 33 A6
Earl Shilton Leics 41 F6
Earl Soham Suffolk 35 B6
Earl Sterndale Derby 50 F2
Earl Stonham Suffolk 34 C5
Earle Northum 78 E4
Earley Wokingham 20 D5
Earlham Norfolk 45 E6
Earlish H'land 109 L8
Earl's Barton Northants 32 B1
Earl's Colne Essex 34 F2
Earl's Croome Worcs 29 D9
Earl's Green Suffolk 34 B4
Earlsdon W Midlands 40 H5
Earlsferry Fife 85 E6
Earlsfield Lincs 42 B2
Earlsford Aberds 99 E8
Earlsheaton W Yorks 57 F7
Earlsmill Moray 103 G8
Earlston Scot Borders 77 D8
Earlston E Ayrs 75 D6
Earlswood Monmouths 17 B9
Earlswood Surrey 22 G2
Earlswood Warwick 30 A3
Earnley W Sussex 12 F2
Earsairidh W Isles 92 F3
Earsdon Tyne/Wear 71 C8
Earshaig Dumf/Gal 76 G3
Earsham Norfolk 45 G7
Earswick C/York 58 C2
Eartham W Sussex 12 E3
Easby N Yorks 64 D3
Easby N Yorks 63 D6
Easdale Arg/Bute 81 C7
Easebourne W Sussex 12 C2
Easenhall Warwick 41 H6
Eashing Surrey 21 G7
Easington Bucks 31 G8
Easington Durham 71 F9
Easington ER Yorks 59 G9
Easington Northum 79 D6
Easington Oxon 31 E6
Easington Oxon 20 B4
Easington Redcar/Clevel'd 64 C5
Easington Colliery Durham 71 F9
Easington Lane Tyne/Wear 71 F8
Easingwold N Yorks 57 B10
Easole Street Kent 15 C7
Eassie Angus 90 G4
East Aberthaw V/Glam 16 E5
East Adderbury Oxon 31 E6
East Allington Devon 5 F8
East Anstey Devon 7 D9
East Appleton N Yorks 63 E7
East Ardsley W Yorks 57 F8
East Ashling W Sussex 12 E2
East Auchronie Aberds 99 H8
East Ayton N Yorks 65 F7
East Barkwith Lincs 52 D4
East Barming Kent 14 C2
East Barnby N Yorks 65 C6
East Barnet London 22 B2
East Barns E Loth 85 G9
East Barsham Norfolk 44 B3
East Beckham Norfolk 44 B5
East Bedfont London 21 D8
East Bergholt Suffolk 34 E4
East Bilney Norfolk 44 D3
East Blatchington E Sussex 13 E8
East Boldre Hants 11 D6
East Brent Som'set 17 F8
East Bridgford Notts 41 A8
East Buckland Devon 7 C7
East Budleigh Devon 8 F2
East Burrafirth Shetl'd 111 H6
East Burton Dorset 9 F10
East Butsfield Durham 71 F6
East Butterwick N Lincs 51 B10
East Cairnbeg Aberds 91 D8
East Calder W Loth 84 H2
East Carleton Norfolk 44 E5
East Carlton Northants 41 G10
East Carlton W Yorks 57 D7
East Chaldon Dorset 9 F9
East Challow Oxon 20 C1
East Chiltington E Sussex 13 D7
East Chinnock Som'set 9 C6
East Chisenbury Wilts 19 F8
East Clandon Surrey 21 F8
East Claydon Bucks 31 F9
East Clyne H'land 103 B8
East Coker Som'set 9 C7
East Combe Som'set 8 A3
East Common N Yorks 58 E2
East Compton Som'set 18 G3
East Cottingwith ER Yorks 58 D3
East Cowes I/Wight 11 E8
East Cowick ER Yorks 58 F2
East Cowton N Yorks 63 D8
East Cramlington Northum 71 C7
East Cranmore Som'set 18 G3
East Creech Dorset 10 F2
East Croachy H'land 96 D4
East Croftmore H'land 97 E7
East Curthwaite Cumb 69 F6
East Dean E Sussex 13 F9
East Dean Hants 10 B5
East Dean W Sussex 12 D3
East Dereham Norfolk 44 D3
East Down Devon 7 B7
East Drayton Notts 51 E9
East Ella Kingston/Hull 59 F6
East End Dorset 10 E2
East End ER Yorks 59 F8
East End Hants 11 E6
East End Hants 11 B9
East End Hants 20 E2
East End Herts 33 F7
East End Kent 14 E3
East End N Som'set 17 D9
East End Oxon 30 G5
East Farleigh Kent 14 C2
East Farndon Northants 41 G9
East Ferry Lincs 51 C10
East Fortune E Loth 85 G7
East Garston W Berks 20 D1
East Ginge Oxon 20 C2
East Goscote Leics 41 D8
East Grafton Wilts 19 E9
East Grimstead Wilts 10 B5
East Grinstead W Sussex 13 B7
East Guldeford E Sussex 14 F4
East Haddon Northants 31 B8
East Hagbourne Oxon 20 C3
East Halton N Lincs 59 G7
East Ham London 22 C4
East Hanney Oxon 20 B2
East Hanningfield Essex 23 A7
East Hardwick W Yorks 57 G9
East Harling Norfolk 44 G3
East Harlsey N Yorks 63 E9
East Harnham Wilts 10 B4
East Harptree Bath/NE Som'set 18 F2
East Hartford Northum 71 C7
East Harting W Sussex 12 D1
East Hatley Cambs 32 C5
East Hauxwell N Yorks 63 E6
East Haven Angus 91 H6
East Heckington Lincs 42 A4
East Hedleyhope Durham 71 F6
East Hendred Oxon 20 C2
East Herrington Tyne/Wear 71 E8
East Heslerton N Yorks 65 G7
East Hoathly E Sussex 13 D9
East Horrington Som'set 18 G2
East Horsley Surrey 21 F8
East Horton Northum 78 D5
East Huntspill Som'set 17 G8
East Hyde Beds 32 G4
East Ilkerton Devon 7 B8
East Ilsley W Berks 20 C2
East Keal Lincs 53 F6
East Kennett Wilts 19 E8
East Keswick W Yorks 57 D8
East Kilbride S Lanarks 75 B8
East Kirkby Lincs 53 F6
East Knapton N Yorks 65 G6
East Knighton Dorset 9 F10
East Knoyle Wilts 10 A1
East Kyloe Northum 78 D5
East Lambrook Som'set 9 C6
East Lamington H'land 103 E6
East Langdon Kent 15 D8
East Langton Leics 41 F9
East Langwell H'land 102 B6
East Lavant W Sussex 12 E2
East Lavington W Sussex 12 D3
East Layton N Yorks 63 D6
East Leake Notts 41 C7
East Learmouth Northum 78 D3
East Leigh Devon 7 F7
East Lexham Norfolk 44 D2
East Lilburn Northum 78 E5
East Linton E Loth 85 G7
East Liss Hants 12 C1
East Looe Cornw'l 4 E3
East Lound N Lincs 51 C9
East Lulworth Dorset 10 F1
East Lutton N Yorks 58 B5
East Lydford Som'set 9 A7
East Mains Aberds 91 B7
East Malling Kent 14 C2
East March Angus 90 H5
East Marden W Sussex 12 D2

Froncysyllte Wrex 38 A3
Frongoch Gwyn 37 B9
Frontierland Western Theme Park, Morecambe Lancs 55 B4
Frostenden Suffolk 45 G8
Frosterley Durham 70 G5
Frotoft Orkney 110 F5
Froxfield Wilts 19 E9
Froxfield Green Hants 11 B10
Froyle Hants 20 G5
Fryerning Essex 23 A6
Fryton N Yorks 64 G4
Fulbeck Lincs 52 G2
Fulbourn Cambs 33 C8
Fulbrook Oxon 30 G4
Fulford Som'set 8 B4
Fulford Staffs 40 B1
Fulford C/York 58 D2
Fulham London 22 D2
Fulking W Sussex 13 D6
Full Sutton ER Yorks 58 C3
Fullarton Glasg C 75 A8
Fullarton N Ayrs 74 D5
Fuller Street Essex 33 G10
Fuller's Moor Ches 48 G5
Fullerton Hants 20 H1
Fulletby Lincs 52 E5
Fullwood E Ayrs 75 B6
Fulmer Bucks 21 C7
Fulmodestone Norfolk 44 B3
Fulnetby Lincs 52 E3
Fulstow Lincs 53 C6
Fulwell Tyne/Wear 71 E8
Fulwood Lancs 55 E5
Fulwood S Yorks 50 D5
Fundenhall Norfolk 44 F5
Fundenhall Street Norfolk 44 F5
Funtington W Sussex 12 E1
Funtley Hants 11 D8
Funtullich Perth/Kinr 83 B8
Funzie Shetl'd 111 D9
Furley Devon 8 D4
Furnace Arg/Bute 81 D10
Furnace Carms 25 F10
Furnace End Warwick 40 F4
Furneaux Pelham Herts 33 F7
Furness Vale Derby 50 D2
Furze Platt Windsor 21 C6
Furzehill Devon 7 B8
Fyfett Som'set 8 C4
Fyfield Essex 33 H8
Fyfield Glos 19 A9
Fyfield Hants 19 G9
Fyfield Oxon 20 B2
Fyfield Wilts 19 E8
Fylingthorpe N Yorks 65 D7
Fyvie Aberds 99 E7

G

Gabhsann bho Dheas W Isles 108 B9
Gabhsann bho Thuath W Isles 108 B9
Gablon H'land 102 C6
Gabroc Hill E Ayrs 75 B6
Gaddesby Leics 41 D8
Gadebridge Herts 32 H3
Gaer Powys 28 F2
Gaerllwyd Monmouths 17 B9
Gaerwen Angl 46 E4
Gagingwell Oxon 31 F6
Gaick Lodge H'land 89 C8
Gailey Staffs 39 D10
Gainford Durham 63 C6
Gainsborough Lincs 51 C10
Gainsborough Suffolk 34 D5
Gainsford End Essex 33 E10
Gairloch H'land 101 E6
Gairlochy H'land 88 C2
Gairney Bank Perth/Kinr 84 E3
Gairnshiel Lodge Aberds 90 A3
Gaisgill Cumb 61 D9
Gaitsgill Cumb 69 F6
Galashiels Scot Borders 77 D7
Galgate Lancs 55 C4
Galhampton Som'set 9 B8
Gallaberry Dumf/Gal 68 B2
Gallachoille Arg/Bute 81 F7
Gallanach Arg/Bute 81 B8
Gallanach Arg/Bute 86 E2
Gallantry Bank Ches 49 G6
Gallatown Fife 84 E4
Galley Common Warwick 40 F5
Galley Hill Cambs 33 B6
Galleyend Essex 23 A7
Galleywood Essex 23 A7
Gallowfauld Angus 90 G5
Gallows Green Staffs 40 A2
Galltair H'land 94 D5
Galmisdale H'land 86 C4
Galmpton Devon 5 F7
Galmpton Torbay 5 E9
Galphay N Yorks 63 G7
Galston E Ayrs 75 D7
Galtrigill H'land 109 M6
Gamblesby Cumb 69 G9
Gamesley Derby 50 C2
Gamlingay Cambs 32 C5
Gammersgill N Yorks 62 F5
Gamrie Aberds 99 B7
Gamston Notts 51 E9
Ganarew Heref'd 29 G6
Ganavan Arg/Bute 81 A8
Gang Cornw'l 4 D4
Ganllwyd Gwyn 37 C7
Gannochy Angus 91 D6
Gannochy Perth/Kinr 84 B3
Gansclet H'land 107 E8
Ganstead ER Yorks 59 E7
Ganthorpe N Yorks 64 G4
Ganton N Yorks 65 G7
Garbat H'land 102 F3
Garbhallt Arg/Bute 81 E10
Garboldisham Norfolk 44 G4
Garden City Flints 48 F4
Garden Village Wrex 48 G4
Garden Village W Yorks 57 E9
Gardens of Gaia, Cranbrook Kent 14 E2
Gardenstown Aberds 99 B7
Garderhouse Shetl'd 111 J6
Gardham ER Yorks 58 D5
Gardin Shetl'd 111 G7
Gare Hill Som'set 18 G4
Garelochhead Arg/Bute 82 E3
Garford Oxon 20 B2
Garforth W Yorks 57 E9
Gargrave N Yorks 56 C4
Gargunnock Stirl 83 E8
Garlic Street Norfolk 45 G6
Garlieston Dumf/Gal 67 F6
Garlinge Green Kent 15 C6
Garlogie Aberds 99 H7
Garmond Aberds 99 C8
Garmony Arg/Bute 87 G6
Garmouth Moray 98 B3
Garn yr erw Torf 28 G3
Garnant Carms 27 G6
Garndiffaith Torf 17 A7
Garndolbenmaen Gwyn 36 A4
Garnedd Conwy 47 G7
Garnett Bridge Cumb 61 E8
Garnfadryn Gwyn 36 B2
Garnkirk N Lanarks 83 H7
Garnlydan Bl Gwent 28 G2
Garnswllt Swan 27 H6
Garrabost W Isles 108 D10
Garragie Lodge H'land 96 E3
Garraron Arg/Bute 81 D8
Garras Cornw'l 3 G6
Garreg Gwyn 37 A6
Garrick Perth/Kinr 83 C9
Garrigill Cumb 70 F2
Garriston N Yorks 63 E6
Garroch Dumf/Gal 67 B7
Garros H'land 100 F2
Garrow Perth/Kinr 89 G9
Garryhorn Dumf/Gal 67 A7
Garsdale Cumb 62 F2
Garsdale Head Cumb 62 E2
Garsdon Wilts 19 C6
Garshall Green Staffs 40 B1
Garsington Oxon 20 A3
Garstang Lancs 55 D4
Garston Mersey 48 D5
Garswood Mersey 49 C6
Gartcosh N Lanarks 83 H7
Garth Bridg 16 B3
Garth Gwyn 46 E5
Garth Powys 27 D9
Garth Shetl'd 111 H5
Garth Wrex 38 A3
Garth Row Cumb 61 E8
Garthamlock Glasg C 83 H7
Garthbrengy Powys 27 E10
Garthdee Aberd C 91 A10
Gartheli Ceredig'n 26 C5
Garthmyl Powys 38 F2
Garthorpe Leics 41 C10
Garthorpe N Lincs 58 G4
Gartly Aberds 98 E5
Gartmore Stirl 83 E6
Gartnagrenach Arg/Bute 73 B7
Gartness N Lanarks 75 A9
Gartness Stirl 83 F6
Gartocharn W Dunb 82 F5
Garton ER Yorks 59 E8
Garton on the Wolds ER Yorks 58 C5
Gartsherrie N Lanarks 83 H8
Gartymore H'land 103 A9
Garvald E Loth 85 G7
Garvamore H'land 88 B6
Garvard Arg/Bute 80 E3
Garvault Hotel H'land 106 F2
Garve H'land 102 F2
Garvestone Norfolk 44 E4
Garvock Aberds 91 D8
Garvock Invercl 82 G3
Garway Heref'd 28 F5
Garway Hill Heref'd 28 F5
Gaskan H'land 87 D7
Gastard Wilts 18 E5
Gasthorpe Norfolk 44 G3
Gatcombe I/Wight 11 F7
Gate Burton Lincs 51 D10
Gate Helmsley N Yorks 58 C2
Gateacre Mersey 48 D5
Gatebeck Cumb 61 F8
Gateford Notts 51 D7
Gateforth N Yorks 58 F1
Gatehead E Ayrs 74 D5
Gatehouse Northum 70 B2
Gatehouse of Fleet Dumf/Gal 67 E8
Gatelawbridge Dumf/Gal 76 H2
Gateley Norfolk 44 C3
Gatenby N Yorks 63 F8
Gateshead Tyne/Wear 71 D7
Gatesheath Ches 48 F5
Gateside Aberds 98 G6
Gateside Angus 90 G5
Gateside E Renf 75 B6
Gateside Fife 84 D3
Gateside N Ayrs 74 B5
Gathurst Gtr Man 49 B6
Gatley Gtr Man 49 D9
Gattonside Scot Borders 77 D8
Gaufron Powys 27 B9
Gaulby Leics 41 E8
Gauldry Fife 84 B5
Gaunt's Common Dorset 10 D3
Gautby Lincs 52 E4
Gavinton Scot Borders 78 B2
Gawber S Yorks 50 B5
Gawcott Bucks 31 E8
Gawsworth Ches 49 F9
Gawthorpe W Yorks 57 F7
Gawthrop Cumb 61 F9
Gawthwaite Cumb 60 F5
Gay Street W Sussex 12 C4
Gaydon Warwick 30 C5
Gayfield Orkney 110 C5
Gayhurst M/Keynes 31 D10
Gayle N Yorks 62 F3
Gayles N Yorks 63 D6
Gayton Mersey 48 D3
Gayton Norfolk 43 D10
Gayton Northants 31 C9
Gayton Staffs 40 C1
Gayton le Marsh Lincs 53 D7
Gayton le Wold Lincs 52 D5
Gayton Thorpe Norfolk 43 D10
Gaywood Norfolk 43 C9
Gazeley Suffolk 33 B10
Geanies House H'land 103 E7
Gearraidh Bhailteas W Isles 92 C3
Gearraidh Bhaird W Isles 108 E8
Gearraidh na h Aibhne W Isles 108 D7
Gearraidh na Monadh W Isles 92 D3
Gearrannan W Isles 108 C6
Geary H'land 109 L7
Geddes House H'land 103 G7
Gedding Suffolk 34 C3
Geddington Northants 42 G1
Gedintailor H'land 94 C2
Gedling Notts 41 A8
Gedney Lincs 43 C7
Gedney Broadgate Lincs 43 C7
Gedney Drove End Lincs 43 C7
Gedney Dyke Lincs 43 C7
Gedney Hill Lincs 43 D6
Gee Cross Gtr Man 50 C1
Geilston Arg/Bute 82 G4
Geirinis W Isles 92 A3
Geise H'land 107 C6
Geisiadar W Isles 108 D6
Geldeston Norfolk 45 F7
Gell Conwy 47 F8
Gelli Pembs 24 E5
Gelli Rh Cyn Taff 16 B4
Gellideg Merth Tyd 27 H10
Gellifor Denbs 48 F2
Gelligaer Caerph 17 B6
Gellilydan Gwyn 37 B6
Gellinudd Neath P Talb 16 A2
Gellyburn Perth/Kinr 90 H1
Gellywen Carms 25 D7
Gelston Dumf/Gal 67 E9
Gelston Lincs 42 A2
Gembling ER Yorks 59 C7
Gentleshaw Staffs 40 D2
Geocrab W Isles 109 H6
George Green Bucks 21 C8
George Nympton Devon 7 D8
George Town Bl Gwent 28 H2
Georgefield Dumf/Gal 68 A5
Georgeham Devon 6 C5
Georth Orkney 110 F4
Gerlan Gwyn 47 F6
Germansweek Devon 6 G5
Germoe Cornw'l 2 G4
Gerrans Cornw'l 3 F7
Gerrards Cross Bucks 21 C8
Gestingthorpe Essex 34 E2
Geuffordd Powys 38 D3
Gib Hill Ches 49 E7
Gibbet Hill Warwick 41 G7
Gibbshill Dumf/Gal 67 C9
Gidea Park London 22 C5
Gidleigh Devon 5 B7
Giffnock E Renf 75 B7
Gifford E Loth 85 H7
Giffordland N Ayrs 74 C4
Giffordtown Fife 84 C4
Giggleswick N Yorks 56 B3
Gilberdyke ER Yorks 58 F4
Gilchriston E Loth 85 H6
Gilcrux Cumb 68 G4
Gildersome W Yorks 57 F7
Gildingwells S Yorks 51 D7
Gileston V/Glam 16 E5
Gilfach Caerph 17 B6
Gilfach Goch Rh Cyn Taff 16 C4
Gilfachrheda Ceredig'n 26 C4
Gillamoor N Yorks 64 F4
Gillar's Green Mersey 48 C5
Gillen H'land 109 M7
Gilling East N Yorks 64 G4
Gilling West N Yorks 63 D6
Gillingham Dorset 9 B10
Gillingham Medway 14 B2
Gillingham Norfolk 45 F8
Gillock H'land 107 D7
Gillow Heath Staffs 49 G9
Gills H'land 107 B8
Gill's Green Kent 14 E2
Gilmanscleuch Scot Borders 77 E6
Gilmerton C/Edinb 84 H4
Gilmerton Perth/Kinr 83 B9
Gilmonby Durham 62 C4
Gilmorton Leics 41 G7
Gilmourton S Lanarks 75 C8
Gilsland Cumb 69 D9
Gilsland Spa Cumb 69 D9
Gilston Scot Borders 77 B7
Gilwern Monmouths 28 G3
Gimingham Norfolk 45 B6
Giosla W Isles 108 E6
Gipping Suffolk 34 B4
Gipsey Bridge Lincs 52 H5
Girdle Toll N Ayrs 74 C5
Girlsta Shetl'd 111 H7
Girsby N Yorks 63 D8
Girtford Beds 32 C4
Girthon Dumf/Gal 67 E8
Girton Cambs 33 B7
Girton Notts 51 F10
Girvan S Ayrs 74 H3
Gisburn Lancs 56 D3
Gisleham Suffolk 45 G9
Gislingham Suffolk 34 A4
Gissing Norfolk 44 G5
Gittisham Devon 8 E3
Gladestry Powys 28 C3
Gladsmuir E Loth 85 G6
Glais Swan 16 A2
Glaisdale N Yorks 64 D5
Glame H'land 94 B2
Glamis Angus 90 G4
Glamis Castle Angus 90 G4
Glan Adda Gwyn 46 E5
Glan Conwy Conwy 47 G8
Glan Conwy Conwy 47 E8
Glan Duar Carms 26 D5
Glan Dwyfach Gwyn 36 A4
Glan Gors Angl 46 E4
Glan rhyd Gwyn 46 G4
Glan traeth Angl 46 E2
Glan y don Flints 48 E2
Glan y nant Powys 37 G9
Glan y wern Gwyn 37 B6
Glan yr afon Angl 47 D6
Glan yr afon Gwyn 37 A9
Glan yr afon Gwyn 37 A10
Glanaman Carms 27 G6
Glandford Norfolk 44 A4
Glandwr Pembs 25 D6
Glandy Cross Carms 24 D6
Glandyfi Ceredig'n 37 F6
Glangrwyney Powys 28 G3
Glanmule Powys 38 F2
Glanrafon Ceredig'n 37 G6
Glanrhyd Gwyn 36 B2
Glanrhyd Pembs 24 B6
Glanton Northum 78 F5
Glanton Pike Northum 78 F5
Glanvilles Wootton Dorset 9 D8
Glapthorn Northants 42 F3
Glapwell Derby 51 F6
Glas allt Shiel Aberds 90 C3
Glasbury Powys 28 E2
Glaschoil H'land 97 C8
Glascoed Denbs 47 E9
Glascoed Monmouths 17 A8
Glascoed Powys 38 D2
Glascorrie Aberds 90 B4
Glascote Staffs 40 E4
Glascwm Powys 28 C2
Glasdrum Arg/Bute 87 G10
Glasfryn Conwy 47 G9
Glasgow Glasg C 83 H6
Glasgow Art Gallery & Museum Glasg C 83 H6
Glasgow Botanic Gardens Glasg C 83 H6
Glasgow Cathedral Glasg C 83 H7
Glashvin H'land 100 F2
Glasinfryn Gwyn 46 F5
Glasnacardoch H'land 94 G3
Glasnakille H'land 94 E2
Glasphein H'land 109 N6
Glaspwll Powys 37 F7
Glassburn H'land 96 C1
Glasserton Dumf/Gal 67 G6
Glassford S Lanarks 75 C9
Glasshouse Hill Glos 29 F8
Glasshouses N Yorks 57 B6
Glasslie Fife 84 D4
Glasson Cumb 68 D5
Glasson Lancs 55 C4
Glassonby Cumb 69 G8
Glasterlaw Angus 91 F6
Glaston Rutl'd 42 E1
Glastonbury Som'set 18 H2
Glastonbury Abbey Som'set 17 H9
Glatton Cambs 42 G4
Glazebrook Warrington 49 C7
Glazebury Warrington 49 C7
Glazeley Shrops 39 G8
Gleadless S Yorks 50 D5
Gleadsmoss Ches 49 F9
Gleann Ghrabhair W Isles 108 F8
Gleann Tholastaidh W Isles 108 C10
Gleaston Cumb 60 G5
Gleiniant Powys 37 F9
Glemsford Suffolk 34 D2
Glen Dumf/Gal 67 E7
Glen Dumf/Gal 67 C10
Glen Auldyn I/Man 54 C4
Glen Bernisdale H'land 109 N9
Glen House Scot Borders 76 D5
Glen Mona I/Man 54 D4
Glen Nevis House H'land 88 D2
Glen of Luce Dumf/Gal 66 E4
Glen Parva Leics 41 F7
Glen Tanar House Aberds 90 B5
Glen Trool Lodge Dumf/Gal 67 B6
Glen Village Falk 83 G9
Glen Vine I/Man 54 E3
Glenamachrie Arg/Bute 81 B9
Glenbarr Arg/Bute 73 D6
Glenbeg H'land 86 E5
Glenbeg H'land 97 D8
Glenbervie Aberds 91 C8
Glenboig N Lanarks 83 H8
Glenborrodale H'land 87 E6
Glenbranter Arg/Bute 82 E2
Glenbreck Scot Borders 76 E3
Glenbrein Lodge H'land 96 E2
Glenbrittle House H'land 93 C10
Glenbuchat Lodge Aberds 98 G3
Glenbuck E Ayrs 75 E9
Glenburn Renf 75 A6
Glencalvie Lodge H'land 102 D3
Glencanisp Lodge H'land 104 G4
Glencaple Dumf/Gal 68 D2
Glencarron Lodge H'land 101 G8
Glencarse Perth/Kinr 84 B3
Glencassley Castle H'land 102 B3
Glenceitlein H'land 88 G2
Glencoe H'land 88 F1
Glencraig Fife 84 E3
Glencripesdale H'land 87 F6
Glencrosh Dumf/Gal 67 B9
Glendavan Ho. Aberds 90 A5
Glendevon Perth/Kinr 84 D1
Glendoe Lodge H'land 96 F2
Glendoebeg H'land 96 F2
Glendoick Perth/Kinr 84 B4
Glendoll Lodge Angus 90 D3
Glenduckie Fife 84 C4
Glendye Lodge Aberds 91 C7
Gleneagles Hotel Perth/Kinr 83 C10
Gleneagles House Perth/Kinr 83 D10
Glenegedale Arg/Bute 72 B3
Glenelg H'land 94 E5
Glenernie Moray 97 B8
Glenfarg Perth/Kinr 84 C3
Glenfarquhar Lodge Aberds 91 C8
Glenferness House H'land 97 B7
Glenfeshie Lodge H'land 89 B9
Glenfiddich Distillery, Dufftown Moray 98 D3
Glenfield Leics 41 E7
Glenfinnan H'land 87 C8
Glenfoot Perth/Kinr 84 C3
Glenfyne Lodge Arg/Bute 82 C3
Glengarnock N Ayrs 74 B5
Glengorm Castle Arg/Bute 86 F4
Glengrasco H'land 93 A10
Glenhead Farm Angus 90 E3
Glenhoul Dumf/Gal 67 B8
Glenhurich H'land 87 E8
Glenkerry Scot Borders 76 F5
Glenkiln Dumf/Gal 67 C10
Glenkindie Aberds 98 G4
Glenlatterach Moray 103 G10
Glenlee Dumf/Gal 67 B8
Glenlichorn Perth/Kinr 83 C8
Glenlivet Moray 97 D9
Glenlochsie Perth/Kinr 90 D1
Glenloig N Ayrs 73 D9
Glenluce Dumf/Gal 66 E4
Glenmallan Arg/Bute 82 E3
Glenmarksie H'land 102 G2
Glenmassan Arg/Bute 82 F2
Glenmavis N Lanarks 83 H8
Glenmaye I/Man 54 E2
Glenmidge Dumf/Gal 68 B1
Glenmore Arg/Bute 81 C8
Glenmore H'land 93 A10
Glenmore Lodge H'land 97 F7
Glenmoy Angus 90 E5
Glenogil Angus 90 E5
Glenprosen Lodge Angus 90 E3
Glenprosen Village Angus 90 E4
Glenquiech Angus 90 E5
Glenreasdell Mains Arg/Bute 73 B8
Glenree N Ayrs 73 E9
Glenridding Cumb 61 C6
Glenrossal H'land 102 B3
Glenrothes Fife 84 D4
Glensanda H'land 87 G8
Glensaugh Aberds 91 D7
Glenshero Lodge H'land 88 B6
Glensluain Arg/Bute 82 E1
Glenstockadale Dumf/Gal 66 D2
Glenstriven Arg/Bute 82 G1
Glentaggart S Lanarks 75 E10
Glentham Lincs 52 C3
Glentirranmuir Stirl 83 E7
Glenton Aberds 98 F6
Glentress Scot Borders 76 D5
Glentromie Lodge H'land 96 G5
Glentrool Village Dumf/Gal 66 C5
Glentruan I/Man 54 B4
Glentruim House H'land 89 B7
Glenturret Distillery, Crieff Perth/Kinr 83 B9
Glentworth Lincs 52 D2
Glenuig H'land 87 D6
Glenurquhart H'land 102 F6
Glespin S Lanarks 75 E10
Gletness Shetl'd 111 H7
Glewstone Heref'd 29 F6
Glinton Peterbro 42 E4
Glooston Leics 41 F9
Glororum Northum 79 D6
Glossop Derby 50 C2
Gloster Hill Northum 79 G7
Gloucester Glos 29 G9
Gloucester Cathedral Glos 29 G9
Gloup Shetl'd 111 C8
Glusburn N Yorks 56 D5
Gluss Shetl'd 111 F6
Glutt Lodge H'land 106 F4
Glutton Bridge Derby 50 F2
Glympton Oxon 31 F6
Glyn Ceiriog Wrex 38 B3
Glyn cywarch Gwyn 37 B6
Glyn Neath Neath P Talb 27 H8
Glynarthen Ceredig'n 25 B8
Glynbrochan Powys 37 G9
Glyncoch Rh Cyn Taff 16 B5
Glyncorrwg Neath P Talb 16 B3
Glynde E Sussex 13 E8
Glyndebourne E Sussex 13 D8
Glyndyfrdwy Denbs 38 A2
Glynogwr Bridg 16 C4
Glyntaff Rh Cyn Taff 16 C5
Glyntawe Powys 27 G8
Gnosall Staffs 39 C9
Gnosall Heath Staffs 39 C9
Goadby Leics 41 F9
Goadby Marwood Leics 41 C9
Goat Lees Kent 14 D5
Goatacre Wilts 19 D7
Goathill Dorset 9 C8
Goathland N Yorks 65 D6
Goathurst Som'set 8 A4
Gobernuisgach Lodge H'land 105 E7
Gobhaig W Isles 108 G5
Gobowen Shrops 38 B4
Godalming Surrey 21 G7
Godley Gtr Man 50 C1
Godmanchester Cambs 32 A5
Godmanston Dorset 9 E8
Godmersham Kent 14 C5
Godney Som'set 17 G9
Godolphin Cross Cornw'l 2 F5
Godre'r graig Neath P Talb 27 H7
Godshill Hants 10 C4
Godshill I/Wight 11 F8
Godstone Surrey 22 F3
Godstone Farm Surrey 22 F3
Godwinscroft Hants 10 E4
Goetre Monmouths 28 H4
Goferydd Angl 46 D2
Goff's Oak Herts 22 A3
Gogar C/Edinb 84 G3
Goginan Ceredig'n 37 G6
Golan Gwyn 36 A5
Golant Cornw'l 4 E2
Golberdon Cornw'l 4 C4
Golborne Gtr Man 49 C7
Golcar W Yorks 57 G6
Gold Hill Cambs 43 F8
Goldcliff Newp 17 C8
Golden Cross E Sussex 13 D9
Golden Green Kent 23 G6
Golden Grove Carms 26 G5
Golden Hill Hants 10 E5
Golden Pot Hants 20 G5
Golden Valley Glos 29 F10
Goldenhill Stoke 49 G9
Golders Green London 22 C2
Goldhanger Essex 34 H3
Golding Shrops 39 E6
Goldington Beds 32 C3
Goldsborough N Yorks 57 C8
Goldsborough N Yorks 65 C6
Goldsithney Cornw'l 2 F4
Goldsworthy Devon 6 D4
Goldthorpe S Yorks 51 B6
Gollanfield H'land 103 G7
Golspie H'land 103 B7
Golval H'land 106 C3
Gomeldon Wilts 19 H8
Gomersal W Yorks 57 F7
Gomshall Surrey 21 G8
Gonalston Notts 51 H8
Gonfirth Shetl'd 111 G6
Good Easter Essex 33 G9
Gooderstone Norfolk 44 E1
Goodleigh Devon 7 C7
Goodmanham ER Yorks 58 D4
Goodnestone Kent 14 B5
Goodnestone Kent 15 C7
Goodrich Heref'd 29 G6
Goodrington Torbay 5 E9
Goodshaw Lancs 56 F3
Goodwick Pembs 24 C4
Goodwood Racecourse W Sussex 12 D2
Goodworth Clatford Hants 20 G1
Goole ER Yorks 58 F3
Goonbell Cornw'l 3 E6
Goonhavern Cornw'l 3 D6
Goose Eye W Yorks 56 D5
Goose Green Gtr Man 49 B6
Goose Green Norfolk 44 G5
Goose Green W Sussex 12 D5
Gooseham Cornw'l 6 E3
Goosey Oxon 20 B1
Goosnargh Lancs 55 E5
Goostrey Ches 49 E8
Gorcott Hill Warwick 30 B2
Gord Shetl'd 111 L7
Gordon Scot Borders 77 C9
Gordonbush H'land 103 B7
Gordonsburgh Moray 98 B4
Gordonstoun Moray 103 F10
Gordonstown Aberds 98 C5
Gordonstown Aberds 99 E7
Gore Kent 15 C8
Gore Cross Wilts 19 F7
Gore Pit Essex 34 G2
Gorebridge Midloth 77 A6
Gorefield Cambs 43 D7
Gorey Jersey 4
Gorgie C/Edinb 84 G4
Goring Oxon 20 C4
Goring by Sea W Sussex 12 E5
Goring Heath Oxon 20 D4
Gorleston on Sea Norfolk 45 E9
Gornalwood W Midlands 39 F10
Gorrachie Aberds 99 C7
Gorran Churchtown Cornw'l 3 E8
Gorran Haven Cornw'l 3 E9
Gorrenberry Scot Borders 77 H7
Gors Ceredig'n 37 H6
Gorse Hill Swindon 19 C8
Gorsedd Flints 48 E2
Gorseinon Swan 25 G10
Gorseness Orkney 110 G5
Gorsgoch Ceredig'n 26 C4
Gorslas Carms 26 G5
Gorsley Glos 29 F7
Gorstan H'land 102 F2
Gorstanvorran H'land 87 D8
Gorsteyhill Staffs 49 G8
Gorsty Hill Staffs 40 C3
Gortantaoid Arg/Bute 80 G3
Gorton Gtr Man 49 C9
Gosbeck Suffolk 34 C5
Gosberton Lincs 42 B5
Gosberton Clough Lincs 42 C4
Gosfield Essex 34 F1
Gosford Heref'd 29 B6
Gosforth Cumb 60 D3
Gosforth Tyne/Wear 71 D7
Gosmore Herts 32 F4
Gosport Hants 11 E9
Gossabrough Shetl'd 111 E8
Gossington Glos 18 A4
Goswick Northum 78 C5
Gotham Notts 41 B7
Gotherington Glos 30 F1
Gott Shetl'd 111 J7
Goudhurst Kent 14 E2
Goulceby Lincs 52 E5
Gourdas Aberds 99 D7
Gourdon Aberds 91 D9
Gourock Invercl 82 G3
Govan Glasg C 83 H6
Govanhill Glasg C 75 A7
Goveton Devon 5 F8
Govilon Monmouths 28 G3
Gowanhill Aberds 99 B10
Gowdall ER Yorks 58 F2
Gowerton Swan 25 G10
Gowkhall Fife 84 F2
Gowthorpe ER Yorks 58 C3
Goxhill ER Yorks 59 D7
Goxhill N Lincs 59 F7
Goxhill Haven N Lincs 59 F7
Goybre Neath P Talb 16 C2
Grabhair W Isles 108 F8
Graby Lincs 42 C3
Grade Cornw'l 3 H6
Graffham W Sussex 12 D3
Grafham Cambs 32 B4
Grafham Surrey 21 G8
Grafton Heref'd 28 E5
Grafton N Yorks 57 B9
Grafton Oxon 19 A9
Grafton Shrops 38 D5
Grafton Worcs 29 B6
Grafton Flyford Worcs 30 C1
Grafton Regis Northants 31 D9
Grafton Underwood Northants 42 G2
Grafty Green Kent 14 D3
Graianrhyd Denbs 48 G3
Graig Conwy 47 E8
Graig Denbs 48 E1
Graig fechan Denbs 48 G2
Grain Medway 23 D8
Grainsby Lincs 52 C5
Grainthorpe Lincs 53 C6
Grampound Cornw'l 3 E8
Grampound Road Cornw'l 3 D8
Gramsdal W Isles 109 M3
Granborough Bucks 31 F9
Granby Notts 41 B9
Grandborough Warwick 31 B6
Grandtully Perth/Kinr 89 F10
Grange Cumb 60 C5
Grange E Ayrs 75 D6
Grange Medway 14 B2
Grange Mersey 48 D3
Grange Perth/Kinr 84 B4
Grange Crossroads Moray 98 C4
Grange Hall Moray 103 F9
Grange Hill Essex 22 B4
Grange Moor W Yorks 57 G7
Grange of Lindores Fife 84 C4
Grange over Sands Cumb 61 G7
Grange Villa Durham 71 E7
Grangemill Derby 50 G4
Grangemouth Falk 83 F10
Grangepans Falk 84 F2
Grangetown Card 17 D6
Grangetown Redcar/Clevel'd 64 B3
Granish H'land 97 E7
Gransmoor ER Yorks 59 C7
Granston Pembs 24 C3
Grantchester Cambs 33 C7
Grantham Lincs 42 B2
Grantley N Yorks 57 B7
Grantlodge Aberds 99 G7
Granton Dumf/Gal 76 G3
Granton C/Edinb 84 G4
Grantown on Spey H'land 97 D8
Grantshouse Scot Borders 85 H10
Grappenhall Warrington 49 D7
Grasby Lincs 52 B3
Grasmere Cumb 61 D6
Grasscroft Gtr Man 50 B1
Grassendale Mersey 48 D4
Grassholme Durham 62 B4
Grassington N Yorks 56 B5
Grassmoor Derby 51 F6
Grassthorpe Notts 51 F9
Grateley Hants 19 G9
Gratwich Staffs 40 B2
Graveley Cambs 32 B5
Graveley Herts 32 F5
Gravelly Hill W Midlands 40 F3
Gravels Shrops 38 E4
Graveney Kent 14 B5
Gravesend Kent 23 D6
Grayingham Lincs 52 C2
Grayrigg Cumb 61 E8
Grays Thurr'k 23 D6
Grayshott Hants 12 B2
Grayswood Surrey 12 B3
Graythorp Hartlep'l 64 B3
Grazeley Wokingham 20 E4
Greasbrough S Yorks 51 C6
Greasby Mersey 48 D3
Great Abington Cambs 33 D8
Great Addington Northants 32 A2
Great Alne Warwick 30 C3
Great Altcar Lancs 48 B4
Great Amwell Herts 33 G6
Great Asby Cumb 61 C9
Great Ashfield Suffolk 34 B3
Great Ayton N Yorks 64 C3
Great Baddow Essex 23 A7
Great Bardfield Essex 33 E9
Great Barford Beds 32 C4
Great Barr W Midlands 40 F2
Great Barrington Glos 30 G4
Great Barrow Ches 48 F5
Great Barton Suffolk 34 B2
Great Barugh N Yorks 64 G5
Great Bavington Northum 70 B4
Great Bealings Suffolk 35 D6
Great Bedwyn Wilts 19 E9
Great Bentley Essex 34 F5
Great Billing Northants 31 B10
Great Bircham Norfolk 44 B1
Great Blakenham Suffolk 34 C5
Great Blencow Cumb 69 G7
Great Bolas Telford 39 C7
Great Bookham Surrey 21 F9
Great Bourton Oxon 31 D6
Great Bowden Leics 41 G9
Great Bradley Suffolk 33 C9
Great Braxted Essex 34 G2
Great Bricett Suffolk 34 C4
Great Brickhill Bucks 32 E2
Great Bridgeford Staffs 39 C9
Great Brington Northants 31 B8
Great Bromley Essex 34 F4
Great Broughton Cumb 68 G3
Great Broughton N Yorks 64 D3
Great Budworth Ches 49 E7
Great Burdon D'lington 63 C8
Great Burgh Surrey 22 F2
Great Burstead Essex 23 B6
Great Busby N Yorks 64 D3
Great Canfield Essex 33 G8
Great Carlton Lincs 53 D7
Great Casterton Rutl'd 42 E3
Great Chart Kent 14 D4
Great Chatwell Staffs 39 D8
Great Chesterford Essex 33 D8
Great Cheverell Wilts 19 F6
Great Chishill Cambs 33 E7
Great Clacton Essex 34 G5
Great Cliff W Yorks 57 G8
Great Clifton Cumb 60 B3
Great Coates NE Lincs 52 B5
Great Comberton Worcs 30 D1
Great Corby Cumb 69 E7
Great Cornard Suffolk 34 D2
Great Cowden ER Yorks 59 D8
Great Coxwell Oxon 19 B9
Great Crakehall N Yorks 63 E7
Great Cransley Northants 41 H10
Great Cressingham Norfolk 44 E2
Great Crosby Mersey 48 C4
Great Cubley Derby 40 B3
Great Dalby Leics 41 D9
Great Doddington Northants 32 B1
Great Dunham Norfolk 44 D2
Great Dunmow Essex 33 F9
Great Durnford Wilts 19 H8
Great Easton Essex 33 F9
Great Easton Leics 41 F10
Great Eccleston Lancs 55 D4
Great Edstone N Yorks 64 F5
Great Ellingham Norfolk 44 F4
Great Elm Som'set 18 G4
Great Everdon Northants 31 C7
Great Eversden Cambs 33 C6
Great Fencote N Yorks 63 E7
Great Finborough Suffolk 34 C4
Great Fransham Norfolk 44 D2
Great Gaddesden Herts 32 G3
Great Gidding Cambs 42 G4
Great Givendale ER Yorks 58 C4
Great Glemham Suffolk 35 B7
Great Glen Leics 41 F8
Great Gonerby Lincs 42 B1
Great Gransden Cambs 32 C5
Great Green Norfolk 45 G6
Great Green Suffolk 34 C3
Great Habton N Yorks 64 G5
Great Hale Lincs 42 A4
Great Hampden Bucks 21 A6
Great Harrowden Northants 32 A1
Great Harwood Lancs 56 E2
Great Haseley Oxon 20 A4
Great Hatfield ER Yorks 59 D7
Great Haywood Staffs 40 C2
Great Heath W Midlands 40 G5
Great Heck N Yorks 58 F1
Great Henny Essex 34 E2
Great Hinton Wilts 19 F6
Great Hockham Norfolk 44 F3
Great Holland Essex 35 G6
Great Horkesley Essex 34 E3
Great Hormead Herts 33 F6
Great Horton W Yorks 57 E6
Great Horwood Bucks 31 E9
Great Houghton Northants 31 C9
Great Houghton S Yorks 51 B6
Great Hucklow Derby 50 E3
Great Kelk ER Yorks 59 C7
Great Kimble Bucks 31 H10
Great Kingshill Bucks 21 B6
Great Langton N Yorks 63 E7
Great Leighs Essex 33 G10
Great Lever Gtr Man 49 B8
Great Limber Lincs 52 B4
Great Linford M/Keynes 32 D1
Great Livermere Suffolk 34 A2
Great Longstone Derby 50 E4
Great Lumley Durham 71 F7
Great Lyth Shrops 38 E5
Great Malvern Worcs 29 D8
Great Maplestead Essex 34 E2
Great Marton Blackp'l 55 E3
Great Massingham Norfolk 44 C1
Great Melton Norfolk 44 E5
Great Milton Oxon 20 A4
Great Missenden Bucks 21 A6
Great Mitton Lancs 56 E2
Great Mongeham Kent 15 C8
Great Moulton Norfolk 44 F5
Great Munden Herts 33 F6
Great Musgrave Cumb 62 C2
Great Ness Shrops 38 D4
Great Oakley Essex 34 F5
Great Oakley Northants 42 G1
Great Offley Herts 32 F4
Great Orme Tramway, Llandudno Conwy 47 D7
Great Ormside Cumb 62 C2
Great Orton Cumb 69 E6
Great Ouseburn N Yorks 57 B9
Great Oxendon Northants 41 G9
Great Oxney Green Essex 33 H9
Great Palgrave Norfolk 44 D2
Great Paxton Cambs 32 B5
Great Plumpton Lancs 55 E3
Great Plumstead Norfolk 45 D7
Great Ponton Lincs 42 B2
Great Preston W Yorks 57 F9
Great Raveley Cambs 42 G5
Great Rissington Glos 30 G3
Great Rollright Oxon 30 E5
Great Ryburgh Norfolk 44 C3
Great Ryle Northum 78 F5
Great Ryton Shrops 38 E5
Great Saling Essex 33 F10
Great Salkeld Cumb 69 G8
Great Sampford Essex 33 E9
Great Sankey Warrington 49 D6
Great Saxham Suffolk 34 B1
Great Shefford W Berks 20 D1
Great Shelford Cambs 33 C7
Great Smeaton N Yorks 63 D8
Great Snoring Norfolk 44 B3
Great Somerford Wilts 19 C6
Great Stainton D'lington 63 B8
Great Stambridge Essex 23 B8
Great Staughton Cambs 32 B4
Great Steeping Lincs 53 F7
Great Stonar Kent 15 C8
Great Strickland Cumb 61 B8
Great Stukeley Cambs 32 A5
Great Sturton Lincs 52 E5
Great Sutton Ches 48 E4
Great Sutton Shrops 39 G6
Great Swinburne Northum 70 C4
Great Tew Oxon 30 F5
Great Tey Essex 34 F2
Great Thurkleby N Yorks 63 G9
Great Thurlow Suffolk 33 C9
Great Torrington Devon 6 E5
Great Tosson Northum 78 G5
Great Totham Essex 34 G2
Great Totham Essex 34 G2
Great Tows Lincs 52 C5
Great Urswick Cumb 60 G5
Great Wakering Essex 23 C9
Great Waldingfield Suffolk 34 D3
Great Walsingham Norfolk 44 B3
Great Waltham Essex 33 G9
Great Warley Essex 22 B5
Great Washbourne Glos 30 E1
Great Weldon Northants 42 G2
Great Welnetham Suffolk 34 C2
Great Wenham Suffolk 34 E4
Great Whittington Northum 70 C5
Great Wigborough Essex 34 G3
Great Wilbraham Cambs 33 C8
Great Wishford Wilts 19 H7
Great Witcombe Glos 29 G10
Great Witley Worcs 29 B8
Great Wolford Warwick 30 E4
Great Wratting Suffolk 33 D9
Great Wymondley Herts 32 F5
Great Wyrley Staffs 40 E1
Great Wytheford Shrops 39 D6
Great Yarmouth Norfolk 45 E9
Great Yarmouth Sea Life Centre Norfolk 45 E9
Great Yeldham Essex 34 E1
Greater Doward Heref'd 29 G6
Greatford Lincs 42 D3
Greatgate Staffs 40 A2
Greatham Hants 12 B1
Greatham Hartlep'l 63 B9
Greatham W Sussex 12 D4
Greatstone on Sea Kent 14 F5
Greatworth Northants 31 D7
Greave Lancs 56 F3
Greeba I/Man 54 D3
Green Denbs 48 F1
Green End Beds 32 C4
Green Hammerton N Yorks 57 C9
Green Lane Powys 38 F2
Green Ore Som'set 18 F2
Green St. Green London 22 E4
Green Street Herts 21 B9
Greenbank Shetl'd 111 C8
Greenburn W Loth 76 A2
Greendikes Northum 78 E5
Greenfield Beds 32 E3
Greenfield Flints 48 E2
Greenfield Gtr Man 50 B1
Greenfield H'land 95 F9
Greenfield Oxon 20 B5
Greenford London 21 C9
Greengairs N Lanarks 83 G8
Greenham W Berks 20 E2
Greenhaugh Northum 70 B2
Greenhead Northum 69 D9
Greenhill Falk 83 G9
Greenhill London 21 C9
Greenhill Kent 15 B6
Greenhill Leics 41 D6
Greenhills N Ayrs 74 B5
Greenhithe Kent 22 D5
Greenholm E Ayrs 75 D7
Greenholme Cumb 61 D8
Greenhouse Scot Borders 77 E8
Greenhow Hill N Yorks 57 B6
Greenigo Orkney 110 H5
Greenland H'land 107 C7
Greenlands Bucks 20 C5
Greenlaw Aberds 99 C6
Greenlaw Scot Borders 78 C2
Greenlea Dumf/Gal 68 C3
Greenloaning Perth/Kinr 83 D9
Greenmeadow Community Farm, Pontnewydd Torf 17 B7
Greenmount Gtr Man 56 G2
Greenmow Shetl'd 111 L7
Greenock Invercl 82 G3
Greenock West Invercl 82 G3
Greenodd Cumb 61 F6
Greenrow Cumb 68 E4
Greens Norton Northants 31 D8
Greenside Tyne/Wear 71 D6
Greensidehill Northum 78 F4
Greenstead Green Essex 34 F2
Greensted Essex 22 A5
Greensted Church, Chipping Ongar Essex 22 A5
Greenway Pembs 24 C5
Greenwich London 22 D3
Greet Glos 30 E2
Greete Shrops 29 A6
Greetham Lincs 53 E6
Greetham Rutl'd 42 D2
Greetland W Yorks 56 F5
Gregg Hall Cumb 61 E7
Gregson Lane Lancs 55 F5
Greinetobht W Isles 109 K3
Greinton Som'set 17 H9
Grenaby I/Man 54 E2
Grendon Northants 32 B1
Grendon Warwick 40 E4
Grendon Common Warwick 40 F4
Grendon Green Heref'd 29 C6
Grendon Underwood Bucks 31 F8
Grenofen Devon 4 C5
Grenoside S Yorks 50 C5
Greosabhagh W Isles 109 H6
Gresford Wrex 48 G4
Gresham Norfolk 44 B5
Greshornish H'land 109 M8
Gressenhall Norfolk 44 D3
Gressingham Lancs 55 B5
Gresty Green Ches 49 G8
Greta Bridge Durham 62 C5
Gretna Dumf/Gal 69 D6
Gretna Green Dumf/Gal 69 D6
Gretton Glos 30 E2
Gretton Northants 42 F1
Gretton Shrops 39 F6
Grewelthorpe N Yorks 63 G7
Grey Green N Lincs 51 B9
Greygarth N Yorks 63 G6
Greynor Carms 25 F10
Greysouthen Cumb 60 B3
Greystoke Cumb 69 G7
Greystone Angus 91 G6
Greystone Dumf/Gal 68 C2
Greywell Hants 20 F5
Griais W Isles 108 C9
Grianan W Isles 108 D9
Gribthorpe ER Yorks 58 E3
Gridley Corner Devon 6 G4
Griff Warwick 40 G5
Griffithstown Torf 17 B7
Grimbister Orkney 110 G4
Grimblethorpe Lincs 52 D5
Grimeford Village Lancs 55 G6
Grimethorpe S Yorks 51 B6
Griminis W Isles 109 M2
Grimista Shetl'd 111 J7
Grimister Shetl'd 111 D7
Grimley Worcs 29 B9
Grimness Orkney 110 J5
Grimoldby Lincs 53 D6
Grimpo Shrops 38 C4
Grimsargh Lancs 55 E5
Grimsbury Oxon 31 D6
Grimsby NE Lincs 59 G8
Grimscote Northants 31 C8
Grimscott Cornw'l 6 F3
Grimsthorpe Lincs 42 C3
Grimston ER Yorks 59 E8
Grimston Leics 41 C8
Grimston Norfolk 43 C10
Grimston C/York 58 C2
Grimstone Dorset 9 E8
Grinacombe Moor Devon 6 G5
Grindale ER Yorks 65 G9
Grindigair Orkney 110 H6
Grindiscol Shetl'd 111 K7
Grindle Shrops 39 E8
Grindleford Derby 50 E4
Grindleton Lancs 56 D2
Grindley Staffs 40 C2
Grindley Brook Shrops 39 A6
Grindlow Derby 50 E3
Grindon Northum 78 C4
Grindon Staffs 50 G2
Grindonmoor Gate Staffs 50 G2
Gringley on the Hill Notts 51 C9
Grinsdale Cumb 69 E6
Grinshill Shrops 39 C6
Grinton N Yorks 62 E5
Griomsiadar W Isles 108 E8
Grishipoll Arg/Bute 86 F1
Grisling Common E Sussex 13 C8
Gristhorpe N Yorks 65 F8
Griston Norfolk 44 F3
Gritley Orkney 110 H6
Grittenham Wilts 19 C7
Grittleton Wilts 18 C5
Grizebeck Cumb 60 F5
Grizedale Cumb 61 E6
Grobister Orkney 110 F7
Groby Leics 41 E7
Groes Conwy 47 F10
Groes Neath P Talb 16 C2
Groes faen Rh Cyn Taff 16 C5
Groes lwyd Powys 38 D3
Groesffordd Marli Denbs 47 E10
Groeslon Gwyn 46 F5
Groeslon Gwyn 46 G4
Grogport Arg/Bute 73 C8
Gromford Suffolk 35 C7
Gronant Flints 48 D1
Groombridge E Sussex 13 B9
Grosmont Monmouths 28 F5
Grosmont N Yorks 65 D6
Grosvenor Museum, Chester Ches 48 F5
Groton Suffolk 34 D3
Grouville Jersey 4
Grove Dorset 9 G9
Grove Kent 15 B7
Grove Notts 51 E9
Grove Oxon 20 B2
Grove Park London 22 D4
Grove Vale W Midlands 40 F2
Grovesend Swan 25 F10
Grudie H'land 102 F2
Gruids H'land 102 B4
Gruinard House H'land 101 C7
Grula H'land 93 C9
Gruline Arg/Bute 86 G5
Grunasound Shetl'd 111 K6
Grundisburgh Suffolk 35 C6
Grunsagill Lancs 56 C2
Gruting Shetl'd 111 J5
Gt. Bridge W Midlands 40 F1
Gt. Hallingbury Essex 33 G8
Gt. Parndon Essex 33 H7
Gualachulain H'land 88 G2
Gualin Ho. H'land 105 D6
Guardbridge Fife 85 C6
Guarlford Worcs 29 D9
Guay Perth/Kinr 89 G11
Guestling Green E Sussex 14 G3
Guestling Thorn E Sussex 14 G3
Guestwick Norfolk 44 C4
Guestwick Green Norfolk 44 C4
Guide Blackb'n 56 F2
Guide Post Northum 71 B7
Guilden Morden Cambs 32 D5
Guilden Sutton Ches 48 F5
Guildford Surrey 21 G7
Guildtown Perth/Kinr 84 A3
Guilsborough Northants 31 A8
Guilsfield Powys 38 D3
Guilton Kent 15 C7
Guineaford Devon 7 C6
Guisborough Redcar/Clevel'd 64 C4
Guiseley W Yorks 57 D6
Guist Norfolk 44 C3
Guith Orkney 110 E6
Guiting Power Glos 30 F2
Gulberwick Shetl'd 111 K7
Gullane E Loth 85 F6
Gulval Cornw'l 2 F3
Gulworthy Devon 4 C5
Gumfreston Pembs 24 F6
Gumley Leics 41 F8
Gummow's Shop Cornw'l 3 D7
Gun Hill E Sussex 13 D9
Gunby ER Yorks 58 E3
Gunby Lincs 42 C2
Gundleton Hants 11 A9
Gunn Devon 7 C7
Gunnerside N Yorks 62 E4
Gunnerton Northum 70 C4
Gunness N Lincs 58 G4
Gunnislake Cornw'l 4 C5
Gunnista Shetl'd 111 J8
Gunthorpe Norfolk 44 B4
Gunthorpe Notts 41 A8
Gunthorpe Peterbro 42 E4
Gunville I/Wight 11 F7
Gunwalloe Cornw'l 2 G5
Gurnard I/Wight 11 E7
Gurnett Ches 49 E10
Gurney Slade Som'set 18 G3
Gurnos Powys 27 H7
Gussage All Saints Dorset 10 C3
Gussage St. Michael Dorset 10 C2
Guston Kent 15 D8
Gutcher Shetl'd 111 D8
Guthrie Angus 91 F6
Guyhirn Cambs 43 E6
Guyhirn Gull Cambs 43 E6
Guy's Head Lincs 43 C7
Guy's Marsh Dorset 9 B10
Guyzance Northum 79 G7
Gwaenysgor Flints 48 D1
Gwalchmai Angl 46 E3
Gwaun Cae Gurwen Neath P Talb 27 G7
Gwaun Leision Neath P Talb 27 G7
Gwbert Ceredig'n 25 B6
Gweek Cornw'l 3 G6
Gwehelog Monmouths 17 A8
Gwenddwr Powys 28 D1
Gwennap Cornw'l 3 F6
Gwenter Cornw'l 3 H6
Gwernaffield Flints 48 F3
Gwernesney Monmouths 17 A9
Gwernogle Carms 26 E5
Gwernymynydd Flints 48 F3
Gwersyllt Wrex 48 G4
Gwespyr Flints 48 D2
Gwithian Cornw'l 2 E4
Gwredog Angl 46 D4
Gwyddelwern Denbs 48 H1
Gwyddgrug Carms 25 C9
Gwydyr Uchaf Conwy 47 F7
Gwynfryn Wrex 48 G3
Gwystre Powys 28 B1
Gwytherin Conwy 47 F8
Gyfelia Wrex 48 H4
Gyffin Conwy 47 E7
Gyrn goch Gwyn 46 H4

H

Habberley Shrops 38 E4
Habergham Lancs 56 E3
Habrough NE Lincs 59 G7
Haceby Lincs 42 B3
Hacheston Suffolk 35 C7
Hackbridge London 22 E2
Hackenthorpe S Yorks 51 D6
Hackford Norfolk 44 E4
Hackforth N Yorks 63 E7
Hackland Orkney 110 F4
Hackleton Northants 31 C10
Hackness N Yorks 65 E7
Hackness Orkney 110 J4
Hackney London 22 C3
Hackthorn Lincs 52 D2
Hackthorpe Cumb 61 B8
Haconby Lincs 42 C4
Hacton London 22 C5
Hadden Scot Borders 78 D2
Haddenham Bucks 31 H9
Haddenham Cambs 43 H7
Haddington E Loth 85 G7
Haddington Lincs 52 F2
Haddiscoe Norfolk 45 F8
Haddon Cambs 42 F4
Haddon Ches 50 F1
Haddon Hall Derby 50 F4
Hade Edge W Yorks 50 B3
Hademore Staffs 40 E3
Hadfield Derby 50 C2
Hadham Cross Herts 33 G7
Hadham Ford Herts 33 F7
Hadleigh Essex 23 C8
Hadleigh Suffolk 34 D4
Hadley Telford 39 D7
Hadley End Staffs 40 C3
Hadlow Kent 23 G6
Hadlow Down E Sussex 13 C9
Hadnall Shrops 39 D6
Hadstock Essex 33 D8
Hady Derby 50 E5
Hadzor Worcs 29 B10
Haffenden Quarter Kent 14 D3
Hafod Dinbych Conwy 47 G8
Hafod Iom Conwy 47 E8
Haggate Lancs 56 E3
Haggbeck Cumb 69 C7
Haggerston Northum 78 C5
Haggrister Shetl'd 111 F6
Hagley Heref'd 29 D6
Hagley Worcs 39 G10
Hagworthingham Lincs 53 F6
Haigh Gtr Man 49 B7
Haigh S Yorks 57 G7
Haigh Moor W Yorks 57 F7
Haighton Green Lancs 55 E5
Hail Weston Cambs 32 B4
Haile Cumb 60 D3
Hailes Glos 30 E2
Hailey Herts 33 G6
Hailey Oxon 30 G5
Hailsham E Sussex 13 E9
Haimer H'land 107 C6
Hainault London 22 B4
Hainford Norfolk 45 D6
Hainton Lincs 52 D4
Hairmyres S Lanarks 75 B8
Haisthorpe ER Yorks 59 B7
Hakin Pembs 24 F3
Halam Notts 51 G8
Halbeath Fife 84 F3
Halberton Devon 8 C2
Halcro H'land 107 C7
Hale Gtr Man 49 D8
Hale Halton 48 D5
Hale Hants 10 C4
Hale Bank Halton 48 D5
Hale Street Kent 14 D1
Halebarns Gtr Man 49 D8
Hales Norfolk 45 F7
Hales Staffs 39 B8
Hales Place Kent 15 C6
Halesfield Telford 39 E8
Halesgate Lincs 43 C6
Halesowen W Midlands 40 G1
Halesworth Suffolk 45 H7
Halewood Mersey 48 D5
Halford Shrops 38 G5
Halford Warwick 30 D4
Halfpenny Furze Carms 25 E7
Halfpenny Green Staffs 39 F9
Halfway Carms 27 E6
Halfway Carms 27 E8
Halfway W Berks 20 E2
Halfway Bridge W Sussex 12 C3
Halfway House Shrops 38 D4
Halfway Houses Kent 23 D9
Halifax W Yorks 56 F5
Halket E Ayrs 75 B6
Halkirk H'land 107 D6
Halkyn Flints 48 E3

Hall Dunnerdale *Cumb* 60 E5
Hall Green *W Midlands* 40 G3
Hall Green *W Yorks* 57 G8
Hall Grove *Herts* 32 G5
Hall of the Forest *Shrops* 38 G3
Halland *E Sussex* 13 D8
Hallaton *Leics* 41 F9
Hallatrow *Bath/NE Som'set* 18 F3
Hallbankgate *Cumb* 69 E8
Hallen *S Gloucs* 18 C2
Halliburton *Scot Borders* 77 C9
Hallin *H'land* 109 M7
Halling *Medway* 14 B2
Hallington *Lincs* 53 D6
Hallington *Northum* 70 C4
Halliwell *Gtr Man* 56 G2
Halloughton *Notts* 51 G8
Hallow *Worcs* 29 C9
Hallrule *Scot Borders* 77 F8
Halls *E Loth* 85 G8
Hall's Green *Herts* 32 F5
Hallsands *Devon* 5 G9
Hallthwaites *Cumb* 60 F4
Halltoft End *Lincs* 53 H6
Hallworthy *Cornw'l* 4 B2
Hallyburton House *Perth/Kinr* 90 H3
Hallyne *Scot Borders* 76 C4
Halmer End *Staffs* 49 H8
Halmore *Glos* 18 A3
Halmyre Mains *Scot Borders* 76 C4
Halnaker *W Sussex* 12 E3
Halsall *Lancs* 55 G3
Halse *Northants* 31 D7
Halse *Som'set* 8 B3
Halsetown *Cornw'l* 2 F4
Halsham *ER Yorks* 59 F8
Halsinger *Devon* 7 C6
Halstead *Essex* 34 E2
Halstead *Kent* 22 E4
Halstead *Leics* 41 E9
Halstock *Dorset* 9 D7
Haltham *Lincs* 52 F5
Halton *Bucks* 32 G1
Halton *Halton* 49 D6
Halton *Lancs* 55 B5
Halton *Northum* 70 D4
Halton *Wrex* 38 B4
Halton *W Yorks* 57 E8
Halton East *N Yorks* 56 C5
Halton Gill *N Yorks* 62 G3
Halton Holegate *Lincs* 53 F7
Halton Lea Gate *Northum* 69 E9
Halton West *N Yorks* 56 C3
Haltwhistle *Northum* 70 D2
Halvergate *Norfolk* 45 E8
Halwell *Devon* 5 E8
Halwill *Devon* 6 G5
Halwill Junction *Devon* 6 F5
Ham *Devon* 8 D4
Ham *Glos* 18 B3
Ham *London* 21 D9
Ham *H'land* 107 B7
Ham *Kent* 15 C8
Ham *Shetl'd* 111 K2
Ham *Wilts* 19 E10
Ham Common *Dorset* 9 B10
Ham Green *Heref'd* 29 D8
Ham Green *Kent* 14 F3
Ham Green *Kent* 14 B3
Ham Green *N Som'set* 18 D2
Ham Green *Worcs* 30 B2
Ham Street *Som'set* 9 A7
Hamble le Rice *Hants* 11 D7
Hambleden *Bucks* 20 C5
Hambledon *Hants* 11 C9
Hambledon *Surrey* 12 B3
Hambleton *Lancs* 55 D3
Hambleton *N Yorks* 58 E1
Hambridge *Som'set* 8 B5
Hambrook *S Gloucs* 18 D3
Hambrook *W Sussex* 12 E1
Hameringham *Lincs* 53 F6
Hamerton *Cambs* 42 H4
Hametoun *Shetl'd* 111 K2
Hamilton *S Lanarks* 75 B9
Hamilton Park Racecourse *S Lanarks* 75 B9
Hammer *W Sussex* 12 B2
Hammerpot *W Sussex* 12 E4
Hammersmith *London* 22 D2
Hammerwich *Staffs* 40 E2
Hammerwood *E Sussex* 13 B8
Hammond Street *Herts* 22 A3
Hammoon *Dorset* 9 C10
Hamnavoe *Shetl'd* 111 E5
Hamnavoe *Shetl'd* 111 K6
Hamnavoe *Shetl'd* 111 E7
Hamnavoe *Shetl'd* 111 F7
Hampden Park *E Sussex* 13 E10
Hamperden End *Essex* 33 E8
Hampnett *Glos* 30 G2
Hampole *S Yorks* 57 G10
Hampreston *Dorset* 10 E3
Hampstead *London* 22 C2
Hampstead Norreys *W Berks* 20 D3
Hampsthwaite *N Yorks* 57 C7
Hampton *London* 21 E9
Hampton *Shrops* 39 G8
Hampton *Worcs* 30 D2
Hampton Bishop *Heref'd* 29 E6
Hampton Court Palace, Teddington *London* 21 E9
Hampton Heath *Ches* 48 H5
Hampton in Arden *W Midlands* 40 G4
Hampton Loade *Shrops* 39 G8
Hampton Lovett *Worcs* 29 B9
Hampton Lucy *Warwick* 30 C4
Hampton on the Hill *Warwick* 30 B4
Hampton Poyle *Oxon* 31 G7
Hamrow *Norfolk* 44 C3
Hamsey *E Sussex* 13 D8
Hamsey Green *Surrey* 22 F3
Hamstall Ridware *Staffs* 40 D3
Hamstead *I/Wight* 11 E7
Hamstead *W Midlands* 40 F2
Hamstead Marshall *W Berks* 20 E2
Hamsterley *Durham* 71 G6
Hamsterley *Durham* 71 E6
Hamstreet *Kent* 14 E5
Hamworthy *Poole* 10 E2
Hanbury *Staffs* 40 C3
Hanbury *Worcs* 30 B1
Hanbury Woodend *Staffs* 40 C3
Hanby *Lincs* 42 B3
Hanchurch *Staffs* 39 A9
Handbridge *Ches* 48 F5
Handcross *W Sussex* 13 C6
Handforth *Ches* 49 D9
Handley *Ches* 48 G5
Handsacre *Staffs* 40 D2
Handsworth *S Yorks* 51 D6
Handsworth *W Midlands* 40 F2
Handy Cross *Devon* 6 D5
Hanford *Stoke* 39 A9
Hanging Langford *Wilts* 19 H7
Hangleton *W Sussex* 12 E4
Hanham *S Gloucs* 18 D3
Hankelow *Ches* 49 H7
Hankerton *Wilts* 19 B6
Hankham *E Sussex* 13 E10
Hanley *Stoke* 49 H9
Hanley Castle *Worcs* 29 D9
Hanley Child *Worcs* 29 B7
Hanley Swan *Worcs* 29 D9
Hanley William *Worcs* 29 B7
Hanlith *N Yorks* 56 B4
Hanmer *Wrex* 38 B5
Hannah *Lincs* 53 E8
Hannington *Hants* 20 F3
Hannington *Northants* 31 A10
Hannington *Swindon* 19 B8
Hannington Wick *Swindon* 19 B8
Hansel Village *S Ayrs* 74 D5
Hanslope *M/Keynes* 31 D10
Hanthorpe *Lincs* 42 C3
Hanwell *London* 21 C9
Hanwell *Oxon* 31 D6
Hanwood *Shrops* 38 E5
Hanworth *London* 21 D9
Hanworth *Norfolk* 44 B5
Happendon *S Lanarks* 76 D1
Happisburgh *Norfolk* 45 B7
Happisburgh Common *Norfolk* 45 C7
Hapsford *Ches* 48 E5
Hapton *Lancs* 56 E2
Hapton *Norfolk* 44 F5
Harberton *Devon* 5 E8
Harbertonford *Devon* 5 E8
Harbledown *Kent* 15 C6
Harborne *W Midlands* 40 G2
Harborough Magna *Warwick* 41 H6
Harbottle *Northum* 78 G4
Harbour Park, Littlehampton *W Sussex* 12 F4
Harbury *Warwick* 30 C5
Harby *Leics* 41 B9
Harby *Notts* 52 E1
Harcombe *Devon* 8 E3
Harden *W Midlands* 40 E2
Harden *W Yorks* 56 E5
Hardenhuish *Wilts* 19 D6
Hardgate *Aberds* 91 A8
Hardham *W Sussex* 12 D4
Hardingham *Norfolk* 44 E4
Hardingstone *Northants* 31 C9
Hardington *Som'set* 18 F4
Hardington Mandeville *Som'set* 9 C7
Hardington Marsh *Som'set* 9 D7
Hardley *Hants* 11 D7
Hardley Street *Norfolk* 45 E7
Hardmead *M/Keynes* 32 D2
Hardrow *N Yorks* 62 E3
Hardstoft *Derby* 51 F6
Hardway *Hants* 11 D9
Hardway *Som'set* 9 A9
Hardwick *Bucks* 31 G10
Hardwick *Cambs* 33 C6
Hardwick *Norfolk* 43 D9
Hardwick *Norfolk* 45 G6
Hardwick *Notts* 51 E8
Hardwick *Northants* 32 B1
Hardwick *Oxon* 30 H5
Hardwick *Oxon* 31 F7
Hardwick *W Midlands* 40 F2
Hardwick Hall *Derby* 51 F6
Hardwicke *Glos* 29 G8
Hardwicke *Glos* 29 F10
Hardwicke *Heref'd* 28 D3
Hardy's Green *Essex* 34 F3
Hare Green *Essex* 34 F4
Hare Hatch *Wokingham* 21 D6
Hare Street *Herts* 33 F6
Hareby *Lincs* 53 F6
Hareden *Lancs* 56 C1
Harefield *London* 21 B8
Harehills *W Yorks* 57 E8
Harehope *Northum* 78 E5
Haresceugh *Cumb* 69 F9
Harescombe *Glos* 29 G9
Haresfield *Glos* 29 G9
Hareshaw *N Lanarks* 75 A10
Hareshaw Head *Northum* 70 B3
Harewood *W Yorks* 57 D8
Harewood End *Heref'd* 29 F6
Harewood House, Wetherby *W Yorks* 57 D8
Harford *Carms* 27 D6
Harford *Devon* 5 E7
Hargate *Norfolk* 44 F5
Hargatewall *Derby* 50 E3
Hargrave *Ches* 48 F5
Hargrave *Northants* 32 A3
Hargrave *Suffolk* 34 C1
Harker *Cumb* 69 D6
Harkland *Shetl'd* 111 E7
Harkstead *Suffolk* 34 E5
Harlaston *Staffs* 40 D4
Harlaw Ho. *Aberds* 99 F7
Harlaxton *Lincs* 42 B1
Harle Syke *Lancs* 56 E3
Harlech *Gwyn* 36 B5
Harlech Castle *Gwyn* 36 B5
Harlequin *Notts* 41 B8
Harlescott *Shrops* 39 D6
Harlesden *London* 22 C2
Harleston *Devon* 5 F8
Harleston *Norfolk* 45 G6
Harleston *Suffolk* 34 C4
Harlestone *Northants* 31 B9
Harley *Shrops* 39 E6
Harley *S Yorks* 50 C5
Harleyholm *S Lanarks* 76 D2
Harlington *Beds* 32 E3
Harlington *London* 21 D8
Harlington *S Yorks* 51 B6
Harlosh *H'land* 93 A8
Harlow *Essex* 33 G7
Harlow Car Botanical Gardens, Harrogate *N Yorks* 57 C7
Harlow Hill *Northum* 70 D5
Harlow Hill *N Yorks* 57 C7
Harlthorpe *ER Yorks* 58 E3
Harlton *Cambs* 33 C6
Harman's Cross *Dorset* 10 F2
Harmby *N Yorks* 63 F6
Harmer Green *Herts* 32 G5
Harmer Hill *Shrops* 38 C5
Harmondsworth *London* 21 D8
Harmston *Lincs* 52 F2
Harnham *Northum* 70 C5
Harnhill *Glos* 19 A7
Harold Hill *London* 22 B5
Harold Wood *London* 22 B5
Haroldston West *Pembs* 24 E3
Haroldswick *Shetl'd* 111 B9
Harome *N Yorks* 64 F4
Harpenden *Herts* 32 G4
Harpford *Devon* 8 E2
Harpham *ER Yorks* 59 B6
Harpley *Norfolk* 44 C1
Harpley *Worcs* 29 B7
Harpole *Northants* 31 B8
Harpsdale *H'land* 107 D6
Harpsden *Oxon* 20 C5
Harpswell *Lincs* 52 D2
Harpur Hill *Derby* 50 E2
Harpurhey *Gtr Man* 49 B9
Harraby *Cumb* 69 E7
Harrapool *H'land* 94 D3
Harrier *Shetl'd* 111 J2
Harrietfield *Perth/Kinr* 84 B1
Harrietsham *Kent* 14 C3
Harrington *Cumb* 60 B2
Harrington *Lincs* 53 E6
Harrington *Northants* 41 G9
Harringworth *Northants* 42 F2
Harris *H'land* 93 F9
Harris Museum, Preston *Lancs* 55 F5
Harrogate *N Yorks* 57 C8
Harrold *Beds* 32 C2
Harrow *London* 21 C9
Harrow on the Hill *London* 21 C9
Harrow Street *Suffolk* 34 E3
Harrow Weald *London* 21 B9
Harrowbarrow *Cornw'l* 4 D4
Harrowden *Beds* 32 D3
Harrowgate Hill *D'lington* 63 C7
Harston *Cambs* 33 C7
Harston *Leics* 41 B10
Harswell *ER Yorks* 58 D4
Hart *Hartlep'l* 71 G9
Hart Common *Gtr Man* 49 B7
Hart Hill *Luton* 32 F4
Hart Station *Hartlep'l* 71 G9
Hartburn *Northum* 70 B5
Hartburn *Stockton* 63 C9
Hartest *Suffolk* 34 C2
Hartfield *E Sussex* 13 B8
Hartford *Cambs* 32 A5
Hartford *Ches* 49 E7
Hartford End *Essex* 33 G9
Hartfordbridge *Hants* 20 F5
Hartforth *N Yorks* 63 D6
Harthill *Ches* 49 G6
Harthill *N Lanarks* 76 A2
Harthill *S Yorks* 51 D6
Hartington *Derby* 50 F3
Hartland *Devon* 6 D3
Hartlebury *Worcs* 29 A9
Hartlepool *Hartlep'l* 71 G10
Hartley *Cumb* 62 D2
Hartley *Kent* 23 E6
Hartley *Kent* 14 E2
Hartley *Northum* 71 C8
Hartley Westpall *Hants* 20 F4
Hartley Wintney *Hants* 20 F5
Hartlip *Kent* 14 B3
Hartoft End *N Yorks* 64 E5
Harton *N Yorks* 58 B3
Harton *Shrops* 38 G5
Harton *Tyne/Wear* 71 D8
Hartpury *Glos* 29 F8
Hartshead *W Yorks* 57 F6
Hartshill *Warwick* 40 F5
Hartshorne *Derby* 40 C5
Hartsop *Cumb* 61 C7
Hartwell *Northants* 31 C9
Hartwood *N Lanarks* 75 B10
Harvieston *Stirl* 83 F6
Harvington *Worcs* 30 D2
Harvington Cross *Worcs* 30 D2
Harwell *Oxon* 20 C2
Harwich *Essex* 35 E6
Harwood *Durham* 70 G3
Harwood *Gtr Man* 56 G2
Harwood Dale *N Yorks* 65 E7
Harworth *Notts* 51 C8
Hasbury *W Midlands* 40 G1
Hascombe *Surrey* 21 G7
Haselbech *Northants* 41 H9
Haselbury Plucknett *Som'set* 9 C6
Haseley *Warwick* 30 B4
Haselor *Warwick* 30 C3
Hasfield *Glos* 29 F9
Hasguard *Pembs* 24 F3
Haskayne *Lancs* 48 B4
Hasketon *Suffolk* 35 C6
Hasland *Derby* 50 F5
Haslemere *Surrey* 12 B3
Haslingden *Lancs* 56 F2
Haslingfield *Cambs* 33 C7
Haslington *Ches* 49 G8
Hassall *Ches* 49 G8
Hassall Green *Ches* 49 G8
Hassell Street *Kent* 14 D5
Hassendean *Scot Borders* 77 E8
Hassingham *Norfolk* 45 E7
Hassocks *W Sussex* 13 D6
Hassop *Derby* 50 E4
Hastigrow *H'land* 107 C7
Hastingleigh *Kent* 14 D5
Hastings *E Sussex* 14 H3
Hastings Castle *E Sussex* 14 G3
Hastings Sea Life Centre *E Sussex* 14 H3
Hastingwood *Essex* 33 H7
Hastoe *Herts* 32 H2
Haswell *Durham* 71 F8
Haswell Plough *Durham* 71 F8
Hatch *Beds* 32 D4
Hatch *Hants* 20 F4
Hatch *Wilts* 10 B2
Hatch Beauchamp *Som'set* 8 B5
Hatch End *London* 21 B9
Hatch Green *Som'set* 8 C5
Hatchet Gate *Hants* 11 D6
Hatching Green *Herts* 32 G4
Hatchmere *Ches* 49 E6
Hatcliffe *NE Lincs* 52 B5
Hatfield *Heref'd* 29 C6
Hatfield *Herts* 32 H5
Hatfield *S Yorks* 51 B8
Hatfield *Worcs* 29 C9
Hatfield Broad Oak *Essex* 33 G8
Hatfield Garden Village *Herts* 32 H5
Hatfield Heath *Essex* 33 G8
Hatfield House *Herts* 32 H5
Hatfield Hyde *Herts* 32 G5
Hatfield Peverel *Essex* 34 G1
Hatfield Woodhouse *S Yorks* 51 B8
Hatford *Oxon* 19 B10
Hatherden *Hants* 19 F10
Hatherleigh *Devon* 7 F6
Hathern *Leics* 41 C6
Hatherop *Glos* 30 H3
Hathersage *Derby* 50 D4
Hathershaw *Gtr Man* 49 B10
Hatherton *Ches* 49 H7
Hatherton *Staffs* 40 D1
Hatley St. George *Cambs* 32 C5
Hatt *Cornw'l* 4 D4
Hattingley *Hants* 20 H4
Hatton *Aberds* 99 E10
Hatton *Derby* 40 C4
Hatton *Lincs* 52 E4
Hatton *Shrops* 38 F5
Hatton *Warwick* 30 B4
Hatton *Warrington* 49 D6
Hatton Castle *Aberds* 99 D7
Hatton Country World *Warwick* 30 B4
Hatton Heath *Ches* 48 F5
Hatton of Fintray *Aberds* 99 G8
Hattoncrook *Aberds* 99 F8
Haugh *E Ayrs* 75 E6
Haugh *Gtr Man* 56 G4
Haugh *Lincs* 53 E7
Haugh Head *Northum* 78 E5
Haugh of Glass *Moray* 98 E4
Haugh of Urr *Dumf/Gal* 67 D10
Haugham *Lincs* 53 D6
Haughley *Suffolk* 34 B4
Haughley Green *Suffolk* 34 B4
Haughs of Clinterty *Aberd C* 99 G8
Haughton *Notts* 51 E8
Haughton *Shrops* 39 F7
Haughton *Shrops* 38 C4
Haughton *Shrops* 39 D6
Haughton *Shrops* 39 E8
Haughton *Staffs* 39 C9
Haughton Castle *Northum* 70 C4
Haughton Grn. *Gtr Man* 49 C10
Haughton Le Skerne *D'lington* 63 C8
Haughton Moss *Ches* 49 G6
Haultwick *Herts* 33 F6
Haunn *Arg/Bute* 86 G3
Haunn *W Isles* 92 D3
Haunton *Staffs* 40 D4
Hauxley *Northum* 79 G7
Hauxton *Cambs* 33 C7
Havant *Hants* 11 D10
Haven *Heref'd* 28 C5
Haven Bank *Lincs* 52 G5
Haven Side *ER Yorks* 59 F7
Havenstreet *I/Wight* 11 E8
Havercroft *W Yorks* 57 G8
Haverfordwest *Pembs* 24 E4
Haverhill *Suffolk* 33 D9
Haverigg *Cumb* 60 G4
Havering atte Bower *London* 22 B5
Haveringland *Norfolk* 44 C5
Haversham *M/Keynes* 31 D10
Haverthwaite *Cumb* 61 F6
Haverton Hill *Stockton* 63 B9
Hawarden *Flints* 48 F4
Hawcoat *Cumb* 60 G5
Hawen *Ceredig'n* 25 B8
Hawes *N Yorks* 62 F3
Hawes Side *Blackp'l* 55 E3
Hawes'Green *Norfolk* 45 F6
Hawford *Worcs* 29 B9
Hawick *Scot Borders* 77 F8
Hawk Green *Gtr Man* 50 D1
Hawkchurch *Devon* 8 D5
Hawkedon *Suffolk* 34 C1
Hawkenbury *Kent* 14 D3
Hawkenbury *Kent* 13 B9
Hawkeridge *Wilts* 18 F5
Hawkerland *Devon* 8 F2
Hawkes End *W Midlands* 40 G5
Hawkesbury *S Gloucs* 18 C4
Hawkesbury *Warwick* 40 G5
Hawkesbury Upton *S Gloucs* 18 C4
Hawkhill *Northum* 79 F7
Hawkhurst *Kent* 14 E2
Hawkinge *Kent* 15 E7
Hawkley *Hants* 11 B10
Hawkridge *Som'set* 7 C9
Hawkshead *Cumb* 61 E6
Hawkshead Hill *Cumb* 61 E6
Hawksland *S Lanarks* 75 D10
Hawkswick *N Yorks* 62 G4
Hawksworth *Notts* 41 A9
Hawksworth *W Yorks* 57 D6
Hawksworth *W Yorks* 57 E7
Hawkwell *Essex* 23 B8
Hawley *Hants* 21 F6
Hawley *Kent* 22 D5
Hawling *Glos* 30 F2
Hawnby *N Yorks* 64 F3
Haworth *W Yorks* 56 E5
Hawstead *Suffolk* 34 C2
Hawthorn *Durham* 71 F9
Hawthorn *Rh Cyn Taff* 17 C6
Hawthorn *Wilts* 18 E5
Hawthorn Hill *Brackn'l* 21 D6
Hawthorn Hill *Lincs* 52 G5
Hawthorpe *Lincs* 42 C3
Hawton *Notts* 51 G9
Haxby *C/York* 58 C2
Haxey *N Lincs* 51 B9
Hay Green *Norfolk* 43 D8
Hay on Wye *Powys* 28 D3
Hay Street *Herts* 33 F6
Haydock *Mersey* 49 C6
Haydock Park Racecourse *Mersey* 49 C6
Haydon *Dorset* 9 C8
Haydon Bridge *Northum* 70 D3
Haydon Wick *Swindon* 19 C8
Haye *Cornw'l* 4 D4
Hayes *London* 22 E4
Hayes *London* 21 C9
Hayfield *Derby* 50 D2
Hayfield *Fife* 84 E4
Hayhill *E Ayrs* 75 F6
Hayhillock *Angus* 91 G6
Hayle *Cornw'l* 2 F4
Haynes *Beds* 32 D3
Haynes Church End *Beds* 32 D3
Hayscastle *Pembs* 24 D3
Hayscastle Cross *Pembs* 24 D4
Hayshead *Angus* 91 G7
Hayton *Aberd C* 99 H9
Hayton *Cumb* 68 F4
Hayton *Cumb* 69 E8
Hayton *ER Yorks* 58 D4
Hayton *Notts* 51 D9
Hayton's Bent *Shrops* 39 G6
Haytor Vale *Devon* 5 C8
Hayward Gallery *London* 22 D3
Haywards Heath *W Sussex* 13 C7
Haywood *S Yorks* 58 G1
Haywood Oaks *Notts* 51 G8
Hazel Grove *Gtr Man* 49 D10
Hazel Street *Kent* 14 E1
Hazelbank *S Lanarks* 75 C10
Hazelbury Bryan *Dorset* 9 D9
Hazeley *Hants* 20 F5
Hazelhurst *Gtr Man* 50 B1
Hazelslade *Staffs* 40 D2
Hazelton *Glos* 30 G2
Hazelton Walls *Fife* 84 B5
Hazelwood *Derby* 50 H5
Hazlemere *Bucks* 21 B6
Hazlerigg *Tyne/Wear* 71 C7
Hazlewood *N Yorks* 56 C5
Hazon *Northum* 79 G6
Heacham *Norfolk* 43 B9
Head of Muir *Falk* 83 F9
Headbourne Worthy *Hants* 11 A7
Headbrook *Heref'd* 28 C4
Headcorn *Kent* 14 D3
Headingley *W Yorks* 57 E7
Headington *Oxon* 31 H7
Headlam *Durham* 63 C6
Headless Cross *Worcs* 30 B2
Headley *Hants* 20 E3
Headley *Hants* 12 B2
Headley *Surrey* 22 F2
Headon *Notts* 51 E9
Heads *S Lanarks* 75 C9
Heads Nook *Cumb* 69 E7
Heage *Derby* 50 G5
Healaugh *N Yorks* 57 D9
Healaugh *N Yorks* 62 E5
Heald Green *Gtr Man* 49 D9
Heale *Devon* 7 B7
Heale *Som'set* 18 G3
Healey *Gtr Man* 56 G3
Healey *Northum* 70 E5
Healey *N Yorks* 63 F6
Healing *NE Lincs* 59 G8
Heamoor *Cornw'l* 2 F3
Heanish *Arg/Bute* 86 D2
Heanor *Derby* 51 H6
Heanton Punchardon *Devon* 7 C6
Heapham *Lincs* 52 D1
Hearthstane *Scot Borders* 76 E4
Heasley Mill *Devon* 7 C8
Heast *H'land* 94 E3
Heath *Card* 17 D6
Heath *Derby* 51 F6
Heath and Reach *Beds* 32 F2
Heath End *Hants* 20 E3
Heath End *Surrey* 21 G6
Heath End *Warwick* 30 B4
Heath Hayes *Staffs* 40 D2
Heath Hill *Shrops* 39 D8
Heath House *Som'set* 17 G9
Heath Town *W Midlands* 39 F10
Heathcote *Derby* 50 F3
Heather *Leics* 40 D5
Heatherfield *H'land* 94 B1
Heathfield *Devon* 5 C9
Heathfield *E Sussex* 13 C9
Heathfield *Som'set* 8 B3
Heathhall *Dumf/Gal* 68 C2
Heathstock *Devon* 8 D4
Heathton *Shrops* 39 F9
Heatley *Warrington* 49 D8
Heaton *Lancs* 55 B4
Heaton *Staffs* 50 F1
Heaton *Tyne/Wear* 71 D7
Heaton *W Yorks* 57 E6
Heaton Moor *Gtr Man* 49 C9
Heaverham *Kent* 22 F5
Heaviley *Gtr Man* 49 D10
Heavitree *Devon* 7 G10
Hebburn *Tyne/Wear* 71 D8
Hebden *N Yorks* 56 B5
Hebden Bridge *W Yorks* 56 F4
Hebron *Angl* 46 D4
Hebron *Carms* 25 D6
Hebron *Northum* 71 B6
Heck *Dumf/Gal* 68 B3
Heckfield *Hants* 20 E5
Heckfield Green *Suffolk* 44 H5
Heckfordbridge *Essex* 34 F3
Heckington *Lincs* 42 A4
Heckmondwike *W Yorks* 57 F7
Heddington *Wilts* 19 E6
Heddle *Orkney* 110 G4
Heddon on the Wall *Northum* 71 D6
Hedenham *Norfolk* 45 F7
Hedge End *Hants* 11 C7
Hedgerley *Bucks* 21 C7
Hedging *Som'set* 8 B5
Hedley on the Hill *Northum* 70 E5
Hednesford *Staffs* 40 D2
Hedon *ER Yorks* 59 F7
Hedsor *Bucks* 21 C7
Hedworth *Tyne/Wear* 71 D8
Heeley City Farm, Sheffield *S Yorks* 50 D5
Hegdon Hill *Heref'd* 29 C6
Heggerscales *Cumb* 62 C3
Heglibister *Shetl'd* 111 H6
Heighington *D'lington* 63 B7
Heighington *Lincs* 52 F3
Heights of Brae *H'land* 102 F4
Heights of Kinlochewe *H'land* 101 F8
Heilam *H'land* 105 C7
Heiton *Scot Borders* 78 D2
Hele *Devon* 7 B6
Hele *Devon* 8 D1
Helensburgh *Arg/Bute* 82 F3
Helford *Cornw'l* 3 G6
Helford Passage *Cornw'l* 3 G6
Helhoughton *Norfolk* 44 C2
Helions Bumpstead *Essex* 33 D9
Hellaby *S Yorks* 51 C7
Helland *Cornw'l* 3 B9
Hellesdon *Norfolk* 45 D6
Hellidon *Northants* 31 C7
Hellifield *N Yorks* 56 C3
Hellingly *E Sussex* 13 D9
Hellington *Norfolk* 45 E7
Hellister *Shetl'd* 111 J6
Helm *Northum* 79 H6
Helmdon *Northants* 31 D7
Helmingham *Suffolk* 34 C5
Helmington Row *Durham* 71 G6
Helmsdale *H'land* 106 H5
Helmshore *Lancs* 56 F2
Helmsley *N Yorks* 64 F4
Helperby *N Yorks* 57 B9
Helperthorpe *N Yorks* 65 G7
Helpringham *Lincs* 42 A4
Helpston *Peterbro* 42 E4
Helsby *Ches* 48 E5
Helsey *Lincs* 53 E8
Helston *Cornw'l* 2 G5
Helstone *Cornw'l* 4 B1
Helton *Cumb* 61 B8
Helwith Bridge *N Yorks* 56 B3
Hemblington *Norfolk* 45 D7
Hemel Hempstead *Herts* 32 H3
Hemingbrough *N Yorks* 58 E2
Hemingby *Lincs* 52 E5
Hemingford Abbots *Cambs* 32 A5
Hemingford Grey *Cambs* 32 A5
Hemingstone *Suffolk* 34 C5
Hemington *Leics* 41 C6
Hemington *Northants* 42 G3
Hemington *Som'set* 18 F4
Hemley *Suffolk* 35 D6
Hemlington *Middlesbro'* 64 C3
Hemp Green *Suffolk* 35 B7
Hempholme *ER Yorks* 59 C6
Hempnall *Norfolk* 45 F6
Hempnall Green *Norfolk* 45 F6
Hempriggs House *H'land* 107 E8
Hempstead *Essex* 33 E9
Hempstead *Medway* 14 B2
Hempstead *Norfolk* 44 B5
Hempstead *Norfolk* 45 C8
Hempsted *Glos* 29 G9
Hempton *Norfolk* 44 C3
Hempton *Oxon* 31 E6
Hemsby *Norfolk* 45 D8
Hemswell *Lincs* 52 C2
Hemswell Cliff *Lincs* 52 D2
Hemsworth *W Yorks* 57 G9
Hemyock *Devon* 8 C3
Hen feddau fawr *Pembs* 25 C7
Henbury *Bristol* 18 D2
Henbury *Ches* 49 E9
Hendon *London* 22 C2
Hendon *Tyne/Wear* 71 E9
Hendre *Flints* 48 F2
Hendre ddu *Conwy* 47 F8
Hendreforgan *Rh Cyn Taff* 16 C4
Hendy *Carms* 25 F10
Heneglwys *Angl* 46 E4
Henfield *W Sussex* 13 D6
Henford *Devon* 6 G4
Henghurst *Kent* 14 E4
Hengoed *Caerph* 17 B6
Hengoed *Powys* 28 C3
Hengoed *Shrops* 38 B3
Hengrave *Suffolk* 34 B2
Henham *Essex* 33 F8
Heniarth *Powys* 38 E2
Henlade *Som'set* 8 B4
Henley *Shrops* 39 H6
Henley *Som'set* 9 A6
Henley *Suffolk* 34 C5
Henley *W Sussex* 12 C2
Henley in Arden *Warwick* 30 B3
Henley on Thames *Oxon* 20 C5
Henley's Down *E Sussex* 14 G2
Henllan *Ceredig'n* 25 B8
Henllan *Denbs* 47 F10
Henllan Amgoed *Carms* 25 D6
Henllys *Torf* 17 B7
Henlow *Beds* 32 E4
Hennock *Devon* 5 B9
Henny Street *Essex* 34 E2
Henryd *Conwy* 47 E7
Henry's Moat *Pembs* 24 D5
Hensall *N Yorks* 58 F1
Henshaw *Northum* 70 D2
Hensingham *Cumb* 60 C2
Henstead *Suffolk* 45 G8
Henstridge *Som'set* 9 C9
Henstridge Ash *Som'set* 9 B9
Henstridge Marsh *Som'set* 9 B9
Henton *Oxon* 20 A5
Henton *Som'set* 17 G9
Henwood *Cornw'l* 4 C3
Heogan *Shetl'd* 111 J7
Heol las *Swan* 16 B1
Heol Senni *Powys* 27 F9
Heol y Cyw *Bridg* 16 C4
Hepburn *Northum* 78 E5
Hepple *Northum* 78 G4
Hepscott *Northum* 71 B7
Heptonstall *W Yorks* 56 F4
Hepworth *Suffolk* 34 A3
Hepworth *W Yorks* 50 B3
Herbrandston *Pembs* 24 F3
Hereford *Heref'd* 29 D6
Hereford Cathedral *Heref'd* 29 E6
Hereford Racecourse *Heref'd* 29 D6
Heriot *Scot Borders* 77 B6
Heritage Motor Centre, Gaydon *Warwick* 30 C5
Hermiston *C/Edinb* 84 G3
Hermitage *Scot Borders* 77 H8
Hermitage *Dorset* 9 D8
Hermitage *W Berks* 20 D3
Hermitage *W Sussex* 12 E1
Hermon *Angl* 46 F3
Hermon *Carms* 25 C8
Hermon *Carms* 27 F6
Hermon *Pembs* 25 C7
Herne *Kent* 15 B6
Herne Bay *Kent* 15 B6
Herner *Devon* 7 D6
Hernhill *Kent* 14 B5
Herodsfoot *Cornw'l* 4 D3
Herongate *Essex* 23 B6
Heronsford *S Ayrs* 66 B3
Herriard *Hants* 20 G4
Herringfleet *Suffolk* 45 F8
Herringswell *Suffolk* 33 A10
Hersden *Kent* 15 B7
Hersham *Cornw'l* 6 F3
Hersham *Surrey* 21 E9
Herstmonceux *E Sussex* 13 D10
Herston *Orkney* 110 J5
Hertford *Herts* 33 G6
Hertford Heath *Herts* 33 G6
Hertingfordbury *Herts* 33 G6
Hesket Newmarket *Cumb* 69 G6
Hesketh Bank *Lancs* 55 F4
Hesketh Lane *Lancs* 55 D6
Heskin Green *Lancs* 55 G5
Hesleden *Durham* 71 G9
Hesleyside *Northum* 70 B3
Heslington *C/York* 58 C2
Hessay *C/York* 57 C10
Hessenford *Cornw'l* 4 E4
Hessett *Suffolk* 34 B3
Hessle *ER Yorks* 59 F6
Hest Bank *Lancs* 55 B4
Heston *London* 21 D9
Hestwall *Orkney* 110 G3
Heswall *Mersey* 48 D3
Hethe *Oxon* 31 F7
Hethersett *Norfolk* 44 E5
Hethersgill *Cumb* 69 D7
Hethpool *Northum* 78 E3
Hett *Durham* 71 G7
Hetton *N Yorks* 56 C4
Hetton le Hole *Tyne/Wear* 71 F8
Hetton Steads *Northum* 78 D5
Heugh *Northum* 70 C5
Heugh head *Aberds* 98 G3
Heveningham *Suffolk* 35 A7
Hever *Kent* 22 G4
Hever Castle and Gardens *Kent* 22 G4
Heversham *Cumb* 61 F7
Hevingham *Norfolk* 44 C5
Hewas Water *Cornw'l* 3 E8
Hewelsfield *Glos* 18 A2
Hewish *N Som'set* 17 E9
Hewish *Som'set* 9 D6
Heworth *C/York* 58 C2
Hexham *Northum* 70 D4
Hexham Abbey *Northum* 70 D4
Hexham Racecourse *Northum* 70 D4
Hextable *Kent* 22 D5
Hexton *Herts* 32 E4
Hexworthy *Devon* 5 C7
Hey *Lancs* 56 D3
Heybridge *Essex* 23 B6
Heybridge *Essex* 34 H2
Heybridge Basin *Essex* 34 H2
Heybrook Bay *Devon* 5 F6
Heydon *Cambs* 33 D7
Heydon *Norfolk* 44 C5
Heydour *Lincs* 42 B3
Heylipol *Arg/Bute* 86 D1
Heylor *Shetl'd* 111 E5
Heysham *Lancs* 55 B4
Heyshott *W Sussex* 12 D2
Heyside *Gtr Man* 49 B10
Heytesbury *Wilts* 19 G6
Heythrop *Oxon* 30 F5
Heywood *Gtr Man* 56 G3
Heywood *Wilts* 18 F5
Hibaldstow *N Lincs* 52 B2
Hickleton *S Yorks* 51 B6
Hickling *Norfolk* 45 C8
Hickling *Notts* 41 C8
Hickling Green *Norfolk* 45 C8
Hickling Heath *Norfolk* 45 C8
Hickstead *W Sussex* 13 C6
Hidcote Boyce *Glos* 30 D3
Hidcote Manor Garden, Moreton in Marsh *Glos* 30 D3
High Ackworth *W Yorks* 57 G9
High Angerton *Northum* 70 B5
High Bankhill *Cumb* 69 F8
High Barnes *Tyne/Wear* 71 E8
High Beach *Essex* 22 B4
High Bentham *N Yorks* 56 B1
High Bickington *Devon* 7 D7
High Birkwith *N Yorks* 62 G2
High Blantyre *S Lanarks* 75 B8
High Bonnybridge *Falk* 83 G9
High Bradfield *S Yorks* 50 C4
High Bray *Devon* 7 C7
High Brooms *Kent* 22 G5
High Bullen *Devon* 7 D6
High Buston *Northum* 79 G7
High Callerton *Northum* 71 C6
High Catton *ER Yorks* 58 C3
High Cogges *Oxon* 30 H5
High Coniscliffe *D'lington* 63 C7
High Cross *Hants* 11 B10
High Cross *Herts* 33 G6
High Easter *Essex* 33 G9
High Eggborough *N Yorks* 58 F1
High Ellington *N Yorks* 63 F6
High Ercall *Telford* 39 D6
High Etherley *Durham* 63 B6
High Garrett *Essex* 34 F1
High Grange *Durham* 71 G6
High Green *Norfolk* 44 E5
High Green *S Yorks* 50 C5
High Green *Worcs* 29 D9
High Halden *Kent* 14 E3
High Halstow *Medway* 23 D7
High Ham *Som'set* 9 A6
High Harrington *Cumb* 60 B3
High Hatton *Shrops* 39 C7
High Hawsker *N Yorks* 65 D7
High Hesket *Cumb* 69 F7
High Hesleden *Durham* 71 G9
High Hoyland *S Yorks* 57 G7
High Hunsley *ER Yorks* 58 E5
High Hurstwood *E Sussex* 13 C8
High Hutton *N Yorks* 58 B3
High Ireby *Cumb* 68 G5
High Kelling *Norfolk* 44 A5
High Kilburn *N Yorks* 64 G3
High Lands *Durham* 63 B6
High Lane *Gtr Man* 50 D1
High Lane *Heref'd* 29 B7
High Laver *Essex* 33 H8
High Legh *Ches* 49 D8
High Leven *Stockton* 63 C9
High Littleton *Bath/NE Som'set* 18 F3
High Lorton *Cumb* 60 B4
High Marishes *N Yorks* 65 G6
High Marnham *Notts* 51 E10
High Melton *S Yorks* 51 B7
High Mickley *Northum* 70 D5
High Mindork *Dumf/Gal* 66 E5
High Moorland Visitor Centre, Princetown *Devon* 5 C6
High Newton *Cumb* 61 F7
High Newton by the Sea *Northum* 79 E7
High Nibthwaite *Cumb* 60 F5
High Offley *Staffs* 39 C8
High Ongar *Essex* 22 A5
High Onn *Staffs* 39 D9
High Roding *Essex* 33 G9
High Row *Cumb* 69 G6
High Salvington *W Sussex* 12 E5
High Shaw *N Yorks* 62 E3
High Spen *Tyne/Wear* 71 E6
High Stoop *Durham* 71 F6
High Street *Cornw'l* 3 D8
High Street *Kent* 14 E2
High Street *Suffolk* 35 C8
High Street *Suffolk* 35 A8
High Street *Suffolk* 34 D2
High Street Green *Suffolk* 34 C4
High Throston *Hartlep'l* 71 G9
High Toynton *Lincs* 52 F5
High Trewhitt *Northum* 78 G5
High Westwood *Durham* 71 E6
High Wray *Cumb* 61 E6
High Wych *Herts* 33 G7
High Wycombe *Bucks* 21 B6
Higham *Derby* 50 G5
Higham *Kent* 23 D7
Higham *Lancs* 56 E3
Higham *Suffolk* 34 E4
Higham *Suffolk* 33 B10
Higham Dykes *Northum* 71 C6
Higham Ferrers *Northants* 32 B2
Higham Gobion *Beds* 32 E4
Higham on the Hill *Leics* 40 F5
Higham Wood *Kent* 22 G5
Highampton *Devon* 6 F5
Highbridge *H'land* 88 C2
Highbridge *Som'set* 17 G8
Highbrook *W Sussex* 13 B7
Highburton *W Yorks* 57 G6
Highbury *Som'set* 18 G3
Highclere *Hants* 20 E2
Highcliffe *Dorset* 10 E5
Higher Ansty *Dorset* 9 D9
Higher Ashton *Devon* 5 B9
Higher Ballam *Lancs* 55 E3
Higher Bartle *Lancs* 55 E5
Higher Boscaswell *Cornw'l* 2 F2
Higher Burwardsley *Ches* 49 G6
Higher End *Gtr Man* 49 B6
Higher Kinnerton *Flints* 48 F4
Higher Penwortham *Lancs* 55 F5
Higher Town *I/Scilly* 2 C3
Higher Walreddon *Devon* 4 C5
Higher Walton *Lancs* 55 F5
Higher Walton *Warrington* 49 D6
Higher Wheelton *Lancs* 55 F6
Higher Whitley *Ches* 49 D7
Higher Wincham *Ches* 49 E7
Higher Wych *Ches* 38 A5
Highfield *ER Yorks* 58 E3
Highfield *Gtr Man* 49 B8
Highfield *N Ayrs* 74 B5
Highfield *Oxon* 31 F7
Highfield *S Yorks* 50 D5
Highfield *Tyne/Wear* 71 E6
Highfields *Cambs* 33 C6
Highfields *Northum* 78 B4
Highgate *London* 22 C2
Highlane *Ches* 49 F9
Highlane *Derby* 51 D6
Highlaws *Cumb* 68 F4
Highleadon *Glos* 29 F8
Highleigh *W Sussex* 12 F2
Highley *Shrops* 39 G8
Highmoor Cross *Oxon* 20 C5
Highmoor Hill *Monmouths* 17 C9
Highnam *Glos* 29 G8
Highnam Green *Glos* 29 F8
Highsted *Kent* 14 B4
Highstreet Green *Essex* 34 E1
Hightae *Dumf/Gal* 68 C3
Hightown *Ches* 49 F9
Hightown *Mersey* 48 B4
Hightown Green *Suffolk* 34 C3
Highway *Wilts* 19 D7
Highweek *Devon* 5 C9
Highworth *Swindon* 19 B9
Hilborough *Norfolk* 44 E2
Hilcote *Derby* 51 G6
Hilcott *Wilts* 19 F8
Hilden Park *Kent* 22 G5
Hildenborough *Kent* 22 G5
Hildersham *Cambs* 33 D8
Hilderstone *Staffs* 39 B10
Hilderthorpe *ER Yorks* 59 B7
Hilfield *Dorset* 9 D8
Hilgay *Norfolk* 43 F9
Hill *Pembs* 24 F6
Hill *S Gloucs* 18 B3
Hill *W Midlands* 40 F3
Hill Brow *W Sussex* 12 C1
Hill Dale *Lancs* 55 G4
Hill Dyke *Lincs* 53 H6
Hill End *Durham* 70 G5
Hill End *Fife* 84 E2
Hill End *N Yorks* 56 C5
Hill Head *Hants* 11 D8
Hill Head *Northum* 70 D4
Hill Mountain *Pembs* 24 F4
Hill of Beath *Fife* 84 E3
Hill of Fearn *H'land* 103 E7
Hill of Mountblairy *Aberds* 99 C6
Hill Ridware *Staffs* 40 D2
Hill Top *Durham* 62 B4
Hill Top *Hants* 11 D7
Hill Top *W Midlands* 40 F1
Hill Top *W Yorks* 57 G8
Hill Top, Sawrey *Cumb* 61 E6
Hill View *Dorset* 10 E2
Hillam *N Yorks* 57 F10
Hillbeck *Cumb* 62 C2
Hillborough *Kent* 15 B7
Hillbrae *Aberds* 99 F7
Hillbrae *Aberds* 98 D6
Hillbutts *Dorset* 10 D2
Hillcliffiane *Derby* 50 H4
Hillcommon *Som'set* 8 B3
Hillend *Fife* 84 F3
Hillerton *Devon* 7 G8
Hillesden *Bucks* 31 F8
Hillesley *Glos* 18 C4
Hillfarance *Som'set* 8 B3
Hillhead *Aberds* 98 E5
Hillhead *Devon* 5 E10
Hillhead *S Ayrs* 75 F6
Hillhead of Auchentumb *Aberds* 99 C9
Hillhead of Cocklaw *Aberds* 99 D10
Hillhouse *Scot Borders* 77 B8
Hilliclay *H'land* 107 C6
Hillier Gardens and Arboretum *Hants* 11 B6
Hillingdon *London* 21 C8
Hillington *Glasg C* 75 A7
Hillington *Norfolk* 43 C10
Hillmorton *Warwick* 31 A7
Hillockhead *Aberds* 98 G4
Hillockhead *Aberds* 98 H3
Hillside *Aberds* 91 B10
Hillside *Angus* 91 E8
Hillside *Mersey* 55 G3
Hillside *Shetl'd* 111 G7
Hillswick *Shetl'd* 111 F5
Hillway *I/Wight* 11 F9
Hillwell *Shetl'd* 111 M6
Hilmarton *Wilts* 19 D7
Hilperton *Wilts* 18 F5
Hilsea *Portsm'th* 11 D9
Hilston *ER Yorks* 59 E8
Hilton *Aberds* 99 E9
Hilton *Cambs* 32 B5
Hilton *Cumb* 62 B2
Hilton *Derby* 40 B4
Hilton *Dorset* 9 D9
Hilton *Durham* 63 B6
Hilton *H'land* 103 D6
Hilton *Shrops* 39 F8
Hilton *Stockton* 63 C9
Hilton of Cadboll *H'land* 103 E7
Himbleton *Worcs* 29 C10
Himley *Staffs* 39 F9
Hincaster *Cumb* 61 F8
Hinckley *Leics* 41 F6
Hinderclay *Suffolk* 44 H4
Hinderton *Ches* 48 E4
Hinderwell *N Yorks* 64 C5
Hindford *Shrops* 38 B4
Hindhead *Surrey* 12 B2
Hindley *Gtr Man* 49 B7
Hindley Green *Gtr Man* 49 B7
Hindlip *Worcs* 29 C9
Hindolveston *Norfolk* 44 C4
Hindon *Wilts* 10 A2
Hindringham *Norfolk* 44 B3
Hingham *Norfolk* 44 E4
Hinstock *Shrops* 39 C7
Hintlesham *Suffolk* 34 D4
Hinton *Hants* 10 E5
Hinton *Heref'd* 28 E4
Hinton *Northants* 31 C7
Hinton *Shrops* 38 E5
Hinton *S Gloucs* 18 D4
Hinton Ampner *Hants* 11 B8
Hinton Blewett *Bath/NE Som'set* 18 F2
Hinton Charterhouse *Bath/NE Som'set* 18 F4
Hinton in the Hedges *Northants* 31 E7
Hinton Martell *Dorset* 10 D3
Hinton on the Green *Worcs* 30 D2
Hinton Parva *Swindon* 19 C9
Hinton St. George *Som'set* 9 C6
Hinton St. Mary *Dorset* 9 C9
Hinton Waldrist *Oxon* 20 B1
Hints *Shrops* 29 A7
Hints *Staffs* 40 E3
Hinwick *Beds* 32 B2
Hinxhill *Kent* 14 D5
Hinxton *Cambs* 33 D7
Hinxworth *Herts* 32 D5
Hipperholme *W Yorks* 57 F6
Hipswell *N Yorks* 63 E6
Hirael *Gwyn* 46 E5
Hiraeth *Carms* 25 D6
Hirn *Aberds* 91 A8
Hirnant *Powys* 38 C1
Hirst *N Lanarks* 76 A1
Hirst *Northum* 71 B7
Hirst Courtney *N Yorks* 58 F2
Hirwaen *Denbs* 48 F2
Hirwaun *Rh Cyn Taff* 27 H9
Hiscott *Devon* 7 D6
Histon *Cambs* 33 B7
Hitcham *Suffolk* 34 C3
Hitchin *Herts* 32 F4
Hither Green *London* 22 D3
Hittisleigh *Devon* 7 G8
Hive *ER Yorks* 58 E4
Hixon *Staffs* 40 C2
HMS Victory *Portsm'th* 11 D9
HMY Britannia *C/Edinb* 84 G4
Hoaden *Kent* 15 C7
Hoaldalbert *Monmouths* 28 F4
Hoar Cross *Staffs* 40 C3
Hoarwithy *Heref'd* 29 F6
Hoath *Kent* 15 B7
Hobarris *Shrops* 38 H4
Hobbister *Orkney* 110 H4
Hobkirk *Scot Borders* 77 F8
Hobson *Durham* 71 E6
Hoby *Leics* 41 D8
Hockering *Norfolk* 44 D4
Hockerton *Notts* 51 G9
Hockley *Essex* 23 B8
Hockley Heath *W Midlands* 30 A3
Hockliffe *Beds* 32 F2
Hockwold cum Wilton *Norfolk* 43 G10
Hockworthy *Devon* 8 C2
Hoddesdon *Herts* 33 H6
Hoddlesden *Blackb'n* 56 F2
Hoddom Castle *Dumf/Gal* 68 C4
Hoddomcross *Dumf/Gal* 68 C4
Hodgeston *Pembs* 24 G5
Hodley *Powys* 38 F2
Hodnet *Shrops* 39 C7
Hodthorpe *Derby* 51 E7
Hoe *Hants* 11 C8
Hoe *Norfolk* 44 D3
Hoe Gate *Hants* 11 C9
Hoff *Cumb* 61 C9
Hog Patch *Surrey* 21 G6
Hoggard's Green *Suffolk* 34 C2
Hoggeston *Bucks* 31 F10
Hogha Gearraidh *W Isles* 109 K2
Hoghton *Lancs* 55 F6
Hognaston *Derby* 50 G4
Hogsthorpe *Lincs* 53 E8
Holbeach *Lincs* 43 C6
Holbeach Bank *Lincs* 43 C6
Holbeach Clough *Lincs* 43 C6
Holbeach Drove *Lincs* 43 D6
Holbeach Hurn *Lincs* 43 C6
Holbeach St. Johns *Lincs* 43 D6
Holbeach St. Marks *Lincs* 43 B6
Holbeach St. Matthew *Lincs* 43 B7
Holbeck *Notts* 51 E7
Holbeck *W Yorks* 57 E7
Holbeck Woodhouse *Notts* 51 E7
Holberrow Green *Worcs* 30 C2
Holbeton *Devon* 5 E7
Holborn *London* 22 C3
Holbrook *Derby* 40 A5
Holbrook *Suffolk* 34 E5
Holbrook *S Yorks* 51 D6
Holburn *Northum* 78 D5
Holbury *Hants* 11 D7
Holcombe *Devon* 8 G1
Holcombe *Som'set* 18 G3
Holcombe Rogus *Devon* 8 C2
Holcot *Northants* 31 B9
Holden *Lancs* 56 D2
Holdenby *Northants* 31 B8
Holdenhurst *Bournem'th* 10 E4
Holdgate *Shrops* 39 G6
Holdingham *Lincs* 52 H3
Holditch *Dorset* 8 D5
Hole in the Wall *Heref'd* 29 F7
Holefield *Scot Borders* 78 D3
Holehouses *Ches* 49 E8
Holemoor *Devon* 6 F5
Holestane *Dumf/Gal* 76 H1
Holford *Som'set* 17 G6
Holgate *C/York* 58 C1
Holker *Cumb* 61 G6
Holkham *Norfolk* 44 A2
Hollacombe *Devon* 6 F4
Holland *Orkney* 110 C5
Holland *Orkney* 110 F7
Holland Fen *Lincs* 52 H5
Holland on Sea *Essex* 35 G6
Hollandstoun *Orkney* 110 C8
Hollee *Dumf/Gal* 68 D5
Hollesley *Suffolk* 35 D7
Hollicombe *Torbay* 5 D9
Hollingbourne *Kent* 14 C3
Hollington *Derby* 40 B4
Hollington *E Sussex* 14 G2
Hollington *Staffs* 40 B2
Hollington Grove *Derby* 40 B4
Hollingworth *Gtr Man* 50 C2
Hollins *Gtr Man* 49 B9
Hollins Green *Warrington* 49 C7
Hollins Lane *Lancs* 55 C4
Hollinsclough *Staffs* 50 F2
Hollinwood *Gtr Man* 49 B10
Hollinwood *Shrops* 39 B6
Hollocombe *Devon* 7 E7
Hollow Meadows *S Yorks* 50 D4
Holloway *Derby* 50 G5
Hollowell *Northants* 31 A8
Holly End *Norfolk* 43 E7
Holly Grn. *Worcs* 29 D9
Hollybush *Caerph* 17 A6
Hollybush *E Ayrs* 74 F5
Hollybush *Worcs* 29 E8
Hollym *ER Yorks* 59 F9
Hollywood *Worcs* 40 H2
Holmbridge *W Yorks* 50 B3
Holmbury St. Mary *Surrey* 21 G9
Holmbush *Cornw'l* 3 D9
Holmcroft *Staffs* 39 C10
Holme *Cambs* 42 G4
Holme *Cumb* 61 G8
Holme *Notts* 51 G10
Holme *N Yorks* 63 F8
Holme *W Yorks* 50 B3
Holme Chapel *Lancs* 56 F3
Holme Green *N Yorks* 58 D1
Holme Hale *Norfolk* 44 E2
Holme Lacy *Heref'd* 29 E6
Holme Marsh *Heref'd* 28 C4
Holme next the Sea *Norfolk* 43 A10
Holme on Spalding Moor *ER Yorks* 58 E4
Holme on the Wolds *ER Yorks* 58 D5
Holme Pierrepont *Notts* 41 B8
Holme St. Cuthbert *Cumb* 68 F4
Holme Wood *W Yorks* 57 E6
Holmer *Heref'd* 29 D6
Holmer Green *Bucks* 21 B7
Holmes Chapel *Ches* 49 F8
Holmesfield *Derby* 50 E5
Holmeswood *Lancs* 55 G4
Holmewood *Derby* 51 F6
Holmfirth *W Yorks* 50 B3
Holmhead *Dumf/Gal* 67 B9
Holmhead *E Ayrs* 75 E7
Holmisdal *H'land* 109 N6
Holmpton *ER Yorks* 59 F9
Holmrook *Cumb* 60 E3
Holmsgarth *Shetl'd* 111 J7
Holmwrangle *Cumb* 69 F8
Holne *Devon* 5 D8
Holnest *Dorset* 9 D8
Holsworthy *Devon* 6 F4
Holsworthy Beacon *Devon* 6 F4
Holt *Dorset* 10 D3
Holt *Norfolk* 44 B4
Holt *Wilts* 18 E5
Holt *Worcs* 29 B9
Holt *Wrex* 48 G5
Holt End *Hants* 20 H4
Holt End *Worcs* 30 B2
Holt Fleet *Worcs* 29 B9
Holt Heath *Worcs* 29 B9
Holt Park *W Yorks* 57 D7
Holtby *C/York* 58 C2
Holton *Oxon* 31 H8
Holton *Som'set* 9 B8
Holton *Suffolk* 45 H7
Holton cum Beckering *Lincs* 52 D4
Holton Heath *Dorset* 10 E2
Holton le Clay *Lincs* 52 B5
Holton le Moor *Lincs* 52 C3
Holton St. Mary *Suffolk* 34 E4
Holwell *Dorset* 9 C9
Holwell *Herts* 32 E4
Holwell *Leics* 41 C9
Holwell *Oxon* 30 H4
Holwick *Durham* 62 B4
Holworth *Dorset* 9 F9
Holy Cross *Worcs* 39 H10
Holy Island *Northum* 79 C6
Holybourne *Hants* 20 G5
Holyhead *Angl* 46 D2
Holymoorside *Derby* 50 F5
Holyport *Windsor* 21 D6
Holystone *Northum* 78 G4
Holytown *N Lanarks* 75 A9
Holywell *Cambs* 33 A6
Holywell *Cornw'l* 3 D6
Holywell *Dorset* 9 D7
Holywell *E Sussex* 13 F9
Holywell *Flints* 48 E2
Holywell *Northum* 71 C8
Holywell Bay Fun Park, Newquay *Cornw'l* 3 D6
Holywell Green *W Yorks* 56 G5
Holywell Lake *Som'set* 8 B3
Holywell Row *Suffolk* 43 H10
Holywood *Dumf/Gal* 68 B2
Hom Green *Heref'd* 29 F6
Homer *Shrops* 39 E7
Homersfield *Suffolk* 45 G6
Homington *Wilts* 10 B4
Honey Hill *Kent* 15 B6
Honey Street *Wilts* 19 E8
Honey Tye *Suffolk* 34 E3
Honeyborough *Pembs* 24 F4
Honeybourne *Worcs* 30 D3
Honeychurch *Devon* 7 F7
Honiley *Warwick* 30 A4
Honing *Norfolk* 45 C7
Honingham *Norfolk* 44 D5
Honington *Lincs* 42 A2
Honington *Suffolk* 34 A3
Honington *Warwick* 30 D4
Honiton *Devon* 8 D3
Honley *W Yorks* 57 G6
Hoo *Medway* 23 D7
Hoo Green *Ches* 49 D8
Hood Green *S Yorks* 50 B5
Hooe *E Sussex* 14 H1
Hooe *Plym'th* 5 E6
Hooe Common *E Sussex* 14 G1
Hook *ER Yorks* 58 F3
Hook *London* 21 E9
Hook *Hants* 20 F5
Hook *Pembs* 24 E4
Hook *Wilts* 19 C7
Hook Green *Kent* 14 E1
Hook Green *Kent* 23 E6
Hook Norton *Oxon* 30 E5
Hooke *Dorset* 9 E7
Hookgate *Staffs* 39 B8
Hookway *Devon* 7 G9
Hookwood *Surrey* 22 G2
Hoole *Ches* 48 F5
Hooley *Surrey* 22 F2
Hooton *Ches* 48 E4
Hooton Levitt *S Yorks* 51 C7
Hooton Pagnell *S Yorks* 51 B6
Hooton Roberts *S Yorks* 51 C6
Hop Pole *Lincs* 42 D4
Hope *Derby* 50 D3
Hope *Devon* 5 G7
Hope *Flints* 48 G4
Hope *H'land* 105 D7
Hope *Powys* 38 E3
Hope *Shrops* 38 E4
Hope *Staffs* 50 G3
Hope Bagot *Shrops* 29 A6
Hope Bowdler *Shrops* 38 F5
Hope End Green *Essex* 33 F8
Hope Green *Ches* 49 D10
Hope Mansell *Heref'd* 29 G7
Hope under Dinmore *Heref'd* 29 C6
Hopeman *Moray* 103 F10
Hope's Grn. *Essex* 23 C7
Hopesay *Shrops* 38 G4
Hopley's Green *Heref'd* 28 C4
Hopperton *N Yorks* 57 C9
Hopstone *Shrops* 39 F8
Hopton *Shrops* 38 C4
Hopton *Shrops* 39 C6
Hopton *Staffs* 39 C10
Hopton *Suffolk* 44 H3
Hopton Cangeford *Shrops* 39 G6
Hopton Castle *Shrops* 38 H4
Hopton on Sea *Norfolk* 45 E9
Hopton Wafers *Shrops* 39 H7
Hoptonheath *Shrops* 38 H4
Hopwas *Staffs* 40 E3
Hopwood *Gtr Man* 49 B9
Hopwood *Worcs* 40 H2
Horam *E Sussex* 13 D9
Horbling *Lincs* 42 B4
Horbury *W Yorks* 57 G7
Horcott *Glos* 19 A8
Horden *Durham* 71 F9
Horderley *Shrops* 38 G5
Hordle *Hants* 10 E5
Hordley *Shrops* 38 B4
Horeb *Ceredig'n* 25 B8
Horeb *Carms* 25 F9
Horeb *Carms* 26 F5
Horfield *Bristol* 18 D3
Horham *Suffolk* 35 A6
Horkesley Heath *Essex* 34 F3
Horkstow *N Lincs* 58 G5
Horley *Oxon* 31 D6
Horley *Surrey* 22 G2

Kirkton of Logie Buchan Aberds 99 F9
Kirkton of Maryculter Aberds 91 B9
Kirkton of Menmuir Angus 91 E6
Kirkton of Monikie Angus 91 H6
Kirkton of Oyne Aberds 99 F6
Kirkton of Rayne Aberds 99 F6
Kirkton of Skene Aberds 99 H8
Kirkton of Tough Aberds 98 G6
Kirktonhill Scot Borders 77 B7
Kirktown Aberds 99 C10
Kirktown of Alvah Aberds 99 B6
Kirktown of Deskford Moray 98 B5
Kirktown of Fetteresso Aberds 91 C9
Kirktown of Mortlach Moray 98 E3
Kirktown of Slains Aberds 99 F10
Kirkwall Orkney 110 G5
Kirkwhelpington Northum 70 B4
Kirmington N Lincs 59 G7
Kirmond le Mire Lincs 52 C4
Kirn Arg/Bute 82 G2
Kirriemuir Angus 90 F4
Kirstead Green Norfolk 45 F6
Kirtlebridge Dumf/Gal 68 C5
Kirtleton Dumf/Gal 68 B5
Kirtling Cambs 33 C9
Kirtling Green Cambs 33 C9
Kirtlington Oxon 31 G6
Kirtomy H'land 106 C2
Kirton Lincs 43 B6
Kirton Notts 51 F8
Kirton Suffolk 35 E6
Kirton End Lincs 42 A5
Kirton Holme Lincs 42 A5
Kirton in Lindsey N Lincs 52 C2
Kislingbury Northants 31 C8
Kites Hardwick Warwick 31 B6
Kittisford Som'set 8 B2
Kittle Swan 25 H10
Kitt's Green W Midlands 40 G3
Kitt's Moss Gtr Man 49 D9
Kittybrewster Aberd C 99 H9
Kitwood Hants 11 A9
Kivernoll Heref'd 28 E5
Kiveton Park S Yorks 51 D6
Klibreck H'land 105 F8
Klondyke Orkney 110 J5
Knaith Lincs 51 D10
Knaith Park Lincs 51 D10
Knap Corner Dorset 9 B10
Knaphill Surrey 21 F7
Knapp Perth/Kinr 84 A4
Knapp Som'set 8 B5
Knapthorpe Notts 51 G9
Knapton Norfolk 45 B7
Knapton C/York 58 C1
Knapton Green Heref'd 28 C5
Knapwell Cambs 33 B6
Knaresborough N Yorks 57 C8
Knarsdale Northum 69 E9
Knauchland Moray 98 C5
Knaven Aberds 99 D8
Knayton N Yorks 63 F9
Knebworth Herts 32 F5
Knebworth House, Stevenage Herts 32 F5
Knedlington ER Yorks 58 F3
Kneesall Notts 51 F9
Kneesworth Cambs 33 D6
Kneeton Notts 51 H9
Knelston Swan 25 H9
Knenhall Staffs 39 B10
Knettishall Suffolk 44 G3
Knightacott Devon 7 C7
Knightcote Warwick 30 C5
Knightley Dale Staffs 39 C9
Knighton Devon 5 F6
Knighton Leics C 41 E7
Knighton Powys 28 A3
Knighton Staffs 39 C8
Knighton Staffs 39 A8
Knightshayes Court Devon 8 C1
Knightswood Glasg C 83 H6
Knightwick Worcs 29 C8
Knill Heref'd 28 B3
Knipton Leics 41 B10
Knitsley Durham 71 F6
Kniveton Derby 50 G4
Knock Arg/Bute 86 H5
Knock Cumb 61 B9
Knock Moray 98 C5
Knockally H'land 107 G6
Knockan H'land 101 A10
Knockandhu Moray 98 F2
Knockando Moray 97 B9
Knockando Ho. Moray 98 D2
Knockbain H'land 102 G5
Knockbreck H'land 109 L7
Knockbrex Dumf/Gal 67 F7
Knockdee H'land 107 C6
Knockdolian Castle S Ayrs 66 B3
Knockenkelly N Ayrs 74 E2
Knockentiber E Ayrs 74 D5
Knockespock Ho. Aberds 98 F5
Knockfarrel H'land 102 G4
Knockholt Kent 22 F4
Knockholt Pound Kent 22 F4
Knockie Lodge H'land 96 E2
Knockin Shrops 38 C4
Knockinlaw E Ayrs 75 D6
Knocklearn Dumf/Gal 67 C9
Knocknaha Arg/Bute 73 F6
Knocknain Dumf/Gal 66 D1
Knockrome Arg/Bute 80 G5
Knocksharry I/Man 54 D2
Knodishall Suffolk 35 B8
Knole House & Gardens Kent 22 F5
Knolls Green Ches 49 E9
Knolton Wrex 38 B4
Knolton Bryn Wrex 38 B4
Knook Wilts 19 G6
Knossington Leics 41 E10
Knott End on Sea Lancs 55 D3
Knotting Beds 32 B3
Knotting Green Beds 32 B3
Knottingley W Yorks 57 F10
Knotts Cumb 61 B7
Knotts Lancs 56 C2
Knotty Ash Mersey 48 C5
Knotty Green Bucks 21 B7
Knowbury Shrops 29 A6
Knowe Dumf/Gal 66 C5
Knowehead Dumf/Gal 67 A8
Knowes of Elrick Aberds 98 C6
Knowesgate Northum 70 B4
Knoweton N Lanarks 75 B9
Knowhead Aberds 99 C9
Knowl Hill Windsor 21 D6
Knowle Bristol 18 D3
Knowle Devon 7 F8
Knowle Devon 8 F2
Knowle Devon 6 C5
Knowle Shrops 29 A6
Knowle W Midlands 40 H3
Knowle Green Lancs 56 E1
Knowle Park W Yorks 56 D5
Knowlton Dorset 10 C3
Knowlton Kent 15 C7
Knowsie Aberds 99 C10
Knowsley Mersey 48 C5
Knowsley Safari Park Mersey 48 C5
Knowstone Devon 7 D9
Knox Bridge Kent 14 D2
Knucklas Powys 28 A3
Knuston Northants 32 B2
Knutsford Ches 49 E8
Knutton Staffs 49 H9
Knypersley Staffs 49 G9
Kuggar Cornw'l 3 H6
Kyle of Lochalsh H'land 94 D4
Kyleakin H'land 94 D4
Kylerhea H'land 94 D4
Kylesknoydart H'land 87 B8
Kylesku H'land 104 F5
Kylesmorar H'land 87 B8
Kylestrome H'land 104 F5
Kyllachy House H'land 96 D5
Kynaston Shrops 38 C4
Kynnersley Telford 39 D7
Kyre Magna Worcs 29 B7

L

La Fontenelle Guernsey 4
La Planque Guernsey 4
Labost W Isles 108 C7
Lacasaigh W Isles 108 E8
Lacasdal W Isles 108 D9
Laceby NE Lincs 52 B5
Lacey Green Bucks 21 B6
Lach Dennis Ches 49 E8
Lackford Suffolk 34 A1
Lacock Wilts 19 E6
Ladbroke Warwick 31 C6
Laddingford Kent 14 D1
Lade Bank Lincs 53 G6
Ladock Cornw'l 3 D7
Ladybank Fife 84 C5
Ladykirk Scot Borders 78 C3
Ladysford Aberds 99 B9
Lagalochan Arg/Bute 81 C8
Lagavulin Arg/Bute 72 C4
Lagg Arg/Bute 80 G5
Lagg N Ayrs 73 E9
Laggan Arg/Bute 72 B2
Laggan H'land 95 G9
Laggan H'land 89 B7
Laggan H'land 87 D7
Laggan S Ayrs 66 B4
Lagganulva Arg/Bute 86 G4
Laide H'land 101 C6
Laigh Fenwick E Ayrs 75 C6
Laigh Glengall S Ayrs 74 F5
Laighmuir E Ayrs 75 C6
Laindon Essex 23 C6
Lair H'land 95 B7
Lairg H'land 102 B4
Lairg Lodge H'land 102 B4
Lairg Muir H'land 102 B4
Lairgmore H'land 96 C3
Laisterdyke W Yorks 57 E6
Laithes Cumb 69 G7
Lake I/Wight 11 F8
Lake Wilts 19 H8
Lake Side Cumb 61 F6
Lakenham Norfolk 45 E6
Lakenheath Suffolk 43 G10
Lakesend Norfolk 43 F8
Lakeside and Haverthwaite Railway Cumb 61 F6
Laleham Surrey 21 E8
Laleston Bridg 16 D3
Lamarsh Essex 34 E2
Lamas Norfolk 45 C6
Lambden Scot Borders 78 C2
Lamberhurst Kent 14 E1
Lamberhurst Quarter Kent 14 E1
Lamberton Scot Borders 78 B4
Lambeth London 22 D3
Lambhill Glasg C 83 H6
Lambley Notts 51 H8
Lambley Northum 69 E9
Lamborough Hill Oxon 20 A2
Lambourn W Berks 19 D10
Lambourne End Essex 22 B4
Lambs Green W Sussex 13 B6
Lambston Pembs 24 E4
Lambton Tyne/Wear 71 E7
Lamerton Devon 4 C5
Lamesley Tyne/Wear 71 E7
Lamington H'land 102 E6
Lamington S Lanarks 76 D2
Lamlash N Ayrs 74 D2
Lamloch Dumf/Gal 75 H7
Lamonby Cumb 69 G7
Lamorna Cornw'l 2 G3
Lamorran Cornw'l 3 E7
Lampardbrook Suffolk 35 B6
Lampeter Ceredig'n 26 D5
Lampeter Velfrey Pembs 25 E6
Lamphey Pembs 24 F5
Lamplugh Cumb 60 B3
Lamport Northants 31 A9
Lamyatt Som'set 18 H3
Lana Devon 6 G4
Lanark S Lanarks 76 C1
Lancaster Lancs 55 B4
Lancaster Leisure Park Lancs 55 B4
Lanchester Durham 71 F6
Lancing W Sussex 12 E5
Landbeach Cambs 33 B7
Landcross Devon 6 D5
Landerberry Aberds 91 A8
Landford Wilts 10 C5
Landford Manor Wilts 10 B5
Landimore Swan 25 G9
Landkey Devon 7 C6
Landore Swan 16 B1
Landrake Cornw'l 4 D4
Land's End Cornw'l 2 G2
Landscove Devon 5 D8
Landshipping Pembs 24 E5
Landshipping Quay Pembs 24 E5
Landulph Cornw'l 4 D5
Landwade Suffolk 33 B9
Lane Cornw'l 3 C7
Lane End Bucks 21 B6
Lane End Cumb 60 E4
Lane End Dorset 10 E1
Lane End Hants 11 B8
Lane End I/Wight 11 F9
Lane End Lancs 56 D3
Lane Ends Lancs 56 E2
Lane Ends Lancs 56 C2
Lane Ends N Yorks 56 D4
Lane Head Derby 50 E3
Lane Head Durham 63 C6
Lane Head Gtr Man 49 C7
Lane Head W Yorks 50 B3
Lane Side Lancs 56 F2
Laneast Cornw'l 4 B3
Laneham Notts 51 E10
Lanehead Durham 70 F3
Lanehead Northum 70 B2
Lanercost Cumb 69 D8
Laneshaw Bridge Lancs 56 D4
Lanfach Caerph 17 B7
Langar Notts 41 B9
Langbank Renf 82 G4
Langbar N Yorks 56 C5
Langburnshiels Scot Borders 77 G8
Langcliffe N Yorks 56 B3
Langdale H'land 105 E9
Langdale End N Yorks 65 E7
Langdon Cornw'l 4 B4
Langdon Beck Durham 70 G3
Langdon Hills Essex 23 C6
Langdyke Fife 84 D5
Langenhoe Essex 34 G4
Langford Beds 32 D4
Langford Devon 8 D2
Langford Essex 34 H2
Langford Notts 51 G10
Langford Oxon 19 A9
Langford Budville Som'set 8 B3
Langham Essex 34 E4
Langham Norfolk 44 A4
Langham Rutl'd 41 D10
Langham Suffolk 34 B3
Langhaugh Scot Borders 76 D5
Langho Lancs 56 E2
Langholm Dumf/Gal 69 B6
Langleeford Northum 78 E4
Langley Ches 49 E10
Langley Hants 11 D7
Langley Herts 32 F5
Langley Kent 14 C3
Langley Northum 70 D3
Langley Slough 21 D8
Langley Warwick 30 B3
Langley W Sussex 12 C2
Langley Burrell Wilts 19 D6
Langley Common Derby 40 B4
Langley Heath Kent 14 C3
Langley Lower Green Essex 33 E7
Langley Marsh Som'set 8 B2
Langley Park Durham 71 F7
Langley Street Norfolk 45 E7
Langley Upper Green Essex 33 E7
Langney E Sussex 13 E10
Langold Notts 51 D7
Langore Cornw'l 4 B4
Langport Som'set 9 B6
Langrick Lincs 52 H5
Langridge Bath/NE Som'set 18 E4
Langridge Ford Devon 7 D6
Langrigg Cumb 68 F4
Langrish Hants 11 B10
Langsett S Yorks 50 B4
Langshaw Scot Borders 77 D8
Langside Perth/Kinr 83 C8
Langskaill Orkney 110 D5
Langstone Hants 11 D10
Langstone Newp 17 B8
Langthorne N Yorks 63 E7
Langthorpe N Yorks 57 B8
Langthwaite N Yorks 62 D5
Langtoft ER Yorks 59 B6
Langtoft Lincs 42 D4
Langton Durham 63 C6
Langton Lincs 52 F5
Langton Lincs 53 E6
Langton N Yorks 58 B3
Langton by Wragby Lincs 52 E4
Langton Green Kent 13 B9
Langton Green Suffolk 34 A5
Langton Herring Dorset 9 F8
Langton Matravers Dorset 10 G3
Langtree Devon 6 E5
Langwathby Cumb 69 G8
Langwell Ho. H'land 107 G6
Langwell Lodge H'land 101 B9
Langwith Derby 51 F7
Langwith Junction Derby 51 F7
Langworth Lincs 52 E3
Lanhydrock House, Bodmin Cornw'l 3 C9
Lanivet Cornw'l 3 C9
Lanlivery Cornw'l 3 D9
Lanner Cornw'l 3 F6
Lanreath Cornw'l 4 E2
Lansallos Cornw'l 4 E2
Lansdown Glos 29 F10
Lanteglos Highway Cornw'l 4 E2
Lanton Scot Borders 77 E9
Lanton Northum 78 D4
Lapford Devon 7 F8
Laphroaig Arg/Bute 72 C3
Lapley Staffs 39 D9
Lapworth Warwick 30 A3
Larachbeg H'land 87 G6
Larbert Falk 83 F9
Larden Green Ches 49 G6
Largie Aberds 98 E6
Largiemore Arg/Bute 81 F9
Largoward Fife 85 D6
Largs N Ayrs 74 B4
Largybeg N Ayrs 74 E2
Largymore N Ayrs 74 E2
Larkfield Invercl 82 G3
Larkhall S Lanarks 75 B9
Larkhill Wilts 19 G8
Larling Norfolk 44 G3
Larriston Scot Borders 69 A8
Lartington Durham 62 C5
Lary Aberds 90 A4
Lasham Hants 20 G4
Lashenden Kent 14 D3
Lassington Glos 29 F8
Lassodie Fife 84 E3
Lastingham N Yorks 64 E5
Latcham Som'set 17 G9
Latchford Herts 33 F6
Latchford Warrington 49 D7
Latchingdon Essex 23 A8
Latchley Cornw'l 4 C5
Lately Common Warrington 49 C7
Lathbury M/Keynes 32 D1
Latheron H'land 107 F6
Latheronwheel H'land 107 F6
Latheronwheel Ho. H'land 107 F6
Lathones Fife 85 D6
Latimer Bucks 21 B8
Latteridge S Gloucs 18 C3
Lattiford Som'set 9 B8
Latton Wilts 19 B7
Latton Bush Essex 33 H7
Lauchintilly Aberds 99 G7
Lauder Scot Borders 77 C8
Laugharne Carms 25 E8
Laughterton Lincs 51 E10
Laughton E Sussex 13 D9
Laughton Leics 41 G8
Laughton Lincs 42 B3
Laughton Lincs 51 C10
Laughton Common S Yorks 51 D7
Laughton en le Morthen S Yorks 51 D7
Launcells Cornw'l 6 F3
Launceston Cornw'l 4 B4
Launton Oxon 31 F8
Laurencekirk Aberds 91 D8
Laurieston Dumf/Gal 67 D8
Laurieston Falk 83 G10
Lavendon M/Keynes 32 C2
Lavenham Suffolk 34 D3
Laverhay Dumf/Gal 76 H4
Laversdale Cumb 69 D7
Laverstock Wilts 10 A4
Laverstoke Hants 20 G2
Laverton Glos 30 E2
Laverton N Yorks 63 G7
Laverton Som'set 18 F4
Lavister Wrex 48 G4
Law S Lanarks 75 B10
Lawers Perth/Kinr 89 H7
Lawers Perth/Kinr 83 B8
Lawford Essex 34 E4
Lawhitton Cornw'l 4 B4
Lawkland N Yorks 56 B2
Lawley Telford 39 E7
Lawnhead Staffs 39 C9
Lawrenny Pembs 24 F5
Lawshall Suffolk 34 C2
Lawton Heref'd 28 C5
Laxey I/Man 54 D4
Laxfield Suffolk 35 A6
Laxfirth Shetl'd 111 J7
Laxfirth Shetl'd 111 H7
Laxford Bridge H'land 104 E5
Laxo Shetl'd 111 G7
Laxobigging Shetl'd 111 F7
Laxton ER Yorks 58 F3
Laxton Notts 51 F9
Laxton Northants 42 F2
Laycock W Yorks 56 D5
Layer Breton Essex 34 G3
Layer de la Haye Essex 34 G3
Layer Marney Essex 34 G3
Layham Suffolk 34 D4
Laylands Green W Berks 20 E1
Laytham ER Yorks 58 E3
Layton Blackp'l 55 E3
Lazenby Redcar/Clevel'd 64 B3
Lazonby Cumb 69 G8
Le Planel Guernsey 4
Le Villocq Guernsey 4
Lea Derby 50 G5
Lea Heref'd 29 F7
Lea Lincs 51 D10
Lea Shrops 38 G4
Lea Shrops 38 E5
Lea Wilts 19 C6
Lea Marston Warwick 40 F4
Lea Town Lancs 55 E4
Leabrooks Derby 51 G6
Leac a Li W Isles 109 H6
Leachkin H'land 96 B4
Leadburn Midloth 76 B5
Leaden Roding Essex 33 G8
Leadenham Lincs 52 G2
Leadgate Cumb 70 F2
Leadgate Durham 71 E6
Leadgate Northum 71 E6
Leadhills S Lanarks 76 F1
Leafield Oxon 30 G5
Leagrave Luton 32 F3
Leake N Yorks 63 E9
Leake Commonside Lincs 53 G6
Lealholm N Yorks 64 D5
Lealt Arg/Bute 81 E6
Lealt H'land 100 F3
Leamington Hastings Warwick 31 B6
Leamonsley Staffs 40 E3
Leamside Durham 71 F8
Leanaig H'land 102 G4
Leargybreck Arg/Bute 80 G5
Leasgill Cumb 61 F7
Leasingham Lincs 52 H3
Leasingthorne Durham 63 B7
Leasowe Mersey 48 C3
Leatherhead Surrey 21 F9
Leatherhead Common Surrey 21 F9
Leathley N Yorks 57 D7
Leaton Shrops 38 D5
Leaveland Kent 14 C5
Leavening N Yorks 58 B3
Leaves Green London 22 E4
Leazes Durham 71 E6
Lebberston N Yorks 65 F8
Lechlade Glos 19 B9
Leck Lancs 61 G9
Leckford Hants 20 H1
Leckfurin H'land 106 D2
Leckgruinart Arg/Bute 80 H2
Leckhampstead Bucks 31 E9
Leckhampstead W Berks 20 D2
Leckhampstead Thicket W Berks 20 D2
Leckhampton Glos 29 G10
Leckie H'land 101 F8
Leckmelm H'land 101 C9
Leckwith V/Glam 17 D6
Leconfield ER Yorks 59 D6
Ledaig Arg/Bute 87 H9
Ledburn Bucks 32 F2
Ledbury Heref'd 29 E8
Ledcharrie Stirl 83 B6
Ledgemoor Heref'd 28 C5
Ledicot Heref'd 28 B5
Ledmore H'land 101 A10
Lednagullin H'land 106 C2
Ledsham Ches 48 E4
Ledsham W Yorks 57 F9
Ledston W Yorks 57 F9
Ledston Luck W Yorks 57 E9
Ledwell Oxon 31 F6
Lee Arg/Bute 80 B4
Lee Devon 6 B5
Lee Hants 11 C6
Lee Lancs 55 C5
Lee Shrops 38 B5
Lee Brockhurst Shrops 39 C6
Lee Clump Bucks 21 A7
Lee Mill Devon 5 E7
Lee Moor Devon 5 D6
Lee on the Solent Hants 11 D8
Leeans Shetl'd 111 J6
Leebotten Shetl'd 111 L7
Leebotwood Shrops 38 F5
Leece Cumb 55 B2
Leechpool Pembs 24 E4
Leeds Kent 14 C3
Leeds W Yorks 57 E7
Leeds Castle Kent 14 C3
Leeds City Art Gallery W Yorks 57 E7
Leedstown Cornw'l 2 F5
Leek Staffs 50 G1
Leek Wootton Warwick 30 B4
Leekbrook Staffs 50 G1
Leeming N Yorks 63 F7
Leeming Bar N Yorks 63 E7
Lees Derby 40 B4
Lees Gtr Man 50 B1
Lees W Yorks 56 E5
Leeswood Flints 48 F3
Legbourne Lincs 53 D6
Legerwood Scot Borders 77 C8
Legoland Windsor 21 D7
Legsby Lincs 52 D4
Leicester Leics C 41 E7
Leicester Forest East Leics 41 E7
Leicester Racecourse Leics 41 E8
Leigh Dorset 9 D8
Leigh Glos 29 F9
Leigh Gtr Man 49 B7
Leigh Kent 22 G5
Leigh Shrops 38 E4
Leigh Surrey 22 G2
Leigh Wilts 19 B7
Leigh Worcs 29 C8
Leigh Beck Essex 23 C8
Leigh Common Som'set 9 B9
Leigh Delamere Wilts 18 D5
Leigh Green Kent 14 E4
Leigh on Sea Southend 23 C8
Leigh Park Hants 11 D10
Leigh Sinton Worcs 29 C8
Leigh upon Mendip Som'set 18 G3
Leigh Woods N Som'set 18 D2
Leighswood W Midlands 40 E2
Leighterton Glos 18 B5
Leighton N Yorks 63 G6
Leighton Powys 38 E3
Leighton Shrops 39 E7
Leighton Som'set 18 G4
Leighton Bromswold Cambs 42 H4
Leighton Buzzard Beds 32 F2
Leinthall Earls Heref'd 28 B5
Leinthall Starkes Heref'd 28 B5
Leintwardine Heref'd 28 A5
Leire Leics 41 F7
Leirinmore H'land 105 C7
Leiston Suffolk 35 B8
Leitfie Perth/Kinr 90 G3
Leith C/Edinb 84 G4
Leitholm Scot Borders 78 C2
Lelant Cornw'l 2 F4
Lelley ER Yorks 59 E8
Lem Hill Worcs 29 A8
Lemmington Hall Northum 79 F6
Lempitlaw Scot Borders 78 D2
Lenchwick Worcs 30 D2
Lendalfoot S Ayrs 66 B3
Lendrick Stirl 83 D6
Lenham Kent 14 C3
Lenham Heath Kent 14 D4
Lenie H'land 96 D3
Lennel Scot Borders 78 C3
Lennoxtown E Dunb 83 G7
Lenton Lincs 42 B3
Lenton Nott'ham 41 B7
Lentran Ho. H'land 96 B3
Lenwade Norfolk 44 D4
Leny Ho. Stirl 83 D7
Lenzie E Dunb 83 G7
Leoch Angus 90 H4
Leochel Cushnie Aberds 98 G5
Leominster Heref'd 28 C5
Leonard Stanley Glos 18 A5
Leonardslee Gardens W Sussex 13 C6
Leorin Arg/Bute 72 C3
Lepe Hants 11 E7
Lephin H'land 109 N6
Lephinchapel Arg/Bute 81 E9
Lephinmore Arg/Bute 81 E9
Leppington N Yorks 58 B3
Lepton W Yorks 57 G7
Lerryn Cornw'l 4 E2
Lerwick Shetl'd 111 J7
Lesbury Northum 79 F7
Leslie Aberds 98 F5
Leslie Fife 84 D4
Lesmahagow S Lanarks 75 D10
Lesnewth Cornw'l 6 G2
Lessendrum Aberds 98 D5
Lessingham Norfolk 45 C7
Lessonhall Cumb 68 E5
Leswalt Dumf/Gal 66 D2
Letchmore Heath Herts 21 B9
Letchworth Herts 32 E5
Letcombe Bassett Oxon 20 C1
Letcombe Regis Oxon 20 C1
Letham Angus 91 G6
Letham Falk 83 F9
Letham Fife 84 C5
Letham Perth/Kinr 84 B2
Letham Grange Angus 91 G7
Lethenty Aberds 99 D8
Letheringham Suffolk 35 C6
Letheringsett Norfolk 44 B4
Lettaford Devon 5 B8
Lettan Orkney 110 D8
Letterewe H'land 101 E7
Letterfearn H'land 94 D5
Letterfinlay H'land 88 B3
Lettermorar H'land 87 C7
Lettermore Arg/Bute 86 G4
Letters H'land 101 D9
Letterston Pembs 24 D4
Lettoch H'land 97 E8
Lettoch H'land 97 C8
Letton Heref'd 28 D4
Letton Heref'd 28 A4
Letton Green Norfolk 44 E3
Letty Green Herts 32 G5
Letwell S Yorks 51 D7
Leuchars Fife 85 B6
Leuchars Ho. Moray 98 B2
Leumrabhagh W Isles 108 F8
Levan Invercl 82 G3
Levaneap Shetl'd 111 G7
Levedale Staffs 39 D9
Leven ER Yorks 59 D7
Leven Fife 84 D5
Levencorroch N Ayrs 74 E2
Levens Cumb 61 F7
Levens Green Herts 33 F6
Levenshulme Gtr Man 49 C9
Levenwick Shetl'd 111 L7
Leverington Cambs 43 D7
Leverton Lincs 53 H7
Leverton Highgate Lincs 53 H7
Leverton Lucasgate Lincs 53 H7
Leverton Outgate Lincs 53 H7
Levington Suffolk 35 E6
Levisham N Yorks 65 E6
Levishie H'land 96 E2
Lew Oxon 30 H5
Lewannick Cornw'l 4 B3
Lewdown Devon 4 B5
Lewes E Sussex 13 D8
Leweston Pembs 24 D4
Lewisham London 22 D3
Lewiston H'land 96 D3
Lewistown Bridg 16 C4
Lewknor Oxon 20 B5
Leworthy Devon 6 F4
Leworthy Devon 7 C7
Lewtrenchard Devon 4 B5
Lexden Essex 34 F3
Ley Aberds 98 G5
Ley Cornw'l 4 D2
Leybourne Kent 14 C1
Leyburn N Yorks 63 E6
Leyfields Staffs 40 E4
Leyhill Bucks 21 A7
Leyland Lancs 55 F5
Leylodge Aberds 99 G7
Leymoor W Yorks 57 G6
Leys Aberds 99 C10
Leys Perth/Kinr 90 H3
Leys Castle H'land 96 B4
Leys of Cossans Angus 90 G4
Leysdown on Sea Kent 23 D10
Leysmill Angus 91 G7
Leysters Pole Heref'd 29 B6
Leyton London 22 C3
Leytonstone London 22 C3
Lezant Cornw'l 4 C4
Leziate Norfolk 43 D9
Lhanbryde Moray 98 B2
Liatrie H'land 95 C9
Libanus Powys 27 F9
Libberton S Lanarks 76 C2
Liberton C/Edinb 84 H4
Liceasto W Isles 109 H6
Lichfield Staffs 40 E3
Lichfield Cathedral Staffs 40 D3
Lickey Worcs 40 H1
Lickey End Worcs 30 A1
Lickfold W Sussex 12 C3
Liddel Orkney 110 K5
Liddesdale H'land 87 F7
Liddington Swindon 19 C9
Lidgate Suffolk 33 C10
Lidget S Yorks 51 B8
Lidget Green W Yorks 57 E6
Lidgett Notts 51 F8
Lidlington Beds 32 E2
Lidstone Oxon 30 F5
Lieurary H'land 106 C5
Liff Angus 84 A5
Lifton Devon 4 B4
Liftondown Devon 4 B4
Lighthorne Warwick 30 C5
Lightwater Surrey 21 E7
Lightwater Valley N Yorks 63 G7
Lightwood Stoke 39 A10
Lightwood Green Ches 39 A7
Lightwood Green Wrex 38 A4
Lilbourne Northants 41 H7
Lilburn Tower Northum 78 E5
Lilleshall Telford 39 D8
Lilley Herts 32 F4
Lilley W Berks 20 D2
Lilliesleaf Scot Borders 77 E8
Lillingstone Dayrell Bucks 31 E9
Lillingstone Lovell Bucks 31 D9
Lillington Dorset 9 C8
Lillington Warwick 30 B5
Lilliput Poole 10 E3
Lilstock Som'set 17 G6
Lilyhurst Shrops 39 D8
Limbury Luton 32 F3
Limebrook Heref'd 28 B4
Limefield Gtr Man 56 G3
Limekilnburn S Lanarks 75 B9
Limekilns Fife 84 F2
Limerigg Falk 83 G9
Limerstone I/Wight 11 F7
Limington Som'set 9 B7
Limpenhoe Norfolk 45 E7
Limpley Stoke Wilts 18 E4
Limpsfield Surrey 22 F4
Limpsfield Chart Surrey 22 F4
Linby Notts 51 G7
Linchmere W Sussex 12 B2
Lincluden Dumf/Gal 68 C2
Lincoln Lincs 52 E2
Lincoln Castle Lincs 52 E2
Lincoln Cathedral Lincs 52 E2
Lincomb Worcs 29 B9
Lincombe Devon 5 E8
Lindal in Furness Cumb 60 G5
Lindale Cumb 61 F7
Lindean Scot Borders 77 D7
Lindfield W Sussex 13 C7
Lindford Hants 12 B2
Lindifferon Fife 84 C5
Lindisfarne Priory, Holy Island Northum 79 C6
Lindley W Yorks 57 G6
Lindley Green N Yorks 57 D7
Lindores Fife 84 C4
Lindridge Worcs 29 B7
Lindsell Essex 33 F9
Lindsey Suffolk 34 D3
Linford Hants 10 D4
Linford Thurr'k 23 D6
Lingague I/Man 54 E2
Lingards Wood W Yorks 56 G5
Lingbob W Yorks 56 E5
Lingdale Redcar/Clevel'd 64 C4
Lingen Heref'd 28 B4
Lingfield Surrey 22 G3
Lingfield Park Racecourse Surrey 22 G3
Lingreabhagh W Isles 109 J5
Lingwood Norfolk 45 E7
Linicro H'land 109 L8
Linkenholt Hants 20 F1
Linkhill Kent 14 F3
Linkinhorne Cornw'l 4 C4
Linklater Orkney 110 K5
Linksness Orkney 110 H3
Linktown Fife 84 E4
Linley Shrops 38 F4
Linley Green Heref'd 29 C7
Linlithgow W Loth 84 G2
Linlithgow Bridge W Loth 84 G1
Linshiels Northum 78 G3
Linsiadar W Isles 108 D7
Linsidemore H'land 102 C4
Linslade Beds 32 F2
Linstead Parva Suffolk 45 H7
Linstock Cumb 69 E7
Linthwaite W Yorks 57 G6
Lintlaw Scot Borders 78 B3
Lintmill Moray 98 B5
Linton Scot Borders 78 E2
Linton Cambs 33 D8
Linton Derby 40 D4
Linton Heref'd 29 F7
Linton Kent 14 D2
Linton Northum 71 A7
Linton N Yorks 56 B4
Linton W Yorks 57 D8
Linton on Ouse N Yorks 57 B9
Linwood Hants 10 D4
Linwood Lincs 52 D4
Linwood Renf 75 A6
Lionacleit W Isles 109 N2
Lional W Isles 108 A10
Liphook Hants 12 B2
Liscard Mersey 48 C4
Liscombe Som'set 7 C9
Liskeard Cornw'l 4 D3
L'Islet Guernsey 4
Liss Hants 12 C1
Liss Forest Hants 12 C1
Lissett ER Yorks 59 C7
Lissington Lincs 52 D4
Lisvane Card 17 C6
Liswerry Newp 17 C8
Lit. Hallingbury Essex 33 G7
Litcham Norfolk 44 D2
Litchborough Northants 31 C8
Litchfield Hants 20 F2
Litherland Mersey 48 C4
Litlington Cambs 33 D6
Litlington E Sussex 13 E9
Little Abington Cambs 33 D8
Little Addington Northants 32 A2
Little Alne Warwick 30 B3
Little Altcar Mersey 48 B4
Little Asby Cumb 61 D9
Little Assynt H'land 104 G4
Little Aston Staffs 40 E2
Little Atherfield I/Wight 11 F7
Little Ayre Orkney 110 J4
Little ayre Shetl'd 111 G6
Little Ayton N Yorks 64 C3
Little Baddow Essex 34 H1
Little Badminton S Gloucs 18 C5
Little Ballinluig Perth/Kinr 89 F10
Little Bampton Cumb 68 E5
Little Bardfield Essex 33 E9
Little Barford Beds 32 C4
Little Barningham Norfolk 44 B5
Little Barrington Glos 30 G4
Little Barrow Ches 48 E5
Little Barugh N Yorks 64 G5
Little Bavington Northum 70 C4
Little Bealings Suffolk 35 D6
Little Bedwyn Wilts 19 E9
Little Bentley Essex 34 F5
Little Berkhamsted Herts 32 H5
Little Billing Northants 31 B10
Little Birch Heref'd 29 E6
Little Blakenham Suffolk 34 D5
Little Blencow Cumb 69 G7
Little Bollington Ches 49 D8
Little Bookham Surrey 21 F9
Little Bowden Leics 41 G9
Little Bradley Suffolk 33 C9
Little Brampton Shrops 38 G4
Little Brechin Angus 91 E6
Little Brickhill M/Keynes 32 E2
Little Brington Northants 31 B8
Little Bromley Essex 34 F4
Little Broughton Cumb 68 G3
Little Budworth Ches 49 F6
Little Burstead Essex 23 B6
Little Bytham Lincs 42 D3
Little Carlton Lincs 53 D6
Little Carlton Notts 51 G9
Little Casterton Rutl'd 42 E3
Little Cawthorpe Lincs 53 D6
Little Chalfont Bucks 21 B7
Little Chart Kent 14 D4
Little Chesterford Essex 33 D8
Little Cheverell Wilts 19 F6
Little Chishill Cambs 33 E7
Little Clacton Essex 34 G5
Little Clifton Cumb 60 B3
Little Colp Aberds 99 D7
Little Comberton Worcs 30 D1
Little Common E Sussex 14 H2
Little Compton Warwick 30 E4
Little Cornard Suffolk 34 E2
Little Cowarne Heref'd 29 C7
Little Coxwell Oxon 19 B9
Little Crakehall N Yorks 63 E7
Little Cressingham Norfolk 44 E2
Little Crosby Mersey 48 B4
Little Dalby Leics 41 D9
Little Dawley Telford 39 E7
Little Dens Aberds 99 D10
Little Dewchurch Heref'd 29 E6
Little Downham Cambs 43 G8
Little Driffield ER Yorks 59 C6
Little Dunham Norfolk 44 D2
Little Dunkeld Perth/Kinr 90 G1
Little Dunmow Essex 33 F9
Little Easton Essex 33 F9
Little Eaton Derby 40 A5
Little Eccleston Lancs 55 D4
Little Ellingham Norfolk 44 F4
Little End Essex 22 A5
Little Eversden Cambs 33 C6
Little Fakenham Suffolk 44 H3
Little Faringdon Oxon 19 A9
Little Fencote N Yorks 63 E7
Little Fenton N Yorks 57 E10
Little Finborough Suffolk 34 C4
Little Fransham Norfolk 44 D3
Little Gaddesden Herts 32 G2
Little Gidding Cambs 42 G4
Little Glemham Suffolk 35 C7
Little Glenshee Perth/Kinr 84 A1
Little Gransden Cambs 32 C5
Little Green Som'set 18 G4
Little Grimsby Lincs 53 C6
Little Gruinard H'land 101 D7
Little Habton N Yorks 64 G5
Little Hadham Herts 33 F7
Little Hale Lincs 42 A4
Little Hampden Bucks 21 A6
Little Harrowden Northants 32 A1
Little Haseley Oxon 20 A4
Little Hatfield ER Yorks 59 D7
Little Hautbois Norfolk 45 C6
Little Haven Pembs 24 E3
Little Hay Staffs 40 E3
Little Hayfield Derby 50 D2
Little Haywood Staffs 40 C2
Little Heath W Midlands 40 G5
Little Hereford Heref'd 29 B6
Little Horkesley Essex 34 E3
Little Horsted E Sussex 13 D8
Little Horton W Yorks 57 E6
Little Horwood Bucks 31 E9
Little Houghton Northants 31 C10
Little Houghton S Yorks 51 B6
Little Hucklow Derby 50 E3
Little Hulton Gtr Man 49 B8
Little Humber ER Yorks 59 F7
Little Hungerford W Berks 20 D3
Little Irchester Northants 32 B2
Little Kimble Bucks 31 H10
Little Kineton Warwick 30 C5
Little Kingshill Bucks 21 B6
Little Langdale Cumb 61 D6
Little Langford Wilts 19 H7
Little Laver Essex 33 H8
Little Leigh Ches 49 E7
Little Leighs Essex 33 G10
Little Lever Gtr Man 49 B8
Little London Bucks 31 G8
Little London E Sussex 13 D9
Little London Hants 20 G1
Little London Hants 20 F4
Little London Lincs 42 C5
Little London Lincs 43 C7
Little London Norfolk 44 C5
Little London Powys 37 G10
Little Longstone Derby 50 E3
Little Lynturk Aberds 98 G5
Little Malvern Worcs 29 D8
Little Maplestead Essex 34 E2
Little Marcle Heref'd 29 E7
Little Marlow Bucks 21 C6
Little Marsden Lancs 56 E3
Little Massingham Norfolk 44 C1
Little Melton Norfolk 44 E5
Little Mill Monmouths 17 A8
Little Milton Oxon 20 A4
Little Missenden Bucks 21 B7
Little Musgrave Cumb 62 C2
Little Ness Shrops 38 D5
Little Neston Ches 48 E3
Little Newcastle Pembs 24 D4
Little Newsham Durham 63 C6
Little Oakley Essex 35 F6
Little Oakley Northants 42 G1
Little Orton Cumb 69 E6
Little Ouseburn N Yorks 57 B9
Little Paxton Cambs 32 B4
Little Petherick Cornw'l 3 B8
Little Pitlurg Moray 98 D4
Little Plumpton Lancs 55 E3
Little Plumstead Norfolk 45 D7
Little Ponton Lincs 42 B2
Little Raveley Cambs 42 H5
Little Reedness ER Yorks 58 F4
Little Ribston N Yorks 57 C8
Little Rissington Glos 30 G3
Little Ryburgh Norfolk 44 C3
Little Ryle Northum 78 F5
Little Salkeld Cumb 69 G8
Little Sampford Essex 33 E9
Little Sandhurst Brackn'l 21 E6
Little Saxham Suffolk 34 B1
Little Scatwell H'land 102 G2
Little Sessay N Yorks 63 G9
Little Shelford Cambs 33 C7
Little Singleton Lancs 55 E3
Little Skillymarno Aberds 99 C9
Little Smeaton N Yorks 57 G10
Little Snoring Norfolk 44 B3
Little Sodbury S Gloucs 18 C4
Little Somborne Hants 11 A6
Little Somerford Wilts 19 C6
Little Stainforth N Yorks 56 B3
Little Stainton D'lington 63 B8
Little Stanney Ches 48 E5
Little Staughton Beds 32 B4
Little Steeping Lincs 53 F7
Little Stoke Staffs 39 B10
Little Stonham Suffolk 34 B5
Little Stretton Leics 41 E8
Little Stretton Shrops 38 F5
Little Strickland Cumb 61 C8
Little Stukeley Cambs 42 H5
Little Sutton Ches 48 E4
Little Tew Oxon 30 F5
Little Thetford Cambs 43 H8
Little Thirkleby N Yorks 63 G9
Little Thurlow Suffolk 33 C9
Little Thurrock Thurr'k 23 D6
Little Torboll H'land 103 C6
Little Torrington Devon 6 E5
Little Totham Essex 34 G2
Little Town Cumb 60 C5
Little Town Lancs 56 E1
Little Urswick Cumb 60 G5
Little Wakering Essex 23 C9
Little Walden Essex 33 D8
Little Waldingfield Suffolk 34 D3
Little Walsingham Norfolk 44 B3
Little Waltham Essex 33 G10
Little Warley Essex 23 B6
Little Weighton ER Yorks 58 E5
Little Weldon Northants 42 G2
Little Welnetham Suffolk 34 B2
Little Wenlock Telford 39 E7
Little Whittingham Green Suffolk 45 H6
Little Wilbraham Cambs 33 C8
Little Wishford Wilts 19 H7
Little Witley Worcs 29 B8
Little Wittenham Oxon 20 B3
Little Wolford Warwick 30 E4
Little Wratting Suffolk 33 D9
Little Wymington Beds 32 B2
Little Wymondley Herts 32 F5
Little Wyrley Staffs 40 E2
Little Yeldham Essex 34 E1
Littlebeck N Yorks 65 D6
Littleborough Gtr Man 56 G4
Littleborough Notts 51 D10
Littlebourne Kent 15 C7
Littlebredy Dorset 9 F7
Littlebury Essex 33 E8
Littlebury Green Essex 33 E7
Littledean Glos 29 G7
Littleferry H'land 103 C7
Littleham Devon 8 F2
Littleham Devon 6 D5
Littlehampton W Sussex 12 E4
Littlehempston Devon 5 D9
Littlehoughton Northum 79 F7
Littlemill Aberds 90 B4
Littlemill E Ayrs 75 F6
Littlemill H'land 103 G8
Littlemill Northum 79 F7
Littlemore Oxon 20 A3
Littleover Derby C 40 B5
Littleport Cambs 43 G8
Littlestone on Sea Kent 14 F5
Littlethorpe Leics 41 F7
Littlethorpe N Yorks 57 B8
Littleton Ches 48 F5
Littleton Hants 11 A7
Littleton Perth/Kinr 84 A4
Littleton Som'set 9 A6
Littleton Surrey 21 E8
Littleton Surrey 21 G7
Littleton Drew Wilts 18 C5
Littleton on Severn S Gloucs 18 C2
Littleton Pannell Wilts 19 F7
Littletown Durham 71 F8
Littlewick Green Windsor 21 D6
Littleworth Beds 32 D3
Littleworth Glos 18 A5
Littleworth Oxon 19 B10
Littleworth Staffs 40 D2
Littleworth Worcs 29 C9
Litton Derby 50 E3
Litton N Yorks 62 G4
Litton Som'set 18 F2
Litton Cheney Dorset 9 E7
Liurbost W Isles 108 E8
Liverpool Mersey 48 C4
Liverpool Cathedral (C of E) Mersey 48 D4
Liverpool Cathedral (RC) Mersey 48 C4
Liversedge W Yorks 57 F7
Liverton Devon 5 C9
Liverton Redcar/Clevel'd 64 C5
Livingston W Loth 84 H2
Livingston Village W Loth 84 H2
Lixwm Flints 48 E2
Lizard Cornw'l 3 H6
Llaingoch Angl 46 D2
Llaithddu Powys 38 G1
Llan Powys 37 E8
Llan y pwll Wrex 48 G4
Llanaber Gwyn 37 D6
Llanaelhaearn Gwyn 36 A3
Llanafan Ceredig'n 27 A6
Llanafan fawr Powys 27 C9
Llanallgo Angl 46 D4
Llanarmon Gwyn 36 B4
Llanarmon Dyffryn Ceiriog Wrex 38 B2
Llanarmon yn Ial Denbs 48 G2
Llanarth Ceredig'n 26 C4
Llanarth Monmouths 28 G4
Llanarthne Carms 26 F5
Llanasa Flints 48 D2
Llanbabo Angl 46 D3
Llanbadarn Fawr Ceredig'n 37 G6
Llanbadarn Fynydd Powys 38 H2
Llanbadarn y Garreg Powys 28 D2
Llanbadoc Monmouths 17 B8
Llanbadrig Angl 46 C3
Llanbeder Newp 17 B8
Llanbedr Gwyn 36 C5
Llanbedr Powys 28 D2
Llanbedr Powys 28 F3
Llanbedr Dyffryn Clwyd Denbs 48 G2
Llanbedr y cennin Conwy 47 F7
Llanbedrgoch Angl 46 D5
Llanbedrog Gwyn 36 B3
Llanberis Gwyn 46 F5
Llanbethery V/Glam 16 E5
Llanbister Powys 28 A2
Llanblethian V/Glam 16 D4
Llanboidy Carms 25 D7
Llanbradach Caerph 17 B6
Llanbrynmair Powys 37 E8
Llancarfan V/Glam 16 D5
Llancayo Monmouths 17 A8
Llancloudy Heref'd 28 F5
Llancynfelyn Ceredig'n 37 F6
Llandaff Card 17 D6
Llandanwg Gwyn 36 C5
Llandarcy Neath P Talb 16 B2
Llandawke Carms 25 E7
Llanddaniel Fab Angl 46 E4
Llanddarog Carms 26 G5
Llanddeiniol Ceredig'n 26 A5
Llanddeiniolen Gwyn 46 F5
Llandderfel Gwyn 37 B9
Llanddeusant Angl 46 D3
Llanddeusant Carms 27 F7
Llanddew Powys 28 E1
Llanddewi Swan 25 H9
Llanddewi Brefi Ceredig'n 27 C6
Llanddewi Rhydderch Monmouths 28 G4
Llanddewi Velfrey Pembs 24 E6
Llanddewi'r Cwm Powys 27 D10
Llanddogeb Conwy 47 F8
Llanddona Angl 46 E5
Llanddowror Carms 25 E7
Llanddulas Conwy 47 E9
Llanddwywe Gwyn 36 C5
Llanddyfynan Angl 46 E5
Llandefaelog Fach Powys 27 E10
Llandefaelog tre'r graig Powys 28 F2
Llandefalle Powys 28 E2
Llandegai Gwyn 46 E5
Llandegfan Angl 46 E5
Llandegla Denbs 48 G2
Llandegley Powys 28 B2
Llandegveth Monmouths 17 B8
Llandegwning Gwyn 36 B2
Llandeilo Carms 27 F6
Llandeilo Graban Powys 28 D1
Llandeilo'r Fan Powys 27 E8
Llandeloy Pembs 24 D3
Llandenny Monmouths 17 A9
Llandevenny Monmouths 17 C9
Llandewednock Cornw'l 3 H6
Llandewi Ystradenny Powys 28 B2
Llandinabo Heref'd 29 F6
Llandinam Powys 37 G10
Llandissilio Pembs 24 D6
Llandogo Monmouths 18 A2
Llandough V/Glam 16 D4
Llandough V/Glam 17 D6
Llandovery Carms 27 E7
Llandow V/Glam 16 D4
Llandre Ceredig'n 37 G6
Llandre Carms 27 D6
Llandrillo Denbs 37 B10
Llandrillo yn Rhos Conwy 47 D8
Llandrindod Wells Powys 28 B1
Llandrinio Powys 38 D3
Llandudno Conwy 47 D7
Llandudno Junction Conwy 47 E7
Llandwrog Gwyn 46 G4
Llandybie Carms 27 G6
Llandyfaelog Carms 25 E9
Llandyfan Carms 27 G6
Llandyfriog Ceredig'n 25 B8
Llandyfrydog Angl 46 D4
Llandygwydd Ceredig'n 25 B7
Llandynan Denbs 48 H2
Llandyrnog Denbs 48 F2
Llandysilio Powys 38 D3
Llandyssil Powys 38 F2
Llandysul Ceredig'n 25 B9
Llanedeyrn Card 17 C7
Llanedy Carms 25 F10
Llaneglwys Powys 28 E1
Llanegryn Gwyn 36 E5
Llanegwad Carms 26 F5
Llaneilian Angl 46 C4
Llanelian yn Rhos Conwy 47 E8
Llanelidan Denbs 48 G2
Llanelieu Powys 28 E2
Llanellen Monmouths 28 G4
Llanelli Carms 25 G10
Llanelli Monmouths 28 G3
Llanelltyd Gwyn 37 D7
Llanelly Hill Monmouths 28 G3
Llanelwedd Powys 27 C10
Llanenddwyn Gwyn 36 C5
Llanengan Gwyn 36 C2
Llanerchymedd Angl 46 D4
Llanerfyl Powys 37 E10
Llanfachraeth Angl 46 D3
Llanfachreth Gwyn 37 C7
Llanfaelog Angl 46 E3
Llanfaelrhys Gwyn 36 C2
Llanfaenor Monmouths 28 G5
Llanfaes Angl 47 E6
Llanfaes Powys 27 F10
Llanfaethlu Angl 46 D3
Llanfaglan Gwyn 46 F4
Llanfair Gwyn 36 C5
Llanfair ar y bryn Carms 27 E8
Llanfair Caereinion Powys 38 E2
Llanfair Clydogau Ceredig'n 27 C6
Llanfair Dyffryn Clwyd Denbs 48 G2
Llanfair Nant Gwyn Pembs 25 C6
Llanfair Talhaiarn Conwy 47 E9
Llanfairfechan Conwy 47 E6
Llanfairpwll gwyngyll Angl 46 E5
Llanfairyneubwll Angl 46 E3
Llanfairynghornwy Angl 46 C3
Llanfallteg Carms 25 E6
Llanfaredd Powys 28 C1
Llanfarian Ceredig'n 36 H5
Llanfechain Powys 38 C2
Llanfechan Powys 27 C9
Llanfechell Angl 46 C3
Llanfendigaid Gwyn 36 E5
Llanferres Denbs 48 F2
Llanfflewyn Angl 46 D3
Llanfihangel ar Arth Carms 25 C9
Llanfihangel Crucorney Monmouths 28 F4
Llanfihangel Glyn Myfyr Conwy 47 H9
Llanfihangel Nant Bran Powys 27 E9
Llanfihangel nant Melan Powys 28 C2
Llanfihangel Rhydithon Powys 28 B2
Llanfihangel Rogiet Monmouths 17 C9
Llanfihangel Tal y llyn Powys 28 F2
Llanfihangel uwch Gwili Carms 25 D9
Llanfihangel y Creuddyn Ceredig'n 37 H6
Llanfihangel y pennant Gwyn 36 A5
Llanfihangel y pennant Gwyn 37 E6
Llanfihangel y traethau Gwyn 36 B5
Llanfihangel yn Ngwynfa Powys 38 D1
Llanfihangel yn Nhowyn Angl 46 E3
Llanfilo Powys 28 E2
Llanfoist Monmouths 28 G3
Llanfor Gwyn 37 B9
Llanfrechfa Torf 17 B8
Llanfrothen Gwyn 37 A6
Llanfrynach Powys 28 F1
Llanfwrog Angl 46 D3
Llanfwrog Denbs 48 G2
Llanfyllin Powys 38 D2
Llanfynydd Carms 26 F5
Llanfynydd Flints 48 G3
Llanfyrnach Pembs 25 C7
Llangadfan Powys 37 D10
Llangadog Carms 27 F7
Llangadwaladr Angl 46 F3
Llangadwaladr Powys 38 B2
Llangaffo Angl 46 F4
Llangain Carms 25 E8
Llangammarch Wells Powys 27 D9
Llangan V/Glam 16 D4
Llangarron Heref'd 29 F6
Llangasty Talyllyn Powys 28 F2
Llangathen Carms 26 F5
Llangattock Powys 28 G3
Llangattock Lingoed Monmouths 28 F4
Llangattock nigh Usk Monmouths 28 H4
Llangattock Vibon Avel Monmouths 28 G5
Llangedwyn Powys 38 C2
Llangefni Angl 46 E4
Llangeinor Bridg 16 C4
Llangeitho Ceredig'n 27 C6
Llangeler Carms 25 C8
Llangelynin Gwyn 36 E5
Llangendeirne Carms 25 E9
Llangennech Carms 25 F10
Llangennith Swan 25 G9
Llangenny Powys 28 G3
Llangernyw Conwy 47 F8
Llangian Gwyn 36 C2
Llanglydwen Carms 25 D6
Llangoed Angl 47 E6
Llangoedmor Ceredig'n 25 B6
Llangollen Denbs 38 A3
Llangolman Pembs 24 D6
Llangorse Powys 28 F2
Llangovan Monmouths 28 H5
Llangower Gwyn 37 B9
Llangrannog Ceredig'n 26 C3
Llangristiolus Angl 46 E4
Llangrove Heref'd 29 G6
Llangua Monmouths 28 F4
Llangunllo Powys 28 A3
Llangunnor Carms 25 E9
Llangurig Powys 37 H9
Llangwm Conwy 37 A9
Llangwm Monmouths 17 A9
Llangwm Pembs 24 F4
Llangwnnadl Gwyn 36 B2
Llangwyfan Denbs 48 F2
Llangwyfan isaf Angl 46 F3
Llangwyllog Angl 46 E4
Llangwyryfon Ceredig'n 26 A5
Llangybi Ceredig'n 27 C6
Llangybi Gwyn 36 A4
Llangybi Monmouths 17 B8
Llangyfelach Swan 16 B1
Llangynhafal Denbs 48 F2
Llangynidr Powys 28 G2
Llangynin Carms 25 E7
Llangynog Carms 25 E8
Llangynog Powys 38 C1
Llangynwyd Bridg 16 C3
Llanhamlach Powys 28 F1
Llanharan Rh Cyn Taff 16 C5

Newton Bromshold Northants 32 B2
Newton Burgoland Leics 40 E5
Newton by Toft Lincs 52 D3
Newton Ferrers Devon 5 F6
Newton Flotman Norfolk 45 F6
Newton Hall Northum 70 D5
Newton Harcourt Leics 41 F8
Newton Heath Gtr Man 49 B9
Newton Ho. Aberds 99 F6
Newton Kyme N Yorks 57 D9
Newton le Willows Mersey 49 C6
Newton le Willows N Yorks 63 F7
Newton Longville Bucks 31 E10
Newton Mearns E Renf 75 B7
Newton Morrell N Yorks 63 D7
Newton Mulgrave N Yorks 64 C5
Newton of Ardtoe H'land 87 D6
Newton of Balcanquhal Perth/Kinr 84 C3
Newton of Falkland Fife 84 D4
Newton on Ayr S Ayrs 74 E5
Newton on Ouse N Yorks 57 C10
Newton on Rawcliffe N Yorks 65 E6
Newton on the Moor Northum 79 G6
Newton on Trent Lincs 51 E10
Newton Poppleford Devon 8 F2
Newton Purcell Oxon 31 E8
Newton Regis Warwick 40 E4
Newton Reigny Cumb 69 G7
Newton Solney Derby 40 C4
Newton St. Cyres Devon 7 G9
Newton St. Faith Norfolk 45 D6
Newton St. Loe Bath/NE Som'set 18 E4
Newton St. Petrock Devon 6 E5
Newton Stacey Hants 20 G2
Newton Stewart Dumf/Gal 67 D6
Newton Toney Wilts 19 G9
Newton Tracey Devon 7 D6
Newton under Roseberry Redcar/Clevel'd 64 C3
Newton upon Derwent ER Yorks 58 D3
Newton Valence Hants 11 A10
Newtonairds Dumf/Gal 68 B1
Newtongrange Midloth 77 A6
Newtonhill Aberds 91 B10
Newtonhill H'land 96 B3
Newtonmill Angus 91 E7
Newtonmore H'land 96 G5
Newtown Ches 49 E6
Newtown Cornw'l 3 G6
Newtown Cumb 68 F3
Newtown Cumb 69 D8
Newtown Derby 50 D1
Newtown Devon 7 D8
Newtown Glos 18 A3
Newtown Glos 29 E10
Newtown Hants 10 C5
Newtown Hants 11 B6
Newtown Hants 11 C9
Newtown Hants 20 E2
Newtown Hants 11 C8
Newtown Hants 11 D7
Newtown Heref'd 29 D7
Newtown H'land 96 F1
Newtown I/Man 54 E3
Newtown I/Wight 11 E7
Newtown Lancs 55 G5
Newtown Northum 78 G5
Newtown Northum 78 E5
Newtown Northum 78 D4
Newtown Poole 10 E3
Newtown Powys 38 F2
Newtown Shrops 38 B5
Newtown Staffs 49 F10
Newtown Staffs 50 F2
Newtown Wilts 10 B2
Newtown Linford Leics 41 E7
Newtown St. Boswells Scot Borders 77 D8
Newtown Unthank Leics 41 E6
Newtyle Angus 90 G3
Neyland Pembs 24 F4
Niarbyl I/Man 54 E2
Nibley S Gloucs 18 C3
Nibley Green Glos 18 B4
Nicholashayne Devon 8 C3
Nicholaston Swan 25 H10
Nidd N Yorks 57 B8
Nigg Aberd C 91 A10
Nigg H'land 103 E7
Nightcott Som'set 7 D9
Nilig Denbs 47 G10
Nine Ashes Essex 22 A5
Nine Mile Burn Midloth 76 B4
Nine Wells Pembs 24 D2
Ninebanks Northum 70 E2
Ninfield E Sussex 14 G2
Ningwood I/Wight 11 F6
Nisbet Scot Borders 77 E9
Nisthouse Orkney 110 G4
Niton I/Wight 11 G8
Nitshill Glasg C 75 A7
No Man's Heath Ches 49 H6
No Man's Heath Warwick 40 E4
Noak Hill London 22 B5
Noblethorpe S Yorks 50 B4
Nobottle Northants 31 B8
Nocton Lincs 52 F3
Noke Oxon 31 G7
Nolton Pembs 24 E3
Nolton Haven Pembs 24 E3
Nomansland Devon 7 E9
Nomansland Wilts 10 C5
Noneley Shrops 38 C5
Nonington Kent 15 C7
Norbreck Blackp'l 55 D3
Norbridge Heref'd 29 D8
Norbury Ches 49 H6
Norbury Derby 40 A3
Norbury Shrops 38 F4
Norbury Staffs 39 C8
Nordelph Norfolk 43 E8
Norden Gtr Man 56 G3
Norden Heath Dorset 10 F2
Nordley Shrops 39 F7
Norham Northum 78 C4
Norley Ches 49 E6
Norleywood Hants 11 E6
Norman Cross Cambs 42 F4
Normanby N Lincs 58 G4
Normanby N Yorks 64 F5
Normanby Redcar/Clevel'd 64 C3
Normanby by Spital Lincs 52 D3
Normanby by Stow Lincs 52 D1
Normanby le Wold Lincs 52 C4
Normandy Surrey 21 F7
Norman's Bay E Sussex 14 H1
Norman's Green Devon 8 D2
Normanstone Suffolk 45 F9
Normanton Derby C 40 B5
Normanton Leics 41 A10
Normanton Lincs 52 H2
Normanton Notts 51 G9
Normanton Rutl'd 42 E2
Normanton W Yorks 57 F8
Normanton le Heath Leics 40 D5
Normanton on Soar Notts 41 C7
Normanton on the Wolds Notts 41 B8
Normanton on Trent Notts 51 F9
Normoss Lancs 55 E3
Norney Surrey 21 G7
Norrington Common Wilts 18 E5
Norris Green Mersey 48 C4
Norris Hill Leics 40 D5
North Anston S Yorks 51 D7
North Aston Oxon 31 F6
North Baddesley Hants 11 C6
North Ballachulish H'land 87 E10
North Barrow Som'set 9 B8
North Barsham Norfolk 44 B3
North Benfleet Essex 23 C7
North Bersted W Sussex 12 E3
North Berwick E Loth 85 F7
North Boarhunt Hants 11 C9
North Bovey Devon 5 B8
North Bradley Wilts 18 F5
North Brentor Devon 4 B5
North Brewham Som'set 18 H4
North Buckland Devon 6 B5
North Burlingham Norfolk 45 D7
North Cadbury Som'set 9 B8
North Cairn Dumf/Gal 66 C1
North Carlton Lincs 52 E2
North Carrine Arg/Bute 73 G6
North Cave ER Yorks 58 E4
North Cerney Glos 30 H2
North Charford Wilts 10 C4
North Charlton Northum 79 E6
North Cheriton Som'set 9 B8
North Cliff ER Yorks 59 D8
North Cliffe ER Yorks 58 E4
North Clifton Notts 51 E10
North Coates Lincs 53 B6
North Cockerington Lincs 53 C6
North Coker Som'set 9 C7
North Collafirth Shetl'd 111 E6
North Common E Sussex 13 C7
North Cornelly Bridg 16 C3
North Cove Suffolk 45 G8
North Cowton N Yorks 63 D7
North Crawley M/Keynes 32 D2
North Cray London 22 D4
North Creake Norfolk 44 B2
North Curry Som'set 8 B5
North Dalton ER Yorks 58 C5
North Dawn Orkney 110 H5
North Deighton N Yorks 57 C8
North Duffield N Yorks 58 E2
North Elkington Lincs 52 C5
North Elmham Norfolk 44 C3
North Elmshall W Yorks 57 G9
North End Bucks 31 F10
North End ER Yorks 59 E8
North End Essex 33 G9
North End Hants 20 E2
North End Lincs 42 A5
North End N Som'set 17 E9
North End Portsm'th 11 D9
North End Som'set 8 B4
North End W Sussex 12 E5
North Erradale H'land 100 D5
North Fambridge Essex 23 B8
North Fearns H'land 94 C2
North Featherstone W Yorks 57 F9
North Ferriby ER Yorks 58 F5
North Frodingham ER Yorks 59 C7
North Gorley Hants 10 C4
North Green Norfolk 45 G6
North Green Suffolk 35 B7
North Greetwell Lincs 52 E3
North Grimston N Yorks 58 B4
North Halley Orkney 110 H6
North Halling Medway 14 B2
North Hayling Hants 11 D10
North Hazelrigg Northum 78 D5
North Heasley Devon 7 C8
North Heath W Sussex 12 C4
North Hill Cambs 43 H7
North Hill Cornw'l 4 C3
North Hinksey Oxon 31 H6
North Holmwood Surrey 21 G9
North Howden ER Yorks 58 E3
North Huish Devon 5 E8
North Hykeham Lincs 52 F2
North Johnston Pembs 24 E4
North Kelsey Lincs 52 B3
North Kelsey Moor Lincs 52 B3
North Kessock H'land 96 B4
North Killingholme N Lincs 59 G7
North Kilvington N Yorks 63 F9
North Kilworth Leics 41 G8
North Kirkton Aberds 99 C11
North Kiscadale N Ayrs 74 E2
North Kyme Lincs 52 G4
North Lancing W Sussex 12 E5
North Lee Bucks 31 H10
North Leigh Oxon 30 G5
North Leverton with Habblesthorpe Notts 51 D9
North Littleton Worcs 30 D2
North Lopham Norfolk 44 G4
North Luffenham Rutl'd 42 E2
North Marden W Sussex 12 D2
North Marston Bucks 31 F9
North Middleton Midloth 77 B6
North Middleton Northum 78 E5
North Molton Devon 7 D8
North Moreton Oxon 20 C3
North Mundham W Sussex 12 E2
North Muskham Notts 51 G9
North Newbald ER Yorks 58 E5
North Newington Oxon 31 E6
North Newnton Wilts 19 F8
North Newton Som'set 8 A4
North Nibley Glos 18 B4
North Norfolk Railway, Sheringham Norfolk 44 A5
North Oakley Hants 20 F3
North Ockendon London 22 C5
North Ormesby Middlesbro' 64 B3
North Ormsby Lincs 52 C5
North Otterington N Yorks 63 F8
North Owersby Lincs 52 C3
North Perrott Som'set 9 D6
North Petherton Som'set 8 A4
North Petherwin Cornw'l 4 B3
North Pickenham Norfolk 44 E2
North Piddle Worcs 30 C1
North Poorton Dorset 9 E7
North Port Arg/Bute 81 B10
North Queensferry Fife 84 F3
North Radworthy Devon 7 C8
North Rauceby Lincs 52 H3
North Reston Lincs 53 D6
North Rigton N Yorks 57 D7
North Rode Ches 49 F9
North Roe Shetl'd 111 E6
North Runcton Norfolk 43 D9
North Sandwick Shetl'd 111 D8
North Scale Cumb 55 B1
North Scarle Lincs 52 F1
North Seaton Northum 71 B7
North Shian Arg/Bute 87 G9
North Shields Tyne/Wear 71 D8
North Shoebury Southend 23 C9
North Shore Blackp'l 55 E3
North Side Cumb 60 B3
North Side Peterbro 42 F5
North Skelton Redcar/Clevel'd 64 C4
North Somercotes Lincs 53 C7
North Stainley N Yorks 63 G7
North Stainmore Cumb 62 C3
North Stifford Thurr'k 23 C6
North Stoke Bath/NE Som'set 18 E4
North Stoke Oxon 20 C4
North Stoke W Sussex 12 D4
North Street Hants 11 A9
North Street Kent 14 C5
North Street Medway 23 D8
North Street W Berks 20 D4
North Sunderland Northum 79 D7
North Tamerton Cornw'l 6 G4
North Tawton Devon 7 F7
North Thoresby Lincs 52 C5
North Tidworth Wilts 19 G9
North Togston Northum 79 G7
North Tuddenham Norfolk 44 D4
North Walbottle Tyne/Wear 71 D6
North Walsham Norfolk 45 B6
North Waltham Hants 20 G3
North Warnborough Hants 20 F5
North Water Bridge Angus 91 E7
North Watten H'land 107 D7
North Weald Bassett Essex 22 A4
North Wheatley Notts 51 D9
North Whilborough Devon 5 D9
North Wick Bath/NE Som'set 18 E2
North Willingham Lincs 52 D4
North Wingfield Derby 51 F6
North Witham Lincs 42 C2
North Woolwich London 22 D4
North Wootton Dorset 9 C8
North Wootton Norfolk 43 C9
North Wootton Som'set 18 G2
North Wraxall Wilts 18 D5
North Wroughton Swindon 19 C8
North Yorkshire Moors Railway, Pickering N Yorks 65 F6
Northacre Norfolk 44 F3
Northallerton N Yorks 63 E8
Northam Devon 6 D5
Northam S'thampton 11 C7
Northampton Northants 31 B9
Northaw Herts 22 A2
Northbeck Lincs 42 A3
Northborough Peterbro 42 E4
Northbourne Kent 15 C8
Northbridge Street E Sussex 14 F2
Northchapel W Sussex 12 C3
Northchurch Herts 32 H2
Northcott Devon 6 G4
Northdown Kent 15 A8
Northdyke Orkney 110 F3
Northend Bath/NE Som'set 18 E4
Northend Bucks 20 B5
Northend Warwick 30 C5
Northenden Gtr Man 49 C9
Northfield Aberd C 99 H9
Northfield Scot Borders 85 H11
Northfield ER Yorks 59 F6
Northfield W Midlands 40 H2
Northfields Lincs 42 E3
Northfleet Kent 23 D6
Northgate Lincs 42 C4
Northhouse Scot Borders 77 G7
Northiam E Sussex 14 F3
Northill Beds 32 D4
Northington Hants 20 H3
Northlands Lincs 53 G6
Northlea Durham 71 E9
Northleach Glos 30 G3
Northleigh Devon 8 E3
Northlew Devon 7 G6
Northmoor Oxon 20 A2
Northmoor Green or Moorland Som'set 8 A5
Northmuir Angus 90 F4
Northney Hants 11 D10
Northolt London 21 C9
Northop Flints 48 F3
Northop Hall Flints 48 F3
Northorpe Lincs 42 D3
Northorpe Lincs 42 B5
Northorpe Lincs 52 C1
Northover Som'set 17 H9
Northover Som'set 9 B7
Northowram W Yorks 57 F6
Northport Dorset 10 F2
Northpunds Shetl'd 111 L7
Northrepps Norfolk 45 B6
Northtown Orkney 110 J5
Northumbria Craft Centre, Morpeth Northum 71 B6
Northway Glos 29 E10
Northwich Ches 49 E7
Northwick S Gloucs 18 C2
Northwold Norfolk 44 F1
Northwood Derby 50 F4
Northwood London 21 B8
Northwood I/Wight 11 E7
Northwood Kent 15 B8
Northwood Shrops 38 B5
Northwood Green Glos 29 G8
Norton E Sussex 13 E8
Norton Glos 29 F9
Norton Halton 49 D6
Norton Herts 32 E5
Norton I/Wight 11 F6
Norton Monmouths 28 G5
Norton Notts 51 E7
Norton Northants 31 B8
Norton N Yorks 64 G5
Norton Powys 28 B4
Norton Shrops 38 G5
Norton Shrops 39 E6
Norton Shrops 39 E8
Norton Stockton 63 B9
Norton Suffolk 34 B3
Norton S Yorks 57 G10
Norton Wilts 18 C5
Norton Worcs 29 C9
Norton Worcs 30 D2
Norton W Sussex 12 F2
Norton W Sussex 12 E3
Norton Bavant Wilts 19 G6
Norton Bridge Staffs 39 B9
Norton Canes Staffs 40 E2
Norton Canon Heref'd 28 D4
Norton Corner Norfolk 44 C4
Norton Disney Lincs 52 G1
Norton East Staffs 40 E2
Norton Ferris Wilts 18 H4
Norton Fitzwarren Som'set 8 B3
Norton Green I/Wight 11 F6
Norton Hawkfield Bath/NE Som'set 18 E2
Norton Heath Essex 23 A6
Norton in Hales Shrops 39 B8
Norton in the Moors Stoke 49 G9
Norton Juxta Twycross Leics 40 E5
Norton le Clay N Yorks 63 G9
Norton Lindsey Warwick 30 B4
Norton Malreward Bath/NE Som'set 18 E3
Norton Mandeville Essex 22 A5
Norton St. Philip Som'set 18 F4
Norton sub Hamdon Som'set 9 C6
Norton Woodseats S Yorks 50 D5
Norwell Notts 51 F9
Norwell Woodhouse Notts 51 F9
Norwich Norfolk 45 E6
Norwich Castle Museum Norfolk 45 E6
Norwich Cathedral Norfolk 45 E6
Norwick Shetl'd 111 B9
Norwood Derby 51 D6
Norwood Hill Surrey 22 G2
Norwoodside Cambs 43 F7
Noseley Leics 41 F9
Noss Shetl'd 111 M6
Noss Mayo Devon 5 F6
Nosterfield N Yorks 63 F7
Nostie H'land 94 D5
Notgrove Glos 30 F3
Nothe Fort, Weymouth Dorset 9 G8
Nottage Bridg 16 D3
Nottingham Nott'ham 41 B7
Nottingham Castle Museum Nott'ham 41 A7
Nottingham Racecourse Nott'ham 41 B7
Nottington Dorset 9 F8
Notton Wilts 19 E6
Notton W Yorks 57 G8
Nounsbrough Shetl'd 111 H5
Nounsley Essex 34 G1
Noutard's Green Worcs 29 B8
Novar House H'land 102 F5
Nox Shrops 38 D5
Nuffield Oxon 20 C4
Nun Hills Lancs 56 F3
Nun Monkton N Yorks 57 C10
Nunburnholme ER Yorks 58 D4
Nuncargate Notts 51 G7
Nuneaton Warwick 40 F5
Nuneham Courtenay Oxon 20 B3
Nunney Som'set 18 G4
Nunnington N Yorks 64 G4
Nunnykirk Northum 70 A5
Nunsthorpe NE Lincs 52 B5
Nunthorpe Middlesbro' 64 C3
Nunthorpe C/York 58 C2
Nunton Wilts 10 B4
Nunwick N Yorks 63 G8
Nupend Glos 29 H8
Nursling Hants 11 C6
Nursted Hants 12 C1
Nutbourne W Sussex 12 D4
Nutbourne W Sussex 12 E1
Nutfield Surrey 22 F3
Nuthall Notts 41 A7
Nuthampstead Herts 33 E7
Nuthurst W Sussex 12 C5
Nutley E Sussex 13 C8
Nutley Hants 20 G4
Nutwell S Yorks 51 B8
Nybster H'land 107 C8
Nyetimber W Sussex 12 F2
Nyewood W Sussex 12 C2
Nymans Garden, Crawley W Sussex 13 C6
Nymet Rowland Devon 7 F8
Nymet Tracey Devon 7 F8
Nympsfield Glos 18 A5
Nynehead Som'set 8 B3
Nyton W Sussex 12 E3

O

Oad Street Kent 14 B3
Oadby Leics 41 E8
Oak Cross Devon 7 G6
Oakamoor Staffs 40 A2
Oakbank W Loth 84 H2
Oakdale Caerph 17 B6
Oake Som'set 8 B3
Oaken Staffs 39 E9
Oakenclough Lancs 55 D5
Oakengates Telford 39 D8
Oakenholt Flints 48 E3
Oakenshaw Durham 71 G7
Oakenshaw W Yorks 57 F6
Oakerthorpe Derby 50 G5
Oakes W Yorks 57 G6
Oakfield Torf 17 B8
Oakford Ceredig'n 26 C4
Oakford Devon 7 D10
Oakfordbridge Devon 7 D10
Oakgrove Ches 49 F10
Oakham Rutl'd 42 E1
Oakhanger Hants 12 B1
Oakhill Som'set 18 G3
Oakhurst Kent 22 F5
Oakington Cambs 33 B7
Oaklands Herts 32 G5
Oaklands Powys 27 C10
Oakle Street Glos 29 G8
Oakley Beds 32 C3
Oakley Bucks 31 G8
Oakley Fife 84 F2
Oakley Hants 20 F3
Oakley Oxon 20 A5
Oakley Poole 10 E3
Oakley Suffolk 44 H5
Oakley Green Windsor 21 D7
Oakley Park Powys 37 G9
Oakmere Ches 49 F6
Oakridge Glos 19 A6
Oakridge Hants 20 F4
Oaks Shrops 38 E5
Oaks Green Derby 40 B3
Oaksey Wilts 19 B6
Oakthorpe Leics 40 D5
Oakwood Adventure Park, Narberth Pembs 24 E5
Oakwoodhill Surrey 12 B5
Oakworth W Yorks 56 E5
Oape H'land 102 B3
Oare Kent 14 B5
Oare Som'set 7 B9
Oare W Berks 20 D3
Oare Wilts 19 E8
Oasby Lincs 42 B3
Oathlaw Angus 90 F5
Oatlands N Yorks 57 C8
Oban Arg/Bute 81 B8
Oban H'land 87 C8
Oborne Dorset 9 C8
Obthorpe Lincs 42 D3
Occlestone Green Ches 49 F7
Occold Suffolk 34 A5
Ocean Beach Amusement Park, Rhyl Denbs 47 D9
Ochil Hills Hospital Perth/Kinr 84 D2
Ochiltree E Ayrs 75 E7
Ochtermuthill Perth/Kinr 83 C9
Ochtertyre Perth/Kinr 83 B9
Ockbrook Derby 41 B6
Ockham Surrey 21 F8
Ockle H'land 86 D5
Ockley Surrey 12 B5
Ocle Pychard Heref'd 29 D6
Octon ER Yorks 59 B6
Octon Cross Roads ER Yorks 59 B6
Odcombe Som'set 9 C7
Odd Down Bath/NE Som'set 18 E4
Oddendale Cumb 61 C8
Odder Lincs 52 E2
Oddingley Worcs 29 C10
Oddington Glos 30 F4
Oddington Oxon 31 G7
Odell Beds 32 C2
Odie Orkney 110 F7
Odiham Hants 20 F5
Odstock Wilts 10 B4
Odstone Leics 40 E5
Offchurch Warwick 30 B5
Offenham Worcs 30 D2
Offham E Sussex 13 D7
Offham Kent 14 C1
Offham W Sussex 12 E4
Offord Cluny Cambs 32 B5
Offord Darcy Cambs 32 B5
Offton Suffolk 34 D4
Offwell Devon 8 E3
Ogbourne Maizey Wilts 19 D8
Ogbourne St. Andrew Wilts 19 D8
Ogbourne St. George Wilts 19 D9
Ogil Angus 90 E5
Ogle Northum 71 C6
Ogmore V/Glam 16 D3
Ogmore by Sea V/Glam 16 D3
Ogmore Vale Bridg 16 B4
Okeford Fitzpaine Dorset 9 C10
Okehampton Devon 7 G6
Okehampton Camp Devon 7 G6
Okraquoy Shetl'd 111 K7
Old Northants 31 A9
Old Aberdeen Aberd C 99 H9
Old Alresford Hants 11 A8
Old Arley Warwick 40 F4
Old Basford Nott'ham 41 A7
Old Basing Hants 20 F4
Old Bewick Northum 78 E5
Old Blacksmith's Shop Centre, Gretna Green Dumf/Gal 69 D6
Old Bolingbroke Lincs 53 F6
Old Bramhope W Yorks 57 D7
Old Brampton Derby 50 E5
Old Bridge of Urr Dumf/Gal 67 D9
Old Buckenham Norfolk 44 F4
Old Burghclere Hants 20 F2
Old Byland N Yorks 64 F3
Old Cassop Durham 71 G8
Old Castleton Scot Borders 69 A8
Old Catton Norfolk 45 D6
Old Clee NE Lincs 52 B5
Old Cleeve Som'set 16 G5
Old Clipstone Notts 51 F8
Old Colwyn Conwy 47 E8
Old Coulsdon London 22 F3
Old Crombie Aberds 98 C5
Old Dailly S Ayrs 74 H4
Old Dalby Leics 41 C8
Old Deer Aberds 99 D9
Old Denaby S Yorks 51 C6
Old Edlington S Yorks 51 C7
Old Eldon Durham 63 B7
Old Ellerby ER Yorks 59 E7
Old Felixstowe Suffolk 35 E7
Old Fletton Peterbro 42 F4
Old Glossop Derby 50 C2
Old Goole ER Yorks 58 F3
Old Hall Powys 37 G9
Old Heath Essex 34 F4
Old Heathfield E Sussex 13 C9
Old Hill W Midlands 40 G1
Old House, Rochford Essex 23 B8
Old Hunstanton Norfolk 43 A9
Old Hutton Cumb 61 F8
Old Kea Cornw'l 3 E7
Old Kilpatrick W Dunb 82 G5
Old Kinnernie Aberds 99 H7
Old Knebworth Herts 32 F5
Old Langho Lancs 56 E2
Old Laxey I/Man 54 D4
Old Leake Lincs 53 G7
Old Malton N Yorks 64 G5
Old Micklefield W Yorks 57 E9
Old Milton Hants 10 E5
Old Milverton Warwick 30 B4
Old Monkland N Lanarks 75 A9
Old Netley Hants 11 D7
Old Philpstoun W Loth 84 G2
Old Quarrington Durham 71 G8
Old Radnor Powys 28 C3
Old Rattray Aberds 99 C10
Old Rayne Aberds 99 F6
Old Romney Kent 14 F5
Old Sarum, Salisbury Wilts 10 A4
Old Scone Perth/Kinr 84 B3
Old Sodbury S Gloucs 18 C4
Old Somerby Lincs 42 B2
Old Stratford Northants 31 D9
Old Thirsk N Yorks 63 F9
Old Town Cumb 69 F7
Old Town Cumb 61 F8
Old Town Northum 70 A3
Old Town I/Scilly 2 C3
Old Trafford Gtr Man 49 C9
Old Tupton Derby 50 F5
Old Warden Beds 32 D4
Old Weston Cambs 42 H3
Old Whittington Derby 50 E5
Old Wick H'land 107 D8
Old Windsor Windsor 21 D7
Old Wives Lees Kent 14 C5
Old Woking Surrey 21 F8
Old Woodhall Lincs 52 F5
Oldany H'land 104 F4
Oldberrow Warwick 30 B3
Oldborough Devon 7 F8
Oldbury Shrops 39 F8
Oldbury Warwick 40 F5
Oldbury W Midlands 40 G1
Oldbury on Severn S Gloucs 18 B3
Oldbury on the Hill Glos 18 C5
Oldcastle Bridg 16 D4
Oldcastle Monmouths 28 F4
Oldcotes Notts 51 D7
Oldfallow Staffs 40 D1
Oldfield Worcs 29 B9
Oldford Som'set 18 F4
Oldham Gtr Man 49 B10
Oldhamstocks E Loth 85 G9
Oldhurst Cambs 42 H5
Oldland S Gloucs 18 D3
Oldmeldrum Aberds 99 F8
Oldshore Beg H'land 104 D4
Oldshoremore H'land 104 D5
Oldstead N Yorks 64 F3
Oldtown Aberds 98 F5
Oldtown of Ord Aberds 98 C6
Oldway Swan 25 H10
Oldways End Devon 7 D9
Oldwhat Aberds 99 C8
Olgrinmore H'land 106 D5
Oliver's Battery Hants 11 B7
Ollaberry Shetl'd 111 E6
Ollerton Ches 49 E8
Ollerton Notts 51 F8
Ollerton Shrops 39 C7
Olmarch Ceredig'n 27 C6
Olney M/Keynes 32 C1
Olrig Ho. H'land 107 C6
Olton W Midlands 40 G3
Olveston S Gloucs 18 C3
Olwen Ceredig'n 26 D5
Ombersley Worcs 29 B9
Ompton Notts 51 F8
Onchan I/Man 54 E3
Onecote Staffs 50 G2
Onen Monmouths 28 G5
Ongar Hill Norfolk 43 C8
Ongar Street Heref'd 28 B4
Onibury Shrops 38 H5
Onich H'land 87 E10
Onllwyn Neath P Talb 27 G8
Onneley Staffs 39 A8
Onslow Village Surrey 21 G7
Onthank E Ayrs 75 C6
Openwoodgate Derby 50 H5
Opinan H'land 101 C6
Opinan H'land 100 E5
Orange Lane Scot Borders 78 C2
Orange Row Norfolk 43 C8
Orasaigh W Isles 108 F8
Orbliston Moray 98 C3
Orbost H'land 93 A8
Orby Lincs 53 F7
Orchard Hill Devon 6 D5
Orchard Portman Som'set 8 B4
Orcheston Wilts 19 G7
Orcop Heref'd 28 F5
Orcop Hill Heref'd 28 F5
Ord H'land 94 E3
Ordhead Aberds 99 G6
Ordie Aberds 90 A5
Ordiequish Moray 98 C3
Ordsall Notts 51 D8
Ore E Sussex 14 G3
Oreton Shrops 39 G7
Orford Suffolk 35 D8
Orford Warrington 49 C7
Orgreave Staffs 40 D3
Orlestone Kent 14 E4
Orleton Heref'd 28 B5
Orleton Worcs 29 B7
Orlingbury Northants 32 A1
Ormesby Redcar/Clevel'd 64 C3
Ormesby St. Margaret Norfolk 45 D8
Ormesby St. Michael Norfolk 45 D8
Ormiclate Castle W Isles 92 B3
Ormiscaig H'land 101 C6
Ormiston E Loth 84 H6
Ormsaigbeg H'land 86 E4
Ormsaigmore H'land 86 E4
Ormsary Arg/Bute 81 G7
Ormsgill Cumb 60 G4
Ormskirk Lancs 48 B5
Orphir Orkney 110 H4
Orpington London 22 E4
Orrell Gtr Man 49 B6
Orrell Mersey 48 C4
Orrisdale I/Man 54 C3
Orroland Dumf/Gal 67 F9
Orsett Thurr'k 23 C6
Orslow Staffs 39 D9
Orston Notts 41 A9
Orthwaite Cumb 68 G5
Ortner Lancs 55 C5
Orton Cumb 61 D9
Orton Northants 41 H10
Orton Longueville Peterbro 42 F4
Orton on the Hill Leics 40 E5
Orton Waterville Peterbro 42 F4
Orwell Cambs 33 C6
Osbaldeston Lancs 56 E1
Osbaldwick C/York 58 C2
Osbaston Shrops 38 C4
Osborne House I/Wight 11 E8
Osbournby Lincs 42 B3
Oscroft Ches 49 F6
Ose H'land 93 A9
Osgathorpe Leics 41 D6
Osgodby Lincs 52 C3
Osgodby N Yorks 58 E2
Osgodby N Yorks 65 F8
Oskaig H'land 94 C2
Oskamull Arg/Bute 86 G4
Osmaston Derby 40 A4
Osmaston Derby C 40 B5
Osmington Dorset 9 F9
Osmington Mills Dorset 9 F9
Osmotherley N Yorks 63 E9
Ospisdale H'land 102 D6
Ospringe Kent 14 B5
Ossett W Yorks 57 F7
Ossington Notts 51 F9
Ostend Essex 23 B9
Oswaldkirk N Yorks 64 G4
Oswaldtwistle Lancs 56 F2
Oswestry Shrops 38 C3
Otford Kent 22 F5
Otham Kent 14 C2
Othery Som'set 8 A5
Otley Suffolk 35 C6
Otley W Yorks 57 D7
Otter Ferry Arg/Bute 81 F9
Otterbourne Hants 11 B7
Otterburn Northum 70 A3
Otterburn N Yorks 56 C3
Otterburn Camp Northum 78 H3
Otterham Cornw'l 6 G2
Otterhampton Som'set 17 G7
Ottershaw Surrey 21 E8
Otterswick Shetl'd 111 E8
Otterton Devon 8 F2
Ottery St. Mary Devon 8 E3
Ottinge Kent 15 D6
Ottringham ER Yorks 59 F8
Oughterby Cumb 68 E5
Oughtershaw N Yorks 62 F3
Oughterside Cumb 68 F4
Oughtibridge S Yorks 50 C5
Oughtrington Warrington 49 D7
Oulston N Yorks 64 G3
Oulton Cumb 68 E5
Oulton Norfolk 44 C5
Oulton Staffs 39 B10
Oulton Suffolk 45 F9
Oulton W Yorks 57 F8
Oulton Broad Suffolk 45 F9
Oulton Street Norfolk 44 C5
Oundle Northants 42 G3
Ousby Cumb 69 G9
Ousdale H'land 106 G5
Ousden Suffolk 33 C10
Ousefleet ER Yorks 58 F4
Ouston Durham 71 E7
Ouston Northum 70 C5
Out Newton ER Yorks 59 F9
Out Rawcliffe Lancs 55 D4
Outertown Orkney 110 G3
Outgate Cumb 61 E6
Outhgill Cumb 62 D2
Outlane W Yorks 56 G5
Outwell Norfolk 43 E8
Outwick Hants 10 C4
Outwood Surrey 22 G3
Outwood W Yorks 57 F8
Outwoods Staffs 39 D8
Ovenden W Yorks 56 F5
Ovenscloss Scot Borders 77 D7
Over Cambs 33 A6
Over Ches 49 F7
Over S Gloucs 18 C2
Over Compton Dorset 9 C7
Over Green W Midlands 40 F3
Over Haddon Derby 50 F4
Over Hulton Gtr Man 49 B7
Over Kellet Lancs 61 G8
Over Kiddington Oxon 31 F6
Over Knutsford Ches 49 E8
Over Monnow Monmouths 29 G6
Over Norton Oxon 30 F5
Over Peover Ches 49 E8
Over Silton N Yorks 63 E9
Over Stowey Som'set 17 H6
Over Stratton Som'set 9 C6
Over Tabley Ches 49 D8
Over Wallop Hants 19 H9
Over Whitacre Warwick 40 F4
Over Worton Oxon 31 F6
Overbister Orkney 110 D7
Overbury Worcs 30 E1
Overcombe Dorset 9 F8
Overgreen Derby 50 E5
Overleigh Som'set 17 H9
Overley Green Warwick 30 C2
Overpool Ches 48 E4
Overscaig Hotel H'land 105 G7
Overseal Derby 40 D4
Oversland Kent 14 C5
Overstone Northants 31 B10
Overstrand Norfolk 45 A6
Overthorpe Northants 31 D6
Overton Aberd C 99 G8
Overton Ches 49 E6
Overton Dumf/Gal 68 D2
Overton Hants 20 G3
Overton Lancs 55 C4
Overton N Yorks 58 C1
Overton Shrops 29 A6
Overton Swan 25 H9
Overton Wrex 38 A4
Overton W Yorks 57 G7
Overton Bridge Wrex 38 A4
Overtown N Lanarks 75 B10
Oving Bucks 31 F9
Oving W Sussex 12 E3
Ovingdean Brighton/Hove 13 E7
Ovingham Northum 70 D5
Ovington Durham 63 C6
Ovington Essex 34 D1
Ovington Hants 11 A8
Ovington Norfolk 44 E3
Ovington Northum 70 D5
Ower Hants 11 C6
Owermoigne Dorset 9 F9
Owlbury Shrops 38 F4
Owler Bar Derby 50 E4
Owlerton S Yorks 50 D5
Owl's Green Suffolk 35 B6
Owlswick Bucks 31 H9
Owmby Lincs 52 B3
Owmby by Spital Lincs 52 D3
Owslebury Hants 11 B8
Owston Leics 41 E9
Owston S Yorks 58 G1
Owston Ferry N Lincs 51 B10
Owstwick ER Yorks 59 E8
Owthorne ER Yorks 59 F9
Owthorpe Notts 41 B8
Oxborough Norfolk 43 E10
Oxburgh Hall Norfolk 43 E10
Oxcombe Lincs 53 E6
Oxen Park Cumb 61 F6
Oxenholme Cumb 61 F8
Oxenhope W Yorks 56 E5
Oxenton Glos 30 E1
Oxenwood Wilts 19 F10
Oxford Oxon 31 H7
Oxford University Botanic Garden Oxon 31 H7
Oxhey Herts 21 B9
Oxhill Warwick 30 D5
Oxley W Midlands 39 E10
Oxley Green Essex 34 G3
Oxley's Green E Sussex 14 F1
Oxnam Scot Borders 78 F2
Oxshott Surrey 21 E9
Oxspring S Yorks 50 B4
Oxted Surrey 22 F3
Oxton Scot Borders 77 B7
Oxton Notts 51 G8
Oxwich Swan 25 H9
Oxwick Norfolk 44 C3
Oykel Bridge H'land 102 B2
Oyne Aberds 99 F6

P

Pabail Iarach W Isles 108 D10
Pabail Uarach W Isles 108 D10
Pace Gate N Yorks 57 C6
Packington Leics 40 D5
Padanaram Angus 90 F5
Padbury Bucks 31 E9
Paddington London 22 C2
Paddlesworth Kent 15 E6
Paddock Wood Kent 14 D1
Paddockhaugh Moray 98 C2
Paddockhole Dumf/Gal 68 B5
Padfield Derby 50 C2
Padiham Lancs 56 E2
Padog Conwy 47 G8
Padside N Yorks 57 C6
Padstow Cornw'l 3 B8
Padworth W Berks 20 E4
Page Bank Durham 71 G7
Pagelsham Eastend Essex 23 B9
Pagham W Sussex 12 F2
Paglesham Churchend Essex 23 B9
Paibeil W Isles 109 L2
Paible W Isles 109 H5
Paignton Torbay 5 D9
Paignton & Dartmouth Steam Railway Devon 5 D9
Paignton Zoo Devon 5 E9
Pailton Warwick 41 G6
Painscastle Powys 28 D2
Painshawfield Northum 70 D5
Painsthorpe ER Yorks 58 C4
Painswick Glos 29 H9
Pairc Shiaboist W Isles 108 C7
Paisley Renf 75 A6
Pakefield Suffolk 45 F9
Pakenham Suffolk 34 B3
Palace House, Beaulieu Hants 11 D6
Palace of Holyroodhouse C/Edinb 84 G4
Pale Gwyn 37 B9
Palestine Hants 19 G9
Paley Street Windsor 21 D6
Palfrey W Midlands 40 F2
Palgowan Dumf/Gal 66 B5
Palgrave Suffolk 44 H5
Pallion Tyne/Wear 71 E8
Palmarsh Kent 15 E6
Palnackie Dumf/Gal 67 E10
Palnure Dumf/Gal 67 D6
Palterton Derby 51 F6
Pamber End Hants 20 F4
Pamber Green Hants 20 F4
Pamber Heath Hants 20 E4
Pamphill Dorset 10 D2
Pampisford Cambs 33 D7
Pan Orkney 110 J4
Panbride Angus 91 H6
Pancrasweek Devon 6 F3
Pandy Gwyn 37 E6
Pandy Monmouths 28 F4
Pandy Powys 37 E9
Pandy Wrex 38 B2
Pandy Tudur Conwy 47 F8
Panfield Essex 33 F10
Pangbourne W Berks 20 D4
Pannal N Yorks 57 C8
Panshanger Herts 32 G5
Pant Shrops 38 C3
Pant glas Carms 26 F5
Pant glas Gwyn 46 H4
Pant glâs Powys 37 F7
Pant glas Shrops 38 B3
Pant gwyn Carms 26 F5
Pant Mawr Powys 37 G8
Pant teg Carms 25 D9
Pant y Caws Carms 25 D6
Pant y dwr Powys 37 H9
Pant y ffridd Powys 38 E2
Pant y Wacco Flints 48 E2
Pant yr awel Bridg 16 C4
Pantgwyn Ceredig'n 25 B7
Pantlasau Swan 16 B1
Panton Lincs 52 E4
Pantperthog Gwyn 37 E7
Pantyffynnon Carms 27 G6
Pantymwyn Flints 48 F2
Panxworth Norfolk 45 D7
Papcastle Cumb 68 G4
Papigoe H'land 107 D8
Papil Shetl'd 111 K6
Papley Orkney 110 J5
Papple E Loth 85 G7
Papplewick Notts 51 G7
Papworth Everard Cambs 32 B5
Papworth St. Agnes Cambs 32 B5
Par Cornw'l 3 D9
Paradise Wildlife Park, Broxbourne Herts 33 H6
Parbold Lancs 55 G4
Parbrook Som'set 18 H2
Parbrook W Sussex 12 C4
Parc Gwyn 37 B8
Parc y rhôs Carms 26 D5
Parcllyn Ceredig'n 26 C2
Pardshaw Cumb 60 B3
Parham Suffolk 35 B7
Park Dumf/Gal 68 A2
Park Corner Oxon 20 C4
Park Corner Windsor 21 C6
Park End Middlesbro' 64 C3
Park End Northum 70 C3
Park Gate Hants 11 D8
Park Hill Notts 51 G8
Park Hill N Yorks 57 B8
Park Rose Pottery and Leisure Park, Bridlington ER Yorks 59 B7
Park Street W Sussex 12 B5
Parkdargue Aberds 98 D6
Parkend Glos 29 H7
Parkeston Essex 35 E6
Parkgate Ches 48 E3
Parkgate Dumf/Gal 68 B3
Parkgate Kent 14 E3
Parkgate Surrey 22 G2
Parkham Devon 6 D4
Parkham Ash Devon 6 D4
Parkhill Ho. Aberds 99 G8
Parkhouse Monmouths 17 A9
Parkhouse Green Derby 51 F6
Parkhurst I/Wight 11 E7
Parkmill Swan 25 H10
Parkneuk Aberds 91 D8
Parkstone Poole 10 E3
Parley Cross Dorset 10 E3
Parracombe Devon 7 B7
Parrog Pembs 24 C5
Parsley Hay Derby 50 F3
Parson Cross S Yorks 50 C5
Parson Drove Cambs 43 E6
Parsonage Green Essex 33 H10
Parsonby Cumb 68 G4
Parson's Heath Essex 34 F4
Partick Glasg C 83 H6
Partington Gtr Man 49 C8
Partney Lincs 53 F7
Parton Cumb 60 B2
Parton Dumf/Gal 67 C8
Parton Glos 29 F9
Partridge Green W Sussex 12 D5
Parwich Derby 50 G3
Passenham Northants 31 E9
Paston Norfolk 45 B7
Patchacott Devon 6 G5
Patcham Brighton/Hove 13 E7
Patching W Sussex 12 E4
Patchole Devon 7 B7
Patchway S Gloucs 18 C3
Pateley Bridge N Yorks 57 B6
Paternoster Heath Essex 34 G3
Path of Condie Perth/Kinr 84 C2
Pathe Som'set 8 A5
Pathhead Aberds 91 E8
Pathhead E Ayrs 75 F8
Pathhead Fife 84 E4
Pathhead Midloth 77 A6
Pathstruie Perth/Kinr 84 C2
Patmore Heath Herts 33 F7
Patna E Ayrs 75 F6
Patney Wilts 19 F7
Patrick I/Man 54 D2
Patrick Brompton N Yorks 63 E7
Patrington ER Yorks 59 F9
Patrixbourne Kent 15 C6
Patterdale Cumb 61 C6
Pattingham Staffs 39 F9
Pattishall Northants 31 C8
Pattiswick Green Essex 34 F2
Patton Bridge Cumb 61 E8
Paul Cornw'l 2 G3
Paulerspury Northants 31 D9
Paull ER Yorks 59 F7
Paulton Bath/NE Som'set 18 F3
Paultons Park, Totton Hants 11 C6
Pavenham Beds 32 C2
Pawlett Som'set 17 G8
Pawston Northum 78 D3
Paxford Glos 30 E3
Paxton Scot Borders 78 B4
Payhembury Devon 8 D2
Paythorne Lancs 56 C3
Peacehaven E Sussex 13 E8
Peak Dale Derby 50 E2
Peak Forest Derby 50 E3
Peakirk Peterbro 42 E4
Pearsie Angus 90 F4
Pease Pottage W Sussex 13 B6
Peasedown St. John Bath/NE Som'set 18 F4
Peasemore W Berks 20 D2
Peasenhall Suffolk 35 B7
Peaslake Surrey 21 G8
Peasley Cross Mersey 49 C6
Peasmarsh E Sussex 14 F3
Peaston E Loth 84 H6
Peaston Bank E Loth 84 H6
Peat Inn Fife 85 D6
Peathill Aberds 99 B9
Peatling Magna Leics 41 F7
Peatling Parva Leics 41 G7
Peaton Shrops 39 G6
Peats Corner Suffolk 34 B5
Pebmarsh Essex 34 E2
Pebworth Worcs 30 D3
Pecket Well W Yorks 56 F4
Peckforton Ches 49 G6
Peckham London 22 D3
Peckleton Leics 41 E6
Pedlinge Kent 15 E6
Pedmore W Midlands 39 G10
Pedwell Som'set 17 H9
Peebles Scot Borders 76 C5
Peel I/Man 54 D2
Peel Common Hants 11 D8
Peel Park S Lanarks 75 B8
Peening Quarter Kent 14 F3
Pegsdon Beds 32 E4
Pegswood Northum 71 B7
Pegwell Kent 15 B8
Peinchorran H'land 94 C2
Peinlich H'land 109 M9
Pelaw Tyne/Wear 71 D7
Pelcomb Bridge Pembs 24 E4
Pelcomb Cross Pembs 24 E4
Peldon Essex 34 G3
Pellon W Yorks 56 F5
Pelsall W Midlands 40 E2
Pelton Durham 71 E7
Pelutho Cumb 68 F4
Pelynt Cornw'l 4 E3
Pemberton Gtr Man 49 B6
Pembrey Carms 25 F9
Pembridge Heref'd 28 C4
Pembroke Pembs 24 F4
Pembroke Castle Pembs 24 F4
Pembroke Dock Pembs 24 F4
Pembury Kent 23 G6
Pen bont Rhydybeddau Ceredig'n 37 G6
Pen clawdd Swan 25 G10
Pen ffordd Pembs 24 D5
Pen groes oped Monmouths 28 H4
Pen llyn Angl 46 D3
Pen lon Angl 46 F4
Pen sarn Gwyn 36 A4
Pen sarn Gwyn 36 C5
Pen twyn Monmouths 29 H6
Pen y banc Carms 27 F6
Pen y bont Carms 25 D8
Pen y bont Gwyn 37 E7
Pen y bont Gwyn 37 C6
Pen y bont Powys 38 C3
Pen y bryn Gwyn 37 D6
Pen y bryn Pembs 25 B6
Pen y cae Powys 27 G8
Pen y cae mawr Monmouths 17 B9
Pen y cefn Flints 48 E2
Pen y clawdd Monmouths 28 H5
Pen y coedcae Rh Cyn Taff 16 C5
Pen y fai Bridg 16 C3
Pen y garn Ceredig'n 37 G6
Pen y garn Carms 26 E5
Pen y garnedd Angl 46 E5
Pen y gop Conwy 37 A9
Pen y graig Gwyn 36 B1
Pen y groes Carms 26 G5
Pen y groeslon Gwyn 36 B2
Pen y Gwryd Hotel Gwyn 47 G6
Pen y stryt Denbs 48 G2
Pen yr heol Monmouths 28 G5
Pen yr Heolgerrig Merth Tyd 27 H10
Penallt Monmouths 29 G6
Penally Pembs 24 G6
Penalt Heref'd 29 F6
Penare Cornw'l 3 E8
Penarth V/Glam 17 D6
Penbryn Ceredig'n 26 C2
Pencader Carms 25 C9
Pencaenewydd Gwyn 36 A4
Pencaitland E Loth 84 H6
Pencarnisiog Angl 46 E3
Pencarreg Carms 26 D5
Pencelli Powys 28 F1
Pencoed Bridg 16 C4
Pencombe Heref'd 29 C6
Pencoyd Heref'd 29 F6
Pencraig Heref'd 29 F6
Pencraig Powys 37 C10
Pendeen Cornw'l 2 F2
Pendennis Castle Cornw'l 3 F7
Penderyn Rh Cyn Taff 27 H9
Pendine Carms 25 F7
Pendlebury Gtr Man 49 B8
Pendleton Lancs 56 E2
Pendock Worcs 29 E8
Pendoggett Cornw'l 3 B9
Pendomer Som'set 9 C7
Pendoylan V/Glam 16 D5
Pendre Bridg 16 C4
Penegoes Powys 37 E7
Pengam Caerph 17 B6
Penge London 22 D3
Pengenffordd Powys 28 E2
Pengorffwysfa Angl 46 C4
Pengover Green Cornw'l 4 D3
Penhale Cornw'l 2 H5
Penhale Cornw'l 3 D8
Penhalvaen Cornw'l 3 F6
Penhill Swindon 19 C8
Penhow Newp 17 B9
Penhurst E Sussex 14 G1
Peniarth Gwyn 37 E6
Penicuik Midloth 76 A5
Peniel Carms 25 D9
Peniel Denbs 47 F10
Penifiler H'land 94 B1
Peninver Arg/Bute 73 E7
Penisarwaun Gwyn 46 F5
Penistone S Yorks 50 B4
Penjerrick Cornw'l 3 F6
Penketh Warrington 49 D6
Penkill S Ayrs 74 H4
Penkridge Staffs 39 D10
Penley Wrex 38 B5
Penllergaer Swan 25 G11
Penllyn V/Glam 16 D4
Penmachno Conwy 47 G7
Penmaen Swan 25 H10
Penmaenan Conwy 47 E7
Penmaenmawr Conwy 47 E7
Penmaenpool Gwyn 37 D6
Penmark V/Glam 16 E5
Penmarth Cornw'l 3 F6
Penmon Angl 47 D6
Penmore Mill Arg/Bute 86 F4
Penmorfa Ceredig'n 26 C3
Penmorfa Gwyn 36 A5
Penmynydd Angl 46 E5
Penn Bucks 21 B7
Penn Street Bucks 21 B7
Pennal Gwyn 37 E7
Pennan Aberds 99 B8
Pennant Ceredig'n 26 B5
Pennant Denbs 37 B10
Pennant Denbs 47 G10
Pennant Powys 37 F8
Pennant Melangell Powys 37 C10
Pennar Pembs 24 F4
Pennard Swan 25 H10
Pennerley Shrops 38 F4
Pennington Cumb 60 G5
Pennington Gtr Man 49 C7
Pennington Hants 11 E6
Penny Bridge Cumb 61 F6
Pennycross Arg/Bute 80 B5
Pennygate Norfolk 45 C7
Pennygown Arg/Bute 86 G5
Pennymoor Devon 7 E9
Pennywell Tyne/Wear 71 E8
Penparc Ceredig'n 25 B7
Penparc Pembs 24 C3
Penparcau Ceredig'n 36 G5
Penperlleni Monmouths 17 A8
Penpillick Cornw'l 3 D9
Penpol Cornw'l 3 F7
Penpoll Cornw'l 4 E2
Penpont Dumf/Gal 67 A10
Penpont Powys 27 F9
Penrherber Carms 25 C7
Penrhiw goch Carms 26 G5
Penrhiw llan Ceredig'n 25 B8
Penrhiw pâl Ceredig'n 25 B8
Penrhiwceiber Rh Cyn Taff 16 B5
Penrhos Gwyn 36 B3
Penrhôs Monmouths 28 G5
Penrhos Powys 27 G7
Penrhosfeilwo Angl 46 D2
Penrhyn Bay Conwy 47 D8
Penrhyn Castle Gwyn 47 E6
Penrhyn coch Ceredig'n 37 G6
Penrhyndeudraeth Gwyn 37 B6
Penrhynside Conwy 47 D8
Penrice Swan 25 H9
Penrith Cumb 69 G8
Penrose Cornw'l 3 B7
Penruddock Cumb 61 B7
Penryn Cornw'l 3 F6
Pensarn Conwy 47 E9
Pensarn Carms 25 E9
Pensax Worcs 29 B8
Pensby Mersey 48 D3
Penselwood Som'set 9 A9
Pensford Bath/NE Som'set 18 E3
Penshaw Tyne/Wear 71 E8
Penshurst Kent 22 G5
Pensilva Cornw'l 4 D3
Penston E Loth 84 G6
Pentewan Cornw'l 3 E9
Pentir Gwyn 46 F5
Pentire Cornw'l 3 C6
Pentlow Essex 34 D2
Pentney Norfolk 43 D10
Penton Mewsey Hants 19 G10
Pentraeth Angl 46 E5
Pentre Carms 26 G5
Pentre Powys 38 G1
Pentre Powys 38 F3
Pentre Rh Cyn Taff 16 B4
Pentre Shrops 38 D4
Pentre Wrex 38 A3
Pentre Wrex 38 B2
Pentre bâch Ceredig'n 26 D5
Pentre bach Powys 27 E9
Pentre Berw Angl 46 E4
Pentre bont Conwy 47 G7
Pentre celyn Denbs 48 G2
Pentre Celyn Powys 37 E8
Pentre chwyth Swan 16 B1
Pentre cwrt Carms 25 C8
Pentre Dolau Honddu Powys 27 D9
Pentre dwr Swan 16 B1
Pentre galar Pembs 25 C6
Pentre Gwenlais Carms 27 G6
Pentre Gwynfryn Gwyn 36 C5

Pentre Halkyn Flints 48 E3
Pentre Isaf Conwy 47 F8
Pentre Llanrhaeadr Denbs 48 F1
Pentre llwyn llwyd Powys 27 C9
Pentre llyn Ceredig'n 27 A6
Pentre llyn cymmer Conwy 47 G9
Pentre Meyrick V/Glam 16 D2
Pentre poeth Newp 17 C7
Pentre rhew Ceredig'n 27 C6
Pentre tafarn y fedw Conwy 47 F8
Pentre ty gwyn Carms 27 E8
Pentrebach Merth Tyd 16 A5
Pentrebach Swan 25 F11
Pentrebeirdd Powys 38 D2
Pentrecagal Carms 25 B8
Pentredwr Denbs 48 H2
Pentrefelin Conwy 47 E8
Pentrefelin Ceredig'n 27 D6
Pentrefelin Carms 26 F5
Pentrefelin Gwyn 36 B5
Pentrefoelas Conwy 47 G8
Pentregat Ceredig'n 26 C3
Pentreheyling Shrops 38 F3
Pentre'r Felin Conwy 47 F8
Pentre'r felin Powys 27 E9
Pentrich Derby 50 G5
Pentridge Dorset 10 C3
Pentyrch Card 17 C6
Penuchadre V/Glam 16 D3
Penuwch Ceredig'n 26 B5
Penwithick Cornw'l 3 D9
Penwyllt Powys 27 G8
Penybanc Carms 27 G6
Penybont Powys 28 B2
Penybontfawr Powys 38 C1
Penycae Wrex 48 H3
Penycwm Pembs 24 D3
Penyffordd Flints 48 F4
Penyffridd Gwyn 46 G5
Penygarnedd Powys 38 C2
Penygraig Rh Cyn Taff 16 B4
Penygroes Gwyn 46 G4
Penygroes Pembs 25 C6
Penyrheol Caerph 17 C6
Penysarn Angl 46 C4
Penywaun Rh Cyn Taff 16 A4
Penzance Cornw'l 2 F3
People's Palace Glasg C 75 A8
Peopleton Worcs 29 C10
Peover Heath Ches 49 E8
Peper Harow Surrey 21 G7
Perceton N Ayrs 67 B6
Percie Aberds 91 B6
Percyhorner Aberds 99 B9
Periton Som'set 16 G4
Perivale London 21 C9
Perkinsville Durham 71 E7
Perlethorpe Notts 51 E8
Perranarworthal Cornw'l 3 F6
Perranporth Cornw'l 3 D6
Perranuthnoe Cornw'l 2 G4
Perranzabuloe Cornw'l 3 D6
Perry Barr W Midlands 40 F2
Perry Green Herts 33 G7
Perry Green Wilts 19 C6
Perry Street Kent 23 D6
Perryfoot Derby 50 D3
Pershall Staffs 39 B9
Pershore Worcs 29 D10
Pert Angus 91 E7
Pertenhall Beds 32 B3
Perth Perth/Kinr 84 B3
Perth Racecourse Perth/Kinr 84 B3
Perthy Shrops 38 B4
Perton Staffs 39 F9
Pertwood Wilts 18 H5
Peter Tavy Devon 5 C6
Peterborough Peterbro 42 F4
Peterborough Cathedral Peterbro 42 F4
Peterburn H'land 100 D5
Peterchurch Heref'd 28 E4
Peterculter Aberd C 91 A9
Peterhead Aberds 99 D11
Peterlee Durham 71 F9
Peter's Green Herts 32 G4
Peters Marland Devon 6 E5
Petersfield Hants 11 B10
Peterston super Ely V/Glam 16 D5
Peterstone Wentlooge Newp 17 C7
Peterstow Heref'd 29 F6
Petertown Orkney 110 H4
Petham Kent 15 C6
Petrockstow Devon 7 F6
Pett E Sussex 14 G3
Pettaugh Suffolk 34 C5
Petteridge Kent 14 D1
Pettinain S Lanarks 76 C2
Pettistree Suffolk 35 C6
Petton Devon 8 B2
Petton Shrops 38 C5
Petts Wood London 22 E4
Petty Aberds 99 E7
Pettycur Fife 84 E5
Pettymuick Aberds 99 F9
Petworth W Sussex 12 C3
Petworth House W Sussex 12 C3
Pevensey E Sussex 13 E10
Pevensey Bay E Sussex 14 H1
Pewsey Wilts 19 E8
Philham Devon 6 D3
Philiphaugh Scot Borders 77 E7
Phillack Cornw'l 2 F4
Philleigh Cornw'l 3 F7
Philpstoun W Loth 84 G2
Phocle Green Heref'd 29 F7
Phoenix Green Hants 20 F5
Pica Cumb 60 B3
Piccotts End Herts 32 H3
Picheon Green S Yorks 58 G2
Pickering N Yorks 64 F5
Picket Piece Hants 20 G1
Picket Post Hants 10 D4
Pickhill N Yorks 63 F8
Picklescott Shrops 38 F5
Pickletillem Fife 84 B6
Pickmere Ches 49 E7
Pickney Som'set 8 B3
Pickstock Telford 39 C8
Pickwell Devon 6 B5
Pickwell Leics 41 D9
Pickworth Lincs 42 B3
Pickworth Rutl'd 42 D2
Picton Ches 48 E5
Picton Flints 48 D2
Picton N Yorks 63 D9
Piddinghoe E Sussex 13 E8
Piddington Northants 31 C10
Piddington Oxon 31 G8
Piddlehinton Dorset 9 E9
Piddletrenthide Dorset 9 E9
Pidley Cambs 43 H6
Piece Hall, Halifax W Yorks 57 F6
Piercebridge D'lington 63 C7
Pierowall Orkney 110 D5
Pigdon Northum 71 B6
Pikehall Derby 50 G3
Pilgrims Hatch Essex 22 B5
Pilham Lincs 52 C1
Pill N Som'set 18 D2
Pillaton Cornw'l 4 D4
Pillerton Hersey Warwick 30 D5
Pillerton Priors Warwick 30 D4
Pilleth Powys 28 B3
Pilley Hants 11 E6
Pilley S Yorks 50 B5
Pilling Lancs 55 D4
Pilling Lane Lancs 55 D3
Pillowell Glos 29 H7
Pillwell Dorset 9 C9
Pilning S Gloucs 18 C2
Pilsbury Derby 50 F3
Pilsdon Dorset 9 E6
Pilsgate Peterbro 42 E3
Pilsley Derby 50 E4
Pilsley Derby 51 F6
Pilton Devon 7 C6
Pilton Northants 42 G3
Pilton Rutl'd 42 E2
Pilton Som'set 18 G2
Pilton Green Swan 25 H9
Pimperne Dorset 10 D2
Pinchbeck Lincs 42 C5
Pinchbeck Bars Lincs 42 C4
Pinchbeck West Lincs 42 C5
Pinehurst Swindon 19 C8
Pinfold Lancs 55 G3
Pinged Carms 25 F9
Pinhoe Devon 8 E1
Pinkneys Grn. Windsor 21 C6
Pinley W Midlands 40 H5
Pinmill Suffolk 35 E6
Pinminnoch S Ayrs 66 A3
Pinmore S Ayrs 66 A4
Pinmore Mains S Ayrs 66 A4
Pinner London 21 C9
Pinvin Worcs 30 D1
Pinwherry S Ayrs 66 B3
Pinxton Derby 51 G6
Pipe and Lyde Heref'd 29 D6
Pipe Gate Shrops 39 A8
Piperhill H'land 103 G7
Piper's Pool Cornw'l 4 B3
Pipewell Northants 41 G10
Pippacott Devon 7 C6
Pipton Powys 28 E2
Pirbright Surrey 21 F7
Pirnmill N Ayrs 73 C8
Pirton Herts 32 E4
Pirton Worcs 29 D9
Pisgah Ceredig'n 37 H6
Pisgah Stirl 83 D8
Pishill Oxon 20 C5
Pistyll Gwyn 36 A3
Pitagowan Perth/Kinr 89 E9
Pitblae Aberds 99 B10
Pitcairngreen Perth/Kinr 84 B2
Pitcalnie H'land 103 E7
Pitcaple Aberds 99 F7
Pitch Green Bucks 20 A5
Pitch Place Surrey 21 F7
Pitchcombe Glos 29 H9
Pitchcott Bucks 31 F9
Pitchford Shrops 39 E6
Pitcombe Som'set 9 A8
Pitcorthie Fife 85 D7
Pitcox E Loth 85 G8
Pitcur Perth/Kinr 90 H3
Pitfichie Aberds 99 G6
Pitforthie Aberds 91 D9
Pitgrudy H'land 103 C6
Pitkennedy Angus 91 F6
Pitkevy Fife 84 D4
Pitkierie Fife 85 D7
Pitlessie Fife 84 D5
Pitlochry Perth/Kinr 89 F10
Pitmachie Aberds 99 F6
Pitmain H'land 96 F5
Pitmedden Aberds 99 F8
Pitminster Som'set 8 C4
Pitmuies Angus 91 G6
Pitmunie Aberds 99 G6
Pitney Som'set 8 B5
Pitroddie Perth/Kinr 84 B4
Pitscottie Fife 84 C6
Pitsea Essex 23 C7
Pitsford Northants 31 B9
Pitsmoor S Yorks 50 D5
Pitstone Bucks 32 G2
Pitstone Green Bucks 32 G2
Pitt Rivers Museum (See University Museum) Oxon 31 H7
Pittendreich Moray 103 F10
Pittentrail H'land 102 B6
Pittenweem Fife 85 D7
Pitteuchar Fife 84 D5
Pittington Durham 71 F8
Pittodrie Aberds 99 F6
Pitton Wilts 10 A5
Pittswood Kent 23 G6
Pittulie Aberds 99 B9
Pity Me Durham 71 F7
Pityme Cornw'l 3 B8
Pityoulish H'land 97 E7
Pixey Green Suffolk 45 H6
Pixham Surrey 21 F9
Pixley Heref'd 29 E7
Place Newton N Yorks 65 G6
Plaidy Aberds 99 C7
Plains N Lanarks 83 H8
Plaish Shrops 39 F6
Plaistow W Sussex 12 B4
Plaitford Hants 10 C5
Plank Lane Gtr Man 49 C7
Plâs Carms 25 D9
Plas Canol Gwyn 36 D5
Plas Gogerddan Ceredig'n 37 G6
Plas Llwyngwern Powys 37 E7
Plas Nantyr Wrex 38 B2
Plas-yn-Cefn Denbs 47 E10
Plastow Green Hants 20 E3
Platt Kent 23 F6
Platt Bridge Gtr Man 49 B7
Platts Common S Yorks 50 B5
Plawsworth Durham 71 F7
Plaxtol Kent 23 F6
Play Hatch Oxon 20 D5
Playden E Sussex 14 F4
Playford Suffolk 35 D6
Playing Place Cornw'l 3 E7
Playley Green Glos 29 E8
Plealey Shrops 38 E5
Plean Stirl 83 F9
Pleasington Blackb'n 56 F1
Pleasley Derby 51 F7
Pleasure Island Theme Park NE Lincs 53 B6
Pleasureland Mersey 55 G3
Pleasurewood Hills American Theme Park, Lowestoft Suffolk 45 F9
Pleckgate Blackb'n 56 E1
Plenmeller Northum 70 D2
Pleshey Essex 33 G9
Plockton H'land 94 C5
Plocropol W Isles 109 H6
Ploughfield Heref'd 28 D4
Plowden Shrops 38 G4
Ploxgreen Shrops 38 E4
Pluckley Kent 14 D4
Pluckley Thorne Kent 14 D4
Plumbland Cumb 68 G4
Plumley Ches 49 E8
Plumpton Cumb 69 G7
Plumpton E Sussex 13 D7
Plumpton Green E Sussex 13 D7
Plumpton Head Cumb 69 G8
Plumpton Racecourse E Sussex 13 D7
Plumstead London 22 D4
Plumstead Norfolk 44 B5
Plumtree Notts 41 B8
Plungar Leics 41 B9
Plush Dorset 9 D9
Plwmp Ceredig'n 26 C3
Plymouth Plym'th 4 E5
Plympton Plym'th 5 E6
Plymstock Plym'th 5 E6
Plymtree Devon 8 D2
Pockley N Yorks 64 F4
Pocklington ER Yorks 58 D4
Pode Hole Lincs 42 C5
Podimore Som'set 9 B7
Podington Beds 32 B2
Podmore Staffs 39 B8
Point Clear Essex 34 G4
Pointon Lincs 42 B4
Pokesdown Bournem'th 10 E4
Pol a Charra W Isles 92 D3
Polbae Dumf/Gal 66 C4
Polbain H'land 101 A7
Polbathic Cornw'l 4 E4
Polbeth W Loth 76 A3
Polchar H'land 97 F6
Pole Elm Worcs 29 D9
Polebrook Northants 42 G3
Polegate E Sussex 13 E9
Poles H'land 103 C6
Polesden Lacey, Dorking Surrey 21 F9
Polesworth Warwick 40 E4
Polgigga Cornw'l 2 G2
Polglass H'land 101 B8
Polgooth Cornw'l 3 D8
Poling W Sussex 12 E4
Polkerris Cornw'l 3 D9
Polla H'land 105 D6
Pollington ER Yorks 58 G2
Polloch H'land 87 E7
Pollok Glasg C 75 A7
Pollok House Glasg C 75 A7
Pollokshields Glasg C 75 A7
Polmassick Cornw'l 3 E8
Polmont Falk 83 G10
Polnessan E Ayrs 75 F6
Polnish H'land 87 C7
Polperro Cornw'l 4 E3
Polruan Cornw'l 4 E2
Polsham Som'set 18 G2
Polstead Suffolk 34 E3
Poltalloch Arg/Bute 81 E8
Poltimore Devon 8 E1
Polton Midloth 76 A5
Polwarth Scot Borders 78 B2
Polyphant Cornw'l 4 B3
Polzeath Cornw'l 3 B8
Ponders End London 22 B3
Pondersbridge Cambs 42 F5
Pondtail Hants 21 F6
Ponsanooth Cornw'l 3 F6
Ponsworthy Devon 5 C8
Pont Aber Carms 27 F7
Pont Aber Geirw Gwyn 37 C7
Pont ar gothi Carms 26 F5
Pont ar Hydfer Powys 27 F8
Pont ar llechau Carms 27 F7
Pont Cwm Pydew Denbs 37 B10
Pont Cyfyng Conwy 47 G7
Pont Cysyllte Wrex 38 A3
Pont Dolydd Prysor Gwyn 37 B7
Pont faen Powys 27 E9
Pont Fronwydd Gwyn 37 C8
Pont gareg Pembs 24 B6
Pont Henri Carms 25 F9
Pont Llogel Powys 37 D10
Pont Pen y benglog Gwyn 47 F6
Pont Rhyd goch Conwy 47 F6
Pont Rhyd sarn Gwyn 37 C8
Pont Rhyd y cyff Bridg 16 C3
Pont rhyd y groes Ceredig'n 27 A7
Pont rug Gwyn 46 F5
Pont siân Ceredig'n 25 B9
Pont y gwaith Rh Cyn Taff 16 B5
Pont y pant Conwy 47 G7
Pont y Pennant Gwyn 37 C9
Pont yclun Rh Cyn Taff 16 C5
Pont yr Afon Gam Gwyn 37 A7
Pont yr hafod Pembs 24 D4
Pontamman Carms 27 G6
Pontantwn Carms 25 E9
Pontardawe Neath P Talb 16 A2
Pontardulais Swan 25 F10
Pontarsais Carms 25 D9
Pontblyddyn Flints 48 F3
Pontbren Araeth Carms 27 F6
Pontbren Llwyd Rh Cyn Taff 27 H9
Pontefract W Yorks 57 F9
Pontefract Racecourse W Yorks 57 F9
Ponteland Northum 71 C6
Ponterwyd Ceredig'n 37 G7
Pontesbury Shrops 38 E4
Pontfadog Wrex 38 B3
Pontfaen Pembs 24 C5
Pontgarreg Ceredig'n 26 C3
Ponthir Torf 17 B8
Ponthirwaun Ceredig'n 25 B7
Pontllanfraith Caerph 17 B6
Pontlliw Swan 25 F11
Pontllyfni Gwyn 46 G4
Pontlottyn Caerph 28 H2
Pontneddfechan Powys 27 H9
Pontnewydd Torf 17 B7
Pontrhydfendigaid Ceredig'n 27 B7
Pontrhydyfen Neath P Talb 16 B2
Pontrilas Heref'd 28 F4
Pontrobert Powys 38 D2
Ponts Green E Sussex 14 G1
Pontshill Heref'd 29 F7
Pontsticill Merth Tyd 28 G1
Pontwgan Conwy 47 E7
Pontyates Carms 25 F9
Pontyberem Carms 26 G5
Pontycymer Bridg 16 B4
Pontyglasier Pembs 24 C6
Pontypool Torf 17 A7
Pontypridd Rh Cyn Taff 16 C5
Pontywaun Caerph 17 B7
Pooksgreen Hants 11 C6
Pool Cornw'l 2 E5
Pool W Yorks 57 D7
Pool o'Muckhart Clack 84 D2
Pool Quay Powys 38 D3
Poole Poole 10 E3
Poole Keynes Glos 19 B6
Poolend Staffs 50 G1
Poolewe H'land 101 D6
Pooley Bridge Cumb 61 B7
Poolfold Staffs 49 G9
Poolhill Glos 29 F8
Poolsbrook Derby 51 E6
Pootings Kent 22 G4
Pope Hill Pembs 24 E4
Popeswood Brackn'l 21 E6
Popham Hants 20 G3
Poplar London 22 C3
Popley Hants 20 F4
Porchester Notts 41 A7
Porchfield I/Wight 11 E7
Porin H'land 102 G2
Poringland Norfolk 45 E6
Porkellis Cornw'l 2 F5
Porlock Som'set 7 B9
Porlock Weir Som'set 7 B9
Port Ann Arg/Bute 81 F9
Port Appin Arg/Bute 87 G9
Port Askaig Arg/Bute 80 H4
Port Bannatyne Arg/Bute 82 H1
Port Carlisle Cumb 68 D5
Port Charlotte Arg/Bute 72 B2
Port Clarence Stockton 63 B9
Port Dinorwic Gwyn 46 F5
Port Driseach Arg/Bute 81 G9
Port e Vullen I/Man 54 C4
Port Ellen Arg/Bute 72 C3
Port Elphinstone Aberds 99 G7
Port Erin I/Man 54 F1
Port Eynon Swan 25 H9
Port Gaverne Cornw'l 4 B1
Port Glasgow Invercl 82 G4
Port Henderson H'land 100 E5
Port Isaac Cornw'l 3 A8
Port Lamont Arg/Bute 82 G1
Port Lion Pembs 24 F4
Port Logan Dumf/Gal 66 F2
Port Mholair W Isles 108 D10
Port Mor H'land 86 D5
Port Mulgrave N Yorks 64 C5
Port Nan Giuran W Isles 108 D10
Port nan Long W Isles 109 K3
Port Nis W Isles 108 A10
Port of Menteith Stirl 83 D6
Port Quin Cornw'l 3 A8
Port Ramsay Arg/Bute 87 G8
Port St. Mary I/Man 54 F2
Port Sunlight Mersey 48 D4
Port Talbot Neath P Talb 16 B2
Port Tennant Swan 16 B1
Port Wemyss Arg/Bute 72 B1
Port William Dumf/Gal 66 F5
Portachoillan Arg/Bute 73 B7
Portavadie Arg/Bute 81 H9
Portbury N Som'set 18 D2
Portchester Hants 11 D9
Portclair H'land 96 E2
Portencross N Ayrs 74 C3
Portesham Dorset 9 F8
Portessie Moray 98 B4
Portfield Gate Pembs 24 E4
Portgate Devon 4 B5
Portgordon Moray 98 B3
Portgower H'land 103 A9
Porth Cornw'l 3 C7
Porth Rh Cyn Taff 16 B5
Porth Navas Cornw'l 3 G6
Porth y waen Shrops 38 C3
Porthallow Cornw'l 3 G6
Porthallow Cornw'l 4 E3
Porthcawl Bridg 16 D3
Porthcothan Cornw'l 3 B7
Porthcurno Cornw'l 2 G2
Porthgain Pembs 24 C3
Porthill Shrops 38 D5
Porthkerry V/Glam 16 E5
Porthleven Cornw'l 2 G5
Porthllechog Angl 46 C4
Porthmadog Gwyn 36 B5
Porthmeor Cornw'l 2 F3
Portholland Cornw'l 3 E8
Porthoustock Cornw'l 3 G7
Porthpean Cornw'l 3 D9
Porthtowan Cornw'l 2 E5
Porthyrhyd Carms 26 G5
Porthyrhyd Carms 27 E7
Portincaple Arg/Bute 82 E3
Portington ER Yorks 58 E3
Portinnisherrich Arg/Bute 81 C9
Portinscale Cumb 60 B5
Portishead N Som'set 17 D9
Portkil Arg/Bute 82 F3
Portknockie Moray 98 B4
Portlethen Aberds 91 B10
Portling Dumf/Gal 68 E1
Portloe Cornw'l 3 F8
Portmahomack H'land 103 D8
Portmeirion Gwyn 36 B5
Portmeirion Village Gwyn 36 B5
Portmellon Cornw'l 3 E9
Portmore Hants 11 E6
Portnacroish Arg/Bute 87 G9
Portnahaven Arg/Bute 72 B1
Portnalong H'land 93 B9
Portnaluchaig H'land 87 C6
Portnancon H'land 105 C7
Portobello C/Edinb 84 G5
Porton Wilts 19 H8
Portpatrick Dumf/Gal 66 E2
Portreath Cornw'l 2 E5
Portree H'land 94 B1
Portscatho Cornw'l 3 F7
Portsea Portsm'th 11 D9
Portskerra H'land 106 C3
Portskewett Monmouths 18 C2
Portslade Brighton/Hove 13 E6
Portslade by Sea Brighton/Hove 13 E6
Portsmouth Portsm'th 11 D9
Portsmouth W Yorks 56 F4
Portsmouth Sea Life Centre Portsm'th 11 E9
Portsonachan Arg/Bute 82 B1
Portsoy Aberds 98 B5
Portswood S'hampton 11 C7
Portuairk H'land 86 E4
Portway Heref'd 28 E5
Portway Worcs 30 A2
Portwrinkle Cornw'l 4 E4
Poslingford Suffolk 34 D1
Postbridge Devon 5 C7
Postcombe Oxon 20 B5
Postling Kent 15 E6
Postwick Norfolk 45 E6
Potholm Dumf/Gal 69 B6
Potsgrove Beds 32 F2
Pott Row Norfolk 43 C10
Pott Shrigley Ches 49 E10
Potten End Herts 32 H3
Potter Brompton N Yorks 65 G7
Potter Heigham Norfolk 45 D8
Potter Street Essex 33 H7
Potterhanworth Lincs 52 F3
Potterhanworth Booths Lincs 52 F3
Potteries Museum & Art Gallery, Stoke on Trent Stoke 49 H9
Potterne Wilts 19 F6
Potterne Wick Wilts 19 F7
Potternewton W Yorks 57 E8
Potters Bar Herts 22 A2
Potter's Cross Staffs 39 G9
Potterspury Northants 31 D9
Potterton Aberds 99 G9
Potterton W Yorks 57 E9
Potto N Yorks 63 D9
Potton Beds 32 D5
Poughill Cornw'l 6 F3
Poughill Devon 7 F9
Poulshot Wilts 19 F6
Poulton Glos 19 A8
Poulton Mersey 48 C4
Poulton le Fylde Lancs 55 E3
Pound Bank Worcs 29 A8
Pound Green E Sussex 13 C9
Pound Green I/Wight 11 F6
Pound Green Worcs 39 H8
Pound Hill W Sussex 13 B6
Poundfield E Sussex 13 B9
Poundland S Ayrs 66 B3
Poundon Bucks 31 F8
Poundsgate Devon 5 C8
Poundstock Cornw'l 6 G3
Powburn Northum 78 F5
Powderham Devon 8 F1
Powderham Castle Devon 8 F1
Powerstock Dorset 9 E7
Powfoot Dumf/Gal 68 D4
Powick Worcs 29 C9
Powis Castle, Welshpool Powys 38 E3
Powmill Perth/Kinr 84 E2
Poxwell Dorset 9 F9
Poyle Slough 21 D8
Poynings W Sussex 13 D6
Poyntington Dorset 9 C8
Poynton Ches 49 D10
Poynton Green Telford 39 D6
Poystreet Green Suffolk 34 C3
Praa Sands Cornw'l 2 G4
Pratt's Bottom London 22 E4
Praze Cornw'l 2 F4
Praze an Beeble Cornw'l 2 F5
Predannack Wollas Cornw'l 2 H5
Prees Shrops 39 B6
Prees Green Shrops 39 B6
Prees Heath Shrops 39 B6
Prees Higher Heath Shrops 39 B6
Prees Lower Heath Shrops 39 B6
Preesall Lancs 55 D3
Preesgweene Shrops 38 B3
Prenderguest Scot Borders 78 B4
Prendwick Northum 78 F5
Prengwyn Ceredig'n 25 B9
Prenteg Gwyn 36 A5
Prenton Mersey 48 D4
Prescot Mersey 48 C5
Prescott Shrops 38 C5
Pressen Northum 78 D3
Prestatyn Denbs 48 D1
Prestbury Ches 49 E10
Prestbury Glos 30 F1
Presteigne Powys 28 B4
Presthope Shrops 39 F6
Prestleigh Som'set 18 G3
Preston Scot Borders 78 B2
Preston Brighton/Hove 13 E7
Preston Devon 5 C9
Preston Dorset 9 F9
Preston E Loth 85 G7
Preston ER Yorks 59 E7
Preston Glos 19 A7
Preston Glos 29 E7
Preston Herts 32 F4
Preston Kent 14 B5
Preston Kent 15 B7
Preston Lancs 55 F5
Preston Northum 79 E6
Preston Rutl'd 42 E1
Preston Shrops 39 D6
Preston Suffolk 34 C3
Preston Wilts 19 D7
Preston Wilts 19 D9
Preston Bagot Warwick 30 B3
Preston Bissett Bucks 31 F8
Preston Bowyer Som'set 8 B3
Preston Brockhurst Shrops 39 C6
Preston Brook Halton 49 D6
Preston Candover Hants 20 G4
Preston Capes Northants 31 C7
Preston Crowmarsh Oxon 20 B4
Preston Gubbals Shrops 38 D5
Preston Hall Museum Stockton 63 C9
Preston on Stour Warwick 30 D4
Preston on the Hill Halton 49 D6
Preston on Wye Heref'd 28 D4
Preston Plucknett Som'set 9 C7
Preston under Scar N Yorks 62 E5
Preston upon the Weald Moors Telford 39 D7
Preston Wynne Heref'd 29 D6
Prestonmill Dumf/Gal 68 E2
Prestonpans E Loth 84 G5
Prestwich Gtr Man 49 B9
Prestwick Northum 71 C6
Prestwick S Ayrs 74 E5
Prestwood Bucks 21 A6
Price Town Bridg 16 B4
Prickwillow Cambs 43 G8
Priddy Som'set 18 F2
Priest Hutton Lancs 61 G8
Priest Weston Shrops 38 F3
Priesthaugh Scot Borders 77 G7
Primethorpe Leics 41 F7
Primrose Green Norfolk 44 D4
Primrose Valley N Yorks 65 G9
Primrosehill Herts 21 A8
Princes Gate Pembs 24 E6
Princes Risborough Bucks 21 A6
Princethorpe Warwick 31 A6
Princetown Caerph 28 G2
Princetown Devon 5 C6
Prinknash Abbey Glos 29 G9
Prion Denbs 48 F1
Prior Muir Fife 85 C7
Prior Park Northum 78 B4
Priors Frome Heref'd 29 E6
Priors Hardwick Warwick 31 C6
Priors Marston Warwick 31 C6
Priorslee Telford 39 D8
Priory Church, Lancaster Lancs 55 B4
Priory Wood Heref'd 28 D3
Priston Bath/NE Som'set 18 E3
Pristow Green Norfolk 44 G5
Prittlewell Southend 23 C8
Privett Hants 11 B9
Prixford Devon 7 C6
Probus Cornw'l 3 E7
Proncy H'land 103 C6
Prospect Cumb 68 F4
Prudhoe Northum 70 D5
Ptarmigan Lodge Stirl 82 D4
Pubil Perth/Kinr 88 G5
Puckeridge Herts 33 F6
Puckington Som'set 8 C5
Pucklechurch S Gloucs 18 D3
Pucknall Hants 11 B6
Puckrup Glos 29 E9
Puddinglake Ches 49 F8
Puddington Ches 48 E4
Puddington Devon 7 E9
Puddledock Norfolk 44 F4
Puddletown Dorset 9 E9
Pudleston Heref'd 29 C6
Pudsey W Yorks 57 E7
Pulborough W Sussex 12 D4
Puleston Telford 39 C8
Pulford Ches 48 G4
Pulham Dorset 9 D9
Pulham Market Norfolk 44 G5
Pulham St. Mary Norfolk 45 G6
Pulloxhill Beds 32 E3
Pumpherston W Loth 84 H2
Pumsaint Carms 27 D6
Puncheston Pembs 24 D5
Puncknowle Dorset 9 F7
Punnett's Town E Sussex 13 C10
Purbrook Hants 11 D9
Purewell Dorset 10 E4
Purfleet Thurr'k 22 D5
Puriton Som'set 17 G8
Purleigh Essex 23 A8
Purley London 22 E3
Purley W Berks 20 D4
Purlogue Shrops 38 H3
Purls Bridge Cambs 43 G7
Purse Caundle Dorset 9 C8
Purslow Shrops 38 G4
Purston Jaglin W Yorks 57 G9
Purton Glos 18 A3
Purton Glos 18 A3
Purton Wilts 19 C7
Purton Stoke Wilts 19 B7
Pury End Northants 31 D9
Pusey Oxon 20 B1
Putley Heref'd 29 E7
Putney London 22 D2
Putsborough Devon 6 B5
Puttenham Herts 32 G1
Puttenham Surrey 21 G7
Puxton N Som'set 17 E9
Pwll Carms 25 F9
Pwll glas Denbs 48 G2
Pwll Meyric Monmouths 18 B2
Pwll trap Carms 25 E7
Pwll y glaw Neath P Talb 16 B2
Pwllcrochan Pembs 24 F4
Pwllgloyw Powys 27 E10
Pwllheli Gwyn 36 B3
Pycombe W Sussex 13 D6
Pye Corner Herts 33 G7
Pye Corner Newp 17 C8
Pye Green Staffs 40 D1
Pyewipe NE Lincs 59 G8
Pyle Bridg 16 C3
Pyle I/Wight 11 G7
Pylle Som'set 18 H3
Pymoor Cambs 43 G7
Pyrford Surrey 21 F8
Pyrton Oxon 20 B4
Pytchley Northants 32 A1
Pyworthy Devon 6 F4

Q

Quabbs Shrops 38 G3
Quadring Lincs 42 B5
Quainton Bucks 31 G9
Quarley Hants 19 G9
Quarndon Derby 40 A5
Quarrier's Homes Invercl 82 H4
Quarrington Lincs 42 A3
Quarrington Hill Durham 71 G8
Quarry Bank W Midlands 39 G10
Quarry Bank Mill, Wilmslow Ches 49 D9
Quarryford E Loth 85 H7
Quarryhill H'land 102 D6
Quarrywood Moray 103 F10
Quarter S Lanarks 75 B9
Quatford Shrops 39 F8
Quatt Shrops 39 G8
Quebec Durham 71 F6
Quedgeley Glos 29 G9
Queen Adelaide Cambs 43 G8
Queen Camel Som'set 9 B7
Queen Charlton Bath/NE Som'set 18 E3
Queen Dart Devon 7 E9
Queen Oak Dorset 9 A9
Queen Street Kent 14 D1
Queen Street Wilts 19 C7
Queenborough Kent 23 D9
Queenhill Worcs 29 E9
Queen's Head Shrops 38 C4
Queen's Park Beds 32 D3
Queen's Park Northants 31 B9
Queen's View Centre, Loch Tummel Perth/Kinr 89 F9
Queensbury W Yorks 57 E6
Queensferry C/Edinb 84 G3
Queensferry Flints 48 F4
Queenstown Blackp'l 55 E3
Queenzieburn N Lanarks 83 G7
Quemerford Wilts 19 E7
Quendale Shetl'd 111 M6
Quendon Essex 33 E8
Queniborough Leics 41 D8
Quenington Glos 19 A8
Quernmore Lancs 55 C5
Quethiock Cornw'l 4 D4
Quholm Orkney 110 G3
Quicks Green W Berks 20 D3
Quidenham Norfolk 44 G4
Quidhampton Hants 20 F3
Quidhampton Wilts 10 A4
Quilquox Aberds 99 E9
Quina Brook Shrops 39 B6
Quindry Orkney 110 J5
Quinton Northants 31 C9
Quinton W Midlands 40 G1
Quixhill Staffs 40 A3
Quoditch Devon 6 G5
Quoig Perth/Kinr 83 B9
Quorndon Leics 41 D7
Quothquan S Lanarks 76 D2
Quoyloo Orkney 110 F3
Quoys Shetl'd 111 B9
Quoys Shetl'd 111 G7

R

Raasay Ho. H'land 94 C2
Rabbit's Cross Kent 14 D2
Raby Mersey 48 E4
Rachan Mill Scot Borders 76 D4
Rachub Gwyn 47 F6
Rackenford Devon 7 E9
Rackham W Sussex 12 D4
Rackheath Norfolk 45 D6
Racks Dumf/Gal 68 C3
Rackwick Orkney 110 J3
Rackwick Orkney 110 D5
Radbourne Derby 40 B4
Radcliffe Gtr Man 49 B8
Radcliffe Northum 79 G7
Radcliffe on Trent Notts 41 B8
Radclive Bucks 31 E8
Radcot Oxon 19 B9
Raddery H'land 102 G6
Radernie Fife 85 D6
Radford Semele Warwick 30 B5
Radipole Dorset 9 F8
Radlett Herts 21 B9
Radley Oxon 20 B3
Radmanthwaite Notts 51 F7
Radmoor Shrops 39 C7
Radmore Green Ches 49 G6
Radnage Bucks 20 B5
Radstock Bath/NE Som'set 18 F3
Radstone Northants 31 D7
Radway Warwick 30 D5
Radway Green Ches 49 G8
Radwell Beds 32 C3
Radwell Herts 32 E5
Radwinter Essex 33 E9
Radyr Card 17 C6
RAF Museum, Hendon London 22 C2
Rafford Moray 103 G9
Ragdale Leics 41 D8
Raglan Monmouths 28 H5
Ragley Hall Warwick 30 C2
Ragnall Notts 51 E10
Rahane Arg/Bute 82 F3
Rainford Mersey 48 B5
Rainford Junction Mersey 48 B5
Rainham London 22 C5
Rainham Medway 14 B3
Rainhill Mersey 48 C5
Rainhill Stoops Mersey 49 C6
Rainow Ches 50 E1
Rainton N Yorks 63 G8
Rainworth Notts 51 G7
Raisbeck Cumb 61 D9
Raise Cumb 70 F2
Rait Perth/Kinr 84 B4
Raithby Lincs 53 D6
Raithby Lincs 53 F6
Rake W Sussex 12 C2
Rakewood Gtr Man 56 G4
Ram Carms 26 D5
Ram Lane Kent 14 D4
Ramasaig H'land 93 A7
Rame Cornw'l 3 F6
Rame Cornw'l 4 F5
Ramnageo Shetl'd 111 C9
Rampisham Dorset 9 D7
Rampside Cumb 55 B2
Rampton Cambs 33 B7
Rampton Notts 51 E9
Ramsbottom Gtr Man 56 G2
Ramsbury Wilts 19 D9
Ramscraigs H'land 107 G6
Ramsdean Hants 11 B10
Ramsdell Hants 20 F3
Ramsden Oxon 30 G5
Ramsden Bellhouse Essex 23 B7
Ramsden Heath Essex 23 B7
Ramsey Cambs 42 G5
Ramsey Essex 35 E6
Ramsey I/Man 54 C4
Ramsey Forty Foot Cambs 43 G6
Ramsey Heights Cambs 42 G5
Ramsey Island Essex 34 H3
Ramsey Mereside Cambs 42 G5
Ramsey St. Mary's Cambs 42 G5
Ramseycleuch Scot Borders 76 F5
Ramsgate Kent 15 B8
Ramsgill N Yorks 63 G6
Ramshorn Staffs 50 H2
Ramsnest Common Surrey 12 B3
Ranais W Isles 108 E9
Ranby Lincs 52 E5
Ranby Notts 51 D8
Rand Lincs 52 E4
Randwick Glos 29 H9
Ranfurly Renf 74 A5
Rangag H'land 107 E6
Rangemore Staffs 40 C3
Rangeworthy S Gloucs 18 C3
Rankinston E Ayrs 75 F6
Ranmoor S Yorks 50 D5
Ranmore Common Surrey 21 F9
Rannerdale Cumb 60 C4
Rannoch School Perth/Kinr 89 F6
Rannoch Station Perth/Kinr 88 F5
Ranochan H'land 87 C8
Ranskill Notts 51 D8
Ranton Staffs 39 C9
Ranworth Norfolk 45 D7
Raploch Stirl 83 E8
Rapness Orkney 110 D6
Rascal Moor ER Yorks 58 E4
Rascarrel Dumf/Gal 67 F9
Rashiereive Aberds 99 F9
Raskelf N Yorks 63 G9
Rassau Bl Gwent 28 G2
Rastrick W Yorks 57 F6
Ratagan H'land 95 E6
Ratby Leics 41 E7
Ratcliffe Culey Leics 40 F5
Ratcliffe on Soar Leics 41 C6
Ratcliffe on the Wreake Leics 41 D8
Rathen Aberds 99 B10
Rathillet Fife 84 B5
Rathmell N Yorks 56 C3
Ratho C/Edinb 84 G3
Ratho Station C/Edinb 84 G3
Rathven Moray 98 B4
Ratley Warwick 30 D5
Ratlinghope Shrops 38 F5
Rattar H'land 107 B7
Ratten Row Lancs 55 D4
Rattery Devon 5 D8
Rattlesden Suffolk 34 C3
Rattray Perth/Kinr 90 G2
Raughton Head Cumb 69 F6
Raunds Northants 32 A2
Raven Seat N Yorks 62 D3
Ravenfield S Yorks 51 C6
Ravenglass Cumb 60 E3
Ravenglass and Eskdale Railway & Museum Cumb 60 E3
Raveningham Norfolk 45 F7
Ravenscar N Yorks 65 D7
Ravenscraig Invercl 82 G3
Ravensdale I/Man 54 C3
Ravensden Beds 32 C3
Ravenshead Notts 51 G7
Ravensmoor Ches 49 G7
Ravensthorpe Northants 31 A8
Ravensthorpe W Yorks 57 F7
Ravenstone Leics 41 D6
Ravenstone M/Keynes 31 C10
Ravenstonedale Cumb 62 D2
Ravenstown Cumb 61 G6
Ravenstruther S Lanarks 76 C2
Ravensworth N Yorks 63 D6
Raw N Yorks 65 D7
Rawcliffe ER Yorks 58 F2
Rawcliffe C/York 58 C1
Rawcliffe Bridge ER Yorks 58 F2
Rawdon W Yorks 57 E7
Rawmarsh S Yorks 51 C6
Rawreth Essex 23 B7
Rawridge Devon 8 D4
Rawtenstall Lancs 56 F3
Raxton Aberds 99 E8
Raydon Suffolk 34 E4
Raylees Northum 70 A4
Rayleigh Essex 23 B8
Rayne Essex 33 F10
Rayners Lane London 21 C9
Raynes Park London 22 E2
Reach Cambs 33 B8
Read Lancs 56 E2
Reading Reading 20 D5
Reading Street Kent 14 E4
Reagill Cumb 61 C9
Rearquhar H'land 102 C6
Rearsby Leics 41 D8
Reaster H'land 107 C7
Reawick Shetl'd 111 J6
Reay H'land 106 C4
Rechullin H'land 101 G6
Reculver Kent 15 B7
Red Dial Cumb 68 F5
Red Hill Worcs 29 C9
Red Houses Jersey 4
Red Lodge Suffolk 33 A9
Red Rail Heref'd 29 F6
Red Rock Gtr Man 49 B6
Red Roses Carms 25 E7
Red Row Northum 79 H7
Red Street Staffs 49 G9
Red Wharf Bay Angl 46 D5
Redberth Pembs 24 F5
Redbourn Herts 32 G4
Redbourne N Lincs 52 C2
Redbrook Glos 29 G6
Redbrook Wrex 39 A6
Redburn H'land 102 F4
Redburn H'land 97 B7
Redburn Northum 70 D2
Redcar Redcar/Clevel'd 64 B4
Redcar Racecourse Redcar/Clevel'd 64 B4
Redcastle Angus 91 F7
Redcastle H'land 96 B3
Redcliff Bay N Som'set 17 D9
Redding Falk 83 G10
Reddingmuirhead Falk 83 G10
Reddish Gtr Man 49 C9
Redditch Worcs 30 B2
Rede Suffolk 34 C2
Redenhall Norfolk 45 G6
Redesdale Camp Northum 78 H3
Redesmouth Northum 70 B3
Redford Aberds 91 D8
Redford Angus 91 G6
Redford Durham 70 G5
Redfordgreen Scot Borders 77 F6
Redgorton Perth/Kinr 84 B2
Redgrave Suffolk 44 H4
Redhill Aberds 99 E6
Redhill Aberds 91 A8
Redhill N Som'set 18 E2
Redhill Surrey 22 F2
Redhouse Arg/Bute 73 A8
Redhouses Arg/Bute 72 A3
Redisham Suffolk 45 G8
Redland Bristol 18 D2
Redland Orkney 110 F4
Redlingfield Suffolk 34 A5
Redlynch Som'set 9 A9
Redlynch Wilts 10 B5
Redmarley D'Abitot Glos 29 E8
Redmarshall Stockton 63 B8
Redmile Leics 41 B9
Redmire N Yorks 62 E5
Redmoor Cornw'l 3 C9
Rednal Shrops 38 C4
Redpath Scot Borders 77 D8
Redpoint H'land 100 F5
Redruth Cornw'l 2 E5
Redvales Gtr Man 49 B9
Redwick Newp 17 C9
Redwick S Gloucs 18 C2
Redworth D'lington 63 B7
Reed Herts 33 E6
Reedham Norfolk 45 E8
Reedness ER Yorks 58 F3
Reeds Beck Lincs 52 F5
Reepham Lincs 52 E3
Reepham Norfolk 44 C4
Reeth N Yorks 62 E5
Regaby I/Man 54 C4
Regoul H'land 103 G7
Reiff H'land 101 A7
Reigate Surrey 22 F2
Reighton N Yorks 65 G9
Reighton Gap N Yorks 65 G9
Reinigeadal W Isles 109 G7
Reiss H'land 107 D8
Rejerrah Cornw'l 3 D6
Releath Cornw'l 2 F5
Relubbus Cornw'l 2 F4
Relugas Moray 97 B7
Remenham Wokingham 20 C5
Remenham Hill Wokingham 20 C5
Remony Perth/Kinr 89 G8
Rempstone Notts 41 C7
Rendcomb Glos 30 H2
Rendham Suffolk 35 B7
Rendlesham Suffolk 35 C7
Renfrew Renf 83 H6
Renhold Beds 32 C3
Renishaw Derby 51 E6
Rennington Northum 79 F7
Renton W Dunb 82 G4
Renwick Cumb 69 F8
Repps Norfolk 45 D8
Repton Derby 40 C5
Rescobie Angus 91 F6
Resipole H'land 87 E7
Resolis H'land 102 F5
Resolven Neath P Talb 16 A3
Reston Scot Borders 78 A3
Reswallie Angus 91 F6
Retew Cornw'l 3 D8
Retford Notts 51 D9
Rettendon Essex 23 B7
Rettendon Place Essex 23 B7
Revesby Lincs 52 F5
Revesby Bridge Lincs 53 F6
Rew Street I/Wight 11 E7
Rewe Devon 7 G10
Reydon Suffolk 45 H8
Reydon Smear Suffolk 45 H8
Reymerston Norfolk 44 E4
Reynalton Pembs 24 F5
Reynoldston Swan 25 G9
Rezare Cornw'l 4 C4
Rhandirmwyn Carms 27 D7
Rhayader Powys 27 B9
Rhedyn Gwyn 36 B2
Rhemore H'land 86 F5
Rhencullen I/Man 54 C3
Rhes y cae Flints 48 E2
Rhewl Denbs 48 F2
Rhewl Denbs 38 A2
Rhian H'land 105 H8
Rhicarn H'land 104 G3
Rhiconich H'land 104 D5
Rhicullen H'land 102 E5
Rhidorroch Ho. H'land 101 C9
Rhifail H'land 106 E2
Rhigos Rh Cyn Taff 27 H9
Rhilochan H'land 102 B6
Rhiroy H'land 101 D9
Rhiw Gwyn 36 C2
Rhiwbina Card 17 C6
Rhiwbryfdir Gwyn 47 H6
Rhiwderin Newp 17 C7
Rhiwlas Gwyn 46 F5
Rhiwlas Gwyn 37 B9
Rhiwlas Powys 38 B2
Rhodes Gtr Man 49 B9
Rhodes Minnis Kent 15 D6
Rhodesia Notts 51 E7
Rhodiad Pembs 24 D2
Rhondda Rh Cyn Taff 16 B4
Rhonehouse or Kelton Hill Dumf/Gal 67 E9
Rhoose V/Glam 16 E5
Rhôs Carms 25 C8
Rhôs Neath P Talb 16 A2
Rhos fawr Gwyn 36 B3
Rhos hill Pembs 25 B6
Rhos on Sea Conwy 47 D8
Rhos y brithdir Powys 38 C2
Rhos y garth Ceredig'n 27 A6
Rhos y gwaliau Gwyn 37 B9
Rhos y llan Gwyn 36 B2
Rhos y Madoc Wrex 38 A4
Rhos y meirch Powys 28 B3
Rhosaman Carms 27 G7
Rhosbeirio Angl 46 C3
Rhoscefnhir Angl 46 E5
Rhoscolyn Angl 46 E2
Rhoscrowther Pembs 24 F4
Rhosesmor Flints 48 F3
Rhosgadfan Gwyn 46 G5
Rhosgoch Angl 46 D4
Rhosgoch Powys 28 D2
Rhoshirwaun Gwyn 36 C1
Rhoslan Gwyn 36 A4
Rhoslefain Gwyn 36 E5
Rhosllanerchrugog Wrex 48 H3
Rhosmaen Carms 27 F6
Rhosmeirch Angl 46 E4
Rhosneigr Angl 46 E3
Rhosnesni Wrex 48 G4
Rhosrobin Wrex 48 G4
Rhossili Swan 25 H9
Rhosson Pembs 24 D2
Rhostryfan Gwyn 46 G4
Rhostyllen Wrex 48 H4
Rhosybol Angl 46 D4
Rhu Arg/Bute 73 A8
Rhu Arg/Bute 82 F3
Rhuallt Denbs 48 E1
Rhuddall Heath Ches 49 F6
Rhuddlan Ceredig'n 25 B9
Rhuddlan Denbs 47 E10
Rhue H'land 101 C8
Rhulen Powys 28 D2
Rhunahaorine Arg/Bute 73 C7
Rhyd Gwyn 37 A6
Rhyd Powys 37 E9
Rhyd Ddu Gwyn 46 G5
Rhyd moel ddu Powys 38 H1
Rhyd Rosser Ceredig'n 26 B5
Rhyd uchaf Gwyn 37 B9
Rhyd wen Gwyn 37 D7
Rhyd y clafdy Gwyn 36 B3
Rhŷd y foel Conwy 47 E9
Rhyd y fro Neath P Talb 27 H7
Rhyd y gwin Swan 16 A1
Rhyd y meirch Monmouths 28 H4
Rhyd y meudwy Denbs 48 G2
Rhyd y sarn Gwyn 37 A6
Rhyd yr onen Gwyn 37 E6
Rhydargaeau Carms 25 D9
Rhydcymerau Carms 26 E5
Rhydd Worcs 29 D9
Rhydding Neath P Talb 16 B2
Rhydfudr Ceredig'n 26 B5
Rhydlewis Ceredig'n 25 B8
Rhydlios Gwyn 36 B1
Rhydlydan Conwy 47 G8
Rhydnest Powys 28 D2
Rhydowen Ceredig'n 25 B9
Rhydspence Heref'd 28 D3
Rhydtalog Flints 48 G3
Rhydwyn Angl 46 D3
Rhydycroesau Shrops 38 B3
Rhydyfelin Ceredig'n 36 H5
Rhydyfelin Rh Cyn Taff 16 C5
Rhydymain Gwyn 37 C8
Rhydymwyn Flints 48 F3
Rhyl Denbs 47 D10
Rhymney Caerph 28 H2
Rhynd Fife 85 B6
Rhynd Perth/Kinr 84 B3
Rhynie Aberds 98 F4
Rhynie H'land 103 E7
Ribbesford Worcs 29 A8
Ribble Head N Yorks 62 G2
Ribbleton Lancs 55 E5
Ribchester Lancs 56 E1
Ribigill H'land 105 D8
Riby Lincs 52 B4
Riby Cross Roads Lincs 52 B4
Riccall N Yorks 58 E2
Riccarton E Ayrs 75 D6
Richards Castle Heref'd 28 B5
Richings Park Bucks 21 D8
Richmond London 21 D9
Richmond N Yorks 63 D6
Rickarton Aberds 91 C9
Rickinghall Suffolk 44 H4
Rickleton Tyne/Wear 71 E7
Rickling Essex 33 E7
Rickmansworth Herts 21 B8
Riddings Cumb 69 C7
Riddings Derby 51 G6
Riddlecombe Devon 7 E7
Riddlesden W Yorks 56 D5
Riddrie Glasg C 83 H7
Ridge Dorset 10 F2
Ridge Hants 11 C6
Ridge Wilts 10 A2
Ridge Green Surrey 22 G3
Ridge Lane Warwick 40 F4
Ridgebourne Powys 28 B1
Ridgehill N Som'set 18 E2
Ridgeway Cross Heref'd 29 D8
Ridgewell Essex 33 D10
Ridgewood E Sussex 13 D8
Ridgmont Beds 32 E2
Riding Mill Northum 70 D5
Ridleywood Wrex 48 G5
Ridlington Norfolk 45 B7
Ridlington Rutl'd 41 E10
Ridsdale Northum 70 B4
Riechip Perth/Kinr 90 G1
Riemore Perth/Kinr 90 G1
Rienachait H'land 104 F3
Rievaulx N Yorks 64 F3
Rievaulx Abbey N Yorks 64 F3
Rift House Hartlep'l 71 G9
Rigg Dumf/Gal 68 D5
Riggend N Lanarks 83 G8
Rigsby Lincs 53 E7
Rigside S Lanarks 76 D1
Riley Green Lancs 55 F6
Rileyhill Staffs 40 D3
Rilla Mill Cornw'l 4 C3
Rillington N Yorks 65 G6
Rimington Lancs 56 D3
Rimpton Som'set 9 B8
Rimswell ER Yorks 59 F9
Rinaston Pembs 24 D4
Ringasta Shetl'd 111 M6
Ringford Dumf/Gal 67 E8
Ringinglow S Yorks 50 D4
Ringland Norfolk 44 D5
Ringles Cross E Sussex 13 C8
Ringmer E Sussex 13 D8
Ringmore Devon 5 F7
Ringorm Moray 98 D2
Ring's End Cambs 43 E6
Ringsfield Suffolk 45 G8
Ringsfield Corner Suffolk 45 G8
Ringshall Herts 32 G2
Ringshall Suffolk 34 C4
Ringshall Stocks Suffolk 34 C4
Ringstead Norfolk 43 A10
Ringstead Northants 42 H2
Ringwood Hants 10 D4
Ringwould Kent 15 D8
Rinmore Aberds 98 G4
Rinnigill Orkney 110 J4
Rinsey Cornw'l 2 G4
Riof W Isles 108 D6
Ripe E Sussex 13 D9
Ripley Derby 50 G5
Ripley Hants 10 E4
Ripley N Yorks 57 B7
Ripley Surrey 21 F8
Riplingham ER Yorks 58 E5
Ripon N Yorks 63 G8
Ripon Cathedral N Yorks 63 G8
Ripon Racecourse N Yorks 57 B8
Rippingale Lincs 42 C3
Ripple Kent 15 D8
Ripple Worcs 29 E9
Ripponden W Yorks 56 G5
Rireavach H'land 101 C8
Risabus Arg/Bute 72 C3
Risbury Heref'd 29 C6
Risby Suffolk 34 B1
Risca Caerph 17 B7
Rise ER Yorks 59 D7
Riseden E Sussex 13 B10
Risegate Lincs 42 C5
Riseholme Lincs 52 E2
Riseley Beds 32 B3
Riseley Wokingham 20 E5
Rishangles Suffolk 34 B5
Rishton Lancs 56 E2
Rishworth W Yorks 56 G5
Rising Bridge Lancs 56 F2
Risley Derby 41 B6
Risley Warrington 49 C7
Risplith N Yorks 57 B7
Rispond H'land 105 C7
Rivar Wilts 19 E10
Rivenhall End Essex 34 G2
River Bank Cambs 33 B8
Riverhead Kent 22 F5
Rivington Lancs 56 G1
Roa Island Cumb 55 B2
Roachill Devon 7 D9
Road Green Norfolk 45 F6
Roade Northants 31 C9
Roadhead Cumb 69 C8
Roadmeetings S Lanarks 76 C1
Roadside H'land 107 C6
Roadside of Catterline Aberds 91 D9
Roadside of Kinneff Aberds 91 D9
Roadwater Som'set 16 H5
Roag H'land 93 A8
Roath Card 17 D6
Rob Roy and Trossachs Visitor Centre, Callander Stirl 83 D7
Robert Burns Centre Dumf/Gal 68 C2
Roberton Scot Borders 77 F7
Roberton S Lanarks 76 E2
Robertsbridge E Sussex 14 F2
Roberttown W Yorks 57 F6
Robeston Cross Pembs 24 F3
Robeston Wathen Pembs 24 E5
Robin Hood W Yorks 57 F8
Robin Hood's Bay N Yorks 65 D7
Roborough Devon 7 E6
Roborough Devon 5 D6
Roby Mersey 48 C5
Roby Mill Lancs 49 B6
Rocester Staffs 40 B3
Roch Pembs 24 D3
Roch Gate Pembs 24 D3
Rochdale Gtr Man 56 G3
Roche Cornw'l 3 C8
Rochester Medway 14 B2
Rochester Northum 78 H3
Rochester Castle Medway 14 B2
Rochester Cathedral Medway 14 B2
Rochford Essex 23 B8
Rock Cornw'l 3 B8
Rock Northum 79 E7
Rock Worcs 29 A8
Rock W Sussex 12 D5
Rock Ferry Mersey 48 D4
Rockbeare Devon 8 E2
Rockbourne Hants 10 C4
Rockcliffe Cumb 69 D6
Rockcliffe Dumf/Gal 68 E1
Rockfield H'land 103 D8
Rockfield Monmouths 28 G5
Rockford Hants 10 D4
Rockhampton S Gloucs 18 B3
Rockingham Northants 42 F1
Rockland All Saints Norfolk 44 F3
Rockland St. Mary Norfolk 45 E7
Rockland St. Peter Norfolk 44 F3
Rockley Wilts 19 D8
Rockwell End Bucks 20 C5
Rockwell Green Som'set 8 B3
Rodborough Glos 18 A5
Rodbourne Swindon 19 C8
Rodbourne Wilts 19 C6
Rodbourne Cheney Swindon 19 C8
Rodd Heref'd 28 B4
Roddam Northum 78 E5
Rodden Dorset 9 F8
Rode Som'set 18 F5
Rode Heath Ches 49 G9
Rodeheath Ches 49 F9
Roden Telford 39 D6
Rodhuish Som'set 16 H5
Rodington Telford 39 D6
Rodley Glos 29 G8
Rodley W Yorks 57 E7

Rodmarton Glos 19 B6
Rodmell E Sussex 13 E8
Rodmersham Kent 14 B4
Rodney Stoke Som'set 17 F9
Rodsley Derby 40 A4
Rodway Som'set 17 H7
Rodwell Dorset 9 G8
Roe Green Herts 33 E6
Roecliffe N Yorks 57 B8
Roehampton London 22 D2
Roesound Shetl'd 111 G6
Roffey W Sussex 12 B5
Rogart H'land 102 B6
Rogart Station H'land 102 B6
Rogate W Sussex 12 C2
Rogerstone Newp 17 C7
Roghadal W Isles 109 J5
Rogiet Monmouths 17 C9
Rogue's Alley Cambs 43 E6
Roisinis W Isles 92 D3
Roke Oxon 20 B4
Roker Tyne/Wear 71 E9
Rollesby Norfolk 45 D8
Rolleston Leics 41 E9
Rolleston Notts 51 G9
Rolleston on Dove Staffs 40 C4
Rolston ER Yorks 59 D8
Rolvenden Kent 14 E3
Rolvenden Layne Kent 14 E3
Romaldkirk Durham 62 B4
Roman Baths & Pump Room Bath/NE Som'set 18 E4
Romanby N Yorks 63 E8
Romannobridge Scot Borders 76 C4
Romansleigh Devon 7 D8
Romford London 22 C5
Romiley Gtr Man 49 C10
Romney, Hythe and Dymchurch Railway & Museum Kent 15 E6
Romsey Hants 11 B6
Romsey Town Cambs 33 C7
Romsley Shrops 39 G8
Romsley Worcs 40 H1
Ronague I/Man 54 E2
Rookhope Durham 70 F4
Rookley I/Wight 11 F8
Rooks Bridge Som'set 17 F8
Roos ER Yorks 59 E8
Roosebeck Cumb 55 B2
Rootham's Green Beds 32 C4
Rootpark S Lanarks 76 B2
Ropley Hants 11 A9
Ropley Dean Hants 11 A9
Ropsley Lincs 42 B2
Rora Aberds 99 C10
Rorandle Aberds 99 G6
Rorrington Shrops 38 E4
Roscroggan Cornw'l 2 E5
Rose Cornw'l 3 D6
Rose Ash Devon 7 D8
Rose Green W Sussex 12 F3
Rose Grove Lancs 56 E3
Rose Hill E Sussex 13 D8
Rose Hill Lancs 56 E3
Rose Hill Suffolk 34 D5
Roseacre Kent 14 C2
Roseacre Lancs 55 E4
Rosebank S Lanarks 75 C10
Rosebrough Northum 79 E6
Rosebush Pembs 24 D5
Rosecare Cornw'l 6 G2
Rosedale Abbey N Yorks 64 E5
Roseden Northum 78 E5
Rosefield H'land 103 G7
Rosehall H'land 102 B3
Rosehaugh Mains H'land 102 G5
Rosehearty Aberds 99 B9
Rosehill Shrops 39 B7
Roseisle Moray 103 F10
Roselands E Sussex 13 E10
Rosemarket Pembs 24 F4
Rosemarkie H'land 102 G6
Rosemary Lane Devon 8 C3
Rosemount Perth/Kinr 90 G2
Rosenannon Cornw'l 3 C8
Rosewell Midloth 76 A5
Roseworth Stockton 63 B9
Roseworthy Cornw'l 2 F5
Rosgill Cumb 61 C8
Roshven H'land 87 D7
Roskhill H'land 109 N7
Roskill House H'land 102 G5
Rosley Cumb 69 F6
Roslin Midloth 76 A5
Rosliston Derby 40 D4
Rosneath Arg/Bute 82 F3
Ross Dumf/Gal 67 F8
Ross Northum 79 D6
Ross Perth/Kinr 83 B8
Ross on Wye Heref'd 29 F7
Rossett Wrex 48 G4
Rossett Green N Yorks 57 C8
Rossie Ochill Perth/Kinr 84 C2
Rossie Priory Perth/Kinr 84 A4
Rossington S Yorks 51 C8
Rosskeen H'land 102 F5
Rossland Renf 82 G5
Roster H'land 107 F7
Rostherne Ches 49 D8
Rosthwaite Cumb 60 C5
Roston Derby 40 A3
Rosyth Fife 84 F3
Rothbury Northum 78 G5
Rotherby Leics 41 D8
Rotherfield E Sussex 13 C9
Rotherfield Greys Oxon 20 C5
Rotherfield Peppard Oxon 20 C5
Rotherham S Yorks 51 C6
Rothersthorpe Northants 31 C9
Rotherwick Hants 20 F5
Rothes Moray 98 D2
Rothesay Arg/Bute 74 A2
Rothiebrisbane Aberds 99 E7
Rothiemurchus Estate Visitor Centre H'land 97 F7
Rothienorman Aberds 99 E7
Rothiesholm Orkney 110 F7
Rothley Leics 41 D7
Rothley Northum 70 B5
Rothley Shield East Northum 70 A5
Rothmaise Aberds 99 E6
Rothwell Lincs 52 C4
Rothwell Northants 41 G10
Rothwell W Yorks 57 F8
Rothwell Haigh W Yorks 57 F8
Rotsea ER Yorks 59 C6
Rottal Angus 90 E4
Rotten End Suffolk 35 B7
Rottingdean Brighton/Hove 13 E7
Rottington Cumb 60 C2
Rotunda, Folkestone Kent 15 E7
Roud I/Wight 11 F8
Rough Close Staffs 39 B10
Rough Common Kent 15 C6
Rougham Norfolk 44 C2
Rougham Suffolk 34 B3
Rougham Green Suffolk 34 B3
Roughburn H'land 88 C4
Roughlee Lancs 56 D3
Roughley W Midlands 40 F3
Roughsike Cumb 69 C8
Roughton Lincs 52 F5
Roughton Norfolk 45 B6
Roughton Shrops 39 F8
Roughton Moor Lincs 52 F5
Roundhay W Yorks 57 E8
Roundstonefoot Dumf/Gal 76 G4
Roundstreet Common W Sussex 12 C4
Roundway Wilts 19 E7
Rous Lench Worcs 30 C2
Rousdon Devon 8 E4
Routenburn N Ayrs 74 A3
Routh ER Yorks 59 D6
Row Cornw'l 3 B9
Row Cumb 61 F7
Row Green Essex 33 F10
Row Heath Essex 34 G5
Rowanburn Dumf/Gal 69 C7
Rowardennan Stirl 82 E4
Rowde Wilts 19 E6
Rowen Conwy 47 E7
Rowfoot Northum 69 D9
Rowhedge Essex 34 F4
Rowhook W Sussex 12 B5
Rowington Warwick 30 B4
Rowland Derby 50 E4
Rowland's Castle Hants 11 C10
Rowlands Gill Tyne/Wear 71 E6
Rowledge Surrey 21 G6
Rowley ER Yorks 58 E5
Rowley Shrops 38 E4
Rowley Hill W Yorks 57 G6
Rowley Regis W Midlands 40 G1
Rowlstone Heref'd 28 F4
Rowly Surrey 21 G8
Rowney Green Worcs 30 A2
Rownhams Hants 11 C6
Rowrah Cumb 60 C3
Rowsham Bucks 31 G10
Rowsley Derby 50 F4
Rowstock Oxon 20 C2
Rowston Lincs 52 G3
Rowton Ches 48 F5
Rowton Shrops 38 D4
Rowton Telford 39 D7
Roxburgh Scot Borders 78 D2
Roxby N Lincs 58 G5
Roxby N Yorks 64 C5
Roxton Beds 32 C4
Roxwell Essex 33 H9
Royal Botanic Gardens C/Edinb 84 G4
Royal Leamington Spa Warwick 30 B5
Royal Museum of Scotland C/Edinb 84 G4
Royal Oak D'lington 63 B7
Royal Oak Lancs 48 B5
Royal Pavilion Brighton/Hove 13 E7
Royal Tunbridge Wells Kent 13 B9
Royal Welch Fusiliers Regimental Museum (See Caernarfon Castle) Gwyn 46 F4
Royal Worcester Porcelain Worcs 29 C9
Roybridge H'land 88 C3
Roydhouse W Yorks 57 G7
Roydon Essex 33 H7
Roydon Norfolk 43 C10
Roydon Norfolk 44 G4
Roydon Hamlet Essex 33 H7
Royston Herts 33 D6
Royston S Yorks 57 G8
Royton Gtr Man 49 B10
Rozel Jersey 4
Ruabon Wrex 38 A4
Ruadh phort Mor Arg/Bute 80 G4
Ruaig Arg/Bute 86 D2
Ruan Lanihorne Cornw'l 3 E7
Ruan Minor Cornw'l 3 H6
Ruarach H'land 95 D6
Ruardean Glos 29 G7
Ruardean Woodside Glos 29 G7
Rubery Worcs 40 H1
Ruckcroft Cumb 69 F8
Ruckhall Common Heref'd 28 E5
Ruckinge Kent 14 E5
Ruckland Lincs 53 E6
Ruckley Shrops 39 E6
Rudbaxton Pembs 24 D4
Rudby N Yorks 63 D9
Ruddington Notts 41 B7
Rudford Glos 29 F8
Rudge Shrops 39 F9
Rudge Som'set 18 F5
Rudgeway S Gloucs 18 C3
Rudgwick W Sussex 12 B4
Rudhall Heref'd 29 F7
Rudheath Ches 49 E7
Rudley Green Essex 23 A8
Rudry Caerph 17 C6
Rudston ER Yorks 59 B6
Rudyard Staffs 50 G1
Rufford Lancs 55 G4
Rufforth C/York 57 C10
Rugby Warwick 41 H7
Rugeley Staffs 40 D2
Ruglen S Ayrs 74 G4
Ruilick H'land 96 B3
Ruishton Som'set 8 B4
Ruisigearraidh W Isles 109 J4
Ruislip London 21 C8
Ruislip Common London 21 C8
Rumbling Bridge Perth/Kinr 84 E2
Rumburgh Suffolk 45 G7
Rumford Cornw'l 3 B7
Rumney Card 17 D7
Runcorn Halton 49 D6
Runcton W Sussex 12 E2
Runcton Holme Norfolk 43 E9
Rundlestone Devon 5 C6
Runfold Surrey 21 G6
Runhall Norfolk 44 E4
Runham Norfolk 45 E9
Runham Norfolk 45 D8
Runnington Som'set 8 B3
Runsell Green Essex 34 H1
Runswick Bay N Yorks 65 C6
Runwell Essex 23 B7
Ruscombe Wokingham 20 D5
Rush Green London 22 C5
Rushall Heref'd 29 E7
Rushall Norfolk 44 G5
Rushall Wilts 19 F8
Rushall W Midlands 40 E2
Rushbrooke Suffolk 34 B2
Rushbury Shrops 39 F6
Rushden Herts 33 E6
Rushden Northants 32 B2
Rushenden Kent 23 D9
Rushford Norfolk 44 G3
Rushlake Green E Sussex 13 D10
Rushmere Suffolk 45 G8
Rushmere St. Andrew Suffolk 35 D6
Rushmoor Surrey 21 G6
Rushmoor Wilts 10 C2
Rushock Worcs 29 A9
Rusholme Gtr Man 49 C9
Rushton Ches 49 F6
Rushton Northants 41 G10
Rushton Shrops 39 E7
Rushton Spencer Staffs 49 F10
Rushwick Worcs 29 C9
Rushyford Durham 63 B7
Ruskie Stirl 83 D7
Ruskington Lincs 52 G3
Rusland Cumb 61 F6
Rusper W Sussex 13 B6
Ruspidge Glos 29 G7
Russell's Water Oxon 20 C5
Russel's Green Suffolk 35 A6
Rusthall Kent 13 B9
Rustington W Sussex 12 E4
Ruston N Yorks 65 F7
Ruston Parva ER Yorks 59 B6
Ruswarp N Yorks 65 D6
Rutherford Scot Borders 77 D9
Rutherglen S Lanarks 75 A8
Ruthernbridge Cornw'l 3 C9
Ruthin Denbs 48 G2
Ruthin Craft Centre Denbs 48 G2
Ruthrieston Aberd C 91 A10
Ruthven Aberds 98 D5
Ruthven Angus 90 G3
Ruthven H'land 97 C6
Ruthven H'land 96 G5
Ruthven House Angus 90 G4
Ruthvoes Cornw'l 3 C8
Ruthwell Dumf/Gal 68 D3
Ruyton XI Towns Shrops 38 C4
Ryal Northum 70 C5
Ryal Fold Blackb'n 56 F1
Ryall Dorset 9 E6
Ryarsh Kent 14 C1
Rydal Cumb 61 D6
Ryde I/Wight 11 E8
Rye E Sussex 14 F4
Rye Foreign E Sussex 14 F3
Rye Harbour E Sussex 14 G4
Rye Park Herts 33 G6
Rye Street Worcs 29 E8
Ryecroft Gate Staffs 49 F10
Ryehill ER Yorks 59 F8
Ryhall Rutl'd 42 D3
Ryhill W Yorks 57 G8
Ryhope Tyne/Wear 71 E9
Rylstone N Yorks 56 C4
Ryme Intrinseca Dorset 9 C7
Ryther N Yorks 58 E1
Ryton Glos 29 E8
Ryton N Yorks 64 G5
Ryton Shrops 39 E8
Ryton Tyne/Wear 71 D6
Ryton on Dunsmore Warwick 30 A5

S

Sabden Lancs 56 E2
Sacombe Herts 33 G6
Sacriston Durham 71 F7
Sadberge D'lington 63 C8
Saddell Arg/Bute 73 D7
Saddington Leics 41 F8
Saddle Bow Norfolk 43 D9
Saddlescombe W Sussex 13 D6
Sadgill Cumb 61 D7
Saffron Walden Essex 33 E8
Sageston Pembs 24 F5
Saham Hills Norfolk 44 E3
Saham Toney Norfolk 44 E3
Saighdinis W Isles 109 L3
Saighton Ches 48 F5
Saint Hill W Sussex 13 B7
Saint Leonards S Lanarks 75 B8
Saintbury Glos 30 E3
Salcombe Devon 5 G8
Salcombe Regis Devon 8 F3
Salcott Essex 34 G3
Sale Gtr Man 49 C8
Sale Green Worcs 29 C10
Saleby Lincs 53 E7
Salehurst E Sussex 14 F2
Salem Ceredig'n 37 G6
Salem Carms 27 F6
Salen Arg/Bute 86 G5
Salen H'land 87 E6
Salesbury Lancs 56 E1
Salford Beds 32 E2
Salford Gtr Man 49 C9
Salford Oxon 30 F4
Salford Priors Warwick 30 C2
Salfords Surrey 22 G2
Salhouse Norfolk 45 D7
Saline Fife 84 E2
Salisbury Wilts 10 B4
Salisbury Cathedral Wilts 10 B4
Salisbury Racecourse Wilts 10 B3
Sallachan H'land 87 E9
Sallachy H'land 95 C6
Sallachy H'land 102 B4
Salle Norfolk 44 C5
Salmonby Lincs 53 E6
Salmond's Muir Angus 91 H6
Salperton Glos 30 F2
Salph End Beds 32 C3
Salsburgh N Lanarks 75 A10
Salt Staffs 40 C1
Salt End ER Yorks 59 F7
Saltaire W Yorks 57 E6
Saltaire 1853 Gallery W Yorks 57 E6
Saltash Cornw'l 4 E5
Saltburn H'land 102 F6
Saltburn by the Sea Redcar/Clevel'd 64 B4
Saltby Leics 42 C1
Saltcoats Cumb 60 E3
Saltcoats N Ayrs 74 C4
Saltdean Brighton/Hove 13 E7
Salter Lancs 55 B6
Salterforth Lancs 56 D3
Salterswall Ches 49 F7
Saltfleet Lincs 53 C7
Saltfleetby All Saints Lincs 53 C7
Saltfleetby St. Clements Lincs 53 C7
Saltfleetby St. Peter Lincs 53 D7
Saltford Bath/NE Som'set 18 E3
Salthouse Norfolk 44 A4
Saltmarshe ER Yorks 58 F3
Saltney Flints 48 F4
Salton N Yorks 64 G5
Saltwick Northum 71 C6
Saltwood Kent 15 E6
Salum Arg/Bute 86 D2
Salvington W Sussex 12 E5
Salwarpe Worcs 29 B9
Salway Ash Dorset 9 E6
Sambourne Warwick 30 B2
Sambrook Telford 39 C8
Samhla W Isles 109 L2
Samlesbury Lancs 55 E5
Samlesbury Bottoms Lancs 55 F6
Sampford Arundel Som'set 8 C3
Sampford Brett Som'set 16 G5
Sampford Courtenay Devon 7 F7
Sampford Peverell Devon 8 C2
Sampford Spiney Devon 5 C6
Sampool Bridge Cumb 61 F7
Samuelston E Loth 85 G6
Sanachan H'land 94 B5
Sanaigmore Arg/Bute 80 G2
Sancreed Cornw'l 2 G3
Sancton ER Yorks 58 E5
Sand H'land 101 C7
Sand Shetl'd 111 J6
Sand Hole ER Yorks 58 E4
Sand Hutton N Yorks 58 C2
Sandaig H'land 94 F4
Sandal Magna W Yorks 57 G8
Sandale Cumb 68 F5
Sandbach Ches 49 F8
Sandbank Arg/Bute 82 F2
Sandbanks Poole 10 F3
Sandend Aberds 98 B5
Sanderstead London 22 E3
Sandfields Glos 29 F10
Sandford Cumb 62 C2
Sandford Devon 7 F9
Sandford Dorset 10 F2
Sandford I/Wight 11 F8
Sandford N Som'set 17 F9
Sandford Shrops 39 B6
Sandford S Lanarks 75 C9
Sandford on Thames Oxon 20 A3
Sandford Orcas Dorset 9 B8
Sandford St. Martin Oxon 31 F6
Sandfordhill Aberds 99 D11
Sandgarth Orkney 110 G6
Sandgate Kent 15 E6
Sandgreen Dumf/Gal 67 E7
Sandhaven Aberds 99 B9
Sandhead Dumf/Gal 66 F2
Sandhills Surrey 12 B3
Sandhoe Northum 70 D4
Sandholme ER Yorks 58 E4
Sandholme Lincs 43 B6
Sandhurst Brackn'l 21 E6
Sandhurst Glos 29 F9
Sandhurst Kent 14 F2
Sandhurst Cross Kent 14 F2
Sandhutton N Yorks 63 F8
Sandiacre Derby 41 B6
Sandilands Lincs 53 D8
Sandilands S Lanarks 76 D1
Sandiway Ches 49 E7
Sandleheath Hants 10 C4
Sandling Kent 14 C2
Sandlow Green Ches 49 F8
Sandness Shetl'd 111 H4
Sandon Essex 23 A7
Sandon Herts 33 E6
Sandon Staffs 39 B10
Sandown I/Wight 11 F8
Sandown Park Racecourse Surrey 21 E9
Sandplace Cornw'l 4 E3
Sandridge Herts 32 G4
Sandridge Wilts 19 E6
Sandringham Norfolk 43 C9
Sandsend N Yorks 65 C6
Sandside Ho. H'land 106 C4
Sandsound Shetl'd 111 J6
Sandtoft N Lincs 51 B9
Sandway Kent 14 C3
Sandwell W Midlands 40 G2
Sandwich Kent 15 C8
Sandwick Cumb 61 C7
Sandwick Orkney 110 K5
Sandwick Shetl'd 111 L7
Sandwith Cumb 60 C2
Sandy Beds 32 D4
Sandy Carms 25 F9
Sandy Bank Lincs 52 G5
Sandy Haven Pembs 24 F3
Sandy Lane Wilts 19 E6
Sandy Lane Wrex 38 A4
Sandycroft Flints 48 F4
Sandyford Dumf/Gal 68 A5
Sandyford Stoke 49 G9
Sandygate I/Man 54 C3
Sandyhills Dumf/Gal 68 E1
Sandylands Lancs 55 B4
Sandypark Devon 5 B8
Sandysike Cumb 69 D6
Sangobeg H'land 105 C7
Sangomore H'land 105 C7
Sanna H'land 86 E4
Sanndabhaig W Isles 108 D9
Sanndabhaig W Isles 92 A4
Sannox N Ayrs 74 C2
Sanquhar Dumf/Gal 75 G9
Santon N Lincs 58 G5
Santon Bridge Cumb 60 D4
Santon Downham Suffolk 44 G2
Sapcote Leics 41 F6
Sapey Common Heref'd 29 B8
Sapiston Suffolk 44 H3
Sapley Cambs 32 A5
Sapperton Glos 19 A6
Sapperton Lincs 42 B3
Saracen's Head Lincs 43 C6
Sarclet H'land 107 E8
Sardis Carms 25 F10
Sarn Bridg 16 C4
Sarn Powys 38 F3
Sarn Bach Gwyn 36 C3
Sarn Meyllteyrn Gwyn 36 B2
Sarnau Ceredig'n 26 C3
Sarnau Carms 25 E8
Sarnau Gwyn 37 B9
Sarnau Powys 27 E10
Sarnau Powys 38 D3
Sarnesfield Heref'd 28 C4
Saron Carms 25 C8
Saron Carms 27 G6
Saron Denbs 47 F10
Saron Gwyn 46 G4
Saron Gwyn 46 F5
Sarratt Herts 21 B8
Sarre Kent 15 B7
Sarsden Oxon 30 F4
Sarsgrum H'land 105 C6
Satley Durham 71 F6
Satron N Yorks 62 E4
Satterleigh Devon 7 D7
Satterthwaite Cumb 61 E6
Satwell Oxon 20 C5
Sauchen Aberds 99 G6
Saucher Perth/Kinr 84 A3
Sauchie Clack 83 E9
Sauchieburn Aberds 91 E7
Saughall Ches 48 E4
Saughtree Scot Borders 77 H8
Saul Glos 29 H8
Saundby Notts 51 D9
Saundersfoot Pembs 24 F6
Saunderton Bucks 20 A5
Saunton Devon 6 C5
Sausthorpe Lincs 53 F6
Saval H'land 102 B4
Savary H'land 87 G6
Savile Park W Yorks 56 F5
Sawbridge Warwick 31 B7
Sawbridgeworth Herts 33 G7
Sawdon N Yorks 65 F7
Sawley Derby 41 B6
Sawley Lancs 56 D2
Sawley N Yorks 57 B7
Sawston Cambs 33 D7
Sawtry Cambs 42 G4
Saxby Leics 41 D10
Saxby Lincs 52 D3
Saxby All Saints N Lincs 58 G5
Saxelby Leics 41 C9
Saxham Street Suffolk 34 B4
Saxilby Lincs 52 E1
Saxlingham Norfolk 44 B4
Saxlingham Green Norfolk 45 F6
Saxlingham Nethergate Norfolk 45 F6
Saxlingham Thorpe Norfolk 45 F6
Saxmundham Suffolk 35 B7
Saxon Street Cambs 33 C9
Saxondale Notts 41 B8
Saxtead Suffolk 35 B6
Saxtead Green Suffolk 35 B6
Saxthorpe Norfolk 44 B5
Saxton N Yorks 57 E9
Sayers Common W Sussex 13 D6
Scackleton N Yorks 64 G4
Scadabhagh W Isles 109 H6
Scaftworth Notts 51 C8
Scagglethorpe N Yorks 65 G6
Scaitcliffe Lancs 56 F2
Scalasaig Arg/Bute 80 E3
Scalby ER Yorks 58 F4
Scalby N Yorks 65 E8
Scaldwell Northants 31 A9
Scale Houses Cumb 69 F8
Scaleby Cumb 69 D7
Scaleby Hill Cumb 69 D7
Scales Cumb 60 G5
Scales Cumb 61 B6
Scales Lancs 55 E4
Scalford Leics 41 C9
Scaling N Yorks 64 C5
Scaling Dam Redcar/Clevel'd 64 C5
Scallastle Arg/Bute 87 H6
Scalloway Shetl'd 111 K7
Scalpay Ho. H'land 94 D3
Scalpsie Arg/Bute 74 B2
Scamadale H'land 87 B7
Scamblesby Lincs 52 E5
Scamodale H'land 87 D8
Scampston N Yorks 65 G6
Scampton Lincs 52 E2
Scapa Orkney 110 H5
Scapegoat Hill W Yorks 56 G5
Scar Orkney 110 D7
Scarborough N Yorks 65 F8
Scarborough Sea Life Centre N Yorks 65 E8
Scarcliffe Derby 51 F6
Scarcroft W Yorks 57 D8
Scarcroft Hill W Yorks 57 D8
Scardroy H'land 101 G10
Scarff Shetl'd 111 E5
Scarfskerry H'land 107 B7
Scargill Durham 62 C5
Scarinish Arg/Bute 86 D2
Scarisbrick Lancs 55 G3
Scarning Norfolk 44 D3
Scarrington Notts 41 A9
Scartho NE Lincs 52 B5
Scarwell Orkney 110 F3
Scat Ness Shetl'd 111 M6
Scatraig H'land 96 C5
Scawby N Lincs 52 B2
Scawsby S Yorks 51 B7
Scawton N Yorks 64 F3
Scayne's Hill W Sussex 13 C7
Scethrog Powys 28 F2
Scholar Green Ches 49 G9
Scholes W Yorks 50 B3
Scholes W Yorks 57 F6
Scholes W Yorks 57 E8
School Green Ches 49 F7
Science & Industry Museum Gtr Man 49 C9
Science Museum London 22 D2
Scleddau Pembs 24 C4
Sco Ruston Norfolk 45 C6
Scofton Notts 51 D8
Scole Norfolk 44 H5
Scolpaig W Isles 109 K2
Scone Palace Perth/Kinr 84 B3
Sconser H'land 94 C2
Scoonie Fife 84 D5
Scoor Arg/Bute 80 C4
Scopwick Lincs 52 G3
Scoraig H'land 101 C8
Scorborough ER Yorks 59 D6
Scorrier Cornw'l 3 E6
Scorton Lancs 55 D5
Scorton N Yorks 63 D7
Scotbheinn W Isles 109 M3
Scotby Cumb 69 E7
Scotforth Lancs 55 C4
Scothern Lincs 52 E3
Scotland Gate Northum 71 B7
Scotlandwell Perth/Kinr 84 D3
Scotney Castle Garden Kent 14 E1
Scotsburn H'land 102 E6
Scotscalder Station H'land 106 D5
Scotscraig Fife 84 B6
Scots'Gap Northum 70 B5
Scotston Aberds 91 D8
Scotston Perth/Kinr 89 G10
Scotstoun Glasg C 83 H6
Scotstown H'land 87 E8
Scotswood Tyne/Wear 71 D6
Scottas H'land 94 F4
Scotter Lincs 52 B1
Scotterthorpe Lincs 52 B1
Scottlethorpe Lincs 42 C3
Scotton Lincs 52 C1
Scotton N Yorks 63 E6
Scotton N Yorks 57 C8
Scottow Norfolk 45 C6
Scoughall E Loth 85 F8
Scoulag Arg/Bute 74 B3
Scoulton Norfolk 44 E3
Scourie H'land 104 E4
Scourie More H'land 104 E4
Scousburgh Shetl'd 111 M6
Scrabster H'land 106 B5
Scrafield Lincs 53 F6
Scrainwood Northum 78 G4
Scrane End Lincs 43 A6
Scraptoft Leics 41 E8
Scratby Norfolk 45 D9
Scrayingham N Yorks 58 B3
Scredington Lincs 42 A3
Scremby Lincs 53 F7
Scremerston Northum 78 C5
Screveton Notts 41 A9
Scrivelsby Lincs 52 F5
Scriven N Yorks 57 C8
Scrooby Notts 51 C8
Scropton Derby 40 B3
Scrub Hill Lincs 52 G5
Scruton N Yorks 63 E7
Sculcoates Kingston/Hull 59 E6
Sculthorpe Norfolk 44 B2
Scunthorpe N Lincs 58 G4
Scurlage Swan 25 H9
Sea Palling Norfolk 45 C8
Sea Zoo Angl 46 F4
Seaborough Dorset 9 D6
Seacombe Mersey 48 C4
Seacroft Lincs 53 F8
Seacroft W Yorks 57 E8
Seadyke Lincs 43 B6
Seafield S Ayrs 74 E5
Seafield W Loth 84 H2
Seaford E Sussex 13 F8
Seaforth Mersey 48 C4
Seagrave Leics 41 D8
Seaham Durham 71 F9
Seahouses Northum 79 D7
Seal Kent 22 F5
Seal Sanctuary, Gweek Cornw'l 3 G6
Sealand Flints 48 F4
Seale Surrey 21 G6
Seamer N Yorks 63 C9
Seamer N Yorks 65 F8
Seamill N Ayrs 74 C3
Searby Lincs 52 B3
Seasalter Kent 14 B5
Seascale Cumb 60 D3
Seater Orkney 110 D8
Seathorne Lincs 53 F8
Seathwaite Cumb 60 E5
Seathwaite Cumb 60 C5
Seatoller Cumb 60 C5
Seaton Cornw'l 4 E4
Seaton Cumb 68 G3
Seaton Devon 8 F4
Seaton Durham 71 E8
Seaton ER Yorks 59 D7
Seaton Northum 71 C8
Seaton Rutl'd 42 F2
Seaton Burn Tyne/Wear 71 C7
Seaton Carew Hartlep'l 64 B3
Seaton Delaval Northum 71 C8
Seaton Ross ER Yorks 58 D3
Seaton Sluice Northum 71 C8
Seatown Aberds 98 B5
Seatown Dorset 9 E6
Seave Green N Yorks 64 D3
Seaview I/Wight 11 E9
Seaville Cumb 68 E4
Seavington St. Mary Som'set 9 C6
Seavington St. Michael Som'set 9 C6
Sebergham Cumb 69 F6
Seckington Warwick 40 E4
Second Coast H'land 101 C7
Sedbergh Cumb 61 E9
Sedbury Glos 18 B2
Sedbusk N Yorks 62 E3
Sedgeberrow Worcs 30 E2
Sedgebrook Lincs 42 B1
Sedgefield Durham 63 B8
Sedgefield Racecourse Durham 63 B8
Sedgeford Norfolk 43 B10
Sedgehill Wilts 10 B1
Sedgley W Midlands 39 F10
Sedgwick Cumb 61 F8
Sedlescombe E Sussex 14 G2
Sedlescombe Street E Sussex 14 G2
Seend Wilts 19 E6
Seend Cleeve Wilts 19 E6
Seer Green Bucks 21 B7
Seething Norfolk 45 F7
Sefton Mersey 48 B4
Seghill Northum 71 C7
Seifton Shrops 38 G5
Seighford Staffs 39 C9
Seilebost W Isles 109 H5
Seion Gwyn 46 F5
Seisdon Staffs 39 F9
Seisiadar W Isles 108 D10
Selattyn Shrops 38 B3
Selborne Hants 11 A10
Selby N Yorks 58 E2
Selham W Sussex 12 C3
Selhurst London 22 E3
Selkirk Scot Borders 77 E7
Selkirk Glass Scot Borders 77 E7
Sellack Heref'd 29 F6
Sellafield Station Cumb 60 D3
Sellafield Visitors Centre Cumb 60 D3
Sellafirth Shetl'd 111 D8
Sellindge Kent 14 E5
Sellindge Lees Kent 15 E6
Selling Kent 14 C5
Sells Green Wilts 19 E6
Selly Oak W Midlands 40 G2
Selmeston E Sussex 13 E9
Selsdon London 22 E3
Selsey W Sussex 12 F2
Selsfield Common W Sussex 13 B7
Selsted Kent 15 D7
Selston Notts 51 G6
Selworthy Som'set 7 B10
Semblister Shetl'd 111 H6
Semer Suffolk 34 D3
Semington Wilts 18 E5
Semley Wilts 10 B1
Send Surrey 21 F8
Send Marsh Surrey 21 F8
Senghenydd Caerph 17 B6
Sennen Cornw'l 2 G2
Sennen Cove Cornw'l 2 G2
Sennybridge Powys 27 F9
Serlby Notts 51 D8
Sessay N Yorks 63 G9
Setchey Norfolk 43 D9
Setley Hants 11 D6
Setter Shetl'd 111 H6
Setter Shetl'd 111 E7
Setter Shetl'd 111 J8
Settiscarth Orkney 110 G4
Settle N Yorks 56 B3
Settrington N Yorks 65 G6
Seven Kings London 22 C4
Seven Sisters Neath P Talb 27 H8
Sevenhampton Glos 30 F2
Sevenoaks Kent 22 F5
Sevenoaks Weald Kent 22 F5
Severn Beach S Gloucs 18 C2
Severn Stoke Worcs 29 D9
Severn Valley Railway Worcs 39 H8
Severnhampton Swindon 19 B9
Sevington Kent 14 D5
Sewards End Essex 33 E8
Sewardstone Essex 22 B3
Sewardstonebury Essex 22 B3
Sewerby ER Yorks 59 B7
Sewerby Hall and Gardens, Bridlington ER Yorks 59 B8
Seworgan Cornw'l 3 F6
Sewstern Leics 42 C1
Sezincote Glos 30 E3
Sgarasta Mhor W Isles 109 H5
Sgiogarstaigh W Isles 108 A10
Shabbington Bucks 31 H8
Shackerstone Leics 40 E5
Shackleford Surrey 21 G7
Shade W Yorks 56 F4
Shadforth Durham 71 F8
Shadingfield Suffolk 45 G8
Shadoxhurst Kent 14 E4
Shadsworth Blackb'n 56 F2
Shadwell Norfolk 44 G3
Shadwell W Yorks 57 E8
Shaftesbury Dorset 10 B1
Shafton S Yorks 57 G8
Shakespeare's Birthplace, Stratford upon Avon Warwick 30 C4
Shalbourne Wilts 19 E10
Shalcombe I/Wight 11 F6
Shalden Hants 20 G4
Shaldon Devon 5 C10
Shalfleet I/Wight 11 F7
Shalford Essex 33 F10
Shalford Surrey 21 G8
Shalford Green Essex 33 F10
Shallowford Devon 7 B8
Shalmsford Street Kent 14 C5
Shalstone Bucks 31 E8
Shamley Green Surrey 21 G8
Shandon Arg/Bute 82 F3
Shandwick H'land 103 E7
Shangton Leics 41 F9
Shankend Scot Borders 77 G8
Shankhouse Northum 71 C7
Shanklin I/Wight 11 F8
Shanklin Chine I/Wight 11 F8
Shanquhar Aberds 98 E5
Shanzie Perth/Kinr 90 F3
Shap Cumb 61 C8
Shapwick Dorset 10 D2
Shapwick Som'set 17 H9
Shardlow Derby 41 B6
Shareshill Staffs 39 E10
Sharlston W Yorks 57 G8
Sharlston Common W Yorks 57 G8
Sharnbrook Beds 32 C2
Sharnford Leics 41 F6
Sharoe Green Lancs 55 E5
Sharow N Yorks 63 G8
Sharp Street Norfolk 45 C7
Sharpenhoe Beds 32 E3
Sharperton Northum 78 G4
Sharpness Glos 18 A3
Sharpthorne W Sussex 13 B7
Sharrington Norfolk 44 B4
Shatterford Worcs 39 G8
Shaugh Prior Devon 5 D6
Shavington Ches 49 G8
Shaw Gtr Man 49 B10
Shaw W Berks 20 E2
Shaw Wilts 18 E5
Shaw Green Lancs 55 G5
Shaw Mills N Yorks 57 B7
Shawbury Shrops 39 C6
Shawdon Hall Northum 78 F5
Shawell Leics 41 G7
Shawford Hants 11 B7
Shawforth Lancs 56 F3
Shawhead Dumf/Gal 68 C1
Shawhill Dumf/Gal 68 D5
Shawton S Lanarks 75 C8
Shawtonhill S Lanarks 75 C8
Shawwood E Ayrs 75 E7
Shear Cross Wilts 18 G5
Shearington Dumf/Gal 68 D3
Shearsby Leics 41 F8
Shebbear Devon 6 F5
Shebdon Staffs 39 C8
Shebster H'land 106 C5
Sheddens E Renf 75 B7
Shedfield Hants 11 C8
Sheen Staffs 50 F3
Sheepscar W Yorks 57 E8
Sheepscombe Glos 29 G9
Sheepstor Devon 5 D6
Sheepwash Devon 6 F5
Sheepway N Som'set 17 D9
Sheepy Magna Leics 40 E5
Sheepy Parva Leics 40 E5
Sheering Essex 33 G8
Sheerness Kent 23 D9
Sheet Hants 12 C1
Sheffield S Yorks 50 D5
Sheffield Bottom W Berks 20 E4
Sheffield Green E Sussex 13 C8
Sheffield Park, Uckfield E Sussex 13 C8
Shefford Beds 32 E4
Shefford Woodlands W Berks 20 D1
Sheigra H'land 104 C4
Sheinton Shrops 39 E7
Shelderton Shrops 38 H5
Sheldon Derby 50 F3
Sheldon Devon 8 D3
Sheldon W Midlands 40 G3
Sheldwich Kent 14 C5
Shelf W Yorks 57 F6
Shelfanger Norfolk 44 G5
Shelfield Warwick 30 B3
Shelfield W Midlands 40 E2
Shelford Notts 41 A8
Shellacres Northum 78 C3
Shelley Essex 22 A5
Shelley Suffolk 34 E4
Shelley W Yorks 57 G7
Shellingford Oxon 19 B10
Shellow Bowells Essex 33 H9
Shelsley Beauchamp Worcs 29 B8
Shelsley Walsh Worcs 29 B8
Shelthorpe Leics 41 D7
Shelton Beds 32 B3
Shelton Norfolk 45 F6
Shelton Notts 41 A9
Shelton Shrops 38 D5
Shelton Green Norfolk 45 F6
Shelve Shrops 38 F4
Shelwick Heref'd 29 D6
Shenfield Essex 23 B6
Shenington Oxon 30 D5
Shenley Herts 21 A9
Shenley Brook End M/Keynes 31 E10
Shenley Church End M/Keynes 31 E10
Shenleybury Herts 21 A9
Shenmore Heref'd 28 E4
Shennanton Dumf/Gal 66 D5
Shenstone Staffs 40 E3
Shenstone Worcs 29 A9
Shenton Leics 40 E5
Shenval H'land 96 D2
Shenval Moray 98 F2
Shepeau Stow Lincs 43 D6
Shephall Herts 32 F5
Shepherd's Green Oxon 20 C5
Shepherd's Port Norfolk 43 B9
Shepherdswell Kent 15 D7
Shepley W Yorks 50 B3
Shepperdine S Gloucs 18 B3
Shepperton Surrey 21 E8
Shepreth Cambs 33 D6
Shepshed Leics 41 D6
Shepton Beauchamp Som'set 9 C6
Shepton Mallet Som'set 18 G3
Shepton Montague Som'set 9 A8
Shepway Kent 14 C2
Sheraton Durham 71 G9
Sherborne Dorset 9 C8
Sherborne Glos 30 G3
Sherborne St. John Hants 20 F4
Sherbourne Warwick 30 B4
Sherburn Durham 71 F8
Sherburn N Yorks 65 G7
Sherburn Hill Durham 71 F8
Sherburn in Elmet N Yorks 57 E9
Shere Surrey 21 G8
Shereford Norfolk 44 C2
Sherfield English Hants 10 B5
Sherfield on Loddon Hants 20 F4
Sherford Devon 5 F8
Sheriff Hutton N Yorks 58 B2
Sheriffhales Shrops 39 D8
Sheringham Norfolk 44 A5
Sherington M/Keynes 32 D1
Shernal Green Worcs 29 B10
Shernborne Norfolk 43 B10
Sherrington Wilts 19 H6
Sherston Wilts 18 C5
Sherwood Green Devon 7 D6
Shettleston Glasg C 75 A8
Shevington Gtr Man 49 B6
Shevington Moor Gtr Man 55 G5
Shevington Vale Gtr Man 49 B6
Sheviock Cornw'l 4 E4
Shide I/Wight 11 F7
Shiel Bridge H'land 95 E6
Shieldaig H'land 101 G6
Shieldaig H'land 101 E6
Shieldhill Falk 83 G9
Shieldhill S Lanarks 76 C3
Shielfoot H'land 87 E6
Shielhill Angus 90 F5
Shielhill Invercl 82 G3
Shifford Oxon 20 A1
Shifnal Shrops 39 E8
Shilbottle Northum 79 G6
Shildon Durham 63 B7
Shillingford Devon 8 B1
Shillingford Oxon 20 B3
Shillingford St. George Devon 5 B10
Shillingstone Dorset 9 C10
Shillington Beds 32 E4
Shillmoor Northum 78 G3
Shilton Oxon 30 H4
Shilton Warwick 41 G6
Shilvington Northum 71 B6
Shimpling Norfolk 44 G5
Shimpling Suffolk 34 C2
Shimpling Street Suffolk 34 C2
Shincliffe Durham 71 F7
Shiney Row Tyne/Wear 71 E8
Shinfield Wokingham 20 E5
Shingham Norfolk 44 E1
Shingle Street Suffolk 35 D7
Shinner's Bridge Devon 5 D8
Shinness H'land 102 A4
Shipbourne Kent 22 F5
Shipdham Norfolk 44 E3
Shipham Som'set 17 F9
Shiphay Torbay 5 D9
Shiplake Oxon 20 D5
Shipley Derby 41 A6
Shipley Northum 79 F6
Shipley Shrops 39 F9
Shipley W Sussex 12 C5
Shipley W Yorks 57 E6
Shipley Shiels Northum 70 A2
Shipmeadow Suffolk 45 G7
Shippea Hill Sta. Cambs 43 G9
Shippon Oxon 20 B2
Shipston on Stour Warwick 30 D4
Shipton Glos 30 G2
Shipton N Yorks 58 C1
Shipton Shrops 39 F6
Shipton Bellinger Hants 19 G9
Shipton Gorge Dorset 9 E6
Shipton Green W Sussex 12 E2
Shipton Moyne Glos 18 C5
Shipton on Cherwell Oxon 31 G6
Shipton Solers Glos 30 G2
Shipton under Wychwood Oxon 30 G4
Shiptonthorpe ER Yorks 58 D4
Shirburn Oxon 20 B4
Shirdley Hill Lancs 55 G3
Shire Horse Centre, Stratford upon Avon Warwick 30 C4
Shirebrook Derby 51 F7
Shiregreen S Yorks 50 C5
Shirehampton Bristol 18 D2
Shiremoor Tyne/Wear 71 C8
Shirenewton Monmouths 17 B9
Shireoaks Notts 51 D7
Shirkoak Kent 14 E4
Shirl Heath Heref'd 28 C5
Shirland Derby 50 G5
Shirley Derby 40 A4
Shirley London 22 E3
Shirley S'thampton 11 C7
Shirley W Midlands 40 H3
Shirrell Heath Hants 11 C8
Shirwell Devon 7 C6
Shirwell Cross Devon 7 C6
Shiskine N Ayrs 73 E9
Shobdon Heref'd 28 B5
Shobnall Staffs 40 C4
Shobrooke Devon 7 F9
Shoby Leics 41 D8
Shocklach Ches 48 H5
Shoeburyness Southend 23 C9
Sholden Kent 15 C8
Sholing S'thampton 11 C7
Shoot Hill Shrops 38 D5
Shop Cornw'l 6 E3
Shop Cornw'l 3 B7
Shop Corner Suffolk 35 E6
Shore Mill H'land 103 F6
Shoreditch London 22 C3
Shoreham Kent 22 E5
Shoreham By Sea W Sussex 13 E6
Shoresdean Northum 78 C4
Shoreswood Northum 78 C4
Shoreton H'land 102 F5
Shorncote Glos 19 B7
Shorne Kent 23 D6
Short Heath W Midlands 40 E1
Shortacombe Devon 5 B6
Shortgate E Sussex 13 D8
Shortlanesend Cornw'l 3 E7
Shortlees E Ayrs 75 D6
Shortstown Beds 32 D3
Shorwell I/Wight 11 F7
Shoscombe Bath/NE Som'set 18 F4
Shotatton Shrops 38 C4
Shotesham Norfolk 45 F6
Shotgate Essex 23 B7
Shotley Suffolk 35 E6
Shotley Bridge Durham 70 E5
Shotley Gate Suffolk 35 E6
Shotleyfield Northum 70 E5
Shottenden Kent 14 C5
Shottermill Surrey 12 B2
Shottery Warwick 30 C3
Shotteswell Warwick 31 D6
Shottisham Suffolk 35 D7
Shottle Derby 50 H5
Shottlegate Derby 50 H5
Shotton Durham 71 G9
Shotton Flints 48 F4
Shotton Northum 78 D3
Shotton Colliery Durham 71 F8
Shotts N Lanarks 76 A1
Shotwick Ches 48 E4
Shouldham Norfolk 43 E9
Shouldham Thorpe Norfolk 43 E9
Shoulton Worcs 29 C9
Shover's Green E Sussex 14 E1
Shrawardine Shrops 38 D5
Shrawley Worcs 29 B9
Shrewley Common Warwick 30 B4
Shrewsbury Shrops 38 D5
Shrewton Wilts 19 G7
Shripney W Sussex 12 E3
Shrivenham Oxon 19 C9
Shropham Norfolk 44 F3
Shrub End Essex 34 F3
Shucknall Heref'd 29 D6
Shudy Camps Cambs 33 D9
Shulishaderbeg H'land 94 B1
Shurdington Glos 29 G10
Shurlock Row Windsor 21 D6
Shurrery H'land 106 D5
Shurrery Lodge H'land 106 D5
Shurton Som'set 17 G7
Shustoke Warwick 40 F4
Shute Devon 8 E4
Shute Devon 7 F9
Shutford Oxon 30 D5
Shuthonger Glos 29 E9
Shutlanger Northants 31 C9
Shuttington Warwick 40 E4
Shuttlewood Derby 51 E6
Siabost bho Dheas W Isles 108 C7
Siabost bho Thuath W Isles 108 C7
Siadar W Isles 108 B8
Siadar Iarach W Isles 108 B8
Siadar Uarach W Isles 108 B8
Sibbaldbie Dumf/Gal 68 B4
Sibbertoft Northants 41 G8
Sibdon Carwood Shrops 38 G5
Sibford Ferris Oxon 30 E5
Sibford Gower Oxon 30 E5
Sible Hedingham Essex 34 E1
Sibsey Lincs 53 G6
Sibson Cambs 42 F3
Sibson Leics 40 E5
Sibthorpe Notts 51 H9
Sibton Suffolk 35 B7
Sibton Green Suffolk 35 A7
Sicklesmere Suffolk 34 B2
Sicklinghall N Yorks 57 D8
Sid Devon 8 F3
Sidbury Devon 8 E3
Sidbury Shrops 39 G7
Sidcot N Som'set 17 F9
Sidcup London 22 D4
Siddick Cumb 68 G3
Siddington Ches 49 E9
Siddington Glos 19 B7
Sidemoor Worcs 30 A1
Sidestrand Norfolk 45 B6
Sidford Devon 8 E3
Sidlesham W Sussex 12 F2
Sidley E Sussex 14 H2
Sidlow Surrey 22 G2
Sidmouth Devon 8 F3
Sigford Devon 5 C8
Sigglesthorne ER Yorks 59 D7
Sighthill C/Edinb 84 G3
Sigingstone V/Glam 16 D4
Signet Oxon 30 G4
Silchester Hants 20 E4
Sildinis W Isles 108 F7
Sileby Leics 41 D7
Silecroft Cumb 60 F4
Silfield Norfolk 44 F5
Silian Ceredig'n 26 C5
Silk Willoughby Lincs 42 A3
Silkstone S Yorks 50 B4
Silkstone Common S Yorks 50 B4
Silloth Cumb 68 E4
Sills Northum 78 G3
Sillyearn Moray 98 C5
Siloh Carms 27 E7
Silpho N Yorks 65 E7
Silsden W Yorks 56 D5
Silsoe Beds 32 E3
Silver End Essex 34 G2
Silverburn Midloth 76 A5
Silverdale Lancs 61 G7
Silverdale Staffs 49 H9
Silvergate Norfolk 44 C5
Silverhill E Sussex 14 G2
Silverley's Green Suffolk 45 H6
Silverstone Northants 31 D8
Silverton Devon 8 D1
Silvington Shrops 39 H7
Silwick Shetl'd 111 J5
Simmondley Derby 50 C2
Simonburn Northum 70 C3
Simonsbath Som'set 7 C8
Simonstone Lancs 56 E2
Simprim Scot Borders 78 C3
Simpson M/Keynes 32 E1
Simpson Cross Pembs 24 E3
Sinclair's Hill Scot Borders 78 B3
Sinclairston E Ayrs 75 F6
Sinderby N Yorks 63 F8
Sinderhope Northum 70 E3
Sindlesham Wokingham 20 E5
Singdean Scot Borders 77 G8
Singleborough Bucks 31 E9
Singleton Lancs 55 E3
Singleton W Sussex 12 D2
Singlewell Kent 23 D6
Sinkhurst Green Kent 14 D3
Sinnahard Aberds 98 G4
Sinnington N Yorks 64 F5
Sinton Green Worcs 29 B9
Sipson London 21 D8
Sirhowy Bl Gwent 28 G2
Sisland Norfolk 45 F7
Sissinghurst Kent 14 E2
Sissinghurst, Cranbrook Kent 14 E3
Sisterpath Scot Borders 78 C2
Siston S Gloucs 18 D3
Sithney Cornw'l 2 G5
Sittingbourne Kent 14 B3
Six Ashes Staffs 39 G8
Six Hills Leics 41 C8
Six Mile Bottom Cambs 33 C8
Sixhills Lincs 52 D4
Sixpenny Handley Dorset 10 C2
Sizewell Suffolk 35 B8
Skail H'land 106 E2
Skaill Orkney 110 G3
Skaill Orkney 110 E5
Skaill Orkney 110 H6
Skares E Ayrs 75 F7
Skarpigarth Shetl'd 111 J4
Skateraw E Loth 85 G9
Skaw Shetl'd 111 G8
Skeabost H'land 109 N9
Skeabrae Orkney 110 F3
Skeeby N Yorks 63 D7
Skeffington Leics 41 E9
Skeffling ER Yorks 59 G9
Skegby Notts 51 F6
Skegness Lincs 53 F8
Skelberry Shetl'd 111 M6
Skelbo H'land 103 C6
Skelbrooke S Yorks 57 G10
Skeldyke Lincs 43 B6
Skellingthorpe Lincs 52 E2
Skellister Shetl'd 111 H7
Skellow S Yorks 57 G10
Skelmanthorpe W Yorks 57 G7
Skelmersdale Lancs 48 B5
Skelmonae Aberds 99 E8
Skelmorlie N Ayrs 82 H2
Skelmuir Aberds 99 D9
Skelpick H'land 106 D2
Skelton Cumb 69 G7
Skelton ER Yorks 58 F3
Skelton N Yorks 62 D5
Skelton Redcar/Clevel'd 64 C4
Skelton C/York 58 C1
Skelton on Ure N Yorks 57 B8
Skelwick Orkney 110 D5
Skelwith Bridge Cumb 61 D6
Skendleby Lincs 53 F7
Skene Ho. Aberds 99 H7
Skenfrith Monmouths 28 F5
Skerne ER Yorks 59 C6
Skeroblingarry Arg/Bute 73 E7
Skerray H'land 105 C9
Skerton Lancs 55 B4
Sketchley Leics 41 F6
Sketty Swan 16 B1
Skewen Neath P Talb 16 B2
Skewsby N Yorks 64 G4
Skeyton Norfolk 45 C6
Skiag Bridge H'land 104 G5
Skibo Castle H'land 102 D6
Skidbrooke Lincs 53 C7
Skidbrooke North End Lincs 53 C7
Skidby ER Yorks 59 E6
Skilgate Som'set 8 B1
Skillington Lincs 42 C1
Skinburness Cumb 68 E4
Skinflats Falk 83 F10
Skinidin H'land 109 N7
Skinningrove Redcar/Clevel'd 64 B5
Skipness Arg/Bute 73 B8
Skippool Lancs 55 D3
Skipsea ER Yorks 59 C7
Skipsea Brough ER Yorks 59 C7
Skipton N Yorks 56 C4
Skipton on Swale N Yorks 63 G8
Skipwith N Yorks 58 E2
Skirbeck Lincs 43 A6
Skirbeck Quarter Lincs 43 A6
Skirlaugh ER Yorks 59 E7
Skirling Scot Borders 76 D3
Skirmett Bucks 20 C5
Skirpenbeck ER Yorks 58 C3
Skirwith Cumb 69 G9
Skirza H'land 107 C8
Skulamus H'land 94 D3
Skullomie H'land 105 C9
Skyborry Green Shrops 28 A3
Skye of Curr H'land 97 D7
Skyreholme N Yorks 56 B5
Slackhall Derby 50 D2
Slackhead Moray 98 B4
Slad Glos 29 H9
Slade Devon 7 B6
Slade Pembs 24 E4
Slade Green London 22 D5
Slaggyford Northum 69 E9
Slaidburn Lancs 56 C2
Slaithwaite W Yorks 56 G5
Slaley Northum 70 E4
Slamannan Falk 83 G9
Slapton Bucks 32 F2
Slapton Devon 5 F9
Slapton Northants 31 D8
Slatepit Dale Derby 50 F5
Slattocks Gtr Man 49 B9
Slaugham W Sussex 13 C6
Slaughterford Wilts 18 D5
Slawston Leics 41 F9
Sleaford Hants 12 B2
Sleaford Lincs 52 H3
Sleagill Cumb 61 C8
Sleapford Telford 39 D7
Sledge Green Worcs 29 E9
Sledmere ER Yorks 58 B5
Sleightholme Durham 62 C4
Sleights N Yorks 65 D6
Slepe Dorset 10 E2
Slickly H'land 107 C7
Sliddery N Ayrs 73 E9
Sligachan Hotel H'land 94 D1
Slimbridge Glos 18 A4
Slimbridge Wildfowl & Wetlands Centre, Frampton on Severn Glos 29 H8
Slindon Staffs 39 B9
Slindon W Sussex 12 E3
Slinfold W Sussex 12 B5
Sling Gwyn 47 F6
Slingsby N Yorks 64 G4
Slioch Aberds 98 E5
Slip End Beds 32 G3
Slip End Herts 32 E5
Slipton Northants 42 H2
Slitting Mill Staffs 40 D2
Slochd H'land 97 D6
Slockavullin Arg/Bute 81 E8
Sloley Norfolk 45 C6
Sloothby Lincs 53 E7
Slough Slough 21 D7
Slough Green W Sussex 13 C6
Sluggan H'land 97 D6
Slumbay H'land 94 C5
Slyfield Surrey 21 F7
Slyne Lancs 55 B4
Smailholm Scot Borders 77 D9
Small Dole W Sussex 13 D6
Small Hythe Kent 14 E3
Smallbridge Gtr Man 56 G4
Smallburgh Norfolk 45 C7
Smallburn Aberds 99 D10
Smallburn E Ayrs 75 E8
Smalley Derby 41 A6
Smallfield Surrey 22 G3
Smallridge Devon 8 D5
Smannell Hants 20 G1
Smardale Cumb 62 D2
Smarden Kent 14 D3
Smarden Bell Kent 14 D3
Smeatharpe Devon 8 C3
Smeeth Kent 14 E5
Smeeton Westerby Leics 41 F8
Smercleit W Isles 92 D3
Smerral H'land 107 F6
Smethwick W Midlands 40 G2
Smirisary H'land 87 D6